Teaching American Ethnic Literatures

TEACHING AMERICAN ETHNIC LITERATURES

Nineteen Essays

EDITED BY

John R. Maitino

AND

David R. Peck

UNIVERSITY OF NEW MEXICO PRESS
Albuquerque

Library of Congress Cataloging in Publication Data
Teaching American ethnic literatures : nineteen essays / edited by
John R. Maitino and David R. Peck. — 1st ed.
p.   cm.
Includes bibliographical references (p.).
1. American literature—Minority authors—Study and teaching.
2. Pluralism (Social sciences) in literature—Study and teaching.
3. Literature and society—United States—Study and teaching.
4. Hispanic Americans in literature—Study and teaching.
5. Asian Americans in literature—Study and teaching.
6. Afro-Americans in literature—Study and teaching.
7. Ethnic groups in literature—Study and teaching.
8. Minorities in literature—Study and teaching.
9. Ethnicity in literature—Study and teaching.
10. Indians in literature—Study and teaching.
I. Maitino, John R. (John Rocco), 1947–.
II. Peck, David R.
ISBN 0-8263-1686-7 (pa.)
PS153.M56T43 1996
810.9'920693—dc20   95-4439
CIP

For Sue

and for Stan and Hannah

Contents

Teaching American Ethnic Literatures

Introduction

Teaching American Ethnic Literatures has been a labor of love by two teachers of American literature who wanted to learn more about the literature they teach and to expand the range of works they assign. In editing these nineteen essays, we have learned more about teaching ethnic literature than we ever expected, and we only hope that other teachers will get as much out of reading the volume as we have gotten out of compiling it. In this introduction, we spell out our assumptions about ethnic literature and teaching, starting with some suggestions about using the book itself.

How to Use This Book

Teaching American Ethnic Literatures has emerged from the recent wave of interest in ethnic literature and could easily be used in the many courses in multiethnic literature that are being created today on college campuses across this country. But the collection could also be adopted in other classes, particularly in genre courses and in surveys of American literature.

Ethnic American literature, by the way it breaks traditional boundaries, often leads us to new insights about literary genres—about autobiography, for example. Ethnic autobiography pushes the form to its limits and reveals how it is made and what its components are. If a teacher were to center a course on the five autobiographies studied here—*Black Elk Speaks*, Carlos Bulosan's *America Is in the Heart*, Maxine Hong Kingston's *Woman Warrior*, Richard Rodriguez's *Hunger of Memory*, and Richard Wright's *Black Boy*, along with the analyses by Thomas Couser, E. San Juan, Jr., Shirley Lim, Antonio Márquez, and Yoshinobu Hakutani—students would learn much about the range and possibilities of the genre. For ethnic autobiography is autobiography at its least mediated, the stories of American writers engaged in the simultaneous process of assimilation and resistance.

Likewise for fiction. A course on the American short story could use the essays on Sandra Cisneros's *The House on Mango Street* (Julián Olivares), and Hisaye Yamamoto's *Seventeen Syllables* (King-Kok Cheung) and learn a great deal about the development of the short story form since World War II. A course in the twentieth-century American novel that used the essays here by John Purdy on Louise Erdrich's *Love Medicine*, William Thackeray on James Welch's *Winter in the Blood*, Daniel Ross on Alice Walker's *The Color Purple*, and Susan Meisenhelder on Zora Neale Hurston's *Their Eyes Were Watching God* would be a course helping to reassess the form and function of the American novel.

In survey classes, ethnic American literature helps us to redefine the very notion of "American." As these essays show, the borders are being pushed north and south: Mitsuye Yamada's chapter on Joy Kogawa reminds us that the experiences of Japanese Americans were the same on both sides of the borders of North America—interned in both Canada and the United States. The chapters on Native American and Mexican American literatures (the essays on Leslie Marmon Silko and Rudolfo Anaya, for example) remind us that our southern borders have always been fluid and historically arbitrary and continue to separate people who are ethnically related: both Native American and Mexican American populations trace their roots to two sides of the border simultaneously.

In both cases, ethnic American writers are helping us to rethink and reposition our literature—its borders, its subjects, its forms. Perhaps that is because, as Frank Shuffleton has written, ethnicity is a process—a dynamic relationship of assimilation and alienation—and not a product.[1] And this may be the reason why traditional academic literary criticism has not worked as well with ethnic writers. Older criticism functions best with literary works that are finished, completed. Ethnic American literature is itself a process—in its stories of assimilation and resistance, of immigration and oppression—and demands a criticism that is equally flexible and fluid. The essays below are part of the development of that new criticism.

The responses of our students to this literature demonstrate just how alive the issues of this literature are for all of us today. As Julián Olivares writes so eloquently in his essay on Sandra Cisneros, below, the subjects of the essays in this collection are not works of anthropology and sociology but, rather, works of art dealing with issues central to our definitions of ourselves as Americans. Their themes—of marginality, identity, alienation—are still the issues of Americans struggling to understand and come to grips with American life at the end of the twentieth century. And no one understands these themes better than American college students.

All of the essays follow the same basic format. Each essay begins with an analysis of the themes and forms of the work in question, describing its most significant cultural foundations and formal qualities. The second part of each essay discusses various strategies for teaching the work in a classroom, including discussion questions and writing topics.

The third part of each essay provides three separate bibliographies. The first, "Related Works," annotates half a dozen titles that connect to the one under examination in this chapter—other novels, plays, autobiographies that could best be taught with the one at hand. In the second, "Best Criticism," we annotate the half-dozen books and articles that provide the most relevant criticism on this work. In the final bibliography, "Other Sources," we list the remaining works, primary and secondary, that have been used in this chapter.

Reflections on Teaching Ethnic Literature

America is woven of many strands. I would recognize them and let it so remain. . . . Our fate is to become one, and yet many—This is not prophecy but description.

—Ralph Ellison[2]

John: Early in Richard Wright's autobiography, *Black Boy,* the narrator describes the devastation his family suffers after the murder of his uncle by whites who had long wanted his successful Arkansas liquor business.

There was no funeral. There was no music. There was no period of mourning. There were no flowers. There were only silence, quiet weeping, whispers, and fear. I did not know when or where Uncle Hoskins was buried. Aunt Maggie was not even allowed to see his body nor was she able to claim any of his assets. Uncle Hoskins had simply been plucked from our midst and we, figuratively, had fallen on our faces to avoid looking into that white-hot face of terror that we knew loomed somewhere above us. This was as close as white terror had ever come to me and my mind reeled. Why had we not fought back, I asked my mother, and the fear that was in her made her slap me into silence.[3]

When I teach the book, I read this scene, among others, asking students to respond to the language, the events, the behavior of the characters. In one class a decade ago, two students gave an audiovisual presentation directly after I read aloud and we discussed this passage. The students shared a sequence of historical photos of the South, using Langston Hughes's *A Pictorial History of Black America* as their source. Projected onto a large screen, the photos startled the audience.

Student response to the final slide was particularly strong. Titled "Lynching Victims," the photo shows two young black men hung from ropes, their necks twisted, their lifeless forms surrounded by the darkness of the night, as a sea of white faces looks up. One student volunteered an explanation for such lynchings. Several students remarked on the facial expressions of various whites (so many faces looking at the camera, one man sternly pointing at one of the lifeless forms, smiling faces in the lower left corner, unconcerned faces, bored faces). Suddenly a student broke the pattern of responses, asking, "Why isn't anyone in the picture scared or horrified or sick to their stomachs?" Almost nonchalantly, another student answered, "It's the white terror." The student's comment provoked a long and fruitful discussion about the meaning of white terror and its effects on the characters in Wright's autobiography, deepening student understanding of the racism so fundamental to *Black Boy*.

That class, which would be repeated over the next ten years, taught me an important lesson: American ethnic literature is fundamentally unique in the American canon because the cultural and historical context is so strong. Most college classes, including many ethnically mixed classes, do not share that context as a part of their immediate cultural background, which is why it is so important to get behind the words of the literature to the historical assumptions that nourish the work—in Richard Wright's case, to southern history, to Reconstruction, to racism, to murder. And to recover that context requires different strategies in the classroom as in the critical approaches of teachers and scholars to American ethnic literatures. (Yoshinobu Hakutani's insightful essay on *Black Boy*, below, is the simplest proof of this thesis.)

Recently critics have begun to give greater attention to the historical and cultural traditions of ethnic literature, and we regularly now study African American folklore, culture, and history when we read the works of Richard Wright, James Baldwin, Maya Angelou, among others. In the case of Toni Morrison's *Song of Solomon*, for example, the richest readings unfold from an understanding of metaphors, tropes, myths, and patterns rooted in African American tradition. As Linda Wagner-Martin shows in her essay on *Song of Solomon*, African American cultural myths and values--black people who can fly, for example—underpin Milkman Dead's journey in the novel;

"his legendary flight was the stuff of a song that echoed throughout his Virginia province, the mythic community of Shalimar not recorded on maps, living still in the songs and narratives of a vital culture."

When we turn to other ethnic American literatures, we find that the same pattern holds true. Readings of Native American literature, for example, are enriched by an understanding of traditional Indian notions of history and geography and by familiarity with the traumatic changes in Native American cultures after their forced assimilation into white culture. In his essay on *Black Elk Speaks,* for example, Thomas Couser shows how "'natural' phenomena—space and time—are constructed differently by different cultures." Such an analysis in a classroom will not only help students understand the literary work but assist them in seeing their own land and history "through indigenous eyes."

Readings of Asian and Mexican American literatures reap similar rewards when we first grasp the history and traditions of each ethnic group. Our understanding of the stories in Amy Tan's *The Joy Luck Club,* for example, is enhanced by an awareness of how the bonds between mothers and daughters are embedded—as Wendy Ho writes—"in the particular psychological, socioeconomic, cultural, and historical realities of a traditional feudal Confucian society that socialized and oppressed women in China." When we read Rudolfo Anaya's *Bless Me, Ultima,* we discover how the novel's meaning is foregrounded in the context of southwestern Mexican American experience and in the myths and traditions shared among those peoples. The agrarian and pastoral traditions of the Southwest, for instance, give shape to the conflict faced by Antonio, who feels pulled apart by the two traditions. His powerful *curandera,* Ultima, helps him to work through this conflict (as Juan Bruce-Novoa shows in detail in his essay on Anaya's novel).

David: Several years ago, I was teaching Helena María Viramontes's story, "The Moths," and reading aloud that powerful last paragraph, of the young woman "cradling" her dying grandmother in the bathtub.

> Then the moths came. Small, gray ones that came from her soul and out through her mouth fluttering to light, circling the single dull light bulb of the bathroom. . . . The bathroom was filled with moths, and for the first time in a long time I cried, rocking us, crying for her, for me . . . the sobs emerging from the depths of anguish, the misery of feeling half born, sobbing until finally the sobs rippled into circles and circles of sadness and relief. There, there, I said to Abuelita, rocking us gently, there, there.[4]

It suddenly struck me that I had seen that image of women in the tub before, not in a story but in a photograph: Gene Smith's "Tomoko in the Bath," which captures a mother "cradling" her thirty-year-old daughter crippled by industrial poisons dumped near the small seaside Japanese village of Minamata.

I brought the photograph into the next class, and as we talked about the similarities between story and photo—the grief, the love—we discovered what else we were observing, the archetype beneath both story and photograph: Michelangelo's "Pieta," the statue of the Virgin Mary holding the dead body of Christ. It is that fundamental image of grief—of a mother mourning her dead or dying child—which is at the heart of both twentieth-century representations, but which Viramontes reverses with a granddaughter holding her dying *abuelita*.

So, the two modern representations are similar in one way—and so different in another. And that is what our collection here is trying to describe. The Viramontes story and the Smith photograph share a representation of some elemental grief-love. But their contexts are so different. The photograph is part of a series that Smith did in the early 1970s documenting the damage that decades of industrial pollution had wrought to the fragile environment and residents of Minamata. Behind the photograph is anger, not resignation, and anger which resulted, after years of lawsuits, in settlements for many of the victims of the Minamata disaster. And the Viramontes story? It is about three generations of Chicana women, and particularly about the fourteen-year old narrator, coming to an understanding of the duty that is part of adulthood—becoming "half-born" in the same bathtub where her grandmother is dying. But it is also a story infused with the supernatural, with Mexican American folk myths, like the moths flying from her *abuelita's* soul.

The point is a simple one: all art repeats certain ideas and qualities, but to focus exclusively on the similarities between works—the themes and forms they share—is to distort the meaning of the individual work. While one thrust of the Viramontes story is toward the same love and grief that we find in the Smith photo as in the Michelangelo statue, an equally important part of the story (what we are here calling its cultural and historical context) is Chicana, and shares its most crucial values and assumptions with other works of Mexican-American literature—coming of age in a Chicano culture, with its particular mix of Catholicism and mysticism (in Anaya as in Viramontes). Without that understanding of cultural uniqueness, a great part of Viramontes's power is lost. We need to do both reading jobs at the same time, in other words: to recognize the cultural uniqueness of the individual work, and then to look for the links among different works.

For years I've taught Robert Hayden's poem "Those Winter Sundays," especially in my adolescent literature class, where students can appreciate the poem's tension between the sacrifices of the father and the indifference of the poem's young persona. But we would invariably stumble on that ninth line of the poem:

> Sundays too my father got up early
> and put his clothes on in the blueblack cold,
> then with cracked hands that ached
> from labor in the weekday weather made
> banked fires blaze. No one ever thanked him.
>
> I'd wake and hear the cold splintering, breaking.
> When the rooms were warm, he'd call,
> and slowly I would rise and dress,
> fearing the chronic angers of that house,
>
> Speaking indifferently to him,
> who had driven out the cold
> and polished my good shoes as well.
> What did I know, what did I know
> of love's austere and lonely offices?

What *were* "the chronic angers of that house"? Just the normal tension of any family living in this winter weather? The problems of any house with kids?

Does it make any difference, I'd ask my class after we'd been through the poem, that Robert Hayden was an African American poet who grew up in Detroit in the 1920s? Well, no, they'd finally say, for this poem has a universal theme, this could be any family. And then I'd tell them about Hayden's childhood in Detroit, raised by foster parents in a period of great social disruptions, when hundreds of thousands of African Americans were migrating north to cities looking for work and a better life. His family unstable, his neighborhood changing daily—could the poem be referring to those problems, too? The line seems somehow less cryptic, reflecting as it perhaps does the instability of black lives, in both family and community, at that troubled time.

But here's the tricky part, I'd say: are all poems by African Americans from this place and this period going to have this theme, and this particular feeling of Hayden's poem, the "chronic angers"? Obviously not. But this poem, like all literature, does come out of a richly specific ethnic history. Hayden was black in 1920s Detroit, from a broken family in economically troubled times. His poem does reflect some of that ethnic history. We need to see both: the "universal" themes of family sacrifice and love (which we can see in Viramontes as well)—but at the same time the specific ethnic context out of which this theme emerges in this particular work of art.

Situating Ourselves in Ethnic Literary History

But why did we choose these four ethnic groups, and these particular nineteen writers? The simplest answer is that the recent discovery of American ethnic literature has focused on these four groups. European-American literary works—like Abraham Cahan's *The Rise of David Levinsky* (1917), for example, or Anzia Yezierska's *Hungry Hearts* (1920)—have been in print almost continuously since their publication, perhaps in part because they help to reinforce the melting-pot ideology that has predominated during most of this century. (Today, of course, these and other classic ethnic texts of immigration and assimilation are being critically reevaluated and positively revalued, as part of a broader redefinition of what constitutes American "ethnic" literature.)

It has only been in the last few decades, however, that the truly multiethnic nature of American literature has been recognized. African American literature was the first body of ethnic writing to emerge, for writers like Zora Neale Hurston, Richard Wright, Langston Hughes, Ralph Ellison, and James Baldwin could hardly be ignored—although major anthologies of American literature managed to skip the Harlem Renaissance for decades—and serious scholarly study of this literature has been under way since at least Robert Bone's *The Negro Novel in America* (1958) or Edward Margolies's *Native Sons: A Critical Study of Twentieth-Century Black American Authors* (1968).

The literature of other American ethnic groups has begun to receive serious critical attention as well. The year that signals the change is 1968, when the Kiowa writer N. Scott Momaday's *House Made of Dawn* was awarded the Pulitzer Prize for fiction. The emergence of ethnic literature as a force in American culture was confirmed in the following years as writers like Alice Walker and Toni Morrison also won Pulitzers, and Amy Tan, Maxine Hong Kingston, and so many other multicultural authors moved into the best-seller lists.

The critical assessment of this literature has been slower. While major efforts have been launched on Native American literature in the last several decades, both Latino and Asian American literature have only in recent years begun to receive the serious scholarly assessments that one expects in major American literatures. Part of the problem is the heterogeneity of both groups: Latino literature includes both Puerto Ricans and Mexican Americans, as well as the increasing numbers of writers from Central and South America, while Asian American literature is an almost useless term when one considers the contrasts among Chinese American, Japanese American, Korean American, and other Asian American and Pacific Rim literatures.

What we want to do in this volume is to help the scholarship catch up with the ethnic literature that is increasingly becoming a central part of the American literary tradition—to translate for students and teachers alike the cultural assumptions and values that lie just beneath the surface of these important works.

Having established these four groups as those we wanted to focus on in this collection, we then decided to pick the individual ethnic works that were most often being taught in college classrooms but had not yet received the kind of critical study they deserved, especially any approach from the perspective of teaching ethnic literature. Thus, early on we dropped Ralph Ellison's *Invisible Man* from consideration, for while it is arguably the most important African American novel, it is likewise one about which a good half-dozen recent studies have been written, including a 1989 volume (edited by Susan Resnick Parry and Pancho Savery) on teaching the novel. Likewise Baldwin's *Go Tell It on the Mountain.* But we selected the works by Hurston, Walker, Hansberry, Morrison and Wright because they were important volumes that had not received this treatment. We went through a similar process in the other three sections of this book.

But why do teachers need this criticism? The typical teacher of American literature was trained before the recent growth in the popularity of ethnic literature and comes to the scholarship only through journal articles and books like ours. Such teachers were trained in the older canon of American literature and are prepared to teach Melville or James, or any one of a number of (mostly male and white) writers, and in many cases they share a similar ideological background. The historical and religious framework surrounding Nathaniel Hawthorne's *The Scarlet Letter,* for example, comes straight from the Euro-American tradition: a story of immigration (Hester Prynne and Roger Chillingworth are both recent immigrants from England), the novel is steeped in this early Protestant experience. If any religious his-

tory is taught in American schools, it is Puritanism—at least in its historical version—and Hawthorne's notions of sin, isolation, and redemption
are generally familiar to anyone raised in the United States.

Leslie Marmon Silko's *Ceremony,* in contrast—and we could use a number of other works from the contents of this volume to establish this point—
does not come out of this Puritan tradition. Rather, it is a story built on a
foundation of Native American myth and history, and southwestern Laguna myth and history in particular. It is, curiously, another novel about
redemption—but Tayo's journey is informed, not by the religious practices
of Protestant New England, but by Laguna legends of the land, origin stories, and Native American spiritual ceremonies. The result is a powerful
story that draws on a number of American Indian myths and experiences,
as Norma Wilson shows, below, in her essay on Silko

The teacher of Hawthorne—or of Twain, Crane, James, Hemingway, et
al.—does not need extra help in understanding those fundamental American works (which is one reason why the "classics" of the American literary
canon can almost all be taught in high school). But the teachers who are
trying to incorporate Silko or Richard Wright, Maxine Hong Kingston, or
Rudolfo Anaya into their syllabi may need to gain a fresh cultural intelligence, in order to understand the history, the myths and legends, the racial
and ethnic experience behind those works. Likewise, these works demand
fresher approaches in the classroom, to get students inside the experiences
these works depict, to sensitize them to the lives of characters who may be
very different from themselves, to worlds which may be very unlike their
own. Our book performs both these intellectual and pedagogical jobs at
once.

Rethinking Classroom Approaches

If our reading of American ethnic literature demands a new set of critical strategies, our teaching of these literatures, likewise, demands a
reconceptualization of our pedagogical approaches. The very nature of our
classroom and its relationships, in fact, must be transformed to address the
dynamics of ethnicity, race, gender, and class. Our contributors provide a
broad outline of new and innovative teaching approaches that we have sum-
marized and augmented below.

The first approach involves a revision of our traditional notion of reading as it applies to American ethnic literature. Since ethnic literature often
introduces readers to new and unfamiliar cultures, reading becomes a kind

of "process of translation" with certain identifiable difficulties. In his discussion of *Black Elk Speaks,* Tom Couser notes the challenge: "to make the 'other' comprehensible without erasing its difference." In the case of *Black Elk Speaks,* Couser shows that Lakota beliefs can be dismissed as exotic if they are too foreign from mainstream thought, or their deeper significance can be lost if they are translated "too quickly into familiar terms." The presentation of American ethnic texts, in other words, must be guided by both a judicious respect for cultural differences and a willingness to explore analogies as they may help readers to partially understand the "other."

A second approach brings the notion of "ethnicity" itself center stage in the study of American ethnic literature. In his discussion of *Hunger of Memory,* Antonio Márquez argues that ethnicity may be understood as an "invention" rather than a fixed notion, and cites Werner Sollors's suggestion that ethnicity is forever reinvented: "Ethnicity is not merely a matter of cultural (let alone biological) survival; ethnicity is constantly recreated as people (and ethnic authors among them, of course), set up new distinctions, make new boundaries, and form new groups." If students employ this dynamic notion of ethnicity in their reading, they will enrich their understanding of the people and experiences portrayed in particular works, and they will begin to recognize how individuals and ethnic groups struggle with, and define themselves against, the values of the dominant cultural group. They may more easily decode what King-Kok Cheung calls the "unsettling messages" hidden in Hisaye Yamamoto's short story "Seventeen Syllables," messages that reveal themselves only when readers can recognize the particular cultural rituals of Japanese American conversational practices. Students may also discern in *House Made of Dawn, Ceremony, Love Medicine,* and other Native American fiction the recurrent theme of "homing in" that informs the very structure of these works. Helen Jaskoski shows how characters in *House Made of Dawn* and *Ceremony* exit, live in exile, undergo a trial, and return to the reservation; and John Purdy reveals the return of the character June, in *Love Medicine,* not as a physical being, but as a "vivid, warm memory."

A third approach foregrounds cultural and ethnic history as a frame of reference for decoding the often unfamiliar individual and social experience portrayed in American ethnic literature. Such history shapes the conduct of all peoples. Thus, Antonio Márquez can speak of *Hunger of Memory* as a "brief chapter" in the larger ethnic drama of America, locating it among a variety of ethnic works for comparison and contrast: Maya Angelou's *I Know Why the Caged Bird Sings,* Maxine Hong Kingston's *The Woman Warrior,* and N. Scott Momaday's *The Names.* Márquez reminds us that the retrieval of the past is an important feature of ethnic literature, noting that "cultural memory binds these diverse works in a common purpose."

In the classroom, student readings of a variety of ethnic literature can be greatly enhanced by even a brief understanding of the history underpinning those works. Several examples come easily to mind. Linda Wagner-Martin reveals how unquestionably *Song of Solomon* draws on African American history and folklore, whether in its use of tropes, songs, or the African American notion of heroism, not as nobility, but as a process of "learning to become as good a soul as was possible." And Antonio Márquez suggests how the 1848 Treaty of Guadalupe Hidalgo made Mexican Americans "foreigners in their own land," a fact that has strongly shaped Chicano literature.

A fourth approach highlights the role of gender in ethnic literature and experience. A rich body of feminist criticism has developed over the last twenty years, redefining how we read traditional as well as non-canonical texts and helping to revise the canon itself. American ethnic literature raises many gender issues of scholarly and pedagogical interest, as our contributors suggest. Linda Wagner-Martin shows how *Song of Solomon,* ostensibly about the lives of black men, actually tells the story of three women wreaking "havoc with the more recognizable narrative of men's lives." *The Joy Luck Club,* as Wendy Ho argues, presents the personal stories of the mothers and daughters "as a form of counter-memory" against patriarchal power structures. And both *Their Eyes Were Watching God* and *The Color Purple* provoke, as Susan Meisenhelder and Daniel W. Ross illustrate, lively student discussion about gender.

A fifth approach identifies new perspectives that, if effectively integrated into classroom discourse, can diminish the ethnic and cultural isolation of our students. Ethnic literature and criticism themselves help us to rethink the notions we have inherited about ethnicity, immigration, assimilation, and related concepts. Antonio Márquez, for example, establishes a useful definition of autobiography by using Sau-Ling Cynthia Wong's argument that "historical periods and generational differences must be included in valuations of ethnic autobiographies." This distinction helps students understand and explore the very different poses one finds in ethnic writing. Ernesto Galarza's *Barrio Boy,* infused with nostalgia for the narrator's Mexican past, becomes an example of immigrant autobiography; Richard Rodriguez's *Hunger of Memory,* in disavowing his Hispanic heritage for his life as a writer, represents ethnic autobiography. A second example may be found in the concept of assimilation. In his chapter on James Welch's *Winter in the Blood,* William Thackeray identifies the costs of assimilation, suggesting the "near impossibility" that young Indian males can "find a place in the world that suits their traditional cultural heritage as heads of families but also gives them the economic security to assume such a responsible role." In fact, the costs of assimilation are powerfully portrayed (and discussed by contributors) in many of the works covered in our book, including Carlos Bulosan's *America Is in the Heart,* Hisaye Yamamoto's "Epithalamium" from *Seventeen Syllables and Other Stories,* and Rodriguez's *Hunger of Memory.* In each example, students explore ethnic experience through a particular perspective that allows them to understand the forces underpinning ethnic life in the United States.

Some General Teaching Resources

The following five works are among the most useful in the study and teaching of ethnic American literature, and we annotate them for the use of teachers and students alike.

Banks, James A. *Teaching Strategies for Ethnic Studies.* 5th ed. Boston: Allyn and Bacon, 1991. One of the best resources for secondary teachers and college education courses, this study contains three major parts: part I presents a rationale for teaching comparative ethnic studies; part II contains chapters on major ethnic groups in the U.S. (including Indochinese Americans), with bibliographies for both teachers and students; and part III "illustrates how the teacher can use the information and strategies in parts I and II to develop and teach multiethnic units and curricula that focus on two or more ethnic groups."

Candelaria, Cordelia, ed. *Multiethnic Literature of the United States: Critical Introductions and Classroom Resources.* Boulder: Multiethnic Literature Project, University of Colorado, 1989. A collection of essays, poems, and syllabi aimed at overcoming the "Eurocentric partiality" in American scholarship and at helping to recover ethnic diversity. The first part includes articles on Chicana writing, "The Japanese Literature of Internment," and "Reflections of Otherness in Ethnic Literature." The second part, "Classroom Resources," contains three course syllabi (for example, "Literature of Black American Women"). Useful bibliographies throughout.

Lauter, Paul, ed. *Reconstructing American Literature: Courses, Syllabi, Issues.* Old Westbury, N.Y.: Feminist Press, 1983. It is difficult to exaggerate the role that Paul Lauter has played in opening the American literary canon in all directions. General editor of *The Heath Anthology of American Literature* (2d ed., 2 vols., 1994)—the first survey of American literature to reflect accurately the ethnic literary diversity in this country—Lauter has for decades fought for the inclusion of women and ethnic writers in American literary collections and courses. In this earlier volume, there are sixty-seven course syllabi that "change the teaching of American literature and . . . the definition of what we call American culture."

Peck, David R. *American Ethnic Literatures: Native American, African American, Chicano/Latino, and Asian American Writers and Their Backgrounds.* Pasadena, Calif.: Salem Press, 1992. This volume provides a single source for listings of the four primary literatures, plus the most important secondary criticism, including background sources—the best treatments of slavery, immigration, and Native American history. In short, *American Ethnic Literatures* lists not only the major ethnic writers, and the scholarship they have generated, but gives teachers and students the context for their literature: the histories of the four ethnic communities producing that extraordinary work in the United States today.

Ruoff, A. LaVonne Brown, and Jerry W. Ward, eds. *Redefining American Literary History.* New York: Modern Language Association of America, 1990. This crucial volume includes sections on revising the canon, oral dimensions of American literature, critical and historical perspectives on American ethnic literatures, extensive bibliographies of major ethnic literatures (African American, American Indian, Asian American, Chicano, and Puerto Rican), and lists of selected journals and presses. One of the best introductions to multiethnic American literatures for college teachers.

Notes

1. Frank Shuffleton, *A Mixed Race: Ethnicity in Early America* (New York: Oxford University Press, 1993), 7–8.

2. *Invisible Man* (New York: Vintage Random House, 1952), 564.

3. *Black Boy* (New York: Harper Perennial paperback, 1993), 64.

4. In *New Worlds of Literature,* ed. Jerome Beaty and J. Paul Hunter (New York: W. W. Norton and Co., 1993), 813–14.

Native American Literature

Preface

The five chapters in this first section of *Teaching American Ethnic Literatures* treat a remarkably representative sampling of Native American texts. While Thomas Couser's insightful essay on *Black Elk Speaks* raises issues about the genre of autobiography central to all ethnic literatures, it should also remind readers of the particular importance of oral literature in the Native American literary tradition. The remaining essays in this section treat four of the major works of the Native American literary renaissance of the last twenty-five years or so, from N. Scott Momaday's Pulitzer Prize–winning *House Made of Dawn* (1968), through James Welch's *Winter in the Blood* (1974) and Leslie Marmon Silko's *Ceremony* (1977), to Louise Erdrich's *Love Medicine* (1984).

Couser's essay is an appropriate opening, for it models most forcefully the methodology that should be followed in reading not only native literature, but any ethnic literature: the importance of decoding the text, or getting beneath the literary surface to the work's social and historical structures. What all of these essays demonstrate are the depth and complexity of those structures: the Lakota worldview Black Elk revealed, or the spiritual and religious themes that Helen Jaskoski identifies in Momaday and Norma Wilson uncovers in Silko.

These essays alert us not only to the themes of these five works, but to their recurring formal qualities as well: the circular structure in so many, for example, the pattern that John Purdy and Jaskoski both identify as "Homing in" (from William Bevis) and that Wilson calls "accretive" (Paula Gunn Allen). These essays thus introduce us to many of the recurring images and motifs of Native American life, so often replicated in nonlinear literary forms.

Predictably, the essays here point up a number of parallels among the five texts—the ways in which Silko and Momaday and Welch portray the theme of exile and return, for example, or the parallels between the use of tribal cultures in Silko and Erdrich. The teaching sections of the five essays, likewise, develop a number of valuable topics (see Jaskoski and William

Thackeray) in order to get beneath the surface of the works to these important themes and forms.

Each of the essays here has a shape that reflects the work it is treating, and yet each has its own structure as well, from the distinct thematic sections in Jaskoski and Thackeray to the more organic analysis in Purdy. Likewise, the teaching sections reflect not only the individual works, but the successes of individual teachers in approaching them—from the useful background study in Wilson to the description of the process of getting into the culture in Couser and Purdy. Teachers of American literature can learn a great deal from the five fine discussions, not only about these individual works, but about some of the most effective approaches to any literary text.

Indian Preservation:

Teaching *Black Elk Speaks*

G. THOMAS COUSER

A. Analysis of Themes and Forms

Based on interviews conducted in 1931 by John G. Neihardt, Nebraska poet laureate and epic poet of the West, *Black Elk Speaks* (1932) tells the life story of Black Elk, an Oglala Lakota holy man, up to the massacre at Wounded Knee in 1890. Of the three books based on his teachings,[1] *Black Elk Speaks* alone has achieved critical esteem and great popularity among Native Americans and Euro-Americans alike. Much of the book's appeal stems from its vivid accounts of the Battle of Little Big Horn, the death of Crazy Horse, Buffalo Bill's Wild West show, the Ghost Dance religion, and the massacre at Wounded Knee. But the book's popularity probably owes most to its autobiographical dimension and its tragic plot: the story of how Black Elk received his vision of the "flowering of the tree" (the renewal of tribal culture), which authorized his role as holy man and healer; how he communicated that vision to his tribe; and how he and his people failed to realize the promise of that vision. *Black Elk Speaks* affords a unique record, from the indigenous point of view, of the precipitous decline of Plains Indian culture and thus of a defining episode in American history: the subjugation of native peoples by Euro-American intruders. One of its major subjects, then, is the response of a native culture to policies and practices that promised—or threatened—to wipe it out.

As the teachings of a holy man, *Black Elk Speaks* has been described by Vine Deloria, Jr., as a kind of "North American bible of all tribes."[2] As an account of Lakota lifeways, it represents some of what was lost when the West was "won." At the same time, it testifies to the vitality of Lakota culture, which seemed doomed with the shift to reservation life in the 1870s and 1880s. For *Black Elk Speaks* not only reveals that much Lakota lore survived the catastrophe of Wounded Knee; the book itself helped to inspire and facilitate the revitalization of Lakota culture, a process still growing in strength and sophistication today. Thus, the book is not as "tragic" as its "plot" suggests, since plot summary fails to take into account the resilience embodied and expressed in Black Elk's act of collaborative narration and cultural recuperation. (For another view of the narrative's emplotment, see Krupat, 126–34.) Therein lie the value and the challenge of teaching *Black Elk Speaks,* which continues to speak to the situation of contemporary Native Americans—and of other indigenous peoples worldwide.

Unlike much "ethnic" literature, the book does not assume the reader's understanding of its distinctive cultural materials; rather, it is intent upon illuminating and preserving those elements. Thus, though the "ethnic" materials—Black Elk's several visions and his tribe's customs—may be totally unfamiliar, even alien, to most first-time readers, these materials require surprisingly little glossing; to a large extent, the book supplies the key to its own cultural codes. For example, before sharing his story with Neihardt, Black Elk insists on praying and smoking the pipe, and before doing that, he explains the sacred pipe's purpose, its symbolism, and its origins (2–6). He also explains the custom of counting coup (89), the Sun Dance (96ff), the vision quest (181ff), and the role of *heyokas,* or sacred fools (188–93). Black Elk also interprets the symbolism of his visions as he narrates them. (Perhaps because it originated in another tribe, and because Black Elk had doubts about it, the Ghost Dance receives less explanation than it may need.) Aware that his rhetorical situation in the interviews was different from that of the tellers of traditional coup tales, in which hostility toward the enemy could be taken for granted, Black Elk even explains the reasons for violence against whites. All of this explanation is a function of the motive behind Black Elk's radical departure—from tribal custom and personal practice—in sharing his teachings with a white man he barely knew: to make his tribe's traditional culture accessible to the world beyond the reservation and thus to preserve it—perhaps even to revive and disseminate it.

This is not to say that the ethnic materials are completely self-explanatory. But the book's internal explanations will probably suffice in most courses, for several reasons. One is the danger that classes will bog down in explication of details, some of which are idiosyncratic and some of which, as Black Elk reminds us, are not susceptible to verbal explication. Moreover, because Neihardt—a poet and mystic, rather than an anthropologist or expert in Lakota culture—compressed and altered Black Elk's accounts of his visions and rituals for literary effect, *Black Elk Speaks* cannot be taken as an entirely reliable guide to Lakota religious beliefs and customs. Many culturally significant details were lost or changed in the complex process of translating, editing, and revising Black Elk's words. In any case, one cannot hope, or presume, to comprehend Lakota culture through a medium such as this book. (Other books are better suited to that purpose—for example, the transcripts of the interviews, published by Raymond J. DeMallie in 1984.)[3]

But presumably the point of teaching the book—outside of courses in anthropology or comparative religion, at least—is not to educate students in the specifics of Lakota culture. In teaching *Black Elk Speaks*, it is preferable, I think, to address more general themes and issues of Native American/Euro-American relations. Although some aspects of traditional Native American religious beliefs have been absorbed into New Age culture (in compromised and controversial forms), there will be a substantial gap, or gulf, between the worldview of most college students and that expressed in *Black Elk Speaks*. Exploring that gulf, and trying to bridge it, will be more rewarding than trying to account for every detail of Black Elk's dramatic visions.

The basic challenge of teaching *Black Elk Speaks* is, in a way, the challenge inherent in any process of cross-cultural translation: to make the "other" comprehensible without erasing its difference. On the one hand, presenting Lakota beliefs as completely alien to modern mainstream American ideas encourages dismissing them as "exotic" or "superstitious"—evidence that Native American culture was doomed, or that in some sense it deserved, to give way to a culture with a more empirical or, conversely, more *truly* religious worldview. On the other hand, translating Lakota culture too quickly into familiar terms—treating it, for example, as a kind of proto–environmentalism—oversimplifies it and obscures its deeply spiritual cast. The challenge is to avoid these extremes. Analogies or comparisons will be necessary to enable understanding of the other, but students must be reminded that the analogies are always partial, always misleading. (See section B, Teaching the Work, for development of this approach.)

More than the purely "ethnic" materials of the book, college students reading *Black Elk Speaks* will need help with its historical context, the troubled relations between Native Americans and Euro-Americans. For what Black Elk describes as happening in and to his own tribe is part of a world-historical phenomenon that can best be understood if his narrative is seen in a larger perspective—one provided neither by Deloria's introduction to *Black Elk Speaks* nor by DeMallie's to *The Sixth Grandfather*. The following summary should be of help in the crucial task of historicizing Black Elk's narrative.[4]

Aside from their adaptation of horses (c. 1750) and firearms (c. 1790), the Lakota, or Western (Teton) Sioux tribes—the Hunkpapa, Sihasapa (Blackfoot), Minneconjou, Sans Arc, Sicangu (Brule), Oohennonpa (Two Kettle), and Oglala—were relatively unaffected by contact with Euro-Americans until well into the nineteenth century. At that time, however, settlers moving into their territory—or through it (especially via the Bozeman Trail from Fort Laramie to Montana) to the Far West in search of gold or land—impinged on the Lakota way of life. As a result, during the three decades narrated by Black Elk (c. 1860 to 1890), his people were forced to make a traumatic transition from their traditional migratory buffalo-hunting life to sedentary life on reservations. (Maps of the territory in question will be indispensable as graphic supplements to written accounts.)[5] The treatment of the Sioux (and other Plains tribes) recapitulated, at an accelerated pace, the fate of many other tribes; thus, their subjugation may serve as a kind of synecdoche of Indian/white history in North America.

The Plains Indians were subdued by a combination of political, military, legal, and cultural pressures. Federal policy, based on the presumption of the superiority of Euro–American culture and administered by the Bureau of Indian Affairs, was to confine the Plains Indians to reservations, where they were to be "civilized": American Indians would be converted into Indian Americans. An important dimension of this process was the erosion of the legal status of Native American nations. In 1831, the Supreme Court assigned them the status of "domestic dependent nations"—in effect, wards of the government; in 1871, the government discontinued making treaties with the tribes, no longer considered sovereign entities; in 1903, the Supreme Court affirmed the power of Congress to break treaties unilaterally. Authority over tribal affairs was increasingly exerted by agents assigned to tribes and by Indian police (established in 1878); such an approach, of course, undermined the authority of traditional leaders.

The degree and kind of resistance to this process varied considerably among Lakota chiefs and bands. (Black Elk was among the less acquiescent Oglalas, who resisted settling permanently at Indian agencies, preferring to roam and hunt.) An initial period of warfare on the northern Plains in the 1850s and 1860s led to the army's abandonment of forts along the Bozeman Trail. In the Treaty of 1868, the Sioux, under Red Cloud, promised to stop raiding; in return, the U.S. government designated roughly the western half of present-day South Dakota as the Great Sioux Reservation and assured the right to hunt in the Powder River region to the west, which the Sioux considered the last great hunting ground. Red Cloud agreed to settle his Oglalas at an agency established for them in 1873 in the northwest corner of Nebraska (rather than on the Missouri, which federal officials would have preferred).

In 1874, however, after General George Armstrong Custer led his troops into the Black Hills, the government made only token efforts to deter gold miners from following, in violation of the Treaty of 1868. Instead, it offered to buy the Black Hills and declared hostile any Indians who refused to return to their agencies. In response, large numbers of Oglalas, led by Sitting Bull and Crazy Horse, violently resisted white encroachment. In 1876, the Sioux and Cheyenne wiped out Custer's army at the Little Big Horn. The government construed the Indians' defense of their land as aggression invalidating the Treaty of 1868 and pressured agency chiefs into ceding the Black Hills in 1877.[6]

Eventually the Lakota tribes surrendered, impelled not so much by military force as by disease and hunger: the slaughtering of the buffalo reduced the tribes to dependency on government rations distributed at various agencies. One by one, the tribes were dismounted, disarmed, and confined to reservation land. Crazy Horse's Oglala band surrendered (and he was killed by guards) in 1877. Sitting Bull took refuge in Canada, where Black Elk and other Oglalas joined him, but he gave in to pressure from both governments and surrendered in 1881. Despite his determined resistance, in 1889 the Lakota succumbed to pressure to sell off large parts of the Great Sioux Reservation, leaving the tribes on separate reservations, the "islands" to which Black Elk refers.

Having confined the Sioux, the government set out to convert them into true Americans—farmers or ranchers rather than hunters, Christians rather than pagans, individual citizens rather than tribe members. (Official policy was to "kill the Indian" to save "the man.") Under the Dawes (or General Allotment) Act of 1887, tribal lands were allotted to individuals or families, who were granted the status of U.S. citizens. "Surplus" land remaining after allotments could be bought by the federal government; much of it was then leased or sold to whites. Though hailed by some as a victory for reformers, the Dawes Act threatened to destroy reservations as territorial bases for the perpetuation of Indian culture. Many children were removed from their families to be educated at boarding schools. (Black Elk's son, Ben, who translated his father's words for Neihardt in 1931, was the product of the best known of these schools, the Carlisle Indian School in Pennsylvania.) Rituals such as the Sun Dance were outlawed or otherwise suppressed. Native Americans were encouraged, or coerced, to adopt Euro-American customs in clothing, hairstyles, housing, food, and religion.

The destruction of the buffalo herds was not merely an economic blow to the Lakota people; it removed the very foundation of their culture. One of the responses of the defeated tribes to their forced assimilation and to the poverty and hunger endemic on reservations was the Ghost Dance religion. This was a syncretic religion that combined elements of Christianity (the idea of a Messiah) and of native religions (the Round Dance). The Ghost Dance religion, which originated in the late 1880s with the Paiute Messiah Wovoka (also known as Jack Wilson), taught that obedience to God and accommodation to Euro-Americans would be rewarded by reunion with ancestors in the afterlife.

Most scholars see Wovoka's teachings as a pacifistic religion born of a sense of deep cultural crisis, even despair. As it spread to other tribes, however, the Ghost Dance religion took on an apocalyptic and sometimes militant cast. Participants danced themselves into trances in which they envisioned the regeneration of their traditional, pre-contact ways. Whites were to disappear as a result of some natural catastrophe that would spare Indians; dancing and other rituals were thought to hasten this event. Some came to believe that shirts adorned with Ghost Dance symbols and images would render them invulnerable to bullets. Still, Euro-American culture was resisted symbolically, rather than militarily.

The Ghost Dance religion was adopted by many Sioux in 1890, at a time of particular hardship—crops had failed and government rations had been cut off. (Initially suspicious of it, Black Elk eventually convinced himself that it was consistent with his visions.) Interpreting the new religious fervor of the Sioux as threatening violent uprising, government agents forbade its practice. When the dancing continued, federal troops were brought in to suppress it. Sitting Bull was thought to be an instigator of resistance, and when a member of his tribe resisted the Indian policemen who came to arrest him, Sitting Bull was killed. The attempt to capture Big Foot, another "fomenter," and to disarm his band resulted in the massacre at Wounded Knee, the event that decisively "pacified" the Sioux (and that concludes Black Elk's narrative).

Over the next several decades the Sioux, under the authority of reservation agents, continued to adapt to "American" culture. Families were encouraged or forced to live on their allotments; the basis of the economy shifted to farming and cattle ranching, neither of which was supported very well by the arid land. The result of allotment was that much of the better land was leased, and eventually sold, to white ranchers. By 1934, more than half of the Sioux land had been acquired by whites; most of the remainder was in individual, rather than tribal, hands, and much of this was economically unproductive. The Depression further eroded the economic status of the Sioux.

Eventually, dissatisfaction with the obviously destructive effects of the Allotment Act led to sentiment for reform. The Indian Reorganization Act (or Wheeler-Howard Act) of 1934 permitted local tribal self-government, encouraged tribal incorporation for economic development, and lifted the ban on the practice of indigenous religion. The bill's effect was to arrest, rather than to reverse, the policy of forced assimilation; nevertheless, it represented an important shift in the cultural and political climate. It may be more than coincidental that Black Elk's collaboration with Neihardt occurred just when the prevailing federal policy was becoming more tolerant of communal aspects of traditional lifeways.

It is crucial that students understand the background against which the interviews were conducted and that they know something about the forty-year chapter of Black Elk's life that is significantly excluded from the narrative—the period during which he accommodated in various ways to the constraints of reservation life. Thus, students need to know what Neihardt knew, but suppressed: that Black Elk married a Christian woman, converted to Roman Catholicism, and functioned as a Roman Catholic catechist on the reservation for decades before he met John Neihardt and somehow sensed that this man might be the vehicle for the communication of his long-latent vision.

One of the controversies over *Black Elk Speaks*, which Vine Deloria, Jr., too quickly dismisses in the book's introduction, has to do with the nature of the collaboration. As DeMallie and others have demonstrated, Neihardt and Black Elk were to some extent working at cross-purposes. Some scholars see Neihardt as unconsciously imposing his own values on Black Elk— for example, Neihardt consistently minimizes the violence and hostility to Euro-Americans expressed in Black Elk's visions—and unwittingly reenacting the expropriation of Indian culture by presuming to speak for a man who could not read his own words.[7] (DeMallie's publication of the transcripts of the interviews makes it possible for all readers to investigate the complex process of cross-cultural collaboration.) Insofar as the structure of *Black Elk Speaks* suggests that Lakota life suddenly ceased, or went into suspended animation, after Wounded Knee, Neihardt's editing reinforces the sentimental image of the Vanishing American, rather than reflecting the difficult process of Lakota survival on the reservation (which DeMallie's introduction helps to restore to visibility). In any case, *Black Elk Speaks* is autobiography of a sort unknown in Lakota culture because it reflects a sense of individualism not valued by traditional oral cultures (Krupat, 29), and students should be made aware that, in important ways, it is not only or always Black Elk who speaks the words they read.

It is important, then, that the book be presented not as a transparent lens on the life of an Oglala Lakota, but rather as a text mediated by an outsider. It would be both naive and fallacious to present the book as a mere record of events—even one from a rarely accessible viewpoint. The collaboration that produced the book is necessarily implicated in the ongoing conflict between Euro-American and Native American cultures; the Christian mystic and poet of the West who oversaw its production inevitably distorted the culture he attempted to present to a wider public. But the book also intervenes in history: it has inspired veneration of Black Elk in non-Native Americans and Native Americans alike and has helped to underwrite the revitalization of Native American religions.[8] Ideally, teaching *Black Elk Speaks* will enable students to reflect on the way in which Black Elk's collaboration with Neihardt acts out some of the cultural conflicts that it takes as its subject.

B. Teaching the Work

Since *Black Elk Speaks* can be taught in very different contexts, I will try to suggest various approaches. One very important aspect of the work, central to its "ethnic" dimension is that, despite Neihardt's omissions and distortions, it can introduce students to a culture radically different from their own. As suggested above, it is perhaps best to direct students' attention away from enigmatic details and toward underlying cultural differences. For example, when it comes to dating the narrative's events, it is tempting simply to translate Lakota "winters" into Euro-American years and Lakota "moons" into months (as the dates in parentheses do), but it is worth dwelling on the discrepancies between these sets of terms, which are not exactly equivalent. A "winter," the period from first snow to first snow (DeMallie, 101n), does not begin and end when a "year" does, nor does it begin and end on an arbitrary, preestablished date. At the very least, this makes translating dates somewhat problematic: for example, events that fell in different years—December 1876 and January 1877— might occur in the same winter. More important, however, the units are defined on different principles. Asking students to think about how years and "winters," months and "moons" reflect very different ways of conceptualizing time—apparently an objectively quantifiable phenomenon—should help them appreciate the complexity of cross-cultural translation and negotiation.

Differences in the cultural organization of space are also worth consideration. Black Elk's terms for features of the landscape will often be unfamiliar to readers, and maps of the contested terrain will be most helpful if they have modern state borders superimposed on them. Exploration of these elementary facts may help students imagine a world organized not by legal, surveyed borders, which are often invisible, but rather by perceptible features of the landscape deemed significant for cultural reasons. Such a process may help to illuminate the inherent complication of boundaries and treaties in Indian/white relations, for the agreements that divided and ceded the land might be understood quite differently by the two parties. Since Native Americans and Euro-Americans named and organized the landscape very differently, the land was contested in a number of senses and ways. Discussion of these "elementary" matters—when and where the book is "set"—can help to illustrate how "natural" phenomena—space and time—are constructed differently by different cultures. Such discussion may help students see "their land" and their times through indigenous eyes.[9]

Similarly, students might be asked to compare the rituals of Western culture to those described by the narrative. How did exhibitions like Queen Victoria's Golden Jubilee (which Black Elk witnessed) or, in America, the Centennial or the Columbian Exposition represent cultural values in conflict with those of the Lakota, as expressed in rituals or dances Black Elk describes? What did Black Elk learn about Euro–American culture through his participation in Buffalo Bill's Wild West show, and how did that spectacle represent Native Americans?[10]

Placing *Black Elk Speaks* in "literary" context is inherently problematic, for it does not grow out of, or "belong in," a single literary tradition; indeed, the process of its cross-cultural production is the subject of much interest and controversy today. Sources listed in the bibliographies, below, suggest how it combines traditional Lakota oral genres and elements of Euro-American autobiography. Indeed, despite Neihardt's tendency to model Black Elk's life on Western autobiographical prototypes, the narrative incorporates examples of various oral genres—from songs to coup tales and "High Horse's Courting"—that nicely illuminate the very different nature of literary production and reception in a tribal culture. Under most literary texts in the Western tradition, such tales and songs are generally communal and anonymous in authorship; in form as well as content, they reflect a very different sense of the relation between the individual and the community.

Black Elk Speaks can be read, of course, instructively in relation to works from print as well as oral cultures. For example, the book's visionary dimension makes for interesting comparison to some of Whitman's poetry, especially "Song of Myself." As the life story of a holy man, *Black Elk Speaks* can be read in relation to any spiritual autobiography, from Augustine on. The best American example might be Jonathan Edwards's *Personal Narrative*. But it should also be juxtaposed against other autobiographies by Native Americans. For example, the narrative of the eighteenth-century Mohegan, Samson Occom, which was produced without collaboration, includes the story of his conversion to Christianity and his career as a missionary to other Native Americans, a chapter of Black Elk's life that Neihardt omitted from his book. Two accounts of twentieth-century Lakota holy men, *Fools Crow,* by Thomas Mails (1979), and *Lame Deer, Seeker of Visions,* by Richard Erdoes and Lame Deer (1972), testify to the persistence of Lakota religion and can be read as sequels to Black Elk's story. Closer to the present, Mary Crow Dog's *Lakota Woman* (1991) depicts the life of a Lakota woman in contemporary America. A veteran of the occupation of Wounded Knee by AIM in 1976, Crow Dog illustrates the reliance of contemporary Indian activists on traditional beliefs and the intra-tribal political divisions that are the legacy of government policy. Contemporary works of fiction (Thomas Berger's *Little Big Man*) or drama (Arthur Kopit's *Indians*) may also work well with *Black Elk Speaks,* since they treat some of the same events from different points of view and in different media.

Like other Indian autobiography, *Black Elk Speaks* may be read in relation to two other American subgenres of autobiography founded in racial conflict: slave and captivity narratives. In broad terms, its plot is the opposite of the comic plot of the slave narrative, whose protagonist, by definition, moves from slavery to freedom: along with his people, Black Elk starts out "free" and ends up confined to a reservation. His narrative also functions antithetically to narratives of Indian captivity, such as Mary Rowlandson's. The historical irony of this popular and persistent genre is that it perpetuated the image of Euro–Americans surrounded by threatening "savages" even as Native Americans were being confined on reservations or otherwise moved out of the way of "Manifest Destiny." Such narratives thus served to rationalize the expropriation of Indian land and the destruction of Native American culture; *Black Elk Speaks* witnesses, laments, and questions this process.[11]

For reasons suggested above, it is essential that students attend to the process that produced this book: its background (Black Elk's post-conversion career as a catechist), its genesis (how the two collaborators came to work together), and what we might call the politics of the collaboration (the power differential between the two). Close comparison of passages in the transcripts with their equivalents in *Black Elk Speaks* may illuminate the process of cross-cultural translation. A crucial question to ask in this regard is: what are the implications of Neihardt's decision to end the narrative with Wounded Knee, ignoring Black Elk's life on the reservation and his career as Roman Catholic catechist? The issue of the appropriation of Native American speech can be further explored by reference to the case of the speech of Chief Seattle, a text that, over time, has been so freely "adapted" that its current versions are not only anachronistic but in some ways fundamentally inconsistent with the earliest one.

Finally, teachers of *Black Elk Speaks* should embrace and exploit the topical. The text speaks eloquently to developments in contemporary history, most obviously the forced assimilation of culturally distinctive people. An alert teacher will have no trouble finding current news stories that will generate discussion in relation to the issues raised by the book.[12]

C. Bibliographies

1. Related Works

Berger, Thomas. *Little Big Man.* New York: Dial Press, 1964.

Crow Dog, Mary, and Richard Erdoes. *Lakota Woman.* New York: Harper, 1991.

Douglass, Frederick. *Narrative of the Life of Frederick Douglass.* 1845. Reprint, New York: Viking Penguin, 1982.

Edwards, Jonathan. "Personal Narrative." In *The Heath Anthology of American Literature,* ed. Paul Lauter et al., 512–16. Lexington, Mass.: D. C. Heath, 1990.

Kopit, Arthur. *Indians: A Play.* New York: Hill and Wang, 1969.

Lame Deer/John Fire, and Richard Erdoes. *Lame Deer, Seeker of Visions: The Life of a Sioux Medicine Man.* New York: Simon and Schuster, 1972.

Mails, Thomas. *Fools Crow.* New York: Doubleday, 1979.

Occom, Samson. "A Short Narrative of My Life." In *The Heath Anthology,* 728–35.

Rowlandson, Mary. *A Narrative of the Captivity and Restoration of Mrs. Mary Rowlandson.* In *The Heath Anthology,* 317–42.

Seattle. "Speech," and Rudolf Kaiser, "Chief Seattle's Speech(es): American Origins and European Reception." In *Recovering the Word: Essays on Native American Literature,* ed. Brian Swann and Arnold Krupat, 497–536. Berkeley: University of California Press, 1987.

2. Best Criticism

Couser, G. Thomas. *Altered Egos.* New York: Oxford University Press, 1989. Chapter 8, "Black Elk Speaks with Forked Tongue," is concerned with the asymmetry of the collaboration between the Euro-American poet and the Lakota holy man, who was unable—disqualified by his lack of English and not invited by Neihardt—to review the manuscript. I argue that despite Neihardt's intentions, the process of the book's production unwittingly and ironically reenacts the very process of oppression and expropriation that it explicitly condemns. This view should be compared with those of Wong and Brumble, who acknowledge the inequality in the collaboration but emphasize the incorporation of indigenous elements in the narrative.

DeMallie, Raymond J. *The Sixth Grandfather: Black Elk's Teachings as Given to John G. Neihardt.* Lincoln: University of Nebraska Press, 1984. This is an essential resource, since it makes available the transcripts of Neihardt's interviews with Black Elk in 1931 (the basis of *Black Elk Speaks*) and 1944 (the basis of Neihardt's *When the Tree Flowered* [1951]). In 1931, Black Elk's words were translated from Lakota. to English by his son, Ben Black Elk, then recorded stenographically by Neihardt's daughter Enid. Her father worked from Enid's typescripts of her stenographic records. (DeMallie reconstructed the interviews using the typescripts and the stenographic notes.) Although these transcripts are by no means verbatim records of what Black Elk spoke, they are the closest and most reliable version; thus, they offer otherwise unavailable insight into the complex process of editing that produced *Black Elk Speaks. The Sixth Grandfather* also includes an indispensable one-hundred-page biographical introduction that carries Black Elk's story into the twentieth century.

Holler, Clyde. "Lakota Religion and Tragedy: The Theology of Black Elk Speaks." *Journal of American Religion* 52 (1984): 19–45. From studying the transcripts of the interviews, Holler concludes that in *Black Elk Speaks* "Neihardt sacrificed strict reporting of Black Elk's theological convictions in order to express his own. . . . The ultimate message of the book, not merely its details, is Neihardt's, not Black Elk's" (20). In particular, he suggests that Neihardt downplayed the more violent and militant aspects of Black Elk's vision in favor of more pacifistic and universal aspects. Moreover, for

> Neihardt the essential theological point is that the traditional Lakota religion and culture are dead [while] . . . it is precisely Black Elk's intention in collaborating with Neihardt to revive the traditional wisdom and values of the Lakotas. (37)

Krupat, Arnold. *For Those Who Come After: A Study of Native American Autobiography.* Berkeley: University of California Press, 1985. Krupat proceeds from the premise that autobiography, at least as Westerners think of it, is not found in Native American cultures, and from the observation that Indian autobiographies are all, in one way or another, the product of "contact"—which is to say, of defeat. In Chapter 2, "Indian Autobiography, Origins, Type, and Function," Krupat establishes the context that determined the shape of "Indian autobiographies" (autobiographies written in collaboration with Euro–Americans). He offers a subtle and penetrating account of the cross-cultural negotiation by which these "original bicultural composite compositions" were produced. In his final chapter, "History and Transcendence," he argues that Black Elk and Neihardt were ultimately working at cross-purposes: as a Christian mystic, Neihardt was incapable of fully understanding or accepting Black Elk's vision and, as an epic poet, he was ill-equipped to give that vision adequate literary form.

Olson, Paul A. "*Black Elk Speaks* as Epic and Ritual Attempt to Reverse History." In *Vision and Refuge: Essays on the Literature of the Great Plains,* ed. Virginia Faulkner, with Frederick C. Luebke, 3–27. Lincoln: University of Nebraska Press, 1982. Olson concentrates on Black Elk's visions, which he sees in historical context—that is, not as expressions of timeless truths or glimpses of a world beyond this one, but as responses to the crisis facing the Sioux. Thus, although Black Elk's later visions and dances are, in a sense, derived from and consistent with his defining power vision, they also reflect a historical consciousness unavailable to the nine-year-old recipient of that initial vision. Olson thus characterizes the visionary as a political agent who draws on traditional sources of power to intervene in history on behalf of his people.

Stone, Albert E. *Autobiographical Occasions and Original Acts: Versions of American Identity from Henry Adams to Nate Shaw.* Philadelphia: University of Pennsylvania Press, 1982. In a chapter entitled "The Soul and the Self: Black Elk and Thomas Merton," Stone compares *Black Elk Speaks* with *The Seven Storey Mountain.* Stone is more concerned with the psychological and spiritual dimensions of *Black Elk Speaks* than with its historical and political aspects. Though sensitive to its ethnic distinctiveness, Stone argues that its collaborative production "locates this unusual story more within the Western frame of autobiographical reference than might at first be expected" and that the book provides "one paradigm of modern spiritual autobiography" (65). His approach to Black Elk encourages students to relate his spirituality to that of other American autobiographers from very different cultural backgrounds—for example, Thomas Shepard, Jonathan Edwards, John Woolman, Louis Sullivan, Malcolm X, and Annie Dillard.

Wong, Hertha. *Sending My Heart Back across the Years: Tradition and Innovation in Native American Autobiography.* New York: Oxford University Press, 1992. Her treatment of Black Elk begins with a helpful review of the critical reception of the book. As the title of her book promises, her account is best in delineating how the book incorporates and modifies traditional Lakota genres—Ehani Woyakapi (legend) and Woyakapi (history)—by including tales of hunting and battle; she stresses the oral and pictographic features of the narrative (the 1972 Pocket Book edition includes illustrations by Standing Bear). Her account is thus a significant act of recuperation as well as interpretation.

3. Other Sources

Berkhofer, Robert F., Jr. *The White Man's Indian: Images of the American Indian from Columbus to the Present.* New York: Knopf, 1978.

Brown, Dee. *Bury My Heart at Wounded Knee: An Indian History of the American West.* New York: Holt, 1970.

Brown, Joseph Epes. *The Sacred Pipe: Black Elk's Account of the Seven Rites of the Oglala Sioux.* Norman: University of Oklahoma Press, 1963.

Brumble, H. David. *American Indian Autobiography.* Berkeley: University of California Press, 1988.

Buffalo Bill and the Wild West. Brooklyn: Brooklyn Museum, 1981.

Deloria, Vine, Jr. *Custer Died for Your Sins: An Indian Manifesto.* London: Macmillan, 1969.

———. Introduction to *Black Elk Speaks,* by John G. Neihardt, xi–xiv. Lincoln: University of Nebraska Press, 1979.

Kehoe, Alice B. *The North American Indians: A Comprehensive Account.* 2d ed. Englewood Cliffs, N.J.: Prentice Hall, 1992.

Neihardt, John G. *Black Elk Speaks, Being the Life Story of a Holy Man of the Oglala Sioux.* 1932. Reprint, Lincoln: University of Nebraska Press, 1979.

Powers, William K. "When Black Elk Speaks, Everybody Listens." In *Religion in Native North America,* ed. Christopher Vecsey, 136–51. Moscow: University of Idaho Press, 1990.

Rice, Julian. *Black Elk's Story: Distinguishing Its Lakota Purpose.* Albuquerque: University of New Mexico Press, 1991.

Spicer, Edward H. *A Short History of the Indians of the United States.* New York: Van Nostrand, 1969.

Truettner, William, ed. *The West as America: Reinterpreting Images of the Frontier, 1820–1920.* Washington: Smithsonian Institution Press, 1991.

Utley, Robert M. *The Indian Frontier of the American West, 1846–1890.* Albuquerque: University of New Mexico Press, 1984.

Notes

1. Neihardt interviewed Black Elk again in 1944; those interviews (and stories told by Eagle Elk) were the basis of Neihardt's *When the Tree Flowered, the Fictional Biography of Eagle Voice, a Sioux Indian.* (Lincoln: University of Nebraska Press, 1951), a fictionalized account of the history of the Lakota people from its origins through contact with whites, as told by a composite narrator, Eagle Voice. Inspired by *Black Elk Speaks,* Joseph Epes Brown interviewed Black Elk in the late 1940s. Those interviews were the basis of Brown's *The Sacred Pipe* (1953); non-narrative in organization, it explains the sacred rituals of the Lakota.

2. "Introduction" to the 1979 edition of *Black Elk Speaks,* xiii. For the irony of this pronouncement, see Krupat, *For Those Who Come After,* 134.

3. A brief, authoritative account of Lakota beliefs and a gloss on Black Elk's visions can be found in DeMallie's introduction to the 1931 interviews, in his *Sixth Grandfather,* 77–99.

4. This account is based on a number of sources. Chapter 6, "The Prairie-Plains," of Alice B. Kehoe's *North American Indians* provides a good overview of Plains Indians culture and history. Two particularly helpful books—good sources for student reports, written or oral—are Robert M. Utley's *The Indian Frontier of the American West, 1846–1890,* and Robert F. Berkhofer's *The White Man's Indian: Images of the American Indian from Columbus to the Present.* Dee Brown's *Bury My Heart at Wounded Knee: An Indian History of the American West* is an instructive attempt to tell the story from the Native American perspective, and Vine Deloria's *Custer Died for Your Sins* gives a pithy, polemical account of many issues raised by this text.

5. Utley's *Indian Frontier of the American West* has a useful map of the Sioux Wars, 1862–1868, on p. 121; of the northern Plains, 1868–1890, on pp. 152–53; and of the Teton Sioux reservations in 1890 on p. 250. The inset map on p. 250 illustrating the reduction of the Great Sioux Reservation from 1868 to 1889 is worth more than the proverbial one thousand words.

6. The Black Hills—site of Harney Peak, where *Black Elk Speaks* concludes with a ritual prayer, as well as of Mount Rushmore and other tourist attractions—are still considered sacred territory by the Sioux, and efforts to reclaim some of this land continue.

7. The publication of the book, which portrayed Black Elk as entirely committed to traditional Lakota religion, had at least one unanticipated negative consequence: it put Black Elk in an awkward position with reservation Jesuits, for whom he had been a model of assimilation through conversion.

8. There is an irony to this, for, as DeMallie notes, the oldest people on

the Pine Ridge reservation remember Black Elk as a Catholic catechist, while the younger generations know nothing of that phase of his life; they know him only through his book. Black Elk was far more complex than *Black Elk Speaks* suggests.

9. A matter of literary technique or style is relevant here, for one of the strengths of Neihardt's rendering of Black Elk's speech is his retention, or literal translation, of native idioms, such as "yellow metal" for gold. Stripping gold of the connotations accrued by its English name enables or requires the reader to see the substance from the perspective of a people whose culture and economy did not value it; to the Lakota, gold was just another metal.

10. For various perspectives on the Wild West show, see *Buffalo Bill and the Wild West,* which contains essays by Vine Deloria, Jr., Richard Slotkin, Howard Lamar, and others.

11. Visual depictions of the "Vanishing American" are also interesting to consider in relation to *Black Elk Speaks,* as are paintings of the "last stand," a very popular subject at the turn of the century. See William Truettner, *The West as America.*

12. As I write this in the summer of 1993, for example, "ethnic cleansing" continues in the former Yugoslavia, and the massacre of Yanomami Indians by gold miners in the Amazon region parallels all too closely events in Sioux history.

Beauty Before Me:

Notes on *House Made of Dawn* (N. Scott Momaday)

HELEN JASKOSKI

A. Analysis of Themes and Forms

Introduction

This analysis of *House Made of Dawn* focuses on themes that link it with other works of American and world literature, and is meant to complement essential scholarship that addresses the ways in which the novel draws upon specifically American Indian culture and literary precedents. In particular, the works by Evers, Nelson, and Scarberry-Garcia noted in the bibliography are indispensable for comprehending the novel's major ideas.

Synopsis

The action of *House Made of Dawn* takes place between July 20, 1945, and February 28, 1952. The narration comprises an undated prologue and four dated sections set in the pueblo of Walatowa (Jemez), New Mexico (prologue and sections one and four), and the Los Angeles area (sections two and three).

After a brief prologue describing a man named Abel who is running in the southwestern countryside, the story proper opens on July 20, 1945, with Abel's return to his grandfather Francisco in Walatowa. Sickened by alcohol and war, Abel cannot reintegrate himself into the village. He has a brief affair with Angela St. John, a sensuous, pregnant woman taking mineral baths for an undefined neurasthenia. He also participates in a religious festival and is singled out by an ominous-appearing albino man. Meanwhile, the omniscient narration follows a parallel line with the village priest, Father Olguin, as he studies the diary of a predecessor and makes an awkward approach to Angela. On August 1, in a strange, ritualistic encounter, Abel stabs the albino to death in a cornfield.

The two chapters of the second section are dated January 27 and 28, 1952. This portion of the story takes place in Los Angeles and centers on John Big Bluff Tosamah, a Kiowa, a storefront preacher, and a priest of the peyote religion. The chapter for January 27 contains a sermon by Tosamah on a Gospel verse: "In the beginning was the Word"; in his sermon Tosamah maintains that white people have debased and corrupted language. While Tosamah gives this sermon, Abel lies fifteen miles away, having suffered a terrible beating that has mangled his hands. The omniscient narrator intersperses Abel's memories of the past with awareness of his pain-wracked body: he recalls a job, his trial, an earnest social worker named Milly with whom he has had an affair, and life in prison and in the army. This chapter also contains a depiction of a peyote ceremony. Tosamah's language throughout is a strange mixture of sarcasm, street slang, and pontification. The January 28 chapter comprises Tosamah's second sermon, "The Way to Rainy Mountain," in which the preacher meditates on his Kiowa grandmother's life and the history of the magnificent Kiowa culture.

The third section of the novel, dated February 20, 1952, is narrated by Ben Benally, a relocated Navajo friend of Abel and Tosamah. Benally's rambling narration, aided by a bottle of wine, reveals more of Abel's life in Los Angeles as well as fragments of Benally's idealized pastoral youth on the reservation. Benally recalls Angela's visit with Abel in the hospital; now the mother of a son, she told Abel a story with a heroic theme, intimating that he reminded her of the hero. Benally also recollects going with Abel to a party in the hills outside the city, where he sang songs, including the verses beginning "House Made of Dawn" from the sacred Navajo healing ceremony called the Night Chant.

The fourth section of *House Made of Dawn* is two brief chapters dated February 27 and 28, 1952. Abel returns to Walatowa to care for his dying grandfather. Having performed appropriate burial rituals, he begins a ceremonial run into the dawn. The novel has moved in a circle, returning to the event depicted in the prologue.

Circular Form

N. Scott Momaday has commented on the circular form and the importance of circling back in *House Made of Dawn*. After the prologue, each of the four sections is dated and presented in chronological order; then at the end of the book the reader encounters Abel, the protagonist, preparing for the race that he is shown running in the undated prologue—the prologue has really pictured the end of the story. The enclosure of the two Los Angeles sections within the first and last New Mexico sections restates the circular emphasis. Within the two middle sections the nonchronological narration moves back and forth: Abel's awakening on a southern California beach after a vicious beating; fragments of his trial; his affair with Milly; encounters with bureaucrats, landladies, and employers in a rehabilitation attempt; Tosamah's two sermons and the peyote ceremony; and Ben Benally's recollections of his childhood on the reservation, of Abel and the community of relocated Indians in Los Angeles, and of Abel's tentative steps toward healing. All these themes and episodes appear and reappear in the fragmented narrative. Playing with chronology in this way characterizes modern and postmodern literature from many sources, and Momaday's affinity with authors like Faulkner and Joyce resonates in *House Made of Dawn*.

Spatial and geographical circling, however, may be even more important than temporal circularity. William Bevis has pointed out that a recurring theme in contemporary American Indian fiction is the motif of "homing": of exit and exile from the community, adventure and trial, and finally return, reconciliation, and—sometimes—the importation into the community of new wisdom or technology. This is the classical outline of the origin myths of many ceremonies. An example from Apache tradition tells of an old woman cast out by her people because "they did not like her" and she was "good for nothing." Blind, deaf, and mute, she was a burden. Weeping and alone, she was visited by Mountain Spirits who cured her by singing to her. The story explains that she returned to her people with these powerful songs: "Then she performed all of that which had been given to her in exactly their way. And, in this way, the ceremony came to be customarily performed" (Hoijer, 33; rpt., Astrov, 211). This is the governing theme of Leslie Silko's novel *Ceremony*, which also centers on a returning veteran and his debilitating, violence-induced malaise. Abel's return to Walatowa, like Tayo's return to Laguna in *Ceremony*, constitutes a reintegration of himself into the life of the community. However, unlike Tayo or the woman in the Apache story, Abel does not share any new insight or ceremony with his community. His healing experience seems purely personal and individual.

Ambiguity and Point of View

House Made of Dawn is a difficult, complex book, which does not follow a single chronological story line nor remain within a single consistent point of view. The novel challenges the reader to do more than follow (or "swallow") a plot: one must take an active part in the construction of the story, sorting and sifting through different kinds of texts related through varied points of view. The challenge is similar to that of a puzzle, which must be pieced together from random shapes in order for a coherent picture to emerge.

Many of the characters in *House Made of Dawn* are enigmatic and mysterious. Questions recur: Why does Abel kill the albino? Does he fear some personal injury? Or is he trying to rescue the community, as in the traditional tales, by eliminating an evil person? The albino himself is an enigma: he is never seen threatening anyone or in association with any evil that occurs in the village, yet Abel regards him as unquestionably an enemy. The text does not answer another question: Why does the albino apparently go willingly with Abel to his death? Is he consciously acting out some ritual part? Angela St. John is another mysterious character: Is she simply a sinful temptation for Abel? How do the affair they have, and the story she tells him much later, affect his healing process? What about Tosamah, who appears to make fun of everything, including the peyote that centers his worship?

The organization of the book, based on a principle of fragmentation and reconstitution, also lends itself to gaps in plot development. One such gap is the question of who beats up Abel, breaks his hands, and leaves him on the beach. Benally recounts a scene in which Martinez, the sadistic police officer, bludgeons Abel's hands with a flashlight but does not break any bones; Abel leaves the apartment days later announcing he will find the "culebra" and presumably even the score (*culebra* is a term for snake, applied pejoratively). Abel awakens on the beach, which is about fifteen miles from the inner-city neighborhood where he lives, with his hands broken. Later, Abel turns up at the apartment, more dead than alive. Was it Martinez who injured and nearly killed Abel? How did Abel manage to return to the apartment in his semiconscious, mangled condition? This is one of several examples of the discontinuity of the plot, of significant elements that tend to disappear in the interstices of the patchwork narration.

Momaday tends to open sections and chapters with scene-setting omniscient narration. The Prologue, with its panoramic view of Abel running, is an example, as are the paragraphs describing the New Mexico and intermountain plains. This is an authoritative storytelling voice, comparable to the narrative voice in oral tales and myths, with no ambiguity as to reliability. However, the impersonal omniscient narrator frequently segues into a single character's limited point of view. A crucial example is the scene—itself told in several separate fragments—in which Abel awakens on the beach after having endured a brutal beating. The narration follows Abel's consciousness as he tries to sort out the events in his life that have led him to this horrible situation. These passages exemplify the profound ambiguity of the novel, for it is here that Abel justifies his murder of the albino; however, it is also evident that Abel's thinking is distorted by pain as he drifts in and out of consciousness and loses awareness of time and his surroundings. The reader must ponder the question: What validity, if any, does the novel ask us to ascribe to perception of witchcraft as a defense against the accusation of murder? Is Abel's judgment of the albino an expression of a culturally coherent set of values, or is it the product of distorted thinking?

Other episodes in the story are narrated in whole or in part through the points of view of Angela, Father Olguin, Francisco, and Tosamah. In each case the biases and personal agendas of the character must be taken into account as part of the storytelling. The text is destabilized as conflicting points of view subvert the reader's confidence in knowing what is supposed to have happened and how it is supposed to be judged. Stream of consciousness and internal monologue create similar ambiguities. For instance, near the end of the section he narrates, Benally criticizes Tosamah as utterly cynical and without understanding. This judgment must be read against Benally's consumption of a bottle of wine through the night and his uncritical acceptance of the relocation program and its promotion of consumerism and materialism. Benally's section of the novel is represented as his internal monologue. Tosamah's own language, especially in his first sermon, is especially problematic: he moves awkwardly back and forth between street slang, pontification, and poetic revery, subverting his own words in the act of pronouncing them.

Finally, other textual forms also occur in *House Made of Dawn,* giving it the aspect of a modernist collage. Oration and sermon take up most of the Tosamah sections. Excerpts from written diaries form part of the text of the first section. The novel is laced throughout with fragments of bureaucratic forms, questionnaires, and documents. Contrasting with these scraps of written forms are renderings of oral tales and poems. The stories that Father Olguin, Tosamah, Angela, and Benally relate are central to the healing theme, as are the two translations from Navajo. The passages from Navajo ceremonies are incorporated into the story as if they were lyric poems complete in themselves. Navajo is an extremely complex language, and there is much debate over the extent to which these poems—torn from their ceremonial context and translated very cryptically—can be considered authentic representations of Navajo thought. What is evident is that both are English poems of great power. Their stately rhythms, rich imagery, and incantatory structure make them compelling pieces of literature. Moreover, the reader is invited, especially in view of Momaday's appropriation of a line from one of the poems for the novel's title, to regard *House Made of Dawn* as essentially a lyrical text—as much poem as story. This approach to the book requires a meditative, contemplative attitude, the same intense reading that would be required of a poem by Emily Dickinson or Wallace Stevens.

House Made of Dawn and American Romanticism

An emphasis on ambiguity and undecidability suggests the Romantic dimension of the novel, which can be seen to grow out of Momaday's admiration for American Romantic writers of the nineteenth century, especially Melville. Commentators have suggested that the mysterious albino resembles the white whale in *Moby Dick*. The albino man is white, implacable, large in size, and interpreted by Abel and Francisco as malevolent. Abel's decision, then, to "kill such an enemy" would parallel Ahab's quest to destroy his enemy. However, while Melville renders in obsessive detail the power and danger of the whale as emblematic of some cosmic evil, Momaday offers but an abstraction of evil. There is no objective correlative for Abel's belief that the albino is a witch: Francisco's corn is not blighted, and Abel's malaise predates his encounter with the white man. The "white man" is said to be evil, but is never shown to have done anything evil. Indeed, Abel seems more profoundly disordered than Ahab: his calculated assault on the albino man, his cool, detached regard for the body of a human being he has just killed, suggests the Mersault of Camus's *The Stranger* more than the tormented protagonist of Melville's epic. Evers (in "Words and Place") suggests that the albino's whiteness resembles that of the white whale in signifying to Abel an emptiness and meaninglessness that he perceives at the heart of the universe and that is a projection of the emptiness he feels within himself. This is different from the perception of witchcraft, which has to do with injury rather than meaninglessness, and it raises the question of Abel's moral culpability in killing a creature who is not, in actuality, a symbol or projection, but another human being. It is a culpability that Momaday does not have him acknowledge.

Two other Melville comparisons that may illuminate issues in *House Made of Dawn* center on the character of Tosamah. A man of two worlds, educated and functioning in both Indian and non-Indian society, Tosamah relishes the bewilderment of the law in the face of witchcraft as a murder defense. Like the young Indians in Leslie Silko's "Tony's Story" (which is based on the same historical event that the albino episode derives from; see Evers), and as Captain Vere eventually comes to realize in *Billy Budd*, Tosamah recognizes that law has no capacity to confront evil. Law and reason can deal with crime, but not with sin.

The most explicit debt to Melville is the echo of *The Confidence Man* in the character and speech of Tosamah. Portions of this section of the novel were published earlier in *Ramparts* magazine in an article titled "The Morality of Indian Hating," an obvious allusion to the chapters on "The Metaphysics of Indian Hating" in *The Confidence Man*. In the *Ramparts* article, as later in *The Way to Rainy Mountain*—where the excerpt also appears—Momaday is speaking about his own life, his grandmother, and his sense of himself as Kiowa. Behind the mask of the character Tosamah, then, Momaday imports an autobiographical dimension into *House Made of Dawn*. The omniscient narrator comments correctly that Tosamah's language is characterized by "conviction, caricature, callousness" (92). The identification of the author with this tricksterlike character and his manipulative use of language further destabilize the text: Tosamah apparently represents the authorial voice, yet his commentary is unpredictable, contradictory, and subversive of his assertions.

While Tosamah represents one possible tradition-based response to urban life, that of the trickster, Ben Benally represents another, the pastoral idealist. The trickster figures of Native American lore bear some resemblance to Melville's confidence man in being verbal manipulators and opportunists, although the Native American trickster is a much more complex, heroically proportioned figure, participating in the creation of the world and the establishment of human lifeways. Tosamah combines the sacred and comic as the traditional trickster does, and not only survives but flourishes in the urban jungle, yet he does not provide the model Abel needs to find his way in the new, post-war world.

Ben Benally emigrates from a pastoral world, and although Momaday evidently did not know of the autobiography of the Navajo called Left Handed when *House Made of Dawn* was being written, Benally's musings have some of the same serenity as the recollections of Left Handed. The Night Chanter section of *House Made of Dawn* is pastoral in convention as well as in tone: it is a recollection in an urban (though certainly not aristocratic) milieu of an idealized pastoral life. The pastoral Benally evokes lives in his mind and imagination, and is consequently deeply romantic. Indeed, Benally, like Tosamah, is a kind of stand-in for Momaday: the famous passage in *The Way to Rainy Mountain* that advocates contemplation of "the remembered earth" is all about imaginary—not real—landscape. Abel's rejection of both Tosamah's and Benally's solutions—the urban trickster or the imagined pastoral—is also (as Nelson makes clear) a rejection of Romantic constructs in favor of actual relationship to a real, physical place.

Religious Dimensions

House Made of Dawn is an extended meditation on the symptoms and eventual cure of spiritual malaise. The theme of spiritual regeneration is figured in the context of four important religious traditions: the ceremonial life of the Pueblos, Navajo healing chantways, the rituals of the peyote religion, and the Roman Catholicism of the Spanish Southwest. Some of the traditions borrow from each other, but each is distinctive.

Critical events in the novel are tied to the seasonal ceremonies of the pueblo agricultural year. Abel recollects an early sexual encounter at a New Year's ceremonial dance, and as Nelson points out, his sickness of soul manifests itself in his killing of the captured eagle during the Bahkyush Eagle Watchers ceremony, long before he has gone off to war. Angela attends the Cochiti corn dance, a fertility ritual which she, a pregnant woman, perceives as a nihilistic vision—a sign, according to Evers, of her spiritual emptiness ("Words and Place"); Evers also relates Abel's inability to participate fully in the festival of Saint James with an inappropriate response to witchcraft ("Ways of Telling"). At the end of the novel Abel correctly carries out the rituals for burial of his grandfather, and his ability to undertake the dawn run that is a striking emblem throughout the book signifies a reintegration into the whole life of the community.

Like the clan priests who blend Spanish Catholic and indigenous religious traditions in the Walatowa festival of Saint James, Abel incorporates into his dawn run, which is a Jemez ceremony, phrases from a Navajo chant. *House Made of Dawn* takes its title from a prayer that forms part of a long, extremely elaborate Navajo ritual, the Night Chant. This prayer, with other texts and a volume of information about the Night Chant ceremony, was transcribed and edited during the 1890s by an army physician and self-trained anthropologist named Washington Matthews, but Momaday almost certainly encountered the text of the prayer in Margot Astrov's anthology, *American Indian Prose and Poetry,* where it is printed next to the other translated Navajo text that appears in *House Made of Dawn.* Navajo healing chants are not, like pueblo agricultural ceremonies, tied to a seasonal cycle. They are specific for illnesses of various kinds, and how much of a given ceremony is performed for an individual may depend on several factors including how much the patient's family can afford to pay. (The most complete analysis of the medicinal aspects of chantways is Sandner's study; the most extended discussion of *House Made of Dawn* as displaying chantway themes is Scarberry-Garcia's; an exhaustive analysis of the *Nightway* as text and ceremony is in Faris.) In *House Made of Dawn,* Abel is not treated with a full-fledged ceremonial performance, but is "sung over" informally and without public ceremony by Ben Benally; nevertheless, the power of the prayer's words operates, returning at the healing moment of Abel's dawn run.

The need for Abel to have a ceremony is related to his status as a returning warrior. The figure of the warrior is central to much American Indian myth and storytelling. The warrior—and often warrior brothers or warrior twins—figures importantly in traditional lore. *House Made of Dawn* emphasizes the unclean aspects of warmaking: the pollution of mind and spirit that accompanies organized violence. Abel returns from war drunk, alienated, and battered in spirit as he is later to be battered physically in the urban jungle of Los Angeles. Traditionally, a warrior needed to be cleansed and purified after returning home in order to keep the violence of combat from infecting the community and to neutralize or transform the power of the captured spoils. Certain Navajo ceremonials are carried out precisely for this purpose of purification after war; one of these is Blessingway, which some people say was in danger of dying out until after the Second World War, when so many returning veterans needed the ceremony that it was revived and began to be retaught.

House Made of Dawn depicts a purification ritual that Abel undergoes. Traditional rituals take place under the direction of knowledgeable practitioners, who know which forms are correct for a given individual. However, Abel has returned from a new kind of war fought on unknown and alien territory; it seems that his must be a new ritual, worked out in the terms of his own experience. It also appears, as noted above, that unlike traditional ceremonies, Abel's healing process is not a gift for the community but a purely personal transformation.

A third religious tradition depicted in *House Made of Dawn* is the peyote religion. The peyote ritual presided over by Tosamah is the ceremonial expression of a religious movement that originated in north-central Mexico, from where it spread northward through the southern plains and eventually became diffused throughout North America. In the course of adaptation to conditions in the United States, the peyote religion incorporated many Christian elements; it is clear in *House Made of Dawn* that the ceremony is a communion ritual similar to other Christian communion services. The peyote religion of the Native American Church has been described as the first important pan-Indian movement, and early adherents sought to win converts to the peyote religion as an alternative to the pagan practices, which were not only under official attack from government policies but were also perceived as ineffectual in preventing alcoholism and family violence (LaBarre). Until a recent Supreme Court decision, the peyote ceremonies of the Native American Church received the same protection under the First Amendment as other religious services.

There has been a Catholic presence in the Southwest since the arrival of missionaries in the 1500s. In *House Made of Dawn* the village priest, Father Olguin, represents that presence. More than doctrine or creed, it is the decorative aspects of Catholicism that are emphasized in the novel: what Father Olguin wears to say Mass (although he vests in red for a martyr, the date, July 21, is not a martyr's feast); bells, candles, and incense; the quaintness of a folktale about Saint James.

Olguin is important as a parallel with Abel's grandfather, Francisco. Both men have the role of "elder" in their respective traditions. Francisco is a mediating figure as well, being sacristan in the church as well as participant in a traditional Jemez religious society. Francisco and Olguin also resemble the "stricken brothers" in the governing myth of the Night Way chant (the story is related in Matthews). Scarberry-Garcia correlates the myth with Abel and his brother, Vidal, but another parallel with the mythical brothers—one paralyzed and one blind—may be seen in Francisco, who is lame in one leg, and Olguin, who is partially blind. Both Francisco and Olguin also have a high regard for books, especially as records of the past. Francisco keeps a ledger book with illustrations denoting important events of the year. Such ledger books form an important subgenre of the art of nineteenth-century Indians, and Kiowa captives at Fort Marion produced a substantial body of work in this mode. Father Olguin, for his part, scrutinizes the journal of a predecessor, Fray Nicolas; in the journal fragments he finds references to people and events that appear to be part of Abel's story. The text of Nicolas's diary is something of a linguistic tour de force: according to the dates of the story, the friar would have been writing in Spanish in the 1890s, yet the English of these passages has an antique, sixteenth-century cadence to it, as if it were produced by a British colonist like Samuel Sewall or one of the Mathers.

Angela (Mrs. Martin) St. John is the other character associated with Catholicism. She attends Mass but implies that she chooses not to participate: her choice indicates that she is Catholic, as she would not be allowed to decide whether to take communion otherwise. She is as alienated from her tradition as Abel is from his. Angela suffers from spiritual malaise, as does Abel, and she appears to have achieved a personal reconciliation when she visits Abel in the hospital in Los Angeles. Her reintegration into her life anticipates Abel's return and reintegration into the life of his pueblo.

Finally, witchcraft is important to the plot of *House Made of Dawn*. Simmons has documented how belief in witches pervades different cultures of the Southwest. Most studies of the phenomenon among Pueblo Indians emphasize the idea that witchcraft is not inherent in any being, human or otherwise, but is rather a misuse of power that is sacred but morally neutral. As noted above, the witchcraft that Abel attributes to the albino is one of the most enigmatic points in a very ambiguous text.

Federal Relocation Policy

The particular sociopolitical context of the two middle sections of *House Made of Dawn* is never explicitly named in the novel. The urban environment in which Tosamah, Benally,Milly, and Abel exist in Los Angeles is the product of the federal policies of Termination and Relocation, which were fostered especially during the 1950s and never really abandoned in spite of considerable evidence of their failure. The most accessible discussion of these policies is still Vine Deloria's in *Custer Died for Your Sins*. The federal programs were the culmination of assimilationist thinking initiated with the missionary efforts of Puritan immigrants. The intended result was that Indian reservations would be abolished (terminated) and Indian people be integrated into the mainstream society and economy. This outcome would be accomplished largely by the relocation of Indians to urban areas with provision of transition benefits such as job training and health care. As with other Indian programs, funding was never adequate for the benefits side of the program, and thousands of Indians found themselves in the slums and skid rows of inner cities, jobless, poor, and lacking the family and community supports they might have turned to at home. It is just such a marginal inner-city area of Los Angeles in which Tosamah, Benally, and Abel find themselves.

Tosamah and Benally manage accommodations to the new reality, Tosamah by following the model of the trickster and Benally by reliance on pastoral revery. The focus on Abel, however, suggests a rejection of the whole scheme, including the possibilities offered by Tosamah and Benally, and insistence on return to the conservative, traditional, pueblo reservation. It is only in his home place, in the context of the landscape and culture of his birth, that Abel's cure can finally be realized.

B. Teaching *House Made of Dawn*

1. Preparation: Reading and Viewing

Because the different sections of the novel are so diverse in tone, focus, narration, and cultural background (and indeed one has been published separately elsewhere), it is helpful, if the class schedule permits, to read the book twice: read it through once, then read and discuss each section in turn.

Several video and audiotape materials are worth presenting either before studying *House Made of Dawn* or in the course of class discussion of the novel. Source information is in the list of works cited.

Seasons of a Navaho follows a Navajo family through the course of a year. This film emphasizes the timeless, pastoral elements of traditional Navajo life. The film depicts the kind of life that Ben Benally remembers, what he draws upon in memory to maintain his equable demeanor and the source of his healing words for Abel.

Surviving Columbus is an excellent introduction to the history of the Southwest pueblos. The film is narrated entirely by members of the Southwest Indian nations.

There is a film version of *House Made of Dawn,* featuring American Indian actor Larry Littlebird. Momaday worked with the filmmakers on the production, and comparison of film and written texts could address significant issues in the novel. The depiction of the peyote ritual is particularly striking.

Momaday is a powerful speaker, storyteller, and reader of his own works. It is worthwhile for a class to spend at least some time listening to his taped reading of passages from *House Made of Dawn*; the interview with Kay Bonetti on the companion tape is of interest as well.

2. Small Group Activities

a. Panels on each section. If it is not possible to read the book twice, students can be divided into small groups, with one section of the book assigned to each group for study and presentation of their findings to the class.

b. Interviews with Angela St. John, Tosamah, Benally, Father Olguin. One person may be moderator or interviewer; others take on roles of the characters and answer questions based on their reading of the characters they "play." Both interviewer and role players should be able to find support in the text for their questions and replies. There should be moments when the character simply does not or cannot explain him or herself: this to bring out the essential ambiguity of these characters.

c. Research panels: assigning small groups to research the cultures and traditions presented. It is a good idea to provide each group with a brief bibliography.

3. Topics for Discussion and Writing

a. Find (or draw) five pictures, one for each section, that would make appropriate introductory images for the novel's major divisions. Write a brief explanation of your choice for each.

b. Silence has both positive and negative value in *House Made of Dawn*. Compare a passage or an instance of the positive quality of silence, and one showing silence as negative.

c. What does this novel have to say about language? Consider Tosamah's statements about language and its power, the passages excerpted from questionnaires and legal documents, Benally's songs. What makes a given use of language benign or destructive?

d. Momaday is a lyric poet and a painter. Analyze selected passages of description as poetic prose, attending to such elements as metaphor, simile, imagery, and so on.

e. Setting and place are important in this novel. Contrast the settings of Walatowa and Los Angeles as described in the novel: how do descriptions portray the atmosphere and mood of these places?

f. Religion is central to *House Made of Dawn*. Examine the depiction of or references to rituals from these religious traditions: Catholicism, traditional Pueblo religion, the peyote religion, Navajo religion. Again, brief bibliographies will be helpful.

g. Discuss examples of different kinds of writing in *House Made of Dawn* (for instance, Francisco keeps a diary or journal, and Father Olguin reads a diary written by a predecessor). How is writing used and misused?

h. The title's emphasis on sunrise and dawn is elaborated in scenes and images throughout the book. Discuss images of sunrise and dawn and events that take place at this time of day.

i. Storytelling has many functions in both literate and preliterate cultures. Look at two stories that characters in this novel tell. Who tells each story? Who is the audience? How does the story reflect important themes in the novel as a whole? Does telling the story make a difference in what happens?

j. The title of the novel refers to a house. What houses or dwelling places are described in the novel, and how do they relate to the book's major themes?

k. The snake is a creature with ambiguous meaning in *House Made of Dawn*. Trace references to snakes in the novel to determine possible significance(s).

l. If you are familiar with other fiction by American Indian writers, draw comparisons between Abel as returning warrior with figures like Tayo in Leslie Silko's *Ceremony* or Attis McCurtain in Louis Owens's *The Sharpest Sight*.

C. Bibliographies

1. Related Works

House Made of Dawn might be taught in courses focusing on multicultural themes, contemporary literature or contemporary fiction, southwestern or western literature, regionalism, surveys of American literature, religion and literature, modernism and experimentation, war and peace in literature, Pulitzer and other prize-winning novels, and so on. The works listed below are suggested as appropriate for these contexts.

Blowsnake, Sam. *Crashing Thunder: The Autobiography of an American Indian,* ed. Paul Radin. 1926. Reprint, with introduction by Arnold Krupat, Lincoln: University of Nebraska Press, 1983. This autobiography written by a Winnebago man offers some interesting parallels with *House Made of Dawn:* a murder committed by the protagonist, peyote religion, interpolation of traditional texts.

Cather, Willa. *Death Comes for the Archbishop.* 1926. Reprint, New York: Knopf, 1957. Cather's novel is comparable in its loving descriptions of the southwestern landscape; it would be especially appropriate for a course in southwestern literature. Wallace Stegner, a Cather scholar, was director of the fiction-writing program at Stanford when Momaday was a graduate student; the possible direct influence of Cather on Momaday's work has not yet been examined.

Crane, Stephen. *The Red Badge of Courage.* 1895. Reprint, ed. Sculley Bradley, et al. New York: W. W. Norton, 1962. Both Momaday's novel and Crane's are accounts of young men's initiations: Henry Fleming is initiated into war, while Abel must be cleansed from war and reinitiated into a pacifist, agrarian community. Both novels are also interesting literary examples of manipulation of point of view.

Dickinson, Emily. *The Complete Poems,* ed. Thomas H. Johnson. Boston and

Toronto: Little, Brown and Company, 1955. Momaday identifies himself as a poet and visual artist as much as a writer of narrative. He has expressed profound admiration for Emily Dickinson and spent a research year reading her poems in manuscript.

Faulkner, William. *The Bear.* 1942. In *Bear, Man, and God: Seven Approaches to William Faulkner's "The Bear,"* ed. Francis Lee Utley et al. New York: Random House, 1964. Faulkner's influence on Momaday's language has been remarked by several critics, and Momaday has expressed a deep spiritual affinity with bears, which he shares with the protagonist of his later novel, *The Ancient Child.* There are several bear stories in *House Made of Dawn* (see Barry, Scarberry-Garcia), and Momaday's poem titled "The Bear" (*The Gourd Dancer*) may have been inspired by Faulkner's story.

Hawthorne, Nathaniel. "Young Goodman Brown." 1835. In *Mosses from an Old Manse,* ed. William Charvat, Roy Harvey Pearce, et al., 74–90. Athens: Ohio State University Press, 1974.

———. *The Scarlet Letter.* 1850. Reprint, ed. Ross C. Murfin. Boston: Bedford Books of St. Martin's Press, 1991. Hawthorne's themes—on the nature of evil, witchcraft or occult power, scapegoating rituals, and a relationship to nature—are also important in *House Made of Dawn.*

House Made of Dawn. Richardson Morse, director. With Larry Littlebird and John Saxon. New Line Cinema, 1972. This film along with *Seasons of a Navajo* and *Surviving Columbus* (see part 3, below) could be especially effective in an interdisciplinary course. Also, see above, section B, part 1.

Kingston, Maxine Hong. *The Woman Warrior: Memoirs of a Girlhood among Ghosts.* New York: Alfred A. Knopf, 1977. Kingston's development of the idea of "talk story" may be compared with Momaday's use of oral myth and poetry.

Melville, Herman. *Moby Dick.* 1851. Reprint, ed. Harrison Hayford and Hershel Parker. NewYork: W. W. Norton, 1967.

———. *Benito Cereno.* 1855. In *The Piazza Tales and Other Prose Pieces, 1839–1860,* ed. Harrison Hayford et al., 46–117. Evanston and Chicago: Northwestern University Press and the Newberry Library, 1987. As noted above, *House Made of Dawn* resonates with explicit and implicit echoes from Melville's works. Among these one might consider the varieties of text and testimony in Benito Cereno compared with those in House Made of Dawn as well as parallels and contrasts in the court cases at the center of both novels.

———. *The Confidence-Man: His Masquerade.* 1857. Reprint, ed. Hershel Parker. New York: W. W. Norton, 1971.

———. *Billy Budd, Sailor (An Inside Narrative).* 1924. Reprint, ed. Harrison Hayford and Merton M. Sealts, Jr. Chicago: University of Chicago Press, 1962.

Silko, Leslie Marmon. *Ceremony.* New York: Viking, 1977. As indicated above,

Ceremony parallels the theme of *House Made of Dawn* in depicting a ritual for purification after war. Many interesting comparisons can be made with respect to the authors' incorporation of traditional lore, depictions of women, attitude toward landscape and environment, and so on.

Stevens, Wallace. *The Collected Poems.* New York: Knopf, 1954. Reprint, New York: Vintage Books, 1982. Both Stevens and Emily Dickinson were highly admired by Momaday's Stanford mentor, Yvor Winters, and some of Momaday's poems as well as the attitude exemplified in his prose express ideas close to those of Stevens.

2. Criticism

Evers, Lawrence J. "Words and Place: A Reading of *House Made of Dawn*" and "The Killing of a New Mexican State Trooper: Ways of Telling an Historical Event." In *Critical Essays on Native American Literature,* ed. Andrew O. Wiget, 211–30 and 246–61, respectively. Philadelphia: G. K. Hall, 1985. "Words and Place" offers a reading of the novel in the context of Momaday's sources, especially Jemez, Kiowa, and Navajo texts; "The Killing" compares Momaday's fictional treatment of a historical event—the shooting of a highway patrolman—with short stories by Leslie Silko and Simon Ortiz based on the same event.

Nelson, Robert M. *Place and Vision: The Function of Landscape in Native American Fiction.* American Indian Studies, vol. 1. New York: Peter Lang, 1994. Nelson's is the most detailed study of Momaday's precision in locating elements of the story in specific places, particularly in Jemez Pueblo.

Roemer, Kenneth M. *Approaches to Teaching N. Scott Momaday's* The Way To Rainy Mountain. New York: Modern Language Association, 1988. This is mainly useful for the Tosamah section in *House Made of Dawn,* but also contains an excellent bibliography and list of other sources on Momaday generally.

Scarberry-Garcia, Susan. *Landmarks of Healing: A Study of* House Made of Dawn. Albuquerque: University of New Mexico Press, 1990. This is the most extensive discussion yet of the novel in the context of Momaday's use of traditional sources. Scarberry-Garcia relates the novel to the governing myths of several Navajo ceremonials and discusses Momaday's use of anthropological sources.

Schubnell, Mathias. *N. Scott Momaday: The Cultural and Literary Background.* Norman: University of Oklahoma Press, 1985. The most comprehensive general discussion of Momaday's work until the mid-1980s, this study also contains an excellent bibliography of Momaday's publications.

Woodard, Charles L. *Ancestral Voice: Conversations with N. Scott Momaday.* Lincoln: University of Nebraska Press, 1989. Edited transcripts of leisurely conversations carried on over a period of years, this is a rich source for Momaday's sense of the writers, artists, and storytellers who have influenced him, how he relates to his ancestry, and his aesthetics.

3. Other Sources

Astrov, Margot. *American Indian Prose and Poetry.* New York: Capricorn Books, 1962. Originally titled *The Winged Serpent,* 1946.

Barry, Nora Baker. "The Bear's Son Folk Tale in *When the Legends Die* and *House Made of Dawn.*" *Western American Literature* 12, no. 4 (February 1978): 275–87.

Bevis, William. "Native American Novels: Homing In." In *Recovering the Word: Essays on Native American Literature,* ed. Brian Swann and Arnold Krupat, 580–620. Berkeley: University of California Press, 1987.

Camus, Albert. *The Stranger,* trans. Matthew Ward. New York: Vintage Books, 1989.

Deloria, Vine. *Custer Died for Your Sins: An Indian Manifesto.* New York: Macmillan, 1969.

Faris, James C. *The Nightway: A History and a History of Documentation of a Navajo Ceremonial.* Albuquerque: University of New Mexico Press, 1990.

Hoijer, Harry. *Chiricahua and Mescalero Apache Texts.* Chicago: University of Chicago Press, 1938.

LaBarre, Weston. *The Peyote Cult.* 1964. Reprint, New York: Schocken, 1969.

Left Handed. *Son of Old Man Hat: A Navaho Autobiography.* New York: Harcourt Brace, 1938. Reprint, Lincoln: University of Nebraska Press, 1967.

Matthews, Washington. *The Night Chant.* Memoirs of the American Museum of Natural History no. 6. 1902. Reprint, New York: AMS, 1974.

Momaday, N. Scott. *House Made of Dawn.* New York: Harper and Row, 1968. Momaday's own works are the best source for understanding his aesthetic and philosophical ideas, and the following are especially recommended.

———. "The Morality of Indian Hating." *Ramparts* 3, no. 1 (Summer 1964): 29–40.

———. *The Way to Rainy Mountain.* Albuquerque: University of New Mexico Press, 1969.

———. *The Gourd Dancer.* New York: Harper and Row, 1976. Poems.

———. *The Names: A Memoir.* New York: Harper and Row, 1976.

——— N. Scott Momaday Reads "Tsoai and the Shieldmaker" and Excerpts from *House Made of Dawn.* No. 3091. American Audio Prose Library, 1983.

———. Interview with Kay Bonetti. No. 3092. American Audio Prose Library, 1983.

————. *The Ancient Child.* New York: Doubleday, 1989.

————. *In the Presence of the Sun.* New York: St. Martin's Press, 1991. Poems and short prose pieces.

Sandner, Donald, M.D. *Navaho Symbols of Healing.* New York: Harcourt Brace Jovanovich, 1979.

Seasons of a Navajo. John Borden, producer. Phoenix: Peace River Films, 1984.

Silko, Leslie Marmon. "Tony's Story." In *Storyteller.* New York: Seaver Books, 1981.

Simmons, Marc. *Witchcraft in the Southwest: Spanish and Indian Supernaturalism on the Rio Grande.* Flagstaff, Ariz.: Northland Press, 1974.

Surviving Columbus: The Story of the Pueblo People. Albuquerque: KNME, 1992.

Crying for Vision in James Welch's
Winter in the Blood

WILLIAM W. THACKERAY

A. Analysis of Themes and Forms

Perspective for Study of the Novel

Winter in the Blood excites almost as many different reactions from readers and critics as there are different readers and critics. Some view it as realistic, others as comic; some as optimistic, others as pessimistic; some as traditional, others as contemporary; some as originating in the oral tradition, others in the tradition of the American novel. One of the most fruitful perspectives for study of the novel, however, is to examine it as the story of an aimless young Indian man of the sixties who is seeking insight into his cultural life and personal identity by pursuing the ritual steps of the traditional vision quest—to such an extent as that can be done in modern reservation life.

The Author

James Welch was born in 1940 in Browning, Montana, the tribal agency for the Blackfeet Indian Reservation. His father and his paternal grandparents are Piegan, which is the southern band of the Blackfeet or Siksika Nation, the other two bands being located largely in Canada.

However, the setting of his novel *Winter in the Blood* is not the Blackfeet Reservation but the Fort Belknap Reservation, two hundred miles east of Browning. Fort Belknap is the home of the Assiniboine and Gros Ventre or Atsina tribes, where Welch is equally at home since his mother is Gros Ventre. The Gros Ventres were mistakenly referred to as "Big Bellies" by French traders who misunderstood the Plains Indian sign-language designation for the tribe. The tribe regards itself as the White Clay People (*A'ani*), the northern branch of the Great Arapaho Nation.

Welch attended school both at Browning and at Fort Belknap where he met many mixed bloods (like the narrator of his novel), who are sometimes referred to as "halfbreeds," a highly pejorative term. One of the central themes of Welch's novel is the lack of identity of such mixed bloods, many of whom long for a "full-blood" or "pure Indian" ancestry. In a sense, the revelation that the unnamed narrator has a Blackfeet ancestry rather than a mixed-blood ancestry might be regarded as fulfilling this forlorn wish of some mixed-bloods—and indeed some other non-Indians—for an "Indian" identity.

After leaving Montana to graduate from high school in Minneapolis, Welch attended the University of Minnesota for a year. Then he returned to Montana to attend Northern Montana College and the University of Montana, where he came under the tutelage of a noted writing teacher, Joseph L. Keller, and the distinguished Montana poet Richard Hugo. Considering his training with Hugo, it is not surprising that his first major publication is a collection of poems, *Riding the Earthboy 40* (1971). Since the publication of *Winter in the Blood* (1974), Welch has completed three additional novels—*The Death of Jim Loney* (1979), *Fools Crow* (1986), and *The Indian Lawyer* (1990)—with each one relating a different part of the story of Indian life on the northern Plains.

The Story

As the novel opens, the nameless narrator is returning to his mother's farm, the Earthboy Place, on the Fort Belknap Reservation near Harlem, Montana. Although he says they mean nothing to him, he thinks of the members of his family, his mother Teresa First Raise, his grandmother, and his Cree girlfriend whom his mother thinks he has married. When he reaches home, he learns that his girlfriend has returned to Havre, stealing his rifle and razor.

Soon, his mother tells him that she is going to remarry the energetic but unimaginative Lame Bull. After she marries, she tells the narrator, "There isn't enough for you here. . . . You would do well to start looking around" (22). Trying to decide what he is to do, the narrator thinks of his father, First Raise, who repaired machinery for white farmers but froze to death in the barrow pit after a night of drinking. He also recalls the stories his grandmother had once told of her honored first marriage to a renowned Blackfeet leader, Standing Bear, who had died during the starvation winter of the Blackfeet. Then she had married a worthless halfbreed, who he thought was Teresa's father and his own grandfather. He also remembers his beloved brother, Mose, who died in an accident when he was trying to herd a bunch of their father's cows across the highway.

After helping Lame Bull finish up cutting and baling the hay on Teresa's farm, the narrator catches the bus to Dodson, Malta, and Havre, the small high line towns of Montana where he hopes to find his Cree girlfriend, Agnes. He sees her only for a few moments in Havre before some of her relatives beat him up, but along the way he meets a mysterious fugitive, the airplane-man, who tries to convince him to run off to Canada.

This time, when he returns to the reservation, he decides to visit a blind old man named Yellow Calf, who lives alone near the irrigation canal. Yellow Calf tells the narrator that he has a message for him from the deer. The deer have told him, says Yellow Calf, "This earth is cockeyed," and in a cockeyed world "one has to lean into the wind to stand straight" (68–69). But the narrator refuses to believe the communication or to accept the possibility that deer can deliver such a profound message. So Yellow Calf tells him not to bring the gift that would have been appropriate for such a spiritual message. If the novice or student cannot accept the message, the teacher or spirit guide cannot accept a gift as compensation for it.

Once again, he returns to Havre, riding with a middle-aged secretary who graduated from Haskell Indian College but was never able to find work. Again, he meets the airplane-man, who enlists the narrator's help to escape the FBI. While he is waiting for the airplane-man, he recalls the details of his brother's death and the car that hit his own horse and injured his leg so that he had had to go to Portland for therapy. Before they can leave for Canada, the airplane-man is arrested. After he is beaten up in a barroom fight, the narrator returns to the reservation, "hung over, beaten up, or both." Now he is in complete despair: "I had had enough of myself. I wanted to lose myself, to ditch these clothes, to outrun this burning sun, to stand beneath the clouds and have my shadow erased, myself along with it" (125).

This time, he takes a bath to purify himself for a second visit to Yellow Calf. Yellow Calf recalls that he too is Blackfeet and that he traveled with Standing Bear's band during the starvation winter when the Blackfeet band had invaded Gros Ventre country. He describes the death of Standing Bear and the resentment felt against his beautiful young bride, the narrator's grandmother. Suddenly, in an epiphany or vision carried on the "gusting wind" of his horse Old Bird's fart (158), the narrator realizes that Yellow Calf is his real grandfather and that he is not a halfbreed but part of a noble line of Blackfeet warriors. He is really an Indian after all.

Yellow Calf warns him that he will be required to pay for such spiritual insight. Soon, he remembers his grandmother is dead. While preparing for her funeral, he tries to rescue a cow from a bog-hole. In the process, Old

Bird kills himself pulling on the cow and the narrator reinjures his leg. In the storm that accompanies his injury, he again recalls his dead brother Mose and father First Raise, "the only ones I really loved . . . the only ones who were good to be with" (172).

At his grandmother's funeral, the narrator dedicates himself to having his leg repaired and assuming his position as a head of family. To reestablish his ties to the traditional life of his grandmother, he throws her medicine pouch into her grave to be buried with her (176).

Motifs: An Age-Graded Society

The life of the nameless narrator is torn between the seemingly disorganized chaos of the white world and the highly structured but unapproachable promise of traditional Indian culture. The age-graded nature of Gros Ventre culture specifies that males go through a particular life cycle in four-year intervals. Thus, at sixteen years of age (four years multiplied times four), they are expected to begin the achievements that make them a warrior and lead to their manhood. At thirty-two years, their achievements should have literally earned them an adult name in the tribe, thereby preparing them through their achievements and vision for their adult role in the cultural life of the tribe.

Not by accident, the narrator of Welch's novel is specified as being thirty-two years old. At that age in his Gros Ventre culture he should be prepared to accept the adult responsibilities of home, family, marriage, and a place in the adult life of his tribe. The disruption of traditional ritual means for attaining manhood, however, has left him with no direction, no identity, and no feeling for the responsibilities of family, which he should have been ready to assume at the beginning of the novel. But as he says, people and country alike "had created a distance as deep as it was empty." His feeling of distance "came from within me. I was as distant from myself as a hawk from the moon" (2).

Motifs: Animal Allies

There are more animal characters in *Winter in the Blood* than there are human characters, although most of the animals play comparatively minor roles, such as the fish the narrator never catches, the calf that kicks him and follows him, the deer that send him messages, and the lions in the story in *Sports Afield* (12). But two animals in the story play a role important enough that they should be regarded as animal allies of the narrator. Traditional members of the Gros Ventre culture would select such animal allies or have them selected in a vision to protect them in battle and aid them in their quest for status and vision.

One of the narrator's allies is his little pet duck, Amos, who returns to him in his dreams. Teresa, the narrator's mother, says of Amos, who survived when all his brothers and sisters died: "He was lucky. One duck can't be smarter than another. They're like Indians" (15). The other animal ally is his horse, Old Bird, who literally carries the narrator on his way and later helps provide his insight and vision (158).

The Vision Quest: "Crying for Pity" and "The Little Death"

The ritual process by which traditional members of the Gros Ventre/ Arapaho culture prepared themselves for the vision and spiritual insight of adulthood or manhood can be specified as occurring in eight steps, as follows:

1. "Sacrifice," usually occurring over a period of years: Continual sacrifice is necessary to insight and vision in the ritual tradition of the vision quest. The narrator's sacrifice begins with the death of his father and brother, continues with the loss of Amos and the wild Cree girl, and is still going on at the end of the novel with the death of his grandmother and Old Bird and the reinjury of his knee.

2. "Crying for Pity," debasing oneself, occasionally even torturing oneself, so that God will look upon one with pity: The narrator's cries open the novel with his hangover and drunken return home, his mindless affairs with meaningless women, and his aimless plotting with the airplane-man. This humiliation and debasement of oneself is an essential but often misunderstood step in the attainment of visionary insight.

3. "Seeking a grandfather," who may or may not be related by blood but who will serve as a spiritual guide: Aided by his horse, Old Bird, the narrator sets out to seek the spiritual guidance of Yellow Calf, whom he hasn't seen since he was a boy.

4. "Acceptance of Sacrifice" one has made or been compelled to make: The narrator accepts his sacrifice by coming to terms with the deaths of his father and brother and by facing the loss of Amos, his wild Cree girlfriend, Old Bird, and his grandmother.

5. "Little Death," ritual despair or the death of hope, often including the hope for physical death: The narrator's "little death" occurs when he decides he wants to lose himself and have even his "shadow erased, myself along with it" (125).

6. "Purification" or ritual cleansing, which traditionally involved the sweat bath: Before visiting Yellow Calf the second time, the narrator goes through such a purification ritual by taking a steamy bath in a tub in his mother's kitchen.

7. "Vision" or mystic and spiritual insight, usually involving insight into the self and its place in or relationship to the world: In the vision or insight resulting from Old Bird's fart, the narrator has a sudden understanding of his true identity as a descendant of Blackfeet warriors and the actual grandson of Yellow Calf, the Blackfeet spirit guide.

8. "Acceptance of Vision," agreeing that one's visionary insight must be accepted as significant in the conduct of one's own life: The narrator accepts the responsibility for his vision and pays the price of insight by rescuing the drowned heifer and, in the process, killing Old Bird and reinjuring his own knee.

Beginning with the sacrifices of his pet duck, Amos, his brother and his father, and finally his horse, Old Bird, these eight steps can be seen as providing the structural framework for the events of the novel. This structure is reflected in each major transition between events of the narrator's story.

B. Teaching the Work

Critical Approaches

Critical appraisals of James Welch's novel *Winter in the Blood* have utilized various approaches. The most fundamental division between critics of the novel has been between those who examine it largely in terms of its relationship to American literature of the European tradition and those who examine its connection to the traditional literatures and mythologies of Native Americans. The first of these critical traditions was established by Reynolds Price, in his admiring review on the front page of the *New York Times Book Review*, "When Is an Indian Novel Not an Indian Novel?" In his review, Price argues that "'Winter in the Blood' is by no means an Indian novel" (section 7, p. 1).

Other critics suggest it may not be *just* an Indian novel, but Indian in essence it certainly is. Elaine Jahner urges, in her essay "Quick Paces and a Space of Mind," that the novel is a challenge to critics and readers "to understand more about the esthetic foundations of American Indian literature. Welch's novel is a good example of the kind of challenge that American Indian writers pose for the contemporary critic" (34). She might have added that critics can hardly be thought to understand contemporary American literature as a whole without realizing its debt to Native traditions.

In addition to this basic split between critics over its European or American characteristics, there is considerable division over other central elements of the novel. Some critics view it largely as comic in nature (Velie), some as realistic (Price, Ruoff), some as existential pessimism (Lincoln), and some as upbeat and optimistic of the future (Standiford, Thackeray). Whatever their different reactions, critics are agreed that Welch's novel is a challenge to interpretation and is, in the words of Price, "a nearly flawless novel about human life."

Teaching Approaches

There are various topics of discussion that arise from the novel, with some topics relating to minority cultures, some concerning conflicts between traditional and modern Indian culture, and some dealing with universal concerns of poverty, rootlessness, alcoholism, and the responsibilities of growing maturity. The novel deals with the life of a maturing young man on and around a reservation during the 1960s, but it also deals with the universal themes of growing up, accepting adult responsibilities, and leaving parents and adolescent concerns behind.

Perhaps the central theme, however, deals with the near impossibility of young Indian males finding a place in the world that suits their traditional cultural heritage as heads of families but also gives them the economic security to assume such a responsible role. Traditionally, they must be warriors, hunters, and visionaries, but also they must learn a trade or profession in a world that is little interested in their traditional skills or way of life.

Topics of Discussion

1. In traditional American Indian oral stories, such as the stories of "Blood-Clot Boy," blood stands not only for the blood of the individual but also for the very cultural life of the community. Interpret the words of the title, "winter in the blood," with this sense of the frozen state of traditional Indian culture in mind.

2. Think of various reasons why the narrator of *Winter in the Blood* is not given a name. What is the significance of names and of naming in general? What would it be like to have no name? When you answer the above questions, consider the following: (a) the Plains Indian tradition of naming people several times during their lifetime to reflect their new status or a

significant achievement; (b) the Gros Ventre tradition that would deny a young man the right to an adult name until he has earned it through vision and achievement; (c) the namelessness of the narrator as a literary convention that allows him to be "Everyman," a character who stands for universal Indian experience or universal minority experience.

Yet another dimension of his namelessness relates to his invisibility or insignificance not only in the aimless barhopping culture of northern Montana at large, but also within his own family and culture. Compare the narrator with Ralph Ellison's character in his novel, *Invisible Man*, and also to other such aimless, uprooted, or embittered "invisible" figures in modern ethnic fiction. (See section C, part 1, "Related Works," below.)

3. Consider the narrator's mother, Teresa First Raise Lame Bull, as the strong feminine figure that from necessity becomes the head-of-family, typical of such strong female figures in ethnic fiction. But also consider the narrator's remark, "I never expected much from Teresa and I never got it. But neither did anyone else. Maybe that's why First Raise [the narrator's dead father] stayed away so much" (21). Has Teresa sacrificed the feeling and support expected of a mother and wife for her strength and cold determination?

4. Some readers of the novel have objected to referring to the central figure as simply "the narrator." They suggest that his efforts earn him the title of a hero in the convention of mythological references to a "culture hero." Discuss whether the narrator might appropriately be thought of as a culture hero.

5. Compare the ritual elk hunt that the narrator's father planned every fall (7) with the fantasy ritual of the lion hunt described in the article in *Sports Afield* (12). With these ritual events in mind, consider the narrator's efforts to fulfill traditional Indian rituals of purification and so forth in the context of modern, non-Indian society. What are some similar rituals that occur in families in our general society?

6. How is Raymond Long Knife a distinctly different and less admirable character than the narrator (23–30)?

7. When Lame Bull marries his mother Teresa, the narrator says, "Lame Bull had married 360 acres of hay land" (13). Relate this comment to the narrator's resentment of Teresa and the haying ritual performed by Lame Bull and the narrator.

8. Contrast the halfbreed Dougie's reaction to the white drunk with that of the narrator (42–44). What are their different motives in rolling the drunk?

9. Some critics have suggested that Yellow Calf is really more like a ghost or phantasm than a real character. Look at the two scenes where he meets

with the narrator (63–70, 149–59), and consider whether this is a plausible view.

10. Yellow Calf, it turns out, is literally the narrator's genetic grandfather, but also he might be regarded as the spiritual guardian or spirit guide of the narrator, much like the "Grandfather" selected as spirit guides in traditional Gros Ventre culture. What advice does Yellow Calf give the narrator? Is it sound advice? Does the narrator respond appropriately to the advice, or does he largely ignore it?

11. Discuss the reasons for the traditional Indian convention of giving a gift for spiritual advice. Think of other gift-giving conventions in our society, and consider what is expected in return. Are gifts in general a kind of payment for services?

12. How does Yellow Calf prepare the way for the narrator's vision or insight into his cultural position (158)? Why is Yellow Calf's connection to Blackfeet culture and to the heroic band of Standing Bear so important to the narrator?

13. What is the narrator's relationship to the two dead members of his family, his father First Raise and his brother Mose? Does he have to overcome his grief to continue his own life? Discuss grief and sorrow in general as an essential part of life.

14. Describe the three girlfriends in the narrator's life: the wild Cree girl Agnes, the barmaid from Malta, and Marlene. What do they have in common? How do they reflect the narrator's own fruitless efforts to become a responsible head-of-family? In your life, how do courtship and seeking a spouse differ from marriage roles and responsibilities and family life?

15. What does Yellow Calf mean when he tells the narrator, "You'd better hurry . . . It's coming" (159)? Does this remark refer just to the coming storm or is it also a warning of the price the narrator will have to pay for his insight? Relate this conception of the price that must be paid for spiritual gifts to the price that Adam and Eve must pay for eating of the Tree of Knowledge.

16. Why does the narrator go to such heroic efforts to rescue the cow from the bog-hole?

17. Note the comic elements in the description of the funeral of the narrator's grandmother. Why does the author turn this into a comic scene?

18. What are the narrator's prospects for bettering his life at the end of the novel? In answering, consider the following two questions as well: (a) Has he learned anything of value during the course of his experiences? (b) What difference does it make to him that Yellow Calf is really his grandfather?

19. Consider the wish or desire of non-Indians to be Indian or to identify with Indian culture. Think of this wish in the broad context of our culture as well as of the context reflected in the novel. Think of evidence, such as hairstyles, jewelry types, beadwork, clothing, shoe styles, and so on, that reflect an identification with Indian culture. Compare the opening of the film *Little Big Man*, where the white hero captured by Cheyennes says, "I was not just playing Indian; I was living Indian."

20. Relate the novel to the lines from Welch's poem, "In My Lifetime," from which the title *Winter in the Blood* derives:

> Now the fool is dead. His bones go back
> so scarred in time, the buttes are young to look
> for signs that say a man could love his fate,
> that winter in the blood is one sad thing.

C. Bibliographies

1. Related Works

Brave Bird, Mary. *Ohitika Woman*. New York: Harper Collins, 1993. A powerful continuation of the story of Mary Brave Bird Crow Dog after Wounded Knee II and the breakup of her marriage to Lakota spiritual leader Leonard Crow Dog, as described below in *Lakota Woman*.

Crow Dog, Mary. *Lakota Woman*. New York: Harper Collins, 1990. A moving account of the spiritual development of two generations of the remarkable Crow Dog family of the Teton Sioux, father Henry, son Leonard, and Leonard's wife Mary, spiritual leaders and participants in the infamous Wounded Knee II.

Dorris, Michael. *A Yellow Raft in Blue Water*. New York: Warner, 1987. A remarkable psychological portrait of three generations of American Indian women—grandmother, daughter, granddaughter—on the Fort Belknap Reservation in Montana, this novel traces the story of the abiding cultural faith that ties Indians to their traditions and tribal identities.

Lame Deer, John (Fire), and Richard Erdoes. *Lame Deer: Seeker of Visions*. New York: Simon and Schuster, 1972. A great spiritual guide and medicine man of the Teton Sioux, Lame Deer tells his life story with vitality and insight.

Least Heat Moon, William. *Blue Highways*. New York: Little Brown, 1984. On a journey through America, the author describes many life-affirming qualities of contemporary and traditional American Indian life.

Linderman, Frank. *Plenty Coups: Chief of the Crows*. Lincoln: University of Nebraska Press, 1962. This as-told-to autobiography traces the life of one of the great leaders of the Crow Tribe from his earliest visions to his leadership of the Crow as allies of the U.S. Army.

———. *Pretty-Shield: Medicine Woman of the Crows*. Lincoln: University of Nebraska Press, 1974. The woman's counterpart of his life of Plenty-Coups, Linderman describes the traditional and more recent life of a spiritual leader of the Montana Crow Tribe.

McNickle, D'Arcy. *The Surrounded*. 1936. Reprint, Albuquerque: University of New Mexico Press, 1978. A classic Native American novel of the 1930s, this account of a mixed blood's return to his family on the Flathead Reservation of western Montana combines incisive portraits of white and Indian characters that demonstrate the inevitablity of conflict between them.

———. *Wind from an Enemy Sky*. 1978. Reprint, Albuquerque: University of New Mexico Press, 1988. Based on the tribal conflict that erupts between traditional Indians and their "progressive" counterparts over the building of a new earthwork dam on tribal land, this novel deals revealingly with that most contemporary of issues, the disputes between those who argue for economic development and those who argue for preservation of the environment, the land, and the cultural traditions of the tribe.

Mourning Dove (Hum-ishu-ma). *Cogewea: The Half-Blood*. Lincoln: University of Nebraska Press, 1927. The first known novel by a Native American woman, this account of the conflicts of a mixed-blood woman in the region of western Montana near the Flathead Reservation evokes reservation life in the early twentieth century as no other work is able to do.

Radin, Paul. *The Autobiography of a Winnebago Indian*. New York: Dover, 1920. A moving account of the life of a young Winnebago man who is restored to his traditional lifeways by involvement in the Peyote ceremonies of the Native American Church.

Silko, Leslie Marmon. *Ceremony*. 1977. Reprint, New York: Viking Penguin, 1986. A returned veteran (warrior) seeks normalcy in the traditional ceremonies of Pueblo life.

Waters, Frank. *People of the Valley*. Athens, Ohio: Swallow, 1941. The beautiful account of the spiritual training and leadership of a young woman of traditional Pueblo background who in her old age becomes a political force among her people in their fight to prevent the flooding of their valley by a government dam project.

———. *The Man Who Killed the Deer*. Athens, Ohio: Swallow, 1942. A young family head of the Pueblo culture finds difficulty in adjusting his twentieth-century non-Indian training with the traditional mores of the Pueblo.

2. Best Criticism

Jahner, Elaine. "Quick Paces and a Space of Mind." *Denver Quarterly* 14, no. 4
    (1980): 34–47. Concluding that *Winter in the Blood* derives from an epis-
    temology and worldview (weltanschauung) that is primarily Indian,
    Jahner sees the resolution of the novel as positive because the narrator
    learns to come to terms with traditional Blackfeet principles.
Larson, Charles R. "*Winter in the Blood.*" *American Indian Fiction.* Albuquer-
    que: University of New Mexico Press, 1978. Seeing the novel as a "cel-
    ebration of life," Larson contrasts the easy style of the novel with the
    more mannered works of Silko, Momaday, and other Indian novelists,
    and finds one of its themes to be opposition to the federal government
    policies that would terminate Indian reservations.
Larson, Sidney J. "James Welch's *Winter in the Blood.*" *The Indian Historian* 10,
    no. 1 (Winter 1977): 23–30. A member of the Gros Ventre tribe and cousin
    of James Welch, Larson traces elements of family history in Welch's char-
    acters and sees the disappearing-fish motif in the novel as reminiscent of
    the general failure of government Indian policies.
Price, Reynolds. "When Is an Indian Novel Not an Indian Novel?" *New York
    Times Book Review,* 10 November 1974, section 7, p. 1. Confirming the
    universal themes of the novel and its polished technique, Price's original
    front-page review established the "nearly flawless" quality with which
    Winter in the Blood has since been regarded as a novel.
Ruoff, A. LaVonne. "*Winter in the Blood.*" In "American Indian Literatures: A
    Guide to Anthologies, Texts, and Research," *Studies in American Indian
    Literatures,* ed. Paula Gunn Allen, 307–8. New York: Modern Language
    Association, 1983. Contains a valuable bibliographical discussion of *Win-
    ter in the Blood.*
Standiford, Lester A. "Worlds Made of Dawn: Characteristic Image and Inci-
    dent in Native American Imaginative Literature." In *Three American Lit-
    eratures,* ed. Houston A. Baker, Jr. New York: Modern Language
    Association, 1982. Responding to critics who regard *Winter in the Blood*
    as a negative representation of Indian life, Standiford concludes that the
    narrator's "triumph is as total as a human can expect" when the novel is
    judged in terms of Indian values and principles.
Thackeray, William W. "'Crying for Pity' in *Winter in the Blood.*" *MELUS* 7, no.
    1 (Spring 1980): 61–78. I expand on the vision-quest theme of *Winter in
    the Blood.*
————. "*The Death of Jim Loney* as a Half-Breed's Tragedy." *Studies in Ameri-
    can Indian Literature* 5, no. 3–4 (1981): 16–18. I contrast the positive
    Indian qualities represented in *Winter in the Blood* with the tragic, hope-
    less life of the halfbreed in Welch's second novel.

————. "Animal Allies and Transformers of *Winter in the Blood*." *MELUS* 12, no. 1 (Spring 1985): 37–64. Applying the structural theory of myth and animal symbolism to the organization of the novel, I trace the animal characters and transformer figures in *Winter in the Blood* in terms of the vision quest theme central to the novel's structure and conclude that animals in the novel act in accord with their roles as mythic figures in Blackfeet and Gros Ventre oral tradition.

Velie, Alan R. "*Winter in the Blood:* Welch and the Comic Novel." In *Four American Indian Literary Masters*. Norman: University of Oklahoma Press, 1982. Viewing the novel in non-Indian terms as negative and pessimistic, Velie applies the drunken-Indian stereotype and concludes that the narrator's "need for drinks" precludes any chance of his restoration, but also adds useful insights into the novel's comic structure.

3. Other Sources

American Indian Quarterly: A Journal of Anthropology, History, and Literature 4, no. 2 (May 1983): 91–172. A useful collection with essays on women's themes, historical background, and narrative style of *Winter in the Blood* by A. LaVonne Ruoff, Kathleen M. Sands, and others.

McFarland, Ron, ed. *James Welch*. The Confluence American Author Series. Lewiston, Idaho: Confluence, 1986. An anthology of essays on several of Welch's works.

Welch, James. *Riding the Earthboy 40*. 1971. Rev. ed., New York: Harper and Row, 1976.

————. *Winter in the Blood*. New York: Harper and Row, 1974.

————. *The Death of Jim Loney*. New York: Harper and Row, 1979.

Wild, Peter. *James Welch*. Western Writers Series No. 57. Boise, Idaho: Boise State University, 1983. An extended essay of Welch criticism.

Audio-Visual Materials. (Several useful audio cassettes are available containing interviews with Welch on *Winter in the Blood*.)

"Radio Profiles of James Welch and Ivan Doig." Missoula, Mont.: Instructional Materials Service. Background of Welch's life on Fort Belknap Reservation, as well as readings of the scene where the narrator of *Winter in the Blood* learns his ancestry from an encounter with Yellow Calf, his grandfather.

"Montana Writers: Jim Welch—*Winter in the Blood*." Missoula, Mont: Mansfield Library Archives. Discussion by William Bevis and Gary Niles Kimble placing Welch's novel in perspective as part of Indian literature.

Ceremony:

From Alienation to Reciprocity (Leslie Marmon Silko)

NORMA C. WILSON

A. Analysis of Themes and Forms

Ceremony is the best known and most highly acclaimed work of Leslie Marmon Silko, one of the major writers of the American Indian literary renaissance, which began in the late 1960s. Born March 5, 1948, in Albuquerque, New Mexico, Silko grew up on the Laguna Pueblo Reservation in the house where her father, Lee H. Marmon, was born. During her childhood, she spent much time with her great-grandmother, A'mooh (Marie), who lived next door. A'mooh and Silko's Aunt Susie (Mrs. Walter K. Marmon) were primary influences on her, telling her the Laguna traditions and stories that would become the primary resource for her poetry and fiction. Silko also has Plains Indian, Mexican, and Anglo ancestry. Though her great-grandfather, Robert Gunn Marmon, a trader, was elected to one term as governor of the pueblo, the family lived at the edge of the village, occupying a marginal place in the community.

Silko attended grade school at Laguna, but the family took her to Albuquerque daily for the four years of high school. She then attended the University of New Mexico, graduating magna cum laude with a B.A. in English in 1969. After attending three semesters of law school, she decided to devote herself to writing. Silko has taught at Navajo Community College in Many Farms, Arizona, at the University of New Mexico, and at the University of Arizona.

In her first book, *Laguna Woman* (poems, 1974), Silko established many of the themes that she would develop in her later work. Laguna myth, culture, and ceremony are the foundations for the contemporary experience of these poems. In "Prayer to the Pacific," she refers to one of the Laguna creation myths: "Thirty thousand years ago / Indians came riding across the ocean / carried by giant sea turtles." A cyclic view of nature is thus conveyed in this poem, which considers the manner in which the Pacific Ocean not only separates but connects the land masses of North America and China. Similarly in her first novel, *Ceremony* (1977), weather patterns in the Philippine jungles and at Laguna are seen as related to each other as well as to the people living in those places, who are also recognized as re-lated. Other poems, such as "When Sun Came to River Woman," embody nature as both the setting and the result of copulation. Human intercourse, the rain and sun, and the ceremonial songs are all seen as necessary to the bringing of new life—they are interconnected and interdependent. These are important concepts in *Ceremony* as well.

Choices of cultural identity; human responsibilities to the earth, to one-self, and to others; the ravages of racism; the presence of evil and goodness in humanity; the development of nuclear weapons; physical, mental, and spiritual health; war and violence; change as essential to renewal; the nur-turing of children; the recurrence of all that happens—all these are the-matic considerations in *Ceremony*.

The nonchronological prose narrative is told in segments with many flashbacks, similar to the structure of N. Scott Momaday's *House Made of Dawn* (1969). Paula Gunn Allen calls this narrative style "accretive," liken-ing it to the manner in which stories are told in the oral tradition (*Sacred Hoop*, 95). Beginning with a poem centered on the page, in which Silko attributes the story to Ts'its'tsi'nako (Thought Woman)—the Spider Grand-mother, namer/creator of all—and ending with one word, "Sunrise," Silko's narrative is told within a circular frame, with "Sunrise" as its last word. *Ceremony* is a creative blending of poetry with prose, of ancient with con-temporary stories. In this novel and in other writings, Silko participates in the creative expression of an indigenous outlook that is filled with the spirit of place and the ongoing cycle of life that is constantly renewing itself. In the traditional oral literature, there are more healing songs and ceremonies than any other kind. The purpose of *Ceremony* is to heal:

> The only cure
> I know
> is a good ceremony,
> that's what she said. (3)

By juxtaposing the story told in the prose of Tayo, a Laguna veteran of World War II, with verse conveying the ancient Laguna mythology, Silko shows the universality and timeless significance of the old stories to the process of healing.

The prose narrative that follows the introductory poetry is a chaotic and fragmented stream of consciousness in which Tayo's memory and identity are confused and tangled. Tayo has returned to the pueblo after six years, miserably confused, alienated, and sick. In nightmares he hears Spanish, Japanese, and Laguna voices that make no sense to him. Suffering intense depression and grief over the death of his cousin Rocky and the drought on the land he has returned to, Tayo feels personally responsible, blaming himself for both. Having grown up influenced by the traditional ways, he cannot see himself as separate from the environment he lives in. Nor can he disavow the Laguna belief in the power of language. He thinks that by cursing the jungle rain during the war, he has prayed the rain away. And in order to be personally healed, he must learn to pray it back.

The nearly five-hundred-year existence of Laguna Pueblo at its present location has given Silko the potential to write out of a cultural tradition intricately tied to the natural environment. Yet it is a place that has suffered severe trauma in the second half of the twentieth century. The atom bomb was developed at nearby Los Alamos, and the first atom bomb exploded just 150 miles from Laguna. In the early 1950s, the Anaconda Company opened a large, open-pit uranium mine on Laguna land. The danger of nuclear war is a central concern in Ceremony, but Tayo comes to understand that this threat has the effect of reuniting all of the world's people into one clan. Tayo's capacity to see himself in relationship to the entire universe illustrates the very real connections among individuals, cultures, and nature as part of one whole.

Tayo has experienced rejection by his community, due to his halfbreed status. The early loss of his mother and the callous treatment by his aunt, who raised him, have intensified Tayo's alienation. Ironically, Rocky, Tayo's full-blood cousin, with whom he grew up, was the one who rejected traditional ways, determined to make it in the white world that he thought was superior. Out of loyalty to Rocky, Tayo enlisted in the U.S. Army but has returned from the war alone. Rocky has been killed, and Tayo suffers from survivor guilt and a complex of other war-related illnesses. He is physically, emotionally, and spiritually sick.

Tayo's grandmother, who lives with his family, asks a Laguna medicine man, Ku'oosh, to help him. Though he is able to help Tayo, he explains that he cannot cure him: "There are some things we can't cure like we used to . . . not since the white people came. The others who had the Scalp Ceremony, some of them are not better either" (38).

Tayo's experience parallels that of numerous Native American men who have served in foreign wars for the United States military. Having grown up in a non-warlike, Pueblo culture (Pueblos traditionally fought only to defend their villages), Tayo has been severely traumatized by the violence that he has seen on both sides. Deeply conscious of his relationship and responsibility to the whole universe, Tayo rejected the army indoctrination that made some of the other Laguna soldiers into killers. Consequently, because he refused to participate in a firing squad executing Japanese soldiers, Tayo has not served honorably, according to army standards. However, by the end of *Ceremony,* Tayo comes to an understanding and acceptance of himself as well as of his refusal to kill.

Tayo's uncle Josiah, the most influential person during his early life, taught him to respect nature, to observe it carefully and with appreciation, and to be guided by an understanding of the necessity of living in harmony with the creation rather than by a desire to gain social acceptance. While Tayo's immediate refusal to shoot a Japanese soldier—related in a flashback—was due to that soldier's resemblance to his uncle Josiah, Tayo will later come to understand that this refusal to kill was also due to his genetic memory and his relationship to the larger human community beyond Laguna. Josiah has died while Tayo was at war. Tayo returns to his aunt's home, to stay in a room he had shared with her son, Rocky. Tayo is heartsick at the loss of these two close relatives.

Complicating Tayo's recovery is the alcoholism of Emo, Leroy, Harley, and Pinkie, other veterans his age. They spend their time drinking, telling stories of the white women they had in Los Angeles, and continuing the violence of war. World War II stories have replaced the oral tradition in their outlook and values. Tayo understands their drinking: "It was something the old people could not understand. Liquor was medicine for the anger that made them hurt, for the pain of the loss, medicine for tight bellies and choked-up throats" (40). But Tayo is different from the other veterans; he sees through their war stories, and he wants to save life, not destroy it. He realizes the truth in the oral tradition:

> He had believed in the stories for a long time, until the teachers at Indian school taught him not to believe in that kind of "nonsense." But they had been wrong. Josiah had been there, in the jungle; he had come. Tayo had watched him die; and he had done nothing to save him. (19)

Sitting in a bar telling stories and drinking, the other veterans push him to talk about the war, and Tayo tells their real story, the one they don't want to hear:

> " . . . First time you walked down the street in Gallup or Albuquerque, you knew. Don't lie. You knew right away. The war was over, the uniform was gone. All of a sudden that man at the store waits on you last, makes you wait until all the white people bought what they wanted. And the white lady at the bus depot, she's real careful now not to touch your hand when she counts out your change. You

watch it slide across the counter at you, and you know. Goddamn it!
You stupid sonofabitches! You know!" (42)

Another time in a bar, the worst of the veterans, Emo, drives Tayo to the
limit with his taunting and his vicious stories:

> He poured the human teeth out on the table. He looked over at
> Tayo and laughed out loud. . . . They were his war souvenirs, the
> teeth he had knocked out of the corpse of a Japanese soldier. . . .
>   "We were the best. U.S. Army. We butchered every Jap we found.
> . . . We had all kinds of ways to get information out of them before
> they died. Cut off this, cut off these." (60–61)

Sickened by Emo's inhumanity, Tayo screams, "Killer!" Emo retaliates, "You
love Japs the way your mother loved to screw white men." And Tayo breaks
a bottle and tries to stab it into Emo's belly. But the other men pull Tayo
away, preventing him from killing Emo, and the police come and take him
to Albuquerque. He is sent to a hospital for a while, and then returns home.

Tayo stays out of trouble, but he makes little progress in recovering until
the old men of Laguna come to tell Tayo's grandmother that he should seek
help. His grandma learns from Ku'oosh about a Navajo medicine man,
Betonie, and she suggests that Tayo go for help to Betonie, who lives in the
foothills north of the Gallup ceremonial grounds.

Robert, his aunt's husband, provides quiet support for Tayo and accompanies him to Gallup. As they walk from the bus station to Betonie's hogan,
they notice the drunks outside the Gallup bars and the people living in
makeshift shelters scattered along the riverbanks. Though not told precisely
as a personal memory, a story woven into the narrative, of an unnamed boy
who lives in the arroyo from hand to mouth and on food his mother sometimes brings him or on garbage, seems to be the story of Tayo's early childhood spent in Gallup. Mixed with the horrible scenes of being left in bars
and sleeping on tables, waiting for his mother to come back; of being placed
in an institution, perhaps an orphanage; and of living in the arroyo, is the
child's love for his mother—"she came back for him, and she held him very
close" (110); "He would wait for her, and she would come back to him"
(113). After his mother gave him to his aunt to raise, Tayo clung to his
mother's picture until his aunt took it from him. This wrenching separation from his mother seems to have been the beginning of Tayo's sickness.
And only by his reintegration into family, community, and universe can he
be healed.

The whole process of healing, self awareness, and acceptance is very complex. Betonie explains that the ceremonies must change if they are to help
people:

"At one time, the ceremonies as they had been performed were enough for the way the world was then. But after the white people came, elements of the world began to shift; and it became necessary to create new ceremonies. I have made changes in the rituals. The people mistrust this greatly, but only this growth keeps the ceremonies strong." (126)

Betonie explains that the Japanese and the Laguna are genetically related. The ancient myths in the story of the Lagunas arriving on the North American continent on the backs of sea turtles have been borne out by Tayo's twentieth-century experience.

Tayo is understandably bitter at the white world. "I wonder what good Indian ceremonies can do against the sickness which comes from their wars, their bombs, their lies?" he asks Betonie (132). The medicine man then tells Tayo a story in verse form to illustrate the power of evil that has always existed, among Native Americans as well as Europeans. According to the story, Indian witches got together from various tribes and had a "contest / in dark things" (133). The witch who made white people won the prize, thus setting "in motion" the most destructive forces imaginable. During the rest of the novel, it will be increasingly apparent that Emo is a modern witch, who will attempt to torture and kill anyone he cannot control. Betonie's sandpainting ceremony sets Tayo's feet on a path of balance. But the balance will be precarious since Tayo will continue to be confronted by Emo and the other veterans controlled by the witchery.

After the ceremony Tayo sleeps and dreams of the herd of speckled cattle that he and Josiah had started before Tayo went to war. He knows he must find those cattle that have disappeared, both out of respect for Josiah and in order to help support his family and pueblo. On his way home he is picked up by Harley, one of the veterans, who insists on taking him drinking. The episode ends with Tayo attempting to "vomit out everything—all the past, all his life" (168).

Nevertheless, the ceremony has enabled Tayo to dream with vision and has shown him how to fulfill his dreams. On his way up the mountain, looking for the speckled cattle, he meets a woman, T'seh Montano. Essential to Tayo's recovery, she feeds him, makes love to him, and points out the pattern of stars in the sky, identical to the pattern in Betonie's sandpainting. She assists him in getting the cattle back— which had been stolen by a white rancher—and into the family's possession. An herbalist, she also teaches him how to use, protect, and understand the power of medicinal plants. She warns him not to get caught up in Emo's destructive witchery: "'Their highest ambition is to gut human beings while they are still breathing, to hold the heart still beating so the victim will never feel anything again. When they finish, you watch yourself from a distance and you can't even cry—not even for yourself'" (229). She takes him to see the pregnant she-elk, A'moo'ooh. Before Tayo leaves her to go back to the pueblo, she tells him to "'remember everything'" (235).

At the novel's climax, Tayo watches, hidden in the distance, while the other veterans torture Harley for his failure to deliver Tayo as their victim. Horrified, Tayo wants to stop the torture but realizes he would be caught up in the witchery if he gave in to his violent impulse:

> The witchery had almost ended the story according to its plan; Tayo had almost jammed the screwdriver into Emo's skull the way the witchery had wanted, savoring the yielding bone and membrane as the steel ruptured the brain. Their deadly ritual for the autumn solstice would have been completed by him. . . . At home the people would blame the liquor, the Army, and the war, but the blame on the whites would never match the vehemence the people would keep in their own bellies, reserving the greatest bitterness and blame for themselves, for one of themselves they could not save. (253)

Tayo is now able to think clearly. No longer are his thoughts tangled and confused. He can see the nightmare destruction of the real world and can consciously hold himself back from it. Like the rest of humanity, he must avoid getting caught up in the ck'o'yo magic that diverts one's attention from the important human responsibility to nurture the earth because "It isn't very easy / to fix up things again" (256).

Tayo's understanding and acceptance of himself lead to his reintegration into the life of his family and community. Meeting with elders after returning to the pueblo, Tayo tells them of his experience with T'seh Montano and of the she-elk he saw painted on a rock. The elders rejoice—that he has seen her means they "will be blessed / again" (257).

Tayo's story is part of the whole human journey. The witchery is "dead for now" (261), but not forever. The novel ends with a prayer to the sunrise, the beginning of light:

> Sunrise,
> accept this offering,
> Sunrise. (262)

In a ceremonial manner Silko has exerted a positive voice. Yet she acknowledges the negative nuclear threat still hanging over the world. It is significant that at the climax of the novel, before Tayo achieves what might be termed an epiphany at the abandoned uranium mine, he remembers the story his grandma once told him of having seen from a distance the first atomic explosion:

> I had to get up, the way I do, to use the chamber pot. It was still dark; everyone else was still sleeping. But as I walked back from the kitchen to my bed there was a flash of lightning through my window. So big, so bright even my old clouded-up eyes could see it. It must have filled the whole southeast sky. I thought I was seeing the sun rise again . . . (245)

Remembering, and considering the explosion, Grandma asked, "'Why did they make a thing like that?'"

Though he was unable to answer when Grandma asked that question, by this point in his journey Tayo understands, as a working out of the sandpainting ceremony, that the creation of the atomic bomb was a manifestation of the human urge to destroy and that this power must be checked within oneself before one can prevent others from exerting it. Silko emphasizes the importance of being conscious of the destructive forces that exist on this earth, both through Tayo's vision and through the truth of the old Laguna stories. The Laguna people's faith and belief in humanity keeping a watchful eye on the purveyors of destruction is borne out in the old stories when the witchman says, "Ck'o'yo magic won't work / if someone is watching us" (247).

The stories of various characters in *Ceremony* and the Laguna stories woven into the novel provide a strong web of meaning, making it possible for Tayo to understand the significance of his experience and to act accordingly. His own healing process is a step toward cultural survival.

Leslie Silko has offered a ceremony and a prayer of healing in this cyclic novel. While her next novel, *Almanac of the Dead,* has a more episodic structure, a broader terrain, and a larger cast of characters, many of Silko's themes remain the same. Both novels make powerful statements about the necessity of human beings respecting and living in balance with all of nature, including one another.

B. Teaching *Ceremony*

It is important to establish a context for studying *Ceremony.* To do that, one needs to be informed about the geographical setting and the historical and cultural context of the narrative. I often begin by noting the location of Laguna Pueblo, Mount Taylor, Los Alamos, Gallup, and White Sands, as well as other places mentioned in the novel, on a map of New Mexico.

Next, I present a history of Laguna Pueblo, ancient and modern. A particularly helpful book is Bertha P. Dutton and Miriam A. Marmon's *The Laguna Calendar*. One might note that the Laguna names for six months of the year are indicative of the planting, growing, and harvesting of corn. One can also find information about Laguna Pueblo and the Keresan pueblos in general in John R. Swanton's *The Indian Tribes of North America*. Laguna, along with Acoma Pueblo, forms the western group of Keresan Indians. The Keresans trace their origin to the underworld, from which they emerged at a place called Shipapu. From there, they traveled slowly southward to their present locations.

In another, perhaps earlier myth, the Lagunas arrive on the West Coast of what is now North America, on the backs of giant sea turtles. This story was mentioned by Silko's aunt, Mrs. Walter K. Marmon, in a taped interview that is part of the Special Collections in the Zimmerman Library at the University of New Mexico. Silko's first poem, "Prayer to the Pacific," includes this story. I project the poem onto a screen and discuss it with students before beginning a study of *Ceremony*.

Also helpful in providing background is the video, *Running on the Edge of the Rainbow*, which features Leslie Silko sitting on the porch of a house on the reservation, talking about the importance of stories to the life of the community and reading some of her poetry. The scenes of Laguna in this video help one to visualize the scenes in *Ceremony*.

Using Silko's book *Storyteller* and biographical information, I then emphasize the importance of her community, of the stories she heard as a child, and of the landscape in shaping Silko's outlook as a writer. I then trace her development as a writer, from *Laguna Woman* to her most recent publications.

In beginning a close reading of *Ceremony*, I have students look at the novel from a number of perspectives. First, we look at the unusual structure of the book with its juxtapositions of Laguna myth and visionary poetry with contemporary prose narrative. Next, we look at the plot of the novel, the gradual progression of the protagonist Tayo from sickness to health, from alienation to reciprocity. We consider the literary techniques, such as flashbacks, stream of consciousness, and descriptions to further the plot and build the themes of the novel. Finally, we consider the themes.

While it is essential to recognize that *Ceremony* is specific to the Laguna culture, it is helpful to discuss parallels and differences between aspects of Laguna and European culture and mythology. The class can consider the similarities and differences between European writers calling on the muse for inspiration and Silko telling the story that Ts'its'tsi'nako is thinking. The class might consider to what extent the individual imagination is similar, regardless of cultural background, and to what extent the imagination is culturally influenced.

The class might also consider the Laguna creation myth in which two sisters of Ts'its'tsi'nako created the universe. Students will note that females have creative prominence in the Laguna genesis, contrasted with the male creator of Hebrew Genesis. It will also be clear that the capacity to imagine stories and to tell them is so highly regarded in the Laguna culture that it is sister to creating the universe.

After this close reading, I ask students to consider the novel within the larger frameworks of Native American, American, and world literatures. One might compare and contrast *Ceremony* with N. Scott Momaday's *House Made of Dawn* or with Louise Erdrich's *Love Medicine*, both of which contain stories of Native American veterans. While *Ceremony* is set in the post–World War II era, Silko was writing the novel during the Vietnam War. In creating the character Tayo, she was no doubt influenced by veterans near her own age who were returning from Vietnam. Interesting comparisons and contrasts could be drawn between *Ceremony* and many other twentieth-century novels, such as *Catch-22* and *Slaughterhouse Five*, in which war and violence are thematic considerations.

Clearly, while *Ceremony* is culturally specific, the novel has the capacity to speak to an international readership. It can be helpful to read the correspondence between Silko and poet James Wright, later published as *The Delicacy and Strength of Lace* (1986). In his initial letter to Silko, Wright said:

> I could call *Ceremony* one of the four or five best books I ever read about America and I would be speaking the truth. But even this doesn't say just what I mean.
> I think I am trying to say that my very life means more to me than it would have meant if you hadn't written *Ceremony*. (3)

Silko's writing is, as Wright observed and as Norwegian critic Per Seyersted remarked, "deeply moving" (23). It provokes us to think deeply and to act responsibly to fulfill our cultural and human responsibilities.

Study Questions

1. Since the setting and chronology of *Ceremony* are not always familiar or easy to determine, placing the narrative in time and space can be helpful to the reader. Find the setting of *Ceremony* on a map, and trace Tayo's journey in time and place.

2. Since most readers are probably unfamiliar with the history of life on

American Indian reservations, it will help to research the history of Laguna Pueblo, where much of the action of the novel takes place. Consult the Dutton and Marmon or Swanton volumes. (See section C, part 3.)

3. Enumerate the ways in which Native American life and culture have been polluted by American technology or by modern life in general, according to *Ceremony*.

4. Since many of the novel's flashbacks take place during World War II in the Philippines, find out what conditions were like on those islands during the war.

5. What is the function of Laguna oral tradition and of storytelling in *Ceremony*? Illustrate by making specific references to the novel.

6. Consider the structure of the novel *Ceremony*. Is it linear or cyclic? How does Silko utilize a stream of consciousness in the narrative?

7. Identify the destructive forces in Tayo's world and the ways in which they affect his life.

8. Consider what Tayo is personally responsible for in the novel (for example, his own behavior) and what he is not responsible for. According to the novel, how important is an individual's assumption of responsibility to the health of the surrounding community's culture and environment?

9. Identify the positive steps in Tayo's healing process in the course of the novel. Describe each step, and indicate whether it occurs as a result of his own actions, outside influences, or both combined.

10. Consider the female characters in *Ceremony*— Grandma, Auntie, Tayo's mother, Night Swan, T'seh Montano, and Helen Jean. How important are they to the novel's themes? Compare and contrast them to female characters in the broader context of American literature who exhibit similar powers (for example, Ultima in Rudolfo Anaya's *Bless Me, Ultima,* or Pilate in Toni Morrison's *Song of Solomon*).

11. What do the male characters Josiah, Ku'oosh, and Robert give Tayo spiritually? How do their gifts differ from those he receives from the female characters?

12. Name some examples of interdependence in the novel: the novelist and Thought Woman, Tayo and the spotted cattle, and others. Do these imply broader kinds of interdependence?

13. Explore the ways in which *Ceremony* critiques dominant American society. What are the specifically white values and actions in the novel that affect Tayo?

14. Consider the form and content of the poetry that is juxtaposed with the narrative in *Ceremony*. How does the shape and content of the poetry serve to develop and accentuate the theme of this novel?

C. Bibliographies

1. Related Works

Erdrich, Louise. *Love Medicine.* New York: Harper Perennial, 1993. Set between 1957 and 1982 on the Turtle Mountain Chippewa Reservation in North Dakota, this novel contains some of the same types of characters as *Ceremony,* including a Vietnam War veteran who returns psychologically wounded and eventually commits suicide.

McNickle, D'Arcy. *The Surrounded.* 1936. Reprint, Albuquerque: University of New Mexico Press, 1978. The musically talented protagonist, Archilde Leon, born of a Salish mother and a Spanish father, returns to St. Xavier, Montana, intending a short visit, but he stays on and comes to identify with his Salish heritage.

Momaday, N. Scott. *House Made of Dawn.* New York: Harper and Row, 1968. After serving in World War II, Abel, the protagonist, returns to Walatowa, a fictionalized Jemez Pueblo. Within two weeks he kills an albino, referred to in the novel as "the white man." After serving seven years in prison, he spends a short time in the relocation program in Los Angeles before returning, physically beaten, to Walatowa. In the end Abel is running, finally articulating the pueblo tradition he inherited from his grandfather.

Ortiz, Simon J. "Kaiser and the War." In *The Man to Send Rain Clouds,* ed. Kenneth Rosen, 47–60. New York: Vintage Books, 1975. Kaiser, an Acoma Pueblo man, initially resists the draft during World War II. When he decides to enlist, against his paternal grandfather's advice, it is too late. He is imprisoned. While incarcerated, he tries to kill a man and his sentence is increased. When finally released, he wears a prison-issued suit until he wears it out, and upon his death it is returned to the government.

Perea, Robert. "Dragon Mountain." In *The Remembered Earth,* ed. Geary Hobson, 358–65. Albuquerque: University of New Mexico Press, 1987. Narrated from the perspective of a soldier serving in Vietnam, Specialist Fourth Class Ernest Rodriguez, this story is set near the Cambodian border. The vernacular of the narrative authentically relates the experience of the war from a Sioux/Chicano perspective.

Waters, Frank. *The Man Who Killed the Deer.* New York: Pocket Books, 1971. Martiniano, from Taos Pueblo, returns from the boarding-school experience and finds it difficult to conform to traditional customs. After killing a deer out of season, he faces trial by pueblo and federal courts. Gradually, Martiniano comes to understand and take on the traditional ways, and his court case provides a way for the pueblo to be granted title to its sacred Blue Lake.

2. Best Criticism

Allen, Paula Gunn. "The Feminine Landscape of Leslie Marmon Silko's *Cer-emony*." In *Studies in American Indian Literature,* ed. Allen, 127–33. New York: Modern Language Association Press, 1983. This essay on *Ceremony* explains the dualities in the novel.

————. *The Sacred Hoop.* Boston: Beacon Press, 1986. Explains how Silko uses "accretive structuring to build toward comprehensive significance . . . as do traditional storytellers."

————. "Special Problems in Teaching Leslie Marmon Silko's *Ceremony.*" *American Indian Quarterly* 14, no. 4 (Fall 1990): 379–86. Allen, who has La-guna ancestry, considers the use of sacred ceremonies in the novel, and the importance of respecting the Native Americans' exclusive right to those ceremonies.

Owens, Louis. "The Very Essence of Our Lives: Leslie Silko's Webs of Identity." In *Other Destinies: Understanding the American Indian Novel,* 167–91. Norman: University of Oklahoma Press, 1992. This analysis emphasizes the timelessness of truth as a theme in *Ceremony.*

Sands, Kathleen M., ed. "A Special Symposium Issue on Leslie Marmon Silko's *Ceremony.*" *American Indian Quarterly* 5, no. 1 (1979): 1–75. Includes essays by Kathleen Sands, Paula Gunn Allen, Peter Beidler, Susan Scarberry, Carol Mitchell, Elaine Jahner, Robert Bell, A. LaVonne Ruoff, and Larry Evers.

Seyersted, Per. *Leslie Marmon Silko.* Western Writers Series, no. 45. Boise: Boise State University, 1980. Provides a good introduction to Silko's life and early work, including *Ceremony.*

Swann Edith. "Laguna Symbolic Geography and Silko's *Ceremony.*" *American Indian Quarterly* 12, no. 3 (Summer 1988): 229–49. Helpful in illustrat-ing the symbolism that is based on the cultural, seasonal, and geographi-cal context of *Ceremony.*

————. "Healing via the Sunrise Cycle in Silko's *Ceremony.*" *American Indian Quarterly* 12, no. 4 (Fall 1988): 313–28. Clarifies the ceremonial healing process in *Ceremony.*

Turner, Frederick. "Voice out of the Land: Leslie Marmon Silko's *Ceremony,*" In *Spirit of Place: The Making of an American Literary Landscape,* 321–51. San Francisco: Sierra Club Books, 1989. Sheds light on Leslie Marmon Silko's childhood love for the land and the old stories. Turner visited Silko's father, Lee Marmon, and Silko herself; the resultant biographical infor-mation helps explain the genesis of *Ceremony.*

Wiget, Andrew. *Native American Literature.* Boston: Twayne Publishers, 1985. Provides insightful interpretations and statements of Silko's major themes.

3. Other Sources

Dutton, Bertha, and Miriam A. Marmon. *The Laguna Calendar.* Albuquerque: University of New Mexico Press, 1936.

Fisher, Dexter. "Stories and Their Tellers—A Conversation with Leslie Marmon Silko." In *The Third Woman: Minority Women Writers of the United States,* ed. Fisher, 18–23. Boston: Houghton Mifflin, 1980.

Luckert, Karl W. "Interviews with Navajo Medicinemen." *Americans before Columbus.* Special edition (1982): 8, 9, 16.

New Mexico Highway Map. Department of Tourism, P.O. Box 20003, Santa Fe, N.M. 87503.

Silko, Leslie Marmon. The Special Collections Department of the Zimmerman Library at the University of New Mexico, Albuquerque, contains transcriptions and tapes of interviews with a number of Leslie Marmon Silko's family members. Headings include "The life of Alice Marmon Little," "Marmon and Gunn Family History," "Harry Marmon," "Mrs. Walter K. Marmon, and "Walter G. Marmon."

———. *Laguna Woman.* Greenfield Center, N.Y.: Greenfield Review Press, 1974.

———. "An Old-Time Indian Attack Conducted in Two Parts." 1976. In *The Remembered Earth,* 211–16.

———. *Ceremony.* 1977. Reprint, New York: Penguin Books, 1986.

———. *Storyteller.* New York: Seaver Books, 1981.

———. *Almanac of the Dead.* New York: Simon and Schuster, 1991.

Silko, Leslie Marmon, and James Wright. *The Delicacy and Strength of Lace,* ed. Anne Wright. St. Paul: Graywolf Press, 1986.

Swanton, John R. *The Indian Tribes of North America.* Washington, D.C.: Smithsonian Institution Press, 1968.

White, Leslie A. *The Acoma Indians.* Washington, D.C.: Smithsonian Institution Bureau of American Ethnology, 1932.

Building Bridges:

Crossing the Waters to a *Love Medicine* (Louise Erdrich)

JOHN PURDY

A: Analysis of Themes and Forms

Since its publication in 1984, Louise Erdrich's *Love Medicine* has been reprinted several times, including a 1993 edition that reintroduces four chapters excised from the originally published version. In other words, after a decade the book continues to attract new readers as well as those who thirst for more of the story, more of the telling. Although a first novel, *Love Medicine* reveals the strength of Erdrich's gift for storytelling: for involving readers in lives less than glamorous and hardly alluring but that, nonetheless, reveal the transcendent qualities of human nature. She has a talented eye, so it is small wonder her popularity has grown with each successive work.

One of the attractive characteristics of *Love Medicine* is its subtle complexity; it offers a diversity of perceptions through a multilayered narrative in which each character's story is centered in a relatively small, seemingly loose-knit community of characters and events. Much like the novels of modernists such as Woolf or Faulkner (who was one influence upon Erdrich's art and to whom she is most often compared), hers evolves through each successive telling of events, and builds toward understanding by requiring the reader to adopt a participatory role and thereby invest in the lives and events it portrays. This process is enhanced by Erdrich's use of first-person narratives that engage us directly in the discourse. We are spoken to, sometimes like amateur ethnographers and at others like familiar confidants; we are asked to respond; we are required to build connections and patterns; and we are satisfied when our efforts in making the story work out are rewarded. Unlike Faulkner or Woolf, however, Erdrich describes "life on the rez," the funnel end of colonialism in the United States of America, and it is to her credit that she entices non-Native American readers into a network of history and a present largely foreign to them, and she does so in compelling ways. An analysis of how this is accomplished reveals the intricacies of her text, as well as the tetralogy of which *Love Medicine* is but one part.

The novel revolves around four of its characters: June, Marie, Nector, and Lulu. The latter three comprise a "love triangle" that is explicated through a nonlinear, fragmented narrative of events that covers fifty years. It begins with Marie Lazarre who, at fourteen, climbs the hill above town to join the Catholic convent and become a saint. She returns down the same hill a short while later—wounded, triumphant, and remorseful—only to stumble into Nector Kashpaw and—almost inexplicably—become his wife, despite his infatuation with Lulu Nanapush. With Marie's forceful direction, Nector becomes a "success," and even tribal chairman, while in later years he carries on a relationship with his first love. Lulu, like a primal force characterized in mythical narratives, gives birth to sons from several fathers, spreading compassion and love throughout the landscape. As the novel opens, in 1981, Nector is in his dotage, and Marie and Lulu are moving toward a time in their lives when, no longer driven by their concerns for self-image, understanding emerges. Their "triangle" has touched the lives and stories of all the other characters, the extended families the two women share.

However, it is June who is the heart of the novel, a referential "center" for all the other characters, and it is she to whom we are first introduced. Her section of the first chapter is told in the third person and in past tense, which in effect removes her own "voice" (and vision) from the novel. It is also very brief, yet it effectively smooths the ground for all that is to follow and for all that is to become significant. In fact, one means of highlighting the accomplishments of the novel is to read these few opening pages immediately after finishing the last. For instance, the closing line of the novel— "So there was nothing to do but cross the water, and bring her home"—takes on added dimension from the ideas and images presented in June's section, for she is as much the antecedent to the pronoun "her" as the car Lipsha is driving over the bridge on his return home, to the reservation.

The first pages seem to describe a bleak, rootless, unsatisfying life. In fact, they conform to, but engage dramatically, the long-held stereotypes of American Indians found in popular literature written by non-Native writers from Purchas to Thoreau to Kesey. More specifically, Erdrich directly confronts those stereotypes of Native women as "loose" drunks whose ill fates are foregone conclusions. In fact, one early newspaper reviewer clearly demonstrates how pervasive these images have become; for her, June is simply "a drunken prostitute," worthy of mention it seems, but not of understanding, or contextualizing. Thus the popular media perform. To Erdrich's

credit, she does not avoid the fundamental issues behind such easy gener-
alizations, nor the materialistic bias upon which racist stereotypes are based.
Instead, she opens her first novel with this all-too-familiar image of poverty, yet does not allow readers to wallow in the comfort of moralistic judgments from a distance: we cannot dismiss with easy categorization. June,
we learn, is simply looking for love, as she has all her life, to heal the hurt
and loss suffered when her mother dies, leaving her child alone in the "bush"
to fend for herself. June survives, and from this experience comes pain, but
also a strength. In the opening pages, near the end of her life, she is not the
helpless pawn of fate, or of poverty, or of men as much as she is, somehow,
a proud, deliberate force who initiates and directs the actions described. In
effect, Erdrich devotes the remainder of the text to shaking the assumptions upon which ethnocentric pronouncements—based upon false information and emerging through privilege—are made. This is no small task.

Like many other contemporary Native novels, *Love Medicine* begins with
a homecoming, what Bill Bevis has termed a "Homing In." However, unlike
Archilde in D'Arcy McNickle's *The Surrounded*, or Abel in N. Scott
Momaday's *House Made of Dawn*, June's return is subtly veiled, for she does
not return "physically." Instead, she comes home as vivid, warm, unshakable memories for all the characters who speak to us after, or more pointedly, she comes home as a character in the stories they tell, the oral literary
canon they all share that tells them who they are in relation to others. She
dies; at least, we are told that she is brought home and buried, although like
Albertine—June's "niece" who is away at school and whose own homecoming provides us with the initial first-person narrative—we do not "witness"
the act: it is not made an event in the novel. Although it may seem inconse-
quential, this is a significant point for it establishes June as a disembodied,
silent, yet palpable presence—a nebulous yet powerful center—throughout the stories and lives of other characters. Furthermore, it draws attention to the details of the brief description of June's final moments, where
Erdrich presents not June's death, but her transcendence (for lack of a better term). This, of course, should undermine the reader's ability to consider
her death a justifiable punishment for a "freewheeling" lifestyle. Life and
death, particularly on reservations, are not that simple.

Two sections of the text—"Scales" and "The Red Convertible"—were
published as short stories before the idea of the novel materialized. When
asked to submit an entry for the Nelson Algren Award, Erdrich evidently
wrote "The World's Greatest Fishermen" in response, and not only did it
win, but it also provided the impetus to bring these three together (Coltelli,

43). In other words, her first chapter, for which June's section acts as a preface, is a kingpin for the book. We learn later in the chapter that June's son, King, has a hat with an inscription that reads "The World's Greatest Fisherman," so the slight—yet crucial—revision for the chapter's title poses an interesting dilemma. To resolve it, readers must face several possibilities: that the plurality, as opposed to singularity, is significant; perhaps that the Anishinaabe (Chippewa), about whom she writes, are implied; that the evocation of Christ, the "Fisher of Men," is poignant; that the concept of fishing is in some way relevant, perhaps even metaphoric or symbolic. All these possibilities are explored throughout the text, beginning with June's section.

In the opening sentence, Erdrich establishes two critical points. First, she tells us that June is "killing time" before she returns home. Although isolated and alone in a North Dakota boomtown, she still possesses an attachment to a place and family that "home" implies: a plurality. Erdrich also sets June's "time of death." The events described—June's meeting of an Anglo oil worker, their day of drinking, their abortive sexual encounter in his pickup that night—begin on the eve of Easter Sunday. She dies, therefore, at a time synonymous with resurrection, and this initial connection is strengthened by the final lines of the chapter.

Rather than walk back to town after she leaves Andy passed out in his truck, she makes a decisive turn away from the road and toward her home on the reservation. Erdrich carefully emphasizes that she "did not lose her sense of direction. . . . The heavy winds couldn't blow her off course. She continued" (7).[1] She moves through the gathering snowstorm, stepping lightly upon the dry spots of the prairie, avoiding "the slush and rotten, gray banks" as she focuses on home and family, on "Uncle Eli's warm, man-smelling kitchen." She moves deliberately, freely, and almost joyfully, swinging her purse:

> Even when her heart clenched and her skin turned crackling cold it didn't matter, because the pure and naked part of her went on.
>   The snow fell deeper that Easter than it had in forty years, but June walked over it like water and came home. (7)

Her death is described in terms of movement, continuance, and a return, rather than an end. Moreover, this line is echoed in the concluding sentence of the novel, where June's son, Lipsha, also crosses the water "and bring[s] her home." With two lines, Erdrich has established a circular structure, but more importantly an implication of continuance and endurance, tied to home, that provide a precarious counterbalance to the images of loss, disintegration, and assimilation that some readers may initially discern.

June's section is reflective of later sections in the ways in which Erdrich toys with quick interpretations. Given all the obvious Christian references here, one might feel the urge to consider June a "Christlike" figure, one who has been sacrificed to the sins of history. This dramatic revision of the "drunken-prostitute" image may be a useful line of inquiry at first, but it makes her—oddly enough—a much too simple character, the text too didactic. Another possibility exists, one that marks Erdrich's ability to work the points where cultures and traditions, Euro-American and Chippewa, engage. Her text rests upon the reader's ability to winnow kernels of truth from the confusion of human experience, and to interpret events and characters based upon a complex social fabric evoked through the life stories of a very few characters. To accomplish this, she employs repetition of key images and phrases.

The first section provides several of the central, recurrent motifs that string the disparate narratives together like the beads on June's only childhood possession, a rosary: the metaphors and allusions from Christian belief; those dealing with water and fishing; the heart as repository of humanity, in particular the ability for love; the important, attractive power of home and family. These, of course, are universally recognizable to a widely diverse audience, and are therefore useful to engage readers in terms of Western written literary conventions, but Erdrich extends their application by using them so consistently that they become intertwined with very basic definitions of self and ethnicity. Rather than imply the complete assimilation of the Chippewa, however, she presents the ways that cultures borrow from one another and thus change, while maintaining a singular sense of identity.

In an interview with Joseph Bruchac, Erdrich once commented upon the powers of this exchange: "That's one of the strengths of Indian culture, that you can pick and choose and keep and discard" (Bruchac, 79). As she notes in another interview, many family trees on the reservation and in the novel possess "a lot of French, but in particular the French and the Indian had been so blended by that time, it's a new culture" (Coltelli, 45). Rather than dwell upon loss, Erdrich underscores the ways in which people are empowered, even in the most destructive of situations.

Each of the storytellers in the novel defines him- or herself as "Indian," and more specifically by family in an elaborate social structure; even Marie's constant reference to her "white" appearance is referential to the local com-

munity. Yet each speaker also utilizes the same Christian metaphors or allusions: even Lulu, the seemingly least "Christian" of the characters, refers
to angels when she describes her lovemaking (277). In short, the novel takes
us into the lives of mediators, characters who must find satisfying exist-
ences through negotiation. The effects of colonialism are apparent in all
aspects of their lives—in religious, economic, and social interactions—and
in each realm, the teachings of the church, the government, the schools can
clash with basic instincts and emotions that appear to form Erdrich's sense
of the enduring core of Chippewa culture. The insistence upon singular
salvation (or the ancillary damnation, a "personal hell" [53]), or upon personal financial success, or individual academic achievement places undue
stress upon social systems comprised of individuals whose primary concern is with the welfare and health of their families within a community:
their survival, its continuance. In the novel, this stress is revealed through
several conflicts. Lulu's overt sexuality is condemned by some, yet she is,
indeed, the embodiment of love and compassion: "I was in love with the
whole world and all that lived in its rainy arms" (276). As tribal chairman,
Nector signs the papers to force Lulu out of her home to make way for a
factory that will make toy tomahawks, but she realizes the economic scheme
is ultimately doomed, a mockery of tribal values (283). Although called a
hardened criminal by the larger society, Lulu's son, Gerry, possesses admirable, positive human qualities—compassion, an unshakable sense of justice, an ability to love wholeheartedly, a sense of humor—all of which are
related to his mysterious powers that are directly equated to his heritage as
a "Nanapush man," who all have an "odd thing with our hearts" (366). The
tensions within the community emerge from the pulls people feel between
personal achievement and social well-being.

However, there are points at which cultures touch—at least ideally—by
possessing similar values. These are the points at which a borrowing or
sharing may occur, or at least a point at which that potential is heightened,
and these are the "hinge" points of the novel, the moments of convergence
that act as bridges (yet another recurrent motif) for readers into another
worldview. For instance, the image of a "Fisher of Men" is molded into an
apt metaphor used by several of Erdrich's characters. Before their removal
to the West, Lulu tells us, the "Chippewas had started way off on the other
side of the five great lakes" (282). Water and beings of the water figure promi-
nently in Anishinaabe culture, whether the Turtle Mountain band about
whom Erdrich writes or those of the Minnesota lakelands where they once
lived, so the preponderance of fishing metaphors and similes is understandable, although its significance goes much deeper than mere "local color."

Erdrich's husband, Michael Dorris (Modoc), verifies this when he talks about the novel he had a hand in shaping:

> Maybe native tribal culture has changed like all cultures, and *Love Medicine* is a story about a contemporary group of people that are in some ways indistinguishable from other rural North Dakota people who are not rich, but in other ways they are very much unique, very much who they were; they have the same kind of symbols that inspired Chippewas in the past, the water and the water god, and they have the kind of family connection which has always been the core of the tribe. (Coltelli, 45)

This uniqueness emerges as we recognize the ways Erdrich's characters express their perceptions of their place.

Although the underwater being Lipsha tells us about, Missepeshu or Misshipeshu, does not become a central character until the third novel of the tetralogy, *Tracks*, in *Love Medicine* he plays, like June, a significant role without appearing on stage:

> Now there's your God of the Old Testament and there is Chippewa Gods as well. Indian Gods, good and bad, like tricky Nanabozho or the water monster, Missepeshu, who lives over in Matchimanito. That water monster was the last God I ever heard to appear. It had a weakness for young girls and grabbed one of the Pillagers off her rowboat. She got to shore all right, but only after this monster had his way with her. She's an old lady now. Old Lady Pillager. She still doesn't like to see her family fish that lake. (236)

The landscape Erdrich paints has several mythical beings, some good, some bad, some local, some imported. While the Christian god is a contentious sociological force through the presence of the church, in particular the nuns, the indigenous powers still inhabit their place and intervene in human lives. Misshipeshu, it seems, is also perceived as a fisher of people, one whose presence has been reported recently and felt personally, and this presence is maintained through language.

Furthermore, when Lipsha describes his view of Nector's mental incapacity, he does not rely upon Western psychological interpretations; he speaks metaphorically and pointedly for the man who became the apparent embodiment of the "modern Indian," but who is still moved by forces ancient and local: Nector "was fishing in the middle of Matchimanito. And there was big thoughts on his line, and he kept throwing them back for even bigger ones that would explain to him, say, the meaning of how we got here and why we have to leave so soon" (234). When he describes Nector's death, he does so in the same terms: "He was still fishing in the middle of Matchimanito. Big thoughts was on his line and he had half a case of beer in the boat. He waved at me, grinned, and then the bobber went under" (250). Once again, death is described as a continuation, not an end, and its meaning in the scheme of things is not found in church or convent, but in the land.

Of course, Old Lady Pillager's story may be suspect, as are all the personal histories we encounter; we tend to maintain our own perceived image as we revise and tell our stories. Throughout *Love Medicine*, however, readers are confronted with the potential inherent in the landscape that surrounds the lives of the families, a potential that consistently qualifies the intervention of Christianity and provides a point of differentiation for those characters who identify as possessing, or being related to those who possess, an indigenous tradition. This may be discerned through the connections we are asked to make, the bridges we must build. For instance, in the title piece of the novel when Lipsha decides to create a "love medicine" that will tie the aged Nector to Marie forever, that will supply the "staying power" (234) required for a strong relationship, he admits that he dealt with powers he did not fully comprehend. This comprehension, evidently, is no longer widespread (if it ever was), but resides "in the bush" with people like Nector's brother, Eli, or more specifically Old Man Pillager, whom all fear. Although Lipsha's revelations about his power to heal may be construed as equally suspect, as an aspect of his own, revised self-image, we cannot so easily dismiss the possibility when we learn, later from Lulu, that he is the direct descendent of Old Man Pillager, who like Lipsha's father, Gerry, is a "Nanapush man" with inexplicable powers (335). (Nanapush, as other critics have amply noted, is a name strongly reminiscent of the trickster Nanabozho, as are Gerry's powers.) When Lipsha's instincts for such healings take him to a probable ingredient for a love medicine—the hearts of a pair of Canada geese, who mate for life—his intellect gets in his way; he incorrectly surmises that there is no inherent power in the hearts themselves, but merely in people's hope for miracles: "I finally convinced myself that the real actual power to the love medicine was not in the goose heart itself but the faith in the cure" (246). He substitutes a long-dead, frozen turkey heart, and Nector chokes to death on it.

Erdrich speaks to a fundamental issue, a point of differentiation between modern, "scientific" explanations and others based in a Native worldview. The results of Lipsha's rationalization are revealing, when we make connections. On a fishing trip to Matchimanito with Nector, Lipsha learns that he is special because he has his brain in his heart (251). Rather than a Euro-

American dichotomy between the head and heart, reason and emotion, we find the preferential merging of the two: equally a reliance upon the fundamental logic of emotions and a regard for old ways of expressing them. Also, Nector's first encounter with Marie in 1934, as she comes down the hill from the convent and he is focused on his love for Lulu, comes about as he trudges up the hill with two Canada geese strapped to his wrists; within the world of the novel, we cannot help but wonder about the "staying power" of geese. The two come together, despite the revulsion each feels at the idea, and in the scene in which they "mate," the geese become participants as they encumber both Marie's and Nector's movements. They prescribe (pun intended) a love medicine that results in the couple's marriage and the events of fifty years.

The love triangle between Marie, Nector, and Lulu clearly demonstrates the intricate entanglements to be found in life, the forces that create them, and the inadequate nature of personal knowledge in either preparing for events or understanding events of the past. To explore these ideas, Erdrich adopts a spiral structure that circles through time to reveal with each swing more information about past events that tie the narratives together. It is Nector Kashpaw who voices this structure: "And here is where events loop around and tangle again" (128). "Thematic" concerns (more accurately, the issues and views revealed through our involvement with Erdrich's fictionalizing) and "structural" device are inseparable in *Love Medicine*. The story is in the telling and, as in any storytelling event, the audience has a role to play. We must untangle events; we must straighten out the fishing line of lives, for only the reader can recognize all the ties, define the relationships, and discern the patterns. In a way, we are like "the elders," Lulu and Marie at book's end, who, after lifetimes of strife and conflict, have reached an objective distance that affords a better, more expansive perspective of the relationships, politics, and petty goings-on in the community. *Love Medicine* is built from this understanding, and exemplifies how passion and compassion, pride and pity can tie people together in productive, supportive ways and thus lead to strength: what Chippewa author Gerald Vizenor calls the power of survivance.

B. Teaching the Work

Much as in the oral literary traditions of Native cultures, *Love Medicine* is a story that teaches itself, if its audience will commit to employing equal measures of memory and imagination. Likewise, it can be approached in discussion from any number of critical stances: from a close New Critical reading, to archetypal analysis, or reader-response theory. And in the two previous statements lurks the complexity of teaching this novel: it is often read and discussed as both an ethnographic text and a work of fiction derived from Euro-American literary conventions. When asked about her intended audience, Erdrich once responded that she writes for American Indians first, in the hope that they will find her depictions personally poignant (Coltelli, 47). In fact, stylistically the novel is written as a series of "as-told-to" autobiographies, a genre much used in literature written about American Indians. In other words, Erdrich is quite aware of the traditions and conventions that derive from both European and North American sources, and so it seems perfectly logical that we employ a similarly enlightened methodology when addressing her works. To this end, I must provide a preface.

There is a great deal of heated debate about the efficacy of using Western literary theory when studying a work of Native American literatures, either spoken or written. On one side, it is argued that to do so is yet another form of colonialism, an attempt to make American Indian texts conform to Western ideals; on the other, it is argued that literary theory can enlighten any text, from any culture and in any form. (I am, of course, simplifying both stances for the sake of discussion.) This issue may surface in the classroom, as it does quite often at conferences and in articles and reviews. No matter what one's opinion may be on this issue, the debate itself is an effective pedagogical tool, as any debate should be: a provocative point of departure for looking at the intricacies of the text. The binary nature of the debate can truly enlighten, since Erdrich employs a number of equally revealing polarities; *Love Medicine* illustrates the complex failure of either/or thinking, as its narrative moves toward a mediation of cultures.

Like any work of literature, the novel shapes perception, and sometimes alters it dramatically. For this reason, it can be useful for students to keep a reading journal, a reader-response record of their initial reactions to the text and one that will allow them a sense of control over a sometimes disorienting narrative. These early responses can then be compared to later reactions, as more information is gained from within the text itself, and from other readings. These readings should come from a variety of points of view as well, and one way of structuring their presentation is to move from the novel to reviews, to published interviews with Erdrich, to ethnographic materials, and to critical responses. (See the bibliography.) Of course, these fundamental components can be restructured depending upon one's own methodology, but each needs to be incorporated in some way and to some degree for a balanced discussion of the text and for a full understanding of its complexity and relevance to various audiences. These can either be read by all, perhaps in a course packet, or else they can be presented by individual students, or, even better, panels of students during class meetings. Ideally, one would also incorporate the reading of the other novels in the tetralogy, which complete the stories of the characters in *Love Medicine*.

As mentioned above, and in the preceding section of this essay, Erdrich makes ample use of polar opposites, in particular characters who are tied to someone much like themselves but who seem to reflect very different attitudes, doppelgängers of sorts: Marie/Sister Leopolda, Nector/Eli, Marie/Lulu, Lipsha/King, to name a few. These can be discussed quite effectively to focus students' attention on specific scenes in which the characters' differences are underscored, while recurrent symbols and metaphors mark the degree to which they share a common heritage/cultural milieu. Discussion of these will invariably raise issues relevant to Native Americans today, not the least of which is the way that colonialism has impinged upon traditional lifeways. This leads logically to the ways Erdrich presents that influence, and therefore the ways she seeks balance and harmony rather than conflict and disharmony. A close look at critical scenes, then, will call attention to the ways that our perceptions are altered as we become more involved in Erdrich's stories, as we learn from them. One may explicate this alteration using any of several critical theories.

The conflict between Marie and Sister Leopolda provides a representative example of what one can do with other central events and how one can apply available resources. Very early in the text we are confronted with their battle, and the ways Marie reflects upon and expresses her perception of that exchange can establish some very fundamental questions that can then be addressed through discussion. It would not be surprising if students respond in their journals by condemning the Catholic church for its centuries-long subjugation—the "disempowerment"—of indigenous peoples. However, it is not that simple. To discuss the chapter "Saint Marie," one must address the nature of Marie's discourse: she is "speaking" to us in retrospect, providing context by revealing her values, then and now. Also, the title is ironic, and hinges upon the final scene where she has, it appears, become a "saint." We can also discuss the ways she effectively inverts and subverts the church hierarchy, perhaps even the very faith of those who believe in the divinity of its authority, by appearing to have been touched by God while actually the victim of Leopolda's obsession. At the same time, however, Marie exemplifies one of Christianity's central values, one shared by many beliefs: she pities the nun, and does not feel joy at her victory over her tormentor. (In a way, she has an epiphany.) All these points can be established with a close reading of the chapter and the way that "evil" and "sin" are personalized.

To elaborate, we can go beyond the text to several resources. In interviews, Erdrich has commented upon her use of religion in her books:

> I guess I have my beefs about Catholicism. Although you never change once you're raised a Catholic—you've got that. You've got that symbolism, that guilt, you've got the whole works and you can't really change that. That's easy to talk about because you have to exorcise it somehow. That's why there's a lot of Catholicism in [my] books. (Bruchac, 81)

The remainder of Marie's story demonstrates the degree to which she has exorcised the church's influence, and illustrates the values so prominent in the lives of other characters: she has compassion for others; she gives a home to children who need one; she acts as a social critic, as well. Thus, later events—in particular the final meeting between Marie and Leopolda as the nun lay dying—can be used to reassess our first readings of "Saint Marie." The novel's structure calls for this approach, and events from others' stories can equally provide more context from which to interpret this early confrontation: Lipsha's lesson on Chippewa "gods" and the ways they behave, Nector's own telling of his first meeting with Marie, and even Gordie's story of the deer.

We read more expansively as our information base expands, and to this end we may conduct research in Chippewa ethnography. Even preliminary readings can raise questions worthy of consideration. For instance, is there any significance to Marie "going up the hill" to the convent? This is a phrase often used to describe the vision quest in some Plains cultures, so could it be said that she in fact has a vision? (And what is the difference between vision and epiphany?) Does her story reflect similarities or differences in Christian and Chippewa perceptions of evil? How does Erdrich's use of water, fish, and fishing metaphors confuse that simple polarity? Is it significant that Leopolda uses boiling water as a means of enlightenment? Who is the "dark fish?" Is the evil character whom Leopolda can "sniff out" the same being we find in Euro-American mythology? In Chippewa? To answer these questions, one can draw on ethnographic sources, as well as articles that deal with the use of Chippewa oral stories in Erdrich's novels, and since *Love Medicine* is one part of a larger story, these answers may relate to her other novels as well:

The Beet Queen (1986), *Tracks* (1988), and *The Bingo Palace* (1994). (See *Tracks*, in particular, in which Sister Leopolda née Pauline Puyat tells her own story.)

However, this close focus on "the telling"—on scenes that initially hold the potential for various readings—can be applied to any event, not only those pertaining to the dualities of characters. In particular, it can be most revealing to consider motifs garnered from ethnographic sources in rereading events. For instance, in the previous section of this essay, I discussed the scene in which June's final moments are described. If one considers her "transcendence" in light of Chippewa stories of the afterlife, both it and Erdrich's continuous use of the images of bridge and water take on an added dimension. In several stories, and in each of Erdrich's novels, people die and then travel a road toward an afterlife, only to find a bridge (often a log), guarded by a ferocious being(s). Here, one's life is judged. Those who lived evil lives find it too difficult to negotiate the bridge and fall off, to travel— to continue—no more; those whose values were sound in life cross and find themselves once more at "home," surrounded by loved ones who have gone before and whose lifeways are recognizable, that is, like those one experienced before death. "The snow fell deeper that Easter than it had in forty years, but June ['the pure and naked part of her'] walked over it like water and came home." Similar episodes are described in *The Beet Queen*, where a Chippewa war veteran "dies" briefly during a parade; in *Tracks*, in which Fleur Pillager travels the road in an attempt to save the lives of her children; and in *The Bingo Palace*, when June returns along that same road.

In brief, if one allows the story to direct our imaginations and our memories, and if one employs both critical theory of whatever stripe and an expanded awareness of Chippewa culture drawn from ethnographic materials and Erdrich's other writings, one finds that *Love Medicine* can be better appreciated for its complex exploration of the contemporary lives of Anishinaabe people. Moreover, if one reads widely in contemporary American Indian literatures, one will find that it shares some qualities with other texts, many of which make use of verbal arts and oral traditions in modern fiction to address modern times, but also the history of the last five hundred years.

Questions for Discussion

1. What binary constructs can be found in the novel?
2. How does Erdrich make use of characters who appear to be polar opposites?

3. How does Erdrich depict the church's influence on the families of her characters?

4. What Christian allusions/symbols does she use frequently, and in what ways are they employed?

5. Why is understanding family connections so important in this novel? (And why have you attempted a genealogy in your journal?)

6. What are the central, recurrent motifs? (The heart, water, fish, fishing . . .)

7. Discuss the metaphor implied through June's beads.

8. Discuss the ways that Erdrich's portrait of "the human heart in conflict with itself" may be very different from that of Faulkner.

C. Bibliographies

1. Related Works

Erdrich, Louise. *The Beet Queen*. New York: Henry Holt and Company, 1986. The second novel in the tetralogy traces the Euro-American sides of the reservation families, including the early life of Dot, who has a baby by Gerry Nanapush in *Love Medicine*.

———. *Tracks*. New York: Henry Holt and Company, 1988. Turns the story back to the decades before *Love Medicine*, telling the stories of Pauline (Sister Leopolda), Nanapush, and Fleur Pillager, Lulu's mother.

———. *The Bingo Palace*. New York: HarperCollins, 1994. The last novel brings us into the present, and establishes Lipsha as the center for all four families of the tetralogy. Fleur returns and, as his great-grandmother, helps him face the age-old conflict between progress and endurance.

Hogan, Linda (Chickasaw). *Mean Spirit*. New York: Atheneum, 1990. Much like *Love Medicine*, this novel explores the complex interplay between the demands of a modern, colonized existence and the sustaining power of family and tribal ties.

McNickle, D'Arcy (Métis/Salish). *The Surrounded*. Albuquerque: University of New Mexico Press, 1978. Originally published in 1936, McNickle's first novel established the young, mixed-ancestry protagonist as a literary convention. With Archilde, he explores the nature of change, accommodation, and survival.

Ortiz, Simon (Acoma Pueblo). *Earth Power Coming: Short Fiction in Native American Literature*. Tsaile, Ariz.: Navajo Community College Press, 1983. This is a fine collection from authors from several tribal affiliations. It

can provide alternative perspectives on the issues Erdrich explores in her
own novels. (There is one story by Erdrich in the collection.)

Silko, Leslie Marmon (Laguna Pueblo). *Ceremony.* New York: Penguin, 1986.
This first novel makes overt use of Laguna oral traditions and ceremonial
practices in its telling of an ill war veteran searching for a cure. It is an
interesting counterpoint to the muted use of Chippewa culture in *Love
Medicine.*

Vizenor, Gerald (Anishinaabe). *The Heirs of Columbus.* Hanover, N.H.: University Press of New England, 1991. As in most of Vizenor's fiction, here
he turns history, colonialism, and stereotypes on their heads. Although a
difficult text for inexperienced readers, this is a wonderfully witty and
insightful handling of contemporary issues facing Native cultures.

Welch, James (Blackfeet). *Winter in the Blood.* New York: Harper and Row, 1974.
Welch's stark narrative and unnamed protagonist move through a landscape radically altered with the incursion of the Euro-American, and he
draws relationships much like the fictional families found in Erdrich's
works.

2. Best Criticism

Lyons, Gene. "In Indian Territory." *Newsweek*, February 11, 1985, 70–71. Lyons's
review reveals the inadequacy of superficial readings: he does not see the
"central action [that] unifies the narrative" and provides some pronouncements that can initiate discussion of Erdrich's storytelling expertise. (This
review plays well against the following essays.)

Owens, Louis. "Erdrich and Dorris's Mixedbloods and Multiple Narratives." In
Other Destinies: Understanding the American Indian Novel. Norman:
University of Oklahoma Press, 1992. This chapter in Owens's expansive
and well-written discussion effectively places *Love Medicine* in the context of contemporary Native American fiction, while providing useful
insights into Erdrich's narration of mixed-ancestry dilemmas. (Owens is
also a Native novelist of mixed ancestry.)

Pérez Castillo, Susan. "Post-Modernism, Native American Literature and the
Real: The Silko-Erdrich Controversy." *Massachusetts Review* 32, no. 2
(Summer 1991): 285–94. Silko's stinging review of Erdrich's second novel
has raised several issues concerning the latter's works, but also contemporary written Native American literature itself. Perez Castillo explicates
the debate and the issues involved.

Ruppert, James. "Mediation and Multiple Narrative in *Love Medicine.*" *North
Dakota Quarterly* 59, no. 4 (1991): 229–41. Ruppert's use of critical theory
underscores the ways in which Erdrich employs and crafts points of com-
monalty.

Sands, Kathleen Mullen. "Untitled." *Studies in American Indian Literatures* 9, no. 1 (Winter 1985): 12–24. Sands's article, one of the first to address *Love Medicine*, charts the seldom-considered ways in which Erdrich employs gossip, a ubiquitous oral tradition, to help readers participate in "making the story work out right."

Studies in American Indian Literatures 9, no. 1 (Winter 1985), and ibid. (series no. 2) 4, no. 1 (Spring 1992). These two very useful issues of *SAIL* are devoted to Louise Erdrich and her works, with the Winter 1985 number focusing on *Love Medicine*.

Van Dyke, Annette. "Questions of the Spirit: Bloodlines in Louise Erdrich's Chippewa Landscape." *Studies in American Indian Literatures* 4, no. 1 (Spring 1992): 15–27. This is a good recounting of the familial connections to be found in Erdrich's tetralogy.

3. Other Sources

Alabaster, Carol. "Indian voices flow together to indict tribal life." *The Arizona Republic*, February 10, 1985.

Barnett, Marianne. "Dreamstuff: Erdrich's *Love Medicine*." *North Dakota Quarterly* 56, no. 1 (Winter 1988): 82–93.

Barnouw, Victor. *Wisconsin Chippewa Myths and Tales and Their Relation to Chippewa Life*. Madison: University of Wisconsin Press, 1977.

Barry, Nora. "The Triumph of the Brave: *Love Medicine*'s Holistic Vision." *Critique: Studies in Contemporary Fiction* 30, no. 2 (Winter 1989): 123–38.

Beidler, Peter G. "Three Student Guides to Louise Erdrich's *Love Medicine*." *American Indian Culture and Research Journal* 16 (1992): 167–73.

Bevis, William. "Native American Novels: Homing In." In *Recovering the Word: Essays on Native American Literature*, ed. Brian Swann and Arnold Krupat. Berkeley: University of California Press, 1987.

Bonetti, Kay. "An Interview with Louise Erdrich and Michael Dorris." *The Missouri Review* 11, no. 2 (1988): 79–99.

Bruchac, Joseph. "Whatever Is Really Yours: An Interview with Louise Erdrich." In *Survival This Way: Interviews with American Indian Poets*. Tucson: University of Arizona Press, 1987.

Chavkin, Allan, and Nancy Feyl Chavkin. *Conversations with Louise Erdrich and Michael Dorris*. University Press of Mississippi, 1994.

Coltelli, Laura. "Louise Erdrich and Michael Dorris." *Winged Words: American Indian Writers Speak*. Lincoln: University of Nebraska Press, 1990.

Erdrich, Louise. *Jacklight*. New York: Henry Holt and Company, 1984.

———. *Love Medicine*. New York: Holt, Rinehart and Winston, 1984. New and expanded version, New York: Henry Holt and Company, 1993.

———. *Baptism of Desire*. New York: Harper and Row, 1989.

———— and Michael Dorris. *The Crown of Columbus*. New York: Harper Collins 1991.

Flavin, Louise. "Louise Erdrich's *Love Medicine*: Loving over Time and Distance." *Critique: Studies in Contemporary Fiction* 31, no. 1 (Fall 1989): 55–64.

George, Jan. "Interview with Louise Erdrich." *North Dakota Quarterly* 53, no. 2 (Spring 1985): 240–46.

Gleason, William. "'Her Laugh an Ace': The Function of Humor in Louise Erdrich's *Love Medicine*." *American Indian Culture and Research Journal* 11, no. 3 (1987): 51–73.

Howard, James H. *The Plains-Ojibwa or Bungi Hunters and Warriors of the Northern Prairies with Special Reference to the Turtle Mountain Band.* Anthropological Papers, No. 1. Vermillion: South Dakota Museum, 1951.

Jones, William. *Ojibwa Texts*. New York: AMS Press, 1974. Although Jones's collection is only one ethnography, and possesses some of the weaknesses found in ethnography itself, it is bilingual and has a wealth of stories that can reveal not only subject matter but also narrative techniques that enlighten Erdrich's work. Consider "The Youth Who Died and Came Back to Life," in vol. 7, part 2.

Magalaner, Marvin. "Louise Erdrich: Of Cars, Time and the River." In *American Women Writing Fiction: Memory, Identity, Family, Space,* ed. Mickey Pearlman. Lexington: University Press of Kentucky, 1989.

Mitchell, David. "A Bridge to the Past in Louise Erdrich's *Love Medicine*." In *Entering the Nineties: The North American Experience: Proceedings from the Native American Studies Conference at Lake Superior University*, ed. Thomas E. Schirer. Sault Saint Marie: Lake Superior University Press, 1991.

Owens, Louis. "Erdrich and Dorris's Mixedbloods and Multiple Narratives." In *Other Destinies: Understanding the American Indian Novel*. Norman: University of Oklahoma Press, 1992.

Pearlman, Mickey. "A Bibliography of Writings about Louise Erdrich." In *American Women Writing Fiction: Memory, Identity, Family, Space*.

Rainwater, Catherine. "Reading Between Worlds: Narrativity in the Fiction of Louise Erdrich." *American Literature* 62, no. 3 (September 1990): 405–22.

Ruppert, James. "Mediation and Multiple Narrative in *Love Medicine*." *North Dakota Quarterly* 59, no. 4 (1991): 229–41.

Schnieder, Lissa. "*Love Medicine*: A Metaphor for Forgiveness." *Studies in American Indian Literatures* 4, no. 1 (Spring 1992): 1–13.

Silberman, Robert. "Opening the Text: *Love Medicine* and the Return of the Native American Woman." In *Narrative Chance: Post Modern Discourse on Native American Literatures*, ed. Gerald Vizenor. Albuquerque: University of New Mexico Press, 1989.

Stripes, James D. "The Problem(s) of (Anishinaabe) History in the Fiction of
    Louise Erdrich: Voices and Contexts." *The Wicazo Sa Review* 7, no. 2,
    (1991): 26–33.
Towery, Margie. "Continuity and Connection: Characters in Louise Erdrich's
    Fiction." *American Indian Culture and Research Journal* 16, no. 4 (1992):
    99–122.
Van Dyke, Annette. "Questions of the Spirit: Bloodlines in Louise Erdrich's
    Chippewa Landscape." *Studies in American Indian Literatures* 4, no. 1
    (Spring 1992): 15–27.
Vizenor, Gerald. *The People Named the Chippewa: Narrative Histories*. Minne-
    apolis: University of Minnesota Press, 1984.
Wong, Hertha D. "An Interview with Louise Erdrich and Michael Dorris." *North
    Dakota Quarterly* 55, no. 1 (Winter 1987): 196–218.
————. "Adoptive Mothers and Throw-away Children in the Novels of Louise
    Erdrich." *Narrating Mothers: Theorizing Maternal Subjectives*, ed. Maureen
    T. Reddy. Knoxville: University of Tennessee Press, 1991.

Notes

1. This and all subsequent citations are from the most recent, 1993 edition. While it includes four chapters omitted from the original version, it
also makes some subtle additions and revisions elsewhere. While these
changes bring this novel in closer, more obvious alignment with the others
in the tetralogy, they also make it a less engaging read, at least for those who
have worked with the original for so long and who have read the remaining
novels in the tetralogy.

African American Literature

Preface

The paradox of education, as James Baldwin once put it in a talk to teachers, is that "as one begins to become conscious one begins to examine the society in which he is being educated."[1] The five essays that follow invite that kind of examination of society, both through the powerful literary texts they discuss and through the scholarly and teaching approaches they present in those discussions.

Readers will discover a range of genres and historical periods treated in the African American texts covered in these chapters. Zora Neale Hurston's *Their Eyes Were Watching God* (1937), a powerful novel about a young girl's growth into womanhood, was published during the Great Depression. Richard Wright's *Black Boy* (1945) presents a searing autobiographical portrait of the struggle for identity in white society, providing an interesting historical record of the Jim Crow era. Lorraine Hansberry's *A Raisin in the Sun* (1958), one of the great American dramas, presents African American family life in the dawn of the modern civil-rights movement. And the final works, Toni Morrison's *Song of Solomon* (1977) and Alice Walker's *The Color Purple* (1982), each presents fictional stories of black men and women that begin in the earlier part of the century and conclude in the present day.

Readers will also find a diverse range of critical approaches to help them in discovering what Morrison calls the "variety" of voices in African American culture. Daniel W. Ross and Susan Meisenhelder give particular attention to feminist perspectives in their analyses of *The Color Purple* and *Their Eyes Were Watching God*, respectively, while Linda Wagner-Martin provides a powerful discussion of the literary and historical influences on *Song of Solomon*, including the ironic use of the quest pattern (Odysseus) and biblical parallels, and the use of metaphors and tropes (the flying man) rooted in African American history and lore. Yoshinobu Hakutani presents both literary and social commentary on Wright's *Black Boy*, including Wright's use of the "young self as a mask" to express the voiceless Negro boy and his ultimate "transcendence of oppression," his lyricism, and his central theme, "self-creation." And Jeanne-Marie A. Miller's chapter on *A Raisin in the Sun* explores the play's themes and its presentation of the complexity of black family life in the United States, giving historical context to this discussion through a brief history of African Americans from 1619 to the play's 1959 opening on Broadway.

Finally, teachers and their students will find a range of imaginative teaching approaches that will help them to read these texts and write about and discuss them in their classrooms. While Ross outlines a series of very specific teaching approaches and group activities, Wagner-Martin invites rich comparisons (*Song of Solomon* with Anaya's *Bless Me, Ultima* and Wright's *Uncle Tom's Children*), biblical parallels, and opportunities for dramatic and musical performances. Both Hakutani and Meisenhelder suggest broad approaches. Hakutani defines teaching strategies that address style, form, and relations between *Black Boy* and other autobiographies. Meisenhelder provides a long and rich first-person narrative of her own teaching of *Their Eyes Were Watching God,* letting readers visualize her classroom (student-generated questions and discussions, students looking at other writers' perspectives on gender, race, and class). And Miller's questions both invite comparison with other plays (*Death of a Salesman, The Glass Menagerie*) and ask students to assess the play through expository analysis and the acting out of various scenes. These chapters, in other words, will help teachers and students both in understanding these texts and exploring them in creative and rewarding ways.

Notes

1. James Baldwin, "A Talk to Teachers," in *Multi-Cultural Literacy: Opening the American Mind,* ed. Rick Simonson and Scott Walker (St. Paul: Graywolf Press, 1988), p. 4.

Ethnic and Gender Identity in
Zora Neale Hurston's *Their Eyes Were Watching God*

SUSAN MEISENHELDER

A. Analysis of Themes and Forms

In this story of a black woman's search for identity, the main character, Janie, suffers through two unfulfilling marriages to oppressive, materialistic men, who "squinch" her spirit until she meets Tea Cake, a carefree, fun-loving bluesman who encourages her independence and self-expression. Janie leaves behind her "respectable," economically secure life to go with Tea Cake to the Everglades where they enjoy life to the fullest until a hurricane strikes. After this disaster, Janie returns home, comforted by her memories and sustained by the spirit of affirmation with which, despite tragic events, she faces life.

A major theme Hurston develops in the novel (and one characteristic of much of her work) is a celebration of black folklife. In the section of the novel that takes place in the Everglades (on the "Muck"), she depicts a kind of black Eden—a world of equality, exuberance, and vitality drawn in sharp contrast to the materialism and dehumanization many black writers have seen in the dominant, white world. In this respect, the novel is written in the spirit of black cultural affirmation characterizing the Harlem Renaissance of the 1920s and early 1930s. Like such writers as Langston Hughes and Claude McKay, Hurston was often critical of middle-class blacks (who, she felt, imitated whites) and much more interested in the life of the black person "farthest down." In the lives of rural, uneducated blacks Hurston found not only a rich cultural tradition of folklore and music, but a set of values opposed to (and in her mind, superior to) those of the dominant culture. Responding to Hurston's treatment of this theme, Alice Walker has praised the novel for its "racial health; [the] sense of black people as complete, complex, undiminished human beings" (85).

While earlier readers of Hurston's work focused on racial and cultural issues, contemporary critics have investigated the importance of gender in the novel. Janie's search for identity, in fact, involves struggling with her place as black and female. Hurston highlights the racial component of Janie's quest, for instance, by detailing the negative effects that growing up in the backyard of whites has had on Janie's sense of self. She has been given so many names by others that she is finally called Alphabet (9), an indication of her fragmented identity reinforced by the fact that she does not see herself as black and cannot even recognize herself in a photograph. As Janie grows into young womanhood, however, the issue of identity—what it means to be black and a woman—becomes even more complex.

Janie's grandmother (a more sympathetic character for the reader perhaps than for Janie) offers her one vision of the black female self. Nanny's belief that "'de white man is de ruler of everything'" leads her to think of society as a multilayered hierarchy involving both race and sex: "'. . . de white man throw down de load and tell de nigger man tuh pick it up. He pick it up because he have to, but he don't tote it. He hand it to his womenfolks. De nigger woman is de mule of de world as fur as I can see'" (14). Drawing this model of black female identity from her own experience with the harshest forms of racial and sexual oppression (slavery and rape), Nanny dreams of marriage and economic security for Janie. Fearing that Janie may be a mule or a "spit-cup" for men, she seeks protection for her by marrying her off to a well-to-do older man. As that marriage graphically demonstrates, the price is high, for Janie is forced to sacrifice love. In more complex ways, Janie's first two marriages highlight the limitations of Nanny's analysis by revealing the ways in which women can be spit-cups and mules with male protection.

Janie has another vision of female possibility, imaged in her experience under the pear tree (10–11). On one level an obvious metaphor for sexual relationships, the passage is a powerful contrast to Nanny's spit-cup and mule metaphors with their suggestions of rape and female dehumanization. This metaphor for sexuality, on the contrary, is one free of domination and divisions into active and passive: there is no suggestion of rapacious violence on the part of the (male) bee or of passive victimization on the part of the "sister-calyxes [who] arch to meet the love embrace." The relationship imaged here, one between active equals, is not only one of delight, but as the metaphor of pollination implies, one of creativity. This passage is a key one in the novel: not only will Janie, in the search for a "bee for her blossom," measure her relationships against this ideal; but Hurston will associate nearly every black character in the novel with tree imagery to suggest their psychic wholeness or mutilation. Ultimately, the image becomes the novel's ideal for human interaction (sexual, interpersonal, or more broadly social), a model of relationships without hierarchy or domination.

Joe Starks is clearly no "bee" in his relationship with Janie or with the black community. While his role as oppressor is often obvious, much more subtle is Hurston's analysis of the source of his identity. Numerous details, from his white house (an imitation plantation one) to his fancy spittoon, suggest that he draws his model from a white world. He interacts with the townspeople like a slaveowner, talking like a "section foreman" (33) with "bow-down command" (44) in his face. Starks recreates power dynamics of the most oppressive sort in the town, a fact recognized by the residents themselves, who, when forced by Starks to dig ditches, "murmured hotly about slavery being over" (44). He sees himself as God (his most frequent exclamation is, in fact, "I god") and acts the part, even bringing light to the community in a parody of Genesis when he installs the first lightpost.

Despite his superficially solicitous behavior, Starks's treatment of Janie is equally oppressive. He puts Janie on a pedestal, above other black women in the community but decidedly beneath himself. This marriage graphically demonstrates the limitations of Nanny's mule metaphor: merely removing white faces from the social hierarchy changes nothing for Janie, for she is still oppressed by the man above her. Ironically, Janie lives a life with Joe that Nanny worked so hard to avoid for her, enduring what Nanny feared despite having attained the economic circumstances she desired. Hurston emphasizes this shortcoming of Nanny's strategy for black women by having Janie symbolically associated with the situations that Nanny most feared. Race and gender intersect in complex ways, for instance, when Joe demands that Janie bind her hair in a "head-rag" (86), an artifact of the slavery period. Despite her husband's wealth, Janie becomes a spiritual slave in this marriage, a sexual object owned and controlled by her master.

In terms of both racial and gender identity, Tea Cake is portrayed as Starks's antithesis. His feminized nickname promises a "sweeter," gentler kind of masculinity than that suggested by Starks's name. Unlike Starks, who draws his models from a white world, Tea Cake is emphatically black, a man who not only revels in his own cultural traditions but also rejects the hierarchy and crass materialism characterizing Starks's whitewashed world. Also rejecting hierarchy based on sex, he becomes "a bee to Janie's blossom," encouraging Janie to express herself and to experience life more fully. Janie must step down from her pedestal to enter a relationship with Tea Cake, but she steps into one built on reciprocity rather than hierarchy. In teaching Janie to play checkers, to shoot, and to drive, and in inviting her to work alongside of him, Tea Cake breaks down the rigid gender definitions that Joe sought to impose.

In the section on the Muck, Hurston projects this model of ideal relationships onto a larger plane. With the status differences and white values that Starks sought to reinforce absent on the Muck, artificial hierarchical divisions evaporate: Janie is just another person rather than Mrs. Mayor, and the West Indians, instead of being ostracized, are accepted as equals in the community. The hierarchies of Nanny's metaphor are also foreign to this community. With no white man present to toss his load to the black man, black men do not toss theirs on to black women. When Janie goes to work in the fields with Tea Cake, it is not because Tea Cake sees her as a mule but because he wants to be with her. Freely chosen, work for Janie becomes an expression of her equality and vitality rather than her oppression. She and Tea Cake "partake with everything," sharing in both paid labor and domestic work. With Janie and Tea Cake as the Adam and Eve at the center of this garden, the spirit of their relationship is mirrored in the community. The center of this world is not the commercial enterprise of Joe's store, but Janie and Tea Cake's house, the cultural heart of the community where everyone enjoys the guitar-playing and storytelling. Janie is not merely an outside observer, as she had been with Joe, but an active participant and speaker (127–28). In this section, Janie develops both a rich ethnic identity and a vigorous female one.

The exception to the racial health in the community (in fact, the serpent in this Eden) is Mrs. Turner, a woman who, as suggested in her name, rejects her own blackness. Like Starks, she wants to "class off" (135), to elevate herself above other blacks. Cut off from the rich cultural life of the community in her desire to be white, she is depicted as racially and sexually insipid, a pale contrast to the vital people around her.

From this point, critics adopt two different interpretations of the novel. For some, Tea Cake's death is a tragic end to this love story; these critics argue that the last few pages of the novel, filled with Janie's memories of Tea Cake, confirm him as an ideal. Other critics see important changes in Tea Cake while he and Janie are on the Muck and, often, a quite different significance in his death.

Critical to this latter view of Tea Cake is the beating he gives Janie as a result of his unfounded fear that she will be attracted to Mrs. Turner's brother. Clearly, it is not the violence of Tea Cake's act that Hurston pinpoints as problematic, but his motives. Hurston emphasizes this fact in the contrast between Tea Cake's beating of Janie and their earlier fight over Nunkie. When Janie feels jealous of Nunkie, she is more than ready to tackle Tea Cake in an honest expression of her passion: "Janie never thought at all. She just acted on feelings" (131). Tea Cake's violence toward Janie has both a very different motivation and a very different effect. His action is not a spontaneous expression of strong feeling, but a premeditated "brainstorm" (140). Fundamentally manipulative and coercive, the beating is calculated to assert domination over Janie, to demonstrate it to Mrs. Turner and to other men. In subtle ways, Tea Cake's behavior toward Janie changes from this point on, echoing the falsely solicitous actions of Starks. To assert the power of his masculinity by reassuring himself of Janie's passive femininity, he "would not let her go with him to the field. He wanted her to get her rest" (146). When the storm strikes, he not only ignores Janie's warnings but expresses a disconcerting acceptance of white superiority and the racial denigration of Indians (148).

Some critics see Tea Cake's illness as symbolic of changes in his attitude toward Janie. While his behavior is obviously explainable as the result of his disease, careful examination of details shows a sharp contrast to his earlier behavior toward Janie. He begins, for instance, to speak to her as Starks had, even complaining about her housework (166–67). Some critics argue that Tea Cake now poses such a threat to Janie's new-found female identity (symbolized in his delirious attempt to kill her) that Janie's act must be viewed as spiritual, as well as physical, self-defense. Alice Walker, who was perhaps the first to see Janie's shooting of Tea Cake as a blow for her free-dom, argues that Tea Cake's beating of Janie is "the reason Hurston permits Janie to kill Tea Cake" (305). Even critics who see problems with Tea Cake's character toward the end of the novel split on the question of whether Janie achieves complete liberation: some say yes, viewing Janie's attitudes at the end of the novel as evidence of a positive identity (whatever Tea Cake's faults); some offer a more qualified view, suggesting that Janie's dream of Tea Cake at the end demonstrates a denial of reality, but her own spiritual strength nonetheless; and some say no, analyzing the god and idol imagery running throughout the novel to conclude that Janie has created yet an-other false idol in her memory of Tea Cake, just as she had with Jody.

B. Teaching the Work

I think it's important to begin class discussion of this novel with some biographical material on Hurston's life. Hemenway's biography and Hurston's own *Dust Tracks on the Road* are helpful here. (Even though crit-ics tend to agree that Hurston is, in many ways, an unreliable narrator in her autobiography, it at least provides insight into the persona that Hurston wanted to present to her contemporaries.) Born into the security of an all-black town in Florida as the daughter of a minister father and a spunky mother who urged her to "jump at the sun," Hurston found herself alone and unsupported when her mother died while Zora was still a child. By her own account, she was only able to continue her education through a combination of sheer willpower and help from assorted (often white) benefactors and patrons. She was able to finish college and to study anthropology under the direction of Franz Boas. Despite the fact that she never earned a Ph.D., Hurston did extensive fieldwork in anthropology, both in the South and in the Caribbean, publishing two book-length studies of black folkways, *Mules and Men* and *Tell My Horse*. In addition to *Their Eyes Were Watching God*, she published several other novels, *Jonah's Gourd Vine, Moses, Man of the Mountain*, and *Seraph on the Suwanee*, as well as an autobiography and numerous stories and articles. While she was well known during the Harlem Renaissance period, she was never able to make a decent living from her writing and died in obscurity and poverty in 1960. Alice Walker has been a major force in bringing Hurston back into popularity (see bibliography), and Hurston is now recognized by many contemporary black women writers as an important foremother.

Even though Hurston highlights both race and gender in *Their Eyes Were Watching God*, students (especially white students, but not exclusively) tend to highlight gender. They will quickly notice, for instance, that Starks is a chauvinist and Tea Cake is not, but they will need more prodding to see the complicated way in which Hurston comments on the racial identity as well as the masculine identity of both men. With the character of Starks, for instance, instructors may need to direct students to Hurston's many symbolic references to Starks's "whiteness." My students also sometimes overlook the way in which Hurston draws parallels between his oppression of Janie and of the town. While students often accept Starks's view of himself as a "leader" and "developer" of the community, Hurston repeatedly suggests a more sinister motive for his actions, namely a desire to control the town as he has seen white men do elsewhere. For him, the development of the community is not a cultural endeavor, but merely a commercial venture, one from which he will reap the profits. As one resident's bitter comment—"'All he got he done made it offa de rest of us'" (46)—suggests, Starks exploits the community as fully as he does Janie.

Another issue that often arises in discussing Starks is the manner in which Janie frees herself from him. After having been humiliated by him, she (in uncharacteristically blunt language) responds: "'You big-bellies round her and put out a lot of brag, but 'tain't nothin' to it but yo' big voice. Humph! Talkin' 'bout me looking old! When you pull down yo' britches, you look lak de change uh life" (75). Some students (and at least one critic) feel that Janie's emasculating comment here is unnecessarily cruel; in discussing this section, it helps to point out that Joe has humiliated Janie in a similarly sexual and explicit way (74).

The issue of how to evaluate Tea Cake's character always engenders some of the most animated (and heated) discussions of any book I've taught. After reading the novel, some students come to class feeling he's a total fraud and others that he's a romantic ideal. Often these reactions stem from students' beliefs about popular contemporary controversies ("male-bashing" and black women "trashing" black men are, for instance, often alluded to when I begin a discussion by asking students for their reactions to the book). To foster more fruitful discussion grounded in the text, it is helpful to have students meet in small groups with others who view Tea Cake similarly in order to develop a case for their point of view. In addition to having them marshal evidence from the text for their interpretations, I also ask them to develop questions for "the other side" to answer. Asking and answering such questions ("If you believe Tea Cake is so wonderful, then how do you explain his beating of Janie?" or "If you think Tea Cake is so awful, then why does Hurston end the book with such beautiful images to describe him?") is an important part of this exercise because students will tend to leave out evidence that weakens their case. Even though I'm convinced that Hurston meant to suggest flaws in Tea Cake's character, the novel is ambiguous and complex enough in its treatment of issues to bear a number of divergent but plausible interpretations. I've heard admirers of Tea Cake develop quite respectable explanations for the beating episode: "Perhaps," some have argued, "Hurston wanted to highlight the power of sexism by making even a nearly perfect character like Tea Cake momentarily succumb to it. Hurston is writing realism, not romantic fairytale. Even Janie has dandruff, after all."

If students are having difficulty generating specifics, I sometimes turn their attention to particular passages that need to be addressed. I ask students enamored with Tea Cake, for instance, to examine closely the language Hurston uses to describe the beating and its aftermath, especially his statement that "'Janie is wherever *Ah* wants tuh be'" (141). I ask students critical of Tea Cake to examine the imagery of the last part of the book: If Tea Cake is a villain, why does Hurston associate him with seed imagery, so suggestive of rebirth and the powerful pear tree scene. If discussion is going well, I sometimes push students to think about the ambiguity of earlier passages, such as the money-stealing episode that occurs in Jacksonville right after Janie and Tea Cake are married. Although, on the one hand, the threat implicit in that event seems diffused (Tea Cake, at least, spends the money in a very unStarksian fashion by throwing a party and only excludes Janie because he fears her disapproval), he does admit to motivations at odds with the characteristics we most value in him: he throws the party not just for fun, but to let people "know who he was" and "to see how it felt to be a millionaire" (117).

One issue that often comes up in this discussion of Tea Cake's character and his relationship with Janie is the nature of oppression. The reaction of some students—Janie is not oppressed by Tea Cake because she doesn't feel that she is—has often led to interesting discussions in my class about what constitutes oppression. (For students to at least consider the possibility that oppression does not have to be defined in terms of awareness seems crucial to their understanding of many ethnic and women writers.) Students respond even more energetically to more specific discussion of the treatment of romantic love in the novel. More than one critic has suggested that Janie's blindness to Tea Cake's faults is precisely the result of an idealizing love for him. In discussion of this very sensitive issue, Nanny's comments on love always elicit student reaction: love, she argues, is "de prong all us black women gits hung on. Dis love! Dat's just whut's got us uh pullin' and uh haulin' and sweatin' and doin' from can't see in de mornin' till can't see at night" (22). Hurston's own account of the major love affair of her life (the one, in fact, that served as the rough model for *Their Eyes Were Watching God*) also sparks discussion. In the account narrated in *Dust Tracks on the Road,* Hurston not only stresses her adoration of her lover, but the subtle ways in which he became the "master kind" (257) and she "his slave" (258).

One question students nearly always raise about the novel is the function of the "mule talk" section (Chapter 6). Just as critics have, students see it as anomalous, seemingly unrelated to events preceding it and conflicting with the novel's realism when the buzzards speak to one another after the funeral. Given Hurston's emphasis on the black woman as "the mule of the world," however, students can draw some interesting parallels between the mule and Janie. Like the yellow mule who is the superficial focus of the men's concern, the light-skinned Janie, while seemingly pampered by her husband, is elevated for his own aggrandizement. At the mule's funeral, he "stands on [its] distended belly . . . for a platform" (57), just as his status in the community requires him to elevate himself above Janie. Almost as if she senses her affinities with the mule (she is the only person to pity it and speak up for it), Janie soon frees herself from Starks after this episode.

After discussing *Their Eyes Were Watching God,* students benefit from returning to some discussion of Hurston's struggles as a writer. I like to end my study of the novel by drawing on Alice Walker's version (*In Search of Our Mother's Gardens*) of Hurston's life and on her own "discovery" of Hurston's work (all of it out of print when Walker was in college). Students are invariably moved by her comments on the plight of Hurston and other black women writers and by Walker's account of her search for Hurston's unmarked grave.

With its focus on gender, race, and class, *Their Eyes Were Watching God* works extremely well in the classroom in a unit on how writers of different backgrounds view these issues. Richard Wright's *Uncle Tom's Children,* for instance, with a different conception of blackness, offers interesting contrasts to Hurston's treatment of race and also fosters good discussion of the role gender plays in ethnic literature. The reviews each author wrote on the other's book can supplement discussion. In his review, "Between Laughter and Tears," published in the October 1937 issue of *New Masses,* Wright had this to say about *Their Eyes Were Watching God:*

> Miss Hurston *voluntarily* continues in her novel the tradition which was forced upon the Negro in the theater, that is, the minstrel technique that makes the 'white folks' laugh. Her characters eat and laugh and cry and work and kill; they swing like a pendulum eternally in that safe and narrow orbit in which America likes to see the Negro live: between laughter and tears.

His searing comments were matched by Hurston's equally caustic ones in her review of *Uncle Tom's Children,* "Stories of Conflict," published in *Saturday Review,* April 2, 1938: "There is lavish killing here, perhaps enough to satisfy all male black readers" (32).

Three novels that foster discussion highlighting race differences in gender identity are Hurston's *Seraph on the Suwanee* (which echoes many aspects of *Their Eyes Were Watching God* in a treatment of white southern life that emphasizes differences in female oppression in black and white communities); Kate Chopin's *The Awakening* (which, with its notion of selfhood defined in individualistic terms, contrasts with Hurston's communal one); and Tillie Olsen's *Yonnondio* (which offers many possibilities for comparing Maisie and Janie and for analyzing different views of the effect that class has on gender identity).

I have also found several novels by other black women to be fruitful companions to *Their Eyes Were Watching God.* Gloria Naylor's *Mama Day,* a contemporary treatment of a black woman's identity by a writer clearly indebted to Hurston, can be used as another view of how race and sex interact in the lives of black women. The novel also offers rich possibilities for comparing Janie and Tea Cake with the main protagonists in Naylor's novel, Cocoa and George. Nella Larsen's *Quicksand,* written by one of Hurston's contemporaries, provides a sharp contrast both in its emphasis on black female identity in the middle class and its seeming pessimism about the possibilities for black women generally. Finally, *Nervous Conditions,* a novel by a Zimbabwean woman writer, Tsitsi Dangaremgba, also examines the relationship between race and gender through an exploration of the effects of colonialism on black female and male identity.

Questions for Discussion and Writing

1. One of the most poetic chapters in the novel is Hurston's description of Janie's vision under the pear tree (10–11). What ideals does Hurston convey through this image? How does the vegetative imagery Hurston uses throughout the novel relate to this passage?

2. Nanny has a view of black womanhood quite different from Janie's ideal. What is her view? To what extent is it the result of having grown up as a slave? What are the limitations of her point of view? Does the book, in any way, seem to support any of Nanny's opinions?

3. Starks clearly has a negative effect on Janie's self-concept. How is his relationship with and effect on the townspeople similar?

4. In what ways is the world of the Everglades (the Muck) depicted as a black Garden of Eden? What is Mrs. Turner's relation to this community? What do you make of the fact that Tea Cake is the character who expresses the most virulent hatred for her?

5. Contrast Janie's sense of identity as Mrs. Mayor Starks and at the end of the novel. Do you see Janie as a fully liberated woman at the end of the book?

6. Readers often differ in their final assessment of Tea Cake's character. Do you think he represents Hurston's ideal male? If so, how do you account for his beating of Janie (140–41)? What seems to account for his behavior? How do you think Hurston wants us to respond to it? If you feel she portrays him more negatively, why do you suppose she uses such beautiful imagery to describe him at the end of the book?

7. What in Hurston's novel leads Wright to the evaluation he makes in his review of *Their Eyes Were Watching God* (quoted earlier)? Is it a fair one in your view? Hurston's review of Wright's book, *Uncle Tom's Children,* was equally uncomplimentary: "There is lavish killing here, perhaps enough to satisfy all male black readers." On the basis of these quotes and their works,

discuss differences you see in the two authors' treatment of blackness.

8. What role does community play in the different fates of the female protagonists in *Their Eyes Were Watching God* and *The Awakening*?

9. Compare the search for female identity experienced by Janie in *Their Eyes Were Watching God* and Maisie in *Yonnondio*.

10. Nella Larsen, one of Hurston's contemporaries, seems to suggest a much more pessimistic view of the possibilities for black women in her novel, *Quicksand*. What in the two novels seems to explain this difference?

C. Bibliographies

1. Related Works

Chopin, Kate. *The Awakening*. 1899. Reprint, New York: Knopf, 1992. In this novel, published at the turn of the century, Chopin charts the transformation of a conventional well-to-do woman as she awakens to her oppression as a wife, lover, and mother.

Dangarembga, Tsitsi. *Nervous Conditions*. Seattle: Seal Press, 1988. Set in Zimbabwe before Independence, this is the story of a young black girl and her personal struggle growing up in a society dominated by racism, sexism, and colonialism.

Hurston, Zora Neale. *Seraph on the Suwanee*. 1948. Reprint, New York: Harper Collins, 1992. In her only work not focused on black life, Hurston writes a novel about southern whites in which she subtly contrasts the values of upwardly mobile whites with those of the poor blacks she created in *Their Eyes Were Watching God*.

Larsen, Nella. *Quicksand and Passing*. 1928, 1929. Reprint, New Brunswick: Rutgers University Press, 1986. In *Quicksand*, a novel of a black woman's search for identity, Larsen focuses on the issue of sexual freedom for black women and the dilemma they face (being labeled either a "lady" or a "whore") in searching for it.

Naylor, Gloria. *Mama Day*. New York: Vintage, 1988. In *Mama Day*, Naylor examines issues of racial and gender identity for black Americans in a novel that takes place on an island off the coast of South Carolina, a woman-centered place contrasting in almost every way with the dominant American culture.

Olsen, Tillie. *Yonnondio*. New York: Delta, 1974. Focusing on the life of a poor white family during the Depression, Olsen examines the lives of men and women imbued with American ideals but thwarted by poverty from achieving them.

Walker, Alice. *The Color Purple*. New York: Pocket Books, 1982. Cast as a series

of letters written by the main character, this is a story about a black
woman's search for an independent sense of identity, a process that involves finding her own sexual and spiritual values.

Wright, Richard. *Uncle Tom's Children*. 1940. Reprint, New York: Harper and
Row, 1989. A set of related short stories in which Wright chronicles the
devastating effects of racism on blacks.

2. Best Criticism

Awkward, Michael. "'The inaudible voice of it all': Silences, Voice, and Action
in *Their Eyes Were Watching God*." In *Black Feminist Criticism and Critical Theory*, ed. Joe Weixlmann and Houston A. Baker, Jr. Greenwood,
Fla.: Penkevill Publishing, 1988. Awkward emphasizes problems in the
relationship between Tea Cake and Janie and flaws in Tea Cake's character. His article also extensively reviews the diversity of opinion on this
issue.

Bloom, Harold, ed. *Zora Neale Hurston's "Their Eyes Were Watching God."* New
York: Chelsea House, 1987. This is an excellent collection of articles with
the exception of Bloom's condescending introduction.

Hemenway, Robert. *Zora Neale Hurston: A Literary Biography*. Urbana: University of Illinois Press, 1977. Hemenway provides both extensive background
material and thoughtful interpretations of Hurston's work.

Jordan, June. "Feminist Fantasies: Zora Neale Hurston's *Their Eyes Were Watching
God*." *Tulsa Studies in Women's Literature* 7, no, 1 (Spring 1988): 105–17.
Finding problems with Janie's identity (and assuming that Janie echoes
Hurston's views), Jordan argues that the novel does not meet the demands
of black feminism.

Walker, Alice. *In Search of Our Mother's Gardens: Womanist Prose*. New York:
Harcourt Brace Jovanovich, 1983. In "Zora Neale Hurston: A Cautionary
Tale and a Partisan Review" (pp. 83–92), Walker celebrates Hurston's ir-
reverent personality and (until recently) unrecognized genius. In "Looking for Zora" (pp. 93–116), she recounts her own search for Hurston's
unmarked grave.

Wilentz, Gay. "Defeating the False God: Janie's Self-Determination in Zora Neale
Hurston's *Their Eyes Were Watching God*." In *Faith of a (Woman) Writer*,
ed. Alice Kessler-Harris and William McBrien, pp. 286–91. New York:
Greenwood Press, 1988. Wilentz discusses ways in which Janie's search
for identity involves rejection of the false "gods" of a white world.

3. Other Sources

Baker, Houston A. *Modernism and the Harlem Renaissance.* Chicago and London: University of Chicago Press, 1979.

Hurston, Zora Neale. *Their Eyes Were Watching God.* 1937. Reprint, New York: Harper and Row, 1990.

————. *Dust Tracks on a Road.* 1942. Reprint, Urbana and Chicago: University of Illinois Press, 1984.

Roses, Lorrain Elena, and Ruth Elizabeth Randolph. *Harlem Renaissance and Beyond: Literary Biographies of 100 Women Writers, 1900–1945.* Boston: G. K. Hall, 1990.

Schockley, Ann Allen. *Afro-American Women Writers, 1746–1933: An Anthology and Criticial Guide.* New York: Penguin, 1989.

Racial Discourse and Self-Creation:

Richard Wright's *Black Boy*

YOSHINOBU HAKUTANI

A. Analysis of Themes and Forms

Black Boy is acclaimed not only as the finest autobiography written by an African American, but as one of the finest autobiographies written in America. Indeed, many American autobiographies are ethnic. As *Black Boy* discusses the experience of an African American youth who grew up in the South, Theodore Dreiser's *Dawn* treats the life struggle that the son of a German immigrant faced in the North. Benjamin Franklin's *Autobiography* is not ethnic in the usual sense of the word, but his life exemplifies the American dream of the poor boy who made good in Pennsylvania, an English colony. What these autobiographies have in common is not only an eloquent portrayal of early life, but a poignant expression of social and cultural views.

Unlike Dreiser's *Dawn* and Franklin's *Autobiography, Black Boy* features a narrator who takes such an impersonal attitude that the work may not seem like a usual autobiography. As W. E. B. Du Bois noted, there is in *Black Boy* a genuine paucity of personal love or affection expressed toward Wright's mother (Du Bois, 2). Wright does express his awe and wonder at his suffering mother, but he is unable to understand the reason that she was deserted by her husband, broken by paralysis, and overwhelmed by every unimaginable circumstance she had to face. His reaction therefore is intellectual rather than personal. By contrast, in *Dawn* the narrator's wonder at his suffering mother is tinged with personal sorrow and sympathy. Wright's intention in *Black Boy* seems to have been to portray his experience with naturalistic objectivity, rather than firsthand intimacy.

By the time he wrote *Black Boy,* Wright had become a literary naturalist who adopts a milieu from life and projects characters that act in accordance with the milieu. The naturalist records, without comment or interpretation, what actually happens. If Wright regarded himself as a fictional persona in *Black Boy,* he would be less concerned either with his own life or with his own point of view. The focus of his interest in the book would be on the events that occurred outside of his life. It is understandable, then, that Wright's account of his own life would not be entirely authentic. One might even suspect that Wright's self-portrait would abound with fictional accounts, and in fact many differences between *Black Boy* and his life have been pointed out. One reviewer's objection to the book as autobiography is based on discrepancies found between Wright's accounts in the book and "The Ethics of Living Jim Crow" (Murphy, 32–33). In addition, Wright refers in *Black Boy* to his mother as a cook "in the kitchens of the white folks" and describes her as less intellectual than she really was (27). In fact, Ella Wilson, his mother, before her marriage to his father, was considerably well educated and taught school. Edwin R. Embree, an African American writer himself, who was closely acquainted with Wright's youth and early literary career, testifies that Wright's mother was light brown and good-looking, and that book learning enabled her to obtain teaching jobs at twenty-five dollars a month (Embree, 25–26).

These discrepancies, however, are not a major reason for calling *Black Boy* a fictionalized autobiography. Even though parts of the book are fictional, it is largely autobiographical and should not be equated with a novel. No one for a moment can overlook the fact that *Black Boy* portrays Wright himself, and if the work also concerns others, their lives are necessarily intertwined with his life. But the most important feature which distinguishes *Black Boy* as autobiography is Wright's intention to use the young self as a mask. The attitudes and sentiments expressed by the young Wright are not totally his own, but represent the responses of those he called "the voiceless Negro boys" of the South ("Handiest Truth," 3). Such a device makes *Black Boy* a unique autobiography, just as a similar technique makes *Native Son* a unique novel. Speaking of that novel, Wright says, in "How 'Bigger' Was Born," that Bigger Thomas is a conscious composite portrait of numerous African American individuals he knew in his life.

What makes *Black Boy* not only a unique autobiography but, perhaps, the most influential racial discourse in America is its style and artistry. What impresses many readers about the book is that it tells bitter truth about life. Wright cannot be criticized for his subject matter, because he is not responsible for the world he had not made. Above all, *Black Boy* impresses the reader because Wright remains an artist throughout the text. As in his best fiction, his language, unlike the language of a typical naturalist, is terse, lucid, and vivid; his presentation is moving and dramatic. Horace R. Cayton, a sociologist who intimately knew Wright's method, quotes him as saying: "I try to float these facts on a sea of emotion, to drive them home with some degree of artistic power, as much as humanly possible. . . . I want people to enjoy my books but I want them to be moved and conditioned by them" (Cayton, 262–69). In short, a bitter man can be a great artist as well.

The poetic passages characteristic of *Black Boy* thus convey the narrator's various emotional responses to his life in the South. Such language often forms a blend of disparate images that are unified only by the intensity of feeling. Some images—"spotted, black-and-white horses," "long straight rows of red and green vegetables," "the yellow, dreaming waters of the Mississippi River" (14)—all suggest a harmony of nature and society. Others— "the crying strings of wild geese" and "a solitary ant carrying a burden upon a mysterious journey" (14)—allude to racial anxiety and tension. Still others—"a [tortured] delicate, blue-pink crawfish that huddled fearfully in the mudsill of a rusty tin can" (14) and "a chicken [leaping] about blindly after its neck had been snapped by a quick twist of my father's wrist" (15)— depict cruelty and sadism.

In these images Wright interpolates such a statement as: "Each event spoke with a cryptic tongue. And the moments of living slowly revealed their coded meanings" (14). This, however, does not necessarily signal that each of the images evoked has a point-for-point correspondence with a specific event in reality. Wright might or might not have intended "a brace of mountainlike, spotted, black-and-white horses clopping down a dusty road" (14) to allude to miscegenation. The same is true of comparing the chicken leaping with its neck cut off to a victim of racial violence. Wright's imagery often appears unrelated to actuality, because facts of life are elevated to a higher level of consciousness and sensibility. "The relationship between reality and the artistic image," he says in "Blueprint for Negro Writing," "is not always direct and simple. The imaginative conception of a historical period will not be a carbon copy of reality. Image and emotion possess a logic of their own" (*Wright Reader*, 48).

In establishing his own world, then, Wright is able to shape the images at will. He knew what hunger and hatred meant in his youth and he had learned to live with them, but he now had a new hunger for the freedom of the mind. "I seemed forever condemned," he writes, "ringed by walls" (*Black Boy*, 274). This image of imprisonment recurs throughout the book. He remembers that at four he tried to burn down his grandmother's house by setting fire to the white curtains. "I crossed restlessly to the window," he recalls, "and pushed back the long fluffy white curtains—which I had been forbidden to touch—and looked yearningly out into the empty street" (9). As he grew older and was allowed to play in the street, he saw one day a host of chained convicts, all black, dressed in the black-and-white striped clothing, a spectacle that at once reminded him of zebras confined in the zoo.

In addition to imagery, dialogue dramatizes his racial discourse. Wright is at his best when much of the episode is interlaced with revealing dialogue. The narrator deliberately creates a scene where two individuals, usually the young Wright and an opponent, confront each other with an exchange of laconic statements. These remarks not only reveal the gullibility of an antagonist, but compel the reader to identify with the narrator. Wright once encountered in an elevator a black youth who exposed his buttocks for a white man to kick so that he might earn a quarter. Wright says he felt "no anger or hatred, only disgust and loathing," and that he confronted this youth:

> "How in God's name can you do that?"
> "I needed a quarter and I got it," he said soberly, proudly.
> "But a quarter can't pay you for what he did to you," I said.
> "Listen, nigger," he said to me, "my ass is tough and quarters is scarce." (250)

At thirteen, when Wright was forced to seek a job as a houseboy, a white woman, a prospective employer looking for an "honest" black boy, gave him an interview:

> "Now, boy, I want to ask you one question and I want you to tell me the truth," she said.
> "Yes, ma'am," I said, all attention.
> "Do you steal?" she asked me seriously.
> I burst into a laugh, then checked myself.
> "What's so damn funny about that?" she asked.
> "Lady, if I was a thief, I'd never tell anybody." (160)

Wright also heightens his racial discourse with irony. The statement by an antagonist inadvertently betrays more than he wants to say, or there is a marked contrast between what he wants to say and what his words mean to the reader. For example, Wright's boss at an optical company in Jackson, Mississippi, who originally came from Illinois, professed himself unprejudiced and boasted that he wanted to "break a colored boy into the optical trade." The white man, however, cautioned the young Wright: "You're going to have a chance to learn a trade. But remember to keep your head. Remember you're black" (205). Ironically, the white man's warning suggests that rebelling against the Jim Crow law, as Wright was resolved to do, would be considered insane. At times Wright's irony verges on humor. On another occasion, he went up to a hotel room to wait on a white prostitute and a white man lying naked on the bed. The presence of a black man in this situation would awaken in the white people no sense of shame since he was in no way considered "human." The prostitute asked Wright to buy some liquor for them, and slid out of bed and walked naked across the floor. As she searched for her purse, Wright naturally watched her. He was immediately warned by the white man: "Keep your eyes where they belong if you want to be healthy!" (222). Such a statement reveals that a black boy is regarded as subhuman or abnormal in the eyes of white men and women of the South.

These rhetorical skills enable Wright to develop his racial discourse with vigor. As an artist he detaches himself from the scene he depicts; above all, he remains a judicious observer. His aim is to bring home his hard-won conviction that racial problems stem not so much from the individuals involved as from a system inherited from the past. At times, the white race is as much a victim as the black race. Many episodes show that the kind of sympathy white southerners felt for black people was nothing more than racial condescension. Although white people in the South considered themselves decent, compassionate human beings, they had a deep-seated, unconscious attitude reminiscent of Aunt Sally's response to Huck Finn. When Huck reports that a steamboat has just blown out a cylinder head down the river and killed a black man, she replies nonchalantly: "Well, it's lucky; because sometimes people do get hurt . . . " (Twain, 218).

The impersonality of *Black Boy* can be explained in another way. Since the narrator is a spokesman for the voiceless black youths in America, he must be objective and scientific in his observations. This book, though not intended as such, is a convincing sociological study. Like sociology, the study not only analyzes a social problem but offers a solution to the problem it treats. Wright explores the ways in which African American life in the South was determined by environment, and, to borrow Émile Zola's words in "The Experimental Novel," he wants to "disengage the determinism of human and social phenomena so that we may one day control and direct these phenomena" (181). Like Zola, Wright makes his investigation systematic and unbiased. Such writing therefore deals with the specific social forces in the environment of a black boy: white racism, black society, and black family.

James Baldwin assailed Wright for the belief that "in Negro life there exists no tradition, no field of manners, no possibility of ritual or intercourse" (*Notes*, 28). Unlike Baldwin, who grew up in a highly religious black community in Harlem, Wright witnessed in the Deep South "the essential bleakness of black life in America" (*Black Boy*, 45). The central issue, however, is whether such human traits as, in Wright's words, "tenderness, love, honor, loyalty, and the capacity to remember" are innate in the African American tradition, as Baldwin says, or are "fostered, won, struggled and suffered for," as Wright believed (45). Wright says elsewhere that he wrote *Black Boy* "to tell a series of incidents strung through my childhood, but the main desire was to render a judgment on my environment. . . . That judgment was this: the environment the South creates is too small to nourish human beings, especially Negro human beings" ("Handiest Truth," 3). Wright, therefore, squarely places the burden of proof upon white society, contending with enough evidence and justification given in *Black Boy* that the absence of such human qualities in black people as tenderness and love stemmed from years of white oppression.

Not only did white racism succeed in separating black and white people, but it had devastating effects on black life. Critics, both black and white, have complained that Wright in *Black Boy* lacks racial pride. It is true that he is critical of the black community in the South, but it is not true that he places the blame on the black community itself. His intention is to show that a racist system produced the way of life that was forced on black people. In terms of social determinism, *Black Boy* provides a literary experiment to demonstrate uniformity in black behavior under the influence of social forces.

Most black people, he admits, do adjust to their environment for survival. But in so doing they lose individuality, self-respect, and dignity. For Wright, the circumstances in which they find themselves damage their personalities, and this in turn results in various forms of hypocritical, erratic, and despicable behavior. In addressing white men's sexual exploitation of black women, Wright is as critical of black women as of white men, because he believed black women expect and readily condone white men's behavior. Once a black maid, slapped playfully on her buttocks by a white nightwatchman, told the indignant Wright, a witness to the incident: "'They never get any further with us than that, if we don't want 'em to'" (*Black Boy*, 218). Understandably, such portraits of black people made some readers feel that Wright unduly deprived black people of their personal honor and dignity. But Wright explains: "I began to marvel at how smoothly the black boys acted out the roles that the white race had mapped out for them. Most of them were not conscious of living a special, separate, stunted way of life" (216).

In Wright's view, this absence of individuality and self-awareness among black people in the South often leads to the compromise of their character, as also shown in *The Long Dream*, Wright's last novel. Individually, Fishbelly and his father in that novel are powerless in asserting themselves. Although they are not forced or coerced to cooperate with white police, their greed often compromises their moral integrity. Wright presents them as fully aware that their illicit political connections will make them as wealthy as white people.

Structurally, the young Wright's observations on white racism and black life buttress the central theme of *Black Boy*, self-creation. In "Blueprint for Negro Writing," Wright argues that the "theme for Negro writers will rise from understanding the meaning of their being transplanted from a 'savage' to a 'civilized'culture in all of its social, political, economic, and emotional implications" (*Wright Reader*, 47). In *Black Boy*, his chief aim is to show how this youth, whom the South called a "nigger," surmounted his obstacles in the civilized culture. The most painful stance he took in this struggle was to be an intense individualist; he created selfhood and exerted his will at the risk of annihilation. Both black and white communities imposed crushing circumstances upon him, but no matter how unbearable his problems were, he refused to compromise. Thus, Wright's logic becomes clear: only under such pressure does one discover one's self. For others, this process of self-creation might have been aided by chance, but for Wright "it should be a matter of plan" ("Handiest Truth," 3).

The reader could be puzzled by this youth's individuality and fortitude if the seed of manhood had not been sown in the child. *Black Boy*, however, contains ample evidence of the child's precocity and independence. Wright's earlier self is revealed even to the point of betraying his vanity. When he moved to his grandmother's house after his family was deserted by his father, Wright took pride in telling the timid children of the new neighborhood about his train ride, his Mississippi cruise, and his escape from the orphanage (46). Moreover, the young child is presented as a rebel who refused to compromise with the dictates of society and family. Once, he was dismayed to find out that the man who had beaten a black boy was not the boy's father. Although Wright was told by his mother that he was "'too young to understand,'" he responded with a resolution: "'I'm not going to let anybody beat me'" (31).

As early as twelve, Wright held "a sense of the world that was mine and mine alone, a notion . . . that no education could ever alter, a conviction that the meaning of living came only when one was struggling to wring meaning out of meaningless suffering" (112). His decision to leave the South seven years later, his final action, was based upon such conviction, as if the seed of manhood had already been in the child. Without mental companionship to rely on, he withdrew and turned inward like the anti-hero of an existentialist novel. In his recoil, he had once again discovered that the revelation of all truths must come through the action and anguish of the self. It was at this point in his ordeal that he came in contact with the writings of American realists such as H. L. Mencken, Theodore Dreiser, Sinclair Lewis, and Sherwood Anderson. It was their ideas, he says, that literally delivered his brooding sensibility to a brighter horizon, a vision that "America could be shaped nearer to the hearts of those who lived in it" (283). He also at this time decided to head North to discover for himself that one could live with dignity and determine one's own destiny. Because he knew he could not make the world, he sought to make things happen within him and caught a sense of freedom, and in so doing he discovered the new world.

B. Teaching the Work

Black Boy can be approached by discussing its style and technique. Although Wright is known as a writer of fiction and nonfiction, he was also an accomplished poet. His lyricism is evident in the early section of *Black Boy*, in which a young African American seeks a harmony between nature and society. Interested in haiku, a form of verse developed by great Japanese poets like Basho and Buson, Wright in fact wrote four thousand haiku toward the end of his life. One of them, for example—"Don't they make you sad, / Those wild geese winging southward, / O lonely scarecrow?" (*This Other World*, 59)—originates from a passage in *Black Boy*: "There were the echoes of nostalgia I heard in the crying strings of wild geese winging south against a bleak, autumn sky" (*Black Boy*, 14; Tener, 275).

The sense of yearning for the natural world and its order was one of Wright's major motifs in both his life and his work. This sense was as much an aspect of Wright as a young poet as it was a reflection of his response to himself as an African American youth. After a visit to Ghana when he was forty-five, he wrote in *Black Power*:

> The African attitude toward life springs from a natural and poetic grasp of existence and all the emotional implications that such an attitude carries. . . . There is no reason why an African or a person of African descent . . . should abandon his primal outlook upon life if he finds that no other way of life is available, or if he is intimidated in his attempt grasp the new way. (266)

Wright's consciousness of negritude and creativity is reflected in the repetition of specific images that provide insight into his vision. Words and phrases like *sun, earth, black, white, red, green, south, north, day, night, a bleak sky, a dusty road, the simple nakedness of his life, the slow flow of the seasons* abound in Wright's writing. Even his favorite line of poetry from Walt Whitman reflects his feelings about nature: "Not till the sun excludes you do I exclude you" (*Black Power*, ix). Wright's poetic passages can also be interpreted in comparison with Langston Hughes's poems such as "The Negro Speaks of Rivers," "Dream Variations," and "Mulatto."

Wright's poetic style, in turn, reinforces other kinds of style and technique in *Black Boy*. While the objectivity of his vision is reflected in his lyrical response to nature, it is also expressed by dialogue in crucial episodes. In satirizing a black boy, for instance, who has failed to achieve self-identity, the narrator puts on a mask and speaks as an independent thinker. An exchange of views between two such speakers often creates irony and humor. *Black Boy* thus thrives upon these related elements of style and technique.

Another way of teaching *Black Boy* is to focus on its major themes: racial oppression, social determinism, and self-creation. Wright explains racism in terms of a degrading assumption that white people have about black people: black people do not have intellectual capabilities. The young Wright often lost employment because of his intelligence, which posed a threat to the white man's sense of superiority. Throughout the book, Wright demonstrates the fact that white citizens in the South would rather have black people who stole goods and properties than black individuals who were conscious, however vaguely, of the worth of their own intelligence and humanity. He is at pains to show that this racist mentality, derived from slavery, is essentially responsible for racial prejudice and oppression in America. In this respect, *Black Boy* can be compared to such a work as Lorraine Hansberry's *A Raisin in the Sun*.

A reading of *Black Boy* suggests that social determinism takes its heaviest toll in black family life. One would assume that if black boys are mistreated in society at large, they would at least be protected in their family. But in Wright's early childhood his father deserted the mother and children; not only did Wright become a casualty of the broken family, but his father himself was a victim of the racial system in the Deep South. His grandmother's Seventh-Day-Adventist doctrine, as practiced at home, epitomizes this strife. Wright saw "more violent quarrels in our deeply religious home than in the home of a gangster, a burglar, or a prostitute. . . . The naked will to power seemed always to walk in the wake of a hymn" (150). Based on Wright's vision, it seems as though black adults, subjected to racism in white society, in turn felt compelled to rule their children at home.

The adults had grown up in a white-dominated society in which they were permitted no missteps. That Wright's worst punishments, such as regular beatings, verbal abuse, and humiliation, were inflicted by his closest relatives suggests how deeply black life could be dominated by white racism.

Although *Black Boy* is strung with a series of episodes that illustrates forms of racial oppression, the center of attention lies in Wright's transcendence of that oppression. Racial oppression is caused not only by the external forces of society, but by the internal problems of the oppressed. "Some may escape the general plight and grow up," Wright admits, "but it is a matter of luck" ("Handiest Truth," 3). To the hero of *Black Boy,* most of them were victims of racial prejudice, failures in the battle for survival. Individualism and self-creation, the young Wright's twin weapons, helped him transcend racial oppression. The most dramatic episode is the story of an African American woman who had avenged her husband's murder by a racist.

As for Wright, becoming an aspiring rebel inevitably led to being a misfit. In Wright's life, however, it is his innate character that allowed this change to occur. The degree of Wright's self-assertiveness can be best shown in the comparison he draws in *Black Boy* between himself and his playmates. Although he identified himself with a mistreated group, there was a crucial difference between him and other black children. They constantly complained about the petty wrongs they suffered, but they had no desire to question the larger issues of racial oppression. Their stance resembles that of the young Fishbelly in *The Long Dream*; just like his father before him, Fishbelly servilely worships the powerful white citizens. He falls in love with the values of the white world because such demeanor can offer him material rewards and make his manhood easier and less painful to achieve. The young Wright, on the other hand, found among the black boys no sympathy for his inquiring mind; he was forced to contemplate such questions for himself. Other works in American literature also deal with self-creation. Books like Franklin's *Autobiography,* Twain's *Adventures of Huckleberry Finn,* Dreiser's *Dawn,* Richard Rodriguez's *Hunger of Memory,* and Joy Kogawa's *Obasan* can be compared with *Black Boy.*

Finally, *Black Boy* can be taught with a historical approach. In scene after scene, Wright shows that white racism has derived from slavery and its corollary, the superiority complex. As pointed out earlier, this work is regarded as a sociological document as well as an autobiography. At times, such a document also demonstrates that oppressors are as much victims of the elemental design of white racism as are the oppressed. Wright, therefore, is intent upon deciphering the design. For a historical study of slavery and racism, this book might be discussed with Wright's other nonfictional works: *12 Million Black Voices, Black Power, The Color Curtain, White Man, Listen!, American Hunger,* "The Ethics of Living Jim Crow," and "How 'Bigger' Was Born."

C. Bibliographies

1. Related Works

Dreiser, Theodore. *Dawn.* New York: Horace Liveright, 1931. The autobiography of a foremost American realist portrays the early life of the son of a German immigrant. In an episode from *Black Boy,* Wright says that he was inspired by Dreiser's writing, which was to the young Wright "nothing less than a sense of life itself."

Franklin, Benjamin. *The Autobiography.* 1788. Reprint, ed. Leonard W. Labaree et al. New Haven: Yale University Press, 1964. This masterpiece of autobiography in American literature consists of the first section, addressed to Franklin's son William, and the remaining three sections, which were not completed until Franklin's final year. The account ends in 1758, before his finest achievement as a diplomat.

Kingston, Maxine Hong. *The Woman Warrior: Memoirs of a Girlhood among Ghosts.* New York: Alfred A. Knopf, 1976. This nonfictional narrative vividly portrays the experience of a young Chinese American woman with a blend of myth, legend, and contemporary reality.

Kogawa, Joy. *Obasan.* 1981. Reprint, Boston: David R. Godine, 1982. This autobiographical novel, based on the young Kogawa's experience in the World War II relocation places for Japanese Canadians, narrates her life with her aunt (*obasan* in Japanese) and uncle. Kogawa's racial discourse thrives on a singular contrast between her harsh social environment and her lyricism.

Rodriguez, Richard. *Hunger of Memory: The Education of Richard Rodriguez.* Boston: David R. Godine, 1982. This collection of autobiographical essays gives a poignant account of Rodriguez's movements between white society and Mexican American society.

Twain, Mark. *Adventures of Huckleberry Finn.* 1884. Reprint, Boston: Houghton Mifflin, 1962. This classic novel not only depicts the freedom of a black man from slavery, but also shows a series of adventures in which the black man's freedom leads to the white boy's freedom from a corrupt society.

Wright, Richard. *Black Power: A Record of Reactions in a Land of Pathos.* New York: Harper and Brothers, 1954. This nonfictional work is based on

Wright's travel in 1953 to the Gold Coast, a West African colonial state under British rule, at the threshold of its independence. Not only does Wright assail European colonialism and imperialism in Africa, but the book demonstrates Africans' "primal outlook upon life," which contributed to the survival of African culture.

———. *The Long Dream*. 1958. Reprint, New York: Harper and Row, 1987. This novel, based partly on Wright's own experiences in growing up in the Deep South, portrays the life of an African American boy named Fishbelly, son of a prosperous mortician. Like Wright, Fishbelly leaves racially oppressive Mississippi for Paris in search of freedom.

2. Best Criticism

Fabre, Michel. *The Unfinished Quest of Richard Wright*. New York: William Morrow, 1973. As the most comprehensive literary biography of Wright, the book includes an invaluable account of Wright's life in the Deep South.

Hakutani, Yoshinobu. "Creation of the Self in Richard Wright's *Black Boy*." *Black American Literature Forum* 19 (Summer 1985): 70–75. Self-creation, the central theme, buttresses Wright's discourse on race.

———, ed. *Critical Essays on Richard Wright*. Boston: G. K. Hall, 1982. The collection, along with a historical and critical introduction, contains seminal essays on Wright's experiences in the South by Irving Howe, Blyden Jackson, Houston A. Baker, Jr., Donald B. Gibson, James Baldwin, and Ralph Ellison.

Kinnamon, Keneth. *The Emergence of Richard Wright: A Study in Literature and Society*. Urbana: University of Illinois Press, 1972. The book shows, with convincing evidence, that Wright faced more formidable obstacles in his youth than any other American writer and that Wright's experience in the South was the catalyst of his extraordinary accomplishment.

Margolies, Edward. *The Art of Richard Wright*. Carbondale: Southern Illinois University Press, 1969. As the earliest book-length critical study, the work includes an excellent examination of Wright's themes of fear and alienation as reflected in *Black Boy* and *Uncle Tom's Children*.

Reilly, John M. "Afterword" to *Black Boy*, 286–88. New York: Harper and Row, 1966. This brief commentary is the earliest critical estimate of the book.

Smith, Valerie. *Self Discovery and Authority in Afro-American Narrative*. Cambridge: Harvard University Press, 1987. The book contains a chapter, "Alienation and Creativity in the Fiction of Richard Wright," which shows how the young Wright in *Black Boy* and Bigger Thomas in *Native Son* achieve self-creation through the power of language.

Stepto, Robert B. *From Behind the Veil: A Study of Afro-American Narrative*. Urbana: University of Illinois Press, 1979. The book contains a chapter,

"Literacy and Ascent: *Black Boy*," showing that *Black Boy*, like Frederick Douglass's slave narratives, is not an "immersion" narrative but a narrative that dramatizes African Americans' quest for literacy and freedom.

Williams, John A. *The Most Native of Sons: A Biography of Richard Wright*. Garden City, N.Y.: Doubleday, 1970. The work, providing an intimate account of the psychological makeup of an African American writer by another African American writer, is the most perceptive and sympathetic in its discussion of Wright's youth.

3. Other Sources

Anonymous. Review of *Black Boy*. *Newark Evening News*, March 17, 1945.

Baldwin, James. *Notes of a Native Son*. 1955. Reprint, New York: Bantam Books, 1968.

———. *Nobody Knows My Name: More Notes of a Native Son*. New York: Dell, 1961.

Cayton, Horace R. "Discrimination—America: Frightened Children of Frightened Parents." *Twice-a-Year* 12–13 (1945): 262–69.

Du Bois, W. E. B. "Richard Wright Looks Back." *New York Herald Tribune Book Review*. March 4, 1945.

Ellison, Ralph. *Shadow and Act*. New York: Random House, 1964.

Embree, Edwin R. "Richard Wright: Native Son." In *13 Against the Odds*, 25–46. New York: Viking, 1944.

Howe, Irving. *A World More Attractive*. New York: Horizon, 1963.

Hughes, Langston. *Selected Poems of Langston Hughes*. New York: Alfred A. Knopf, 1965.

Kinnamon, Keneth, comp. *A Richard Wright Bibliography: Fifty Years of Criticism and Commentary, 1933–82*. Westport, Conn.: Greenwood Press, 1988.

Murphy, Beatrice M. Review of *Black Boy*. *Pulse* 3 (April 1945): 32–33.

Reilly, John M. "Self-Portraits by Richard Wright." *Colorado Quarterly* 22 (Summer 1971): 31–45.

———, ed. *Richard Wright: The Critical Reception*. New York: Burt Franklin, 1978.

Tener, Robert. "The Where, the When, the What: A Study of Richard Wright's Haiku." In *Critical Essays on Richard Wright*, ed. Yoshinobu Hakutani, 273–98. Boston: G. K. Hall, 1982.

Wright, Richard. "Blueprint for Negro Writing." *New Challenge*, 2 (Fall 1937): 53–65. Reprinted in *Richard Wright Reader*, eds. Ellen Wright and Michel Fabre, 36–49. New York: Harper and Row, 1978.

———. "The Ethics of Living Jim Crow." In *American Stuff: A WPA Writers Anthology*, 39–52. New York: Viking Press, 1937. Reprinted in *Uncle Tom's Children*, 3–15. New York: Harper and Row, 1965.

————. *Uncle Tom's Children.* 1940. Reprint, New York: Harper and Row, 1965.

————. *Native Son.* 1940. Reprint, New York: Harper and Row, 1966.

————. "How 'Bigger' Was Born." *Saturday Review,* June 1, 1940. Reprinted in *Native Son,* vii–xxxiv. New York: Harper and Row, 1965.

————. *12 Million Black Voices.* New York: Viking Press, 1941.

————. *Black Boy: A Record of Childhood and Youth.* 1945. Reprint, New York: Harper and Row, 1966.

————. "The Handiest Truth to Me to Plow Up Was in My Own Hand." *P.M. Magazine,* April 4, 1945.

————. *The Color Curtain: A Report on the Bandung Conference.* Cleveland: World, 1956.

————. *White Man, Listen!* 1957. Reprint, Garden City, N.Y.: Doubleday/Anchor, 1964.

————. *This Other World: Projections in the Haiku Manner,* 1–82. Manuscript. New Haven, Conn.: Beinecke Rare Book and Manuscript Library, Yale University, 1960.

————. *Lawd Today.* New York: Walker, 1963.

————. *American Hunger.* 1977. Reprint, New York: Harper and Row, 1979.

Zola, Émile. "The Experimental Novel." 1880. In *Documents of Modern Literary Realism,* ed. George J. Becker, 162–96. Princeton, N.J.: Princeton University Press, 1963.

"Measure Him Right":

An Analysis of Lorraine Hansberry's
Raisin in the Sun

JEANNE-MARIE A. MILLER

A. Analysis of Themes and Forms

On March 11, 1959, Lorraine Hansberry's *A Raisin in the Sun* opened on Broadway at the Ethel Barrymore Theatre and made theatrical history. The play was the first professional production of an African American woman on Broadway, and it won the prestigious New York Drama Critics Circle Award as the Best Play of the Year. The twenty-eight-year-old Hansberry became the youngest American, the fifth woman, and the first African American to win this award. Since its initial production, the play has been published and produced in approximately thirty countries, and many critics have referred to *A Raisin in the Sun* as a classic and a visionary work. The play was sold to Columbia Pictures in 1959, and the movie won the Gary Cooper Award for "outstanding human values" at the 1961 Cannes Film Festival. In 1973, eight years after Hansberry's untimely death from cancer at the age of thirty-four, the musical *Raisin,* based on the play, was produced and won a Tony Award in 1974 and a Grammy Award for best musical in 1975. The book was by Robert Nemiroff, Hansberry's former husband and literary executor, and Charlotte Zaltzberg.

A realistic drama in three acts, *A Raisin in the Sun* is in the traditional form of the well-made play. Hansberry observes the unities of place, action, and, to a degree, time. All action occurs in the living room of the Younger family's cramped Southside apartment in Chicago. The playwright uses a linear plot and a box set. The action is unified, concentrated, and well organized, and concerns how the family members will solve the problem of what they will do with the ten thousand dollars from the dead father's life-insurance policy. The insurance money acts as a catalyst, projecting the family into a situation that not only causes dramatic conflicts, but tests their individual characters. It is around this check that tension mounts and action swirls as the play progresses. Act I of the play serves as the beginning; Act II, the middle; and Act III, the end, with a resolution of the problem. The unity of time is modified somewhat—from twenty-four hours to one month.

While the structure of *A Raisin in the Sun* is traditional, the themes and ideas are not—at least for a play about African Americans on Broadway up to that time. The late Darwin T. Turner, a literary critic, writes that *A Raisin in the Sun* is "one of the most perceptive presentations of Afro-Americans in the history of American professional theatre" (*Black Drama in America,* 14). Presenting myriad levels of black life, the play is not protest drama and is neither stereotypic nor romantic. It shows, as Turner has written, "the impossibility of typifying the Negro race" ("The Negro Dramatist's Image of the Universe," 73). The title of *A Raisin in the Sun* is taken from "Harlem," a poem by Langston Hughes, in which the poet alludes to the deferred dreams of African Americans and questions the outcome—whether or not these postponed dreams will "dry up / Like a raisin in the sun?" or eventually "*explode.*"

In addition to celebrating the strength and endurance of the human spirit in the face of many obstacles, *A Raisin in the Sun* celebrates black life in all its diversity. The themes include the survival of the African American family, the black man–black woman relationship, black heritage, budding African independence, feminism, and dreams. Through three generations of the Youngers, Hansberry tells the story of an African American working-class family and its struggles to survive with dignity. The older generation, Big Walter and Lena (Mama), had migrated from the South to the North, as had many blacks, to forge a better life for themselves. While living, Big Walter was the head of the household. A man of human frailties—a womanizer and a drinker, for example—he perhaps had died from overwork, but left a legacy: his dreams and a ten-thousand-dollar insurance policy to sustain some of his family's dreams.

The weariness of the room, which is the setting of the play, is fought against by the family to keep liveable as the Youngers fight against the environment in order to survive and to keep their dreams alive. The environment, which is limiting, is symbolized by the only window in the apartment, which lets light in upon Lena's scraggly plant that, like the family, struggles to survive with inadequate light. Lena wants a larger home with a garden that will have ample sunlight for many plants, a home that, above all, will provide healthy space for her family.

Over the present household presides the domineering figure of the sixty-year-old Lena, whom Hansberry links to her African heritage: "Her bearing is perhaps most like the noble bearing of the women of the Hereros of Southwest Africa . . . " (22). Lena has grandeur, strength, courage, patience, and heroic faith, a faith not shared by the younger generation. She is deeply religious and believes strongly in family. This sturdy woman who mightily loves her children, but sometimes meddles in their affairs, teaches them self-respect, pride, and human dignity, and she fights to preserve these qualities. Lena wants to invest a portion of the insurance money in a house that will remove her family from their overcrowded, roach-infested apartment in the ghetto where they are trapped. The house would bring to an end some of the postponements that she and her late husband endured in the quest for their dream. The house would be the harvest of Lena's and her late husband's days. She also wants to put some of the money aside for the medical education of Beneatha, her daughter.

Walter Lee, Jr., Lena's thirty-five-year-old son, who lives with his wife Ruth and their young son Travis in the apartment, is in conflict with his mother over how to invest the insurance money. Lena and Walter are dual protagonists. Having reached a crossroads in his life, Walter sees affluence around him, especially in his job as a chauffeur for rich whites, and he desires a piece of this wealth, a slice of the American dream. He models himself after the white community that he encounters daily and seeks to make his presence felt in the larger American community. He has accepted American values. Julius Lester writes that "Walter has been taught that he should want the world, but because he is black he has been denied the possibility of ever having it. And that only makes the pain of the desire that much more hurting" (7). In America, it is believed that anyone can become anything he or she wants to be. Walter wants a viable stake in the American economic market and is concerned with the economic future and the stability of his family who are in need. He believes in himself and has high expectations and a determination to succeed. In reality, he has been an ignored man, an almost invisible man, a powerless man. Walter longs for an identity and believes that money brings with it power and freedom. As a black man in a dead-end job, he feels that the dream is out of reach. The investment of the insurance money in a liquor store that he wishes to own and his mother opposes for religious reasons will make his dream realizable. An enterprising black man, Walter will make the opportunity if his mother provides the means. If he can become a successful businessman, he thinks that he will be able to hand his son the world—the American dream. He visualizes his manhood as being connected to his ability to support his family in style, and to free himself from drudgery and toil. He equates money and what it symbolizes with life. In his present frustration, Walter blames his wife, his mother, and himself for his lack of personal fulfillment.

Lena's generation had fought for dignity based on human values—to escape white lynchers in the South and segregated seating in the backseats of public transportation, among other things. Lena's values differ from her

son's. Her use of some of the insurance money for a down payment on a
house destroys her son, and explodes his dream of a life of dignity as he
defines it. Walter becomes dejected and starts to drink heavily, dying a spiritual death when his dream ends. His distress causes Lena, compassionately,
to make amends by relinquishing the head of the household to him, along
with the remainder of the money to manage. She tells him to put three
thousand dollars in a savings account for Beneatha's education and the rest
in a checking account with his name on it. Instead, Walter gives the entire
amount to one of his partners-to-be in the liquor store, a con man who
absconds with the money. Walter's passion for a better way of life is thwarted.
Upon losing the money, Walter reaches the lowest depths. He calls Karl
Lindner, the representative of the white neighborhood group who wants to
pay the Youngers not to move into their community, to buy the house from
the family and at a profit to them. The offer had been rejected originally,
but the despairing Walter is now ready to accept. It is Lena who forces her
son to look inward. She links the past to the present by driving home to
him the dignity of his black ancestors:

> Lena: . . . I come from five generations of people who was slaves and
> sharecroppers—but ain't nobody in my family never let nobody pay
> 'em no money that was a way of telling us we wasn't fit to walk the
> earth. We ain't never been that poor. . . . We ain't never been that
> dead inside. (Hansberry 133)

She also admonishes Beneatha not to berate her brother:

> Lena: . . . When you starts measuring somebody, measure him right
> child, measure him right. Make sure you done taken into account
> what hills and valleys he come through before he got to wherever he
> is. (136)

Lena sets in motion her son's painful struggle with himself. Walter, reaching deep inside himself to the values, spirit, and self-respect instilled in him
by his ancestors, refuses Lindner's deal, this time with finality. "In making
this decision," writes Steven A. Carter, "Walter acknowledges his links not
only to his family, but also to his race through past, present, and future
generations and identifies with their mutual struggle against racist restrictions" (24). Walter redefines manhood from his original conception and
shows pride in his family while in the presence of Lindner.

The Youngers will move into the white neighborhood, not with the goal
of integrating it, but because the house is one they need, want, and can
afford. The move not only is practical but is also based on human dignity

and self-respect. Their ancestors have earned the family the right to live there. A deferred dream has been made possible. In the sometimes depressing, restricted, dimly lit environment of the black ghetto, dreams must often die and survive only with difficulty in the spiritual and material poverty surrounding them.

In addition to Lena and Walter Lee, Jr., other characters in *A Raisin in the Sun* are Ruth, Walter's thirty-year-old wife; Beneatha, Lena's twenty-year-old daughter; George Murchison, Beneatha's black, wealthy, and privileged suitor; Joseph Asagai, Beneatha's Nigerian suitor; Travis, Walter and Ruth's son; and Karl Lindner, the representative of the Clybourne Park Improvement Association. Pregnant with a child that she and Walter can ill afford, Ruth unselfishly considers having an abortion. The black ghetto often takes lives. Before the play opens, Walter, Sr., had died from overwork, and he and Lena had lost one child, little Claude, to death. Because of the difficulty of Ruth's own life and that of her husband, the man-woman relationship between them is deteriorating. She is the victim of her husband's exhaustion with his dead-end life and is blamed unfairly, along with other black women, for his failure to achieve his dreams. The deterioration of their marriage is symbolic of the all-too-often painful black male–black female relationship ground down by the pressures of daily living experiences. The communication problems between Ruth and Walter subside somewhat when she begins to comprehend his dream. Her mother-in-law's efforts to buy a larger home bring hope to Ruth, who borders on near hysteria over the idea of moving into a house. In the Younger family, Ruth often ameliorates the misunderstandings that spring up from time to time between the generations.

Beneatha, brash, intelligent, a freethinker, and a budding feminist, has a strong sense of racial pride. A college student, she has had certain privileges that her family lacked—membership in a play-acting group and horseback-riding club, in addition to photography and guitar lessons. Although she is supported by her mother in her dream to become a doctor, her brother chauvinistically believes that she should be a nurse like other women or get married. She is more concerned about a career than marriage at this time, and dreams of administering through medicine to those who suffer in the world. Beneatha clashes violently with Lena in her ideas about God, ideas that her mother considers blasphemous. Beneatha is interested in her African heritage—in African history and culture. An antiassimilationist, she wears with pride the African robe that Asagai has given her, plays African music on the phonograph, tries to imitate an African dance, and becomes conscious of her artificially straightened hair after her Nigerian boyfriend playfully refers to it as "mutilated." Even Walter, in drunken reverie, mystically looks back to Africa with her, as he imagines himself an African warrior with a spear and fighting against enemies.

George Murchison, an assimilationist, represents a materialistic way of life. He dissociates himself from both African and African American culture. When he arrives for his date with Beneatha and finds her in African attire, he is repulsed. To him, Africa represents primitivism: "Let's face it, baby, your heritage is nothing but a bunch of raggedy-assed spirituals and some grass huts" (Hansberry, 72). But into his sarcastic speech Hansberry also inserts information about Africa's greatness: the great Ashanti empires and Songhay civilizations, the wonderful Bénin sculpture, and Bantu poetry. Like Walter, he too is a male chauvinist. George says to Beneatha: "You're a nice-looking girl . . . all over. That's all you need, honey, forget the atmosphere. Guys aren't going to go for the atmosphere—they're going to go for what they see. Be glad for that" (88). To Beneatha, he is a fool. Hansberry uses Murchison to satirize aspects of the black middle class.

Joseph Asagai, a Western-educated Nigerian intellectual, links the Younger family to Africa. He is dedicated to the independence of his country from colonialism and to his country's future. He visualizes a black-ruled Nigeria, and accepts the future and all that it holds for Africa. He is also a male chauvinist. He tells Beneatha: "Between a man and a woman there need be only one kind of feeling," adding, "For a woman [love] should be enough" (49). He offers Beneatha marriage in the future—to one day come home to Nigeria with him. He gives her renewed hope when she feels that her chance for a medical education has been lost. Life has no end, he tells her; one moves on, despite setbacks, despite disappointments. This too has been the philosophic base for the life of the less formally educated Lena, who, though surrounded by life's uncertainties, has never surrendered.

Travis, the sixth generation of his black family in America, represents the future. He embodies the strong values that have been passed on to him, and he, in turn, perhaps with some modifications, will pass on to future generations. In his presence, his father stands up against the white racism of the Clybourne Park Improvement Association, and it is for him that Walter wants a better life.

Karl Lindner, the caller from the neighborhood association and the only white character in the drama, is a symbol of the white outside. He is an intruder in the family and the mouthpiece of white racism. He is presented as an ordinary man, and in that ordinariness lies danger, for he represents the common people. He does not come clad in a Klan uniform, but instead wears a business suit, carries a briefcase, and speaks in a modulated voice. Lindner is a forerunner of the hostility and potential violence that the Youngers will experience in their new neighborhood.

A Raisin in the Sun contains not only various levels of black life, but also cultural diversity in music and speech, for example. Lena likes African American spirituals; Ruth, the blues; and Walter, spirituals and jazz. Hansberry also uses language adeptly in delineating her characters. The discernible differences in their speech patterns are indicative of their social and educational levels. Lena, whose roots are in the South, Walter, Ruth, and Travis speak black English, the language of the community in which they live, the black ghetto. They use nonstandard verb forms and diction and dropped letters. When reaching his lowest level of despair and displaying how he will accept the money from Lindner, Walter temporarily disposes of his racial pride. He employs the mutilated, grotesque language attributed, mainly by white writers, to the debasing stereotypical black comic figures of the early stage, movies, and radio. The college-educated Beneatha and Asagai speak formal English, though Beneatha intersperses her speech with some of the slang of her contemporaries. Hansberry knew well the variety of language used by blacks.

While the Youngers may differ in their ideas on religion, career choices, dreams, and the like in *A Raisin in the Sun*, they come together as one in the fight against steely white racism. In telling her story, Hansberry depicts the difficulties of black life as a natural part of the story line. While certain problems achieve resolution in the drama, others remain unresolved. Problems await the Youngers, who are unwanted in the white neighborhood, but the struggle to survive there looms as a future challenge. Walter discards his original dream, but many African Americans in the next decade were unwilling to follow in his path. The Youngers, like many other African Americans, remain on the distant shore of the mainstream.

B. Teaching the Work

The background materials that may establish a context for teaching *A Raisin in the Sun* and comprehending the drama's African American background are John Hope Franklin's *From Slavery to Freedom: A History of Negro Americans* and Rayford Logan's *The Negro in the United States: A Brief History*. A capsulized history of African Americans to 1959 follows.

The first Africans to land in English America were those twenty who, in 1619, were brought to Jamestown, Virginia, by a Dutch man-of-war. Because slavery did not receive statutory recognition in Virginia until 1661, they were probably servants rather than slaves. But the status of African Americans did crystallize into permanent slavery, and they were governed by codes that varied in their rigidity. They had been brought to this country to provide the cheapest agricultural labor, and their activities were considered indispensable. The explosion between the industrial North and the agricultural slavocracy of the South, known as the Civil War, gave slaves freedom at last. With this freedom, however, came a new set of problems for the former chattel who had little preparation for life in liberty.

During the twelve-year period after the Civil War known as Reconstruction, the federal government tried to give the newly freed men and women equal rights with white citizens. This attempt, however, was met by fierce opposition from Southerners in the form, for example, of the adoption of the "Black Codes" and the rise of the Ku Klux Klan and other terroristic groups.

During the years of World War I, African Americans migrated from the South to the North in search of an improved way of life: higher wages, adequate housing, better schools, the right to vote, and a greater share of justice, freedom, and dignity. But once in the North, most were forced to reside in crowded houses and apartments, with the demand for housing often resulting in inflated rents. Within the city there developed separate black cities.

After World War II, African Americans intensified their drive for equality in the United States. As the nation approached the second half of the twentieth century, the interaction of forces—such as civil rights groups, notably the NAACP; civic, labor, and religious groups; political organizations; the courts, especially the federal courts; and the executive branch of the federal government—made the United States a better place for black Americans. A high point was reached in the battle for civil rights when, in 1954, the United States Supreme Court, in a unanimous decision, outlawed the segregation of pupils according to race in the public schools. In 1957, the first civil-rights act since 1875 was passed by Congress. The advancement of blacks, however, was not without opposition, and their progress, in some instances, was retarded.

Some blacks met with violence when they attempted to move into heretofore white neighborhoods. The 1950s was also the decade of the Montgomery, Alabama, bus boycott, triggered by the drivers' mistreatment of African Americans as passengers on the city bus lines. Other African Americans in other cities found boycotts to be an effective weapon against inequality. Whites, however, fought back.

The White Citizens Councils organized and battled against school desegregation. Economic reprisals were used against blacks who actively sought the desegregation of schools. Some public schools became private in an effort to circumvent the Supreme Court ruling. African Americans, especially in the South, were discouraged from pressing for their rights by dismissals from jobs, foreclosures on mortgages, and, in extreme cases, violence. Homes were bombed, black leaders were murdered, and riots broke out when black students were admitted to previously all-white universities.

Throughout the 1950s, blacks and their white supporters increased their efforts to gain equality for all Americans regardless of color, with some pressures leading to face-to-face confrontations between opposing groups in the streets. Against this backdrop, Hansberry's *A Raisin in the Sun* opened on Broadway in 1959.

Though born into a relatively comfortable and secure existence for a black family in Chicago, Lorraine Hansberry, at an early age, had been exposed to the harsh effects of racial prejudice. One incident stands out. At the age of eight she experienced racial violence in her native Chicago, when her parents moved the family to a house in a hostile white neighborhood. A brick hurled through the window of her new home by a member of an angry mob narrowly missed her. The Hansberrys were evicted from their home after the father, Carl, lost a battle against restrictive covenants in the Illinois courts. In 1940, when the United States Supreme Court declared restrictive covenants illegal (*Hansberry* v. *Lee*, 311 U.S. 32), the victory was only a minor palliative, for the racial experience had so affected the father psychologically and financially that he planned to become an expatriate. He bought a home in Polanco, Mexico, where he wanted to move his family, but in 1946, while in self-exile, he died of a cerebral hemorrhage.

In *A Raisin in the Sun,* the Youngers have hope, however, and they have kept alive their dreams—dreams of a better life for all of them. Lena, the present head of the household, is not only strong but resilient. She has learned to compromise and aspires to moderate aims. Despite obstacles, Lena and her husband dreamed of a better home for their family. After Walter, Jr., loses the insurance money to an untrustworthy friend, Lena plans to make their present dwelling more attractive through modest purchases. Though the Youngers have been the victims of social and racial frustration and their lives have been limited by outside forces, they do not remain stagnant; they act to improve their conditions. Walter, Jr., has grasped the American concept of upward mobility and believes that people have to make their own way. Beneatha has hope of curing mankind through medicine. When the family seems to have lost the means and the hope of moving into a larger home, Ruth clings to the belief that the four adults can support the new home in Clybourne Park.

The African American's diversity of language, as represented by the characters, has been discussed in the section entitled "Analysis of Themes and Forms." The language is often related to the social and educational level of the people. Standard or formal English is used by the better-read and educated blacks, while less formal English is used by the ordinary people. It is not unusual for the styles to be intermingled as they are in Hansberry's *A Raisin in the Sun*.

Satire, to a degree, is used by Hansberry to depict aspects of the black middle class. George Murchison, a member of the black bourgeoisie, is not interested in his black heritage and even ridicules it. He has embraced the standards of upper-class white America and eagerly displays such minutiae as knowledge of curtain time in New York theatres. He is impatient with Beneatha's quest for knowledge of her African heritage and with the thoughts of menials like Walter, Jr. Steven A. Carter notes that the values of the middle class, as represented by Murchison, "are largely those of the money-obsessed and business-oriented sectors of the middle class of any race: a delight in luxury and status, slavish attachment to the latest fashion, contempt for the aims and abilities of the lower class, conformity to a rigid code of social behavior, and pragmatic indifference to knowledge for its own sake" (59).

Through her play, *A Raisin in the Sun*, Hansberry etched into the American consciousness a rich and complex portrait of black family life. The Younger family struggles against formidable obstacles—a history of slavery and segregation, deferred dreams, the deprivations of black life, among other things. Students may gain a fuller appreciation of the play's depth and power through the exploration of a number of subjects in research, writing, discussion, and even dramatic interpretation itself. Some of these subjects follow and include questions and suggested direction for thinking, discussion, and research.

1. The play begins against the backdrop of a bleak historical past that includes slavery, segregation, and fierce resistance to the assimilation of blacks into American life. Explore specific historical periods, including slavery, the Jim Crow era, and the early civil-rights movement, and discuss how the social, economic, and historical conditions of particular periods help us to understand the panoply of problems faced by the Youngers.

2. The drive for equality (in jobs and housing, for example) for black Americans shaped the lives of many black families living in the 1950s and 1960s. What are the conditions for the Younger family, and how do they seek to gain some measure of equality in their lives?

3. Despite an environment that often limits possibilities, how do particular characters (for example, Beneatha and Walter) see themselves in terms of their racial heritage, and how does that sense of identity help or hinder them in establishing and achieving goals?

4. *A Raisin in the Sun* dramatizes the struggle of a family to achieve material success and maintain a sense of dignity. What are the particular family traditions, attitudes, and behaviors that help the Younger family struggle against considerable odds and achieve some measure of success?

5. Given the attitudes, traditions, and strengths in the Younger family, predict in some detail how the family might have fared ten years later, and explain their successes and/or failures in terms of family attitudes, traditions, and the like.

6. *A Raisin in the Sun* shares similar themes with Arthur Miller's *Death of a Salesman* and Tennessee Williams's *The Glass Menagerie,* among other plays. Explore those themes—including dysfunctional family structures, gender roles, generational conflicts, questions of identity, and so forth—as they are presented in several plays, giving attention to differing social classes, ethnic backgrounds, historical periods, and other factors.

7. What are the qualities of stagecraft in *A Raisin in the Sun*—such elements as lighting, stage, music, and set design—and how do they shape the development of the play?

8. Language, including dialect, often serves to distinguish characters, social class, economic aspirations, among other things. Explore Hansberry's use of language as it helps readers and viewers to understand the setting, characters, and action of the play.

9. Explore the similarities in values between the members of other ethnic groups and the black characters in *A Raisin in the Sun.*

10. Examine Hansberry's use of a muted satire to depict certain aspects of black middle-class life through George Murchison, among other characters. What aspects of the black bourgeoisie are critiqued, and how does that critique hold up today in terms of the black middle class?

11. Select a particular scene from the play that highlights an important theme, conflict, or problem, and ask small groups of students to dramatize that scene in short skits. After each dramatization, ask audience members to identify what the skit highlighted, what elements in the staging, dialogue, acting, and voice contributed to that effect, and how this dramatic interpretation was different from others.

In addition to students reading *A Raisin in the Sun,* they can view the play on film or videotape and, if possible, see a live production. Seeing a live production will enable students to more fully understand the playwright's intentions. Seeing a play is a different experience from reading it. In a live performance, the characters come to life. The videocassette of the American Playhouse production of *A Raisin in the Sun* is distributed by Fries Home Video, Fries Entertainment, 6922 Hollywood Blvd., Hollywood, California 90028. Another useful resource is *Lorraine Hansberry: The Black Experience in the Creation of Drama,* which is available from Films for the Humanities and Sciences, P.O. Box 2053, Princeton, New Jersey 08543.

C. Bibliographies

1. Related Works

Ellison, Ralph. *Invisible Man.* 1952. Reprint, New York: Random House, 1972. This novel, in part, deals with the problem of identity.

Fitzgerald, F. Scott. *The Great Gatsby.* 1925. Reprint, New York: Charles Scribner's Sons, 1953. Among other things, this novel treats the appeal of the American dream.

Miller, Arthur. *Death of a Salesman.* 1952. In *Arthur Miller: Eight Plays,* 91–208. Garden City, N.Y.: Nelson Doubleday, 1980. In this drama, the protagonist's quest is for the secret of success. Willy Loman believes in the rags-to-riches segment of the American dream.

Peterson, Louis. *Take a Giant Step.* 1954. In *Black Theater, U.S.A.: Forty-Five Plays by Black Americans, 1847–1974,* 547–84. Ed. James V. Hatch. New York: The Free Press, 1974. This play is an account of a seventeen-year-old youth's coming of age in a middle-class white community in New England, where he is the only black boy.

Walker, Joseph A. *The River Niger.* New York: Hill and Wang,1973. This play treats the problems of an African American family in Harlem during the 1970s.

Ward, Theodore. *Big White Fog.* 1937. In *Black Theater, U.S.A.,* 278–319. This play deals with the racial and economic problems facing a black family in Chicago during the 1920s and the 1930s.

Wright, Richard, and Paul Green. *Native Son.* 1941. In *Black Theater, U.S.A.,* 393–431. This play is a tragedy of a spiritually dead young African American male in Chicago.

2. Best Criticism

Abramson, Doris E. *Negro Playwrights in the American Theatre, 1925–1959,* 239–54. New York: Columbia University Press. 1969. The author presents an overview of *A Raisin in the Sun* with some critical appraisal. She compares the play to Richard Wright and Paul Green's *Native Son.*

Carter, Steven A. *Hansberry's Drama: Commitment amid Complexity,* 19–69. New York: Penguin, 1993. This book has an excellent treatment of the play, including character analyses and the black characters' speech patterns, suggesting the breadth of African American culture. In his discussion, Carter incorporates other drafts of the play.

Cheney, Anne. *Lorraine Hansberry,* 55–71. Boston: Twayne Publishers, 1984. Cheney gives a good overview of *A Raisin in the Sun,* including Hansberry's treatment of Africa and the characters, especially the women.

Keyssar, Helene. *The Curtain and the Veil: Strategies in Black Drama,* 113–46. New York: Burt Franklin and Co., 1981. The author emphasizes the strategies used by Hansberry in writing *A Raisin in the Sun.* To Keyssar, the play points out similarities in values between black and white people.

3. Other Sources

Baraka, Amiri. "A Critical Reevaluation: *A Raisin in the Sun*'s Enduring Passion." In *A Raisin in the Sun (Expanded Twenty-Fifth Anniversary Edition) and The Sign in Sidney Brustein's Window,* ed. Robert Nemiroff, 9–20. New York: New American Library, 1987.

Bigsby, C. W. E. *Confrontation and Commitment: A Study of Contemporary American Drama, 1959–1966,* 156–73. London: MacGibbon and Kee, 1967.

Brown-Guillory, Elizabeth. *Their Place on the Stage: Black Women Playwrights in America.* New York: Greenwood Press, 1988.

Cruse, Harold. *The Crisis of the Negro Intellectual.* New York: Morrow, 1967.

Du Bois, W. E. B. *The Souls of Black Folk.* In *Three Negro Classics.* New York: Avon Books, 1965.

Fabre, Genevieve. *Drumbeats, Masks, and Metaphor: Contemporary Afro-American Theatre.* Cambridge, Mass.: Harvard University Press, 1983.

Franklin, John Hope. *From Slavery to Freedom: A History of Negro Americans.* 5th ed. New York: Alfred A. Knopf, 1980.

Hansberry, Lorraine. *A Raisin in the Sun.* New York: Random House, 1959.

Hooks, Bell. "Raisin in a New Light." *Christianity and Crisis,* February 6, 1989, 21–23.

Lester, Julius. Introduction. *Les Blancs: The Collected Last Plays of Lorraine Hansberry,* ed. Robert Nemiroff, 3–32. New York: Vintage Books, 1973.

Logan, Rayford. *The Negro in the United States: A Brief History.* Princeton, N.J.: D. Van Nostrand Company, 1957.

Miller, Jeanne-Marie A. "Images of Black Women in Plays by Black Playwrights." *CLA Journal* 20 (1977): 494–507.

"Closer to the Edge":

Toni Morrison's *Song of Solomon*

LINDA WAGNER-MARTIN

A. Analysis of Themes and Forms

Now that Toni Morrison has won the Nobel Prize for Literature—surely the apex of any writer's career, much less that of a black woman writer whose first novel, *The Bluest Eye,* appeared scarcely twenty-five years ago—all her fiction will begin to receive the serious critical attention it has long deserved. Of Morrison's earlier works, only the 1977 *Song of Solomon* garnered the kind of response it merited—it was a Book-of-the-Month Club selection; it won awards. Most importantly, it identified Morrison as a black writer who saw her culture as integral to her art. *Song of Solomon* showed that it was largely through her intimate knowledge of the culture of her black characters that Morrison herself had come to expression. In this work there was no envy of traditional mainstream fiction, no attempt to craft a narrative that would be compared with work by Ernest Hemingway or Saul Bellow or John Barth. As she explained in her 1993 *Paris Review* interview, "I would like to write novels that were unmistakably mine, but nevertheless fit first into African-American traditions and second of all, this whole thing called literature" (Schappell, 118). When the interviewer asked why African American took precedence, Morrison replied of that culture, "It's richer. It has more complex sources. It pulls from something that's closer to the edge, it's much more modern. It has a human future" (ibid.).

In her own terms, then, *Song of Solomon* was an exemplary text—there was little question that it was rich, telling a number of complex stories, drawing a quantity of realistic but hauntingly idiosyncratic characters. It relied for its metaphoric impact on various African American tropes—that of the flying man, the powerful father, the scapegoat, the love-obsessed woman, as well as the woman as healer and spiritual guide—and in some cases, on Morrison's reversals of expected patterns, as when knowledge comes from a journey *south* rather than north, and from divesting oneself of material wealth rather than acquiring it. And in its emphasis on nonintellectual ways of knowing, as Morrison consistently privileged Pilate's understanding of the human condition rather than her brother Macon's materialistic success, the novel spoke for a healthy, if primitive, finding of the self. *Song of Solomon* also bespeaks that "human future," a glimpse into a world where people recognize their need for each other; and in that respect it is newly modern, circling away from the core of absurdity that postmodernism posits. Morrison's novel suggests that flip nonanswers to human problems can be only temporarily interesting.

The suggesting Morrison achieves through her fiction is never didactic; in fact, much of the interest in her narratives comes in the process of unraveling story. As she had in *The Bluest Eye,* Morrison started *Song of Solomon* obliquely, by telling the story of insurance agent Robert Smith's attempt at flight. His 1931 suicide metaphorically introduced Morrison's primary narrative, the story of Macon Dead's family, a family that needed the courage to act for the good of others. Ducking and dodging the reader's expectations, Morrison's novel is as multi-plotted as it is multi-voiced, and part of the reader's involvement with the text becomes the simple allure of mystery: what happens next, to whom, and why?

As Mr. Smith stands near the cupola of No Mercy hospital, wearing his "wide blue silk wings curved forward around his chest" and meditating on his proposed flight, Ruth Foster Dead and her daughters Lena and Corinthians scatter their red velvet roses on the snow beneath him, as Ruth's labor pains begin. The birth of her only son, Milkman, was immanent. Accompanying Smith's leap is the "Sugarman done fly away" folksong, sung by an unnamed woman in the crowd who is later identified as Pilate; sent for help by the nervous white nurse is the young black child, Guitar, who grows to become Milkman's friend and, eventually, his adversary. In one brief scene, the cast is assembled for this all too American story.

Morrison suggests that she wanted a visual pattern of red, white, and blue to introduce the narrative of the *failure* of the American dream: one man beaten economically who dies; another (Macon Dead) who, despite his perverted name, "succeeds" but grows less human in the process. Similarly, one woman—Ruth Dead—ostensibly Christian, giving birth while mourning her godlike father so desperately that she skewers her own family relationships; the other, Pilate, a kind of pagan, wandering the earth, restlessly searching for the literal bones of her sire, but giving moral life to Ruth's drifting son in the process. As the twentieth century moves relentlessly to crush the black lower class, the few people who can escape do so—often by copying the objectionable ethics of the white business world. But the pervasive metaphor of *Song of Solomon* is not Macon Dead's financial success so much as it is the flight of the man who knows himself.

Although Robert Smith dies a suicide, or a failed flyer, the crowd watching applauds his imagination. Three hundred and some pages later, the purposely ambiguous ending forces the reader to see that Milkman too flies—and, more important, to see that whether Guitar dies, or Milkman dies, or both, or neither, the significance of their struggle has been in their journey. While Guitar accepts a rigidly prescriptive and senseless plan for avenging the whites' killing of blacks, his awakened political consciousness serves no real purpose. He murders Pilate, the only capable and sane character in the book, in his vendetta to kill his own friend, Milkman. Milkman's hegira as he moves from a tardy and extended machismo adolescence comes to fulfillment very near its end. Traveling at his father's insistence into a southern culture that threatens his hypocritical superiority, Milkman plays the archetypal role of Telemachus to his wrongheaded father. What he finally learns—and this from Pilate—is that the valuable is the human; it is love, not gold, that people thirst for. And all too often, the loss of love is the crippling element in lives. Once Milkman sees that his disdain for a woman's love has killed her, once he has admitted his guilt, he can begin to grow.

The metaphors, tropes, and patterns that shape the reader's understanding of Morrison's novel are all rooted in African American beliefs and lore. As Trudier Harris points out so accurately, it is sometimes possible to use a scaffolding of classic myth to explore Morrison's texts, but such a tactic must remain secondary. By drawing from the African American body of knowledge, the author emphasizes dualism, a worldview that "presupposes an intertwining of the secular and sacred realms of existence" (Harris, 87). In that perspective, the myth of the flying man was never questioned. To quote Morrison, "my meaning is specific: it is about black people who could fly. That was always part of the folklore of my life; flying was one of our gifts. I don't care how silly it may seem. It is everywhere—people used to talk about it, it's in the spirituals and gospels" (LeClair, 26–27).

Morrison questioned the notion of "hero" throughout the book, but by inverting the idea of the quest as a means of instructing the protagonist she also undermined the trope of consistent forward progress. If Milkman was a hero figure, searching for meaning as he made the journeys his father had sent him on, then he would have learned from those treks. But his primary impulse to understand came again and again from the influence of Pilate rather than from his father—and he could have learned what Pilate had to teach him with much less traveling. Part of the African American vision was that being heroic did not mandate nobility; it rather reflected the process of learning to become as good a soul as was possible. Milkman, therefore, did not need to erase the tawdry life he had lived on the way to becoming a man Pilate could be proud of, a man who could take up her role as singer of the song of the family's history—a role he assumes at the moment of her death.

In 1977, Morrison's *Song of Solomon* was valued more than her two earlier books had been because it was ostensibly a text about black men. Both Milkman and Guitar could have been fairly typical bildungsroman heroes, kids finding themselves despite cultural pressures to avoid maturing. Guitar, a classic ghetto adolescent, looks for a sense of identity and belonging through the harshest of criminal bonds. Milkman, better fixed economically through working for his pompous father, grows further and further from becoming either adult or human. But in the subtly quiet inter-chapters of the book, where Morrison tells the story of Pilate, Reba, and Hagar, she wreaks havoc with the more recognizable narrative of men's lives.

Pilate, her daughter, and her granddaughter are the poor of the earth, but they are also its salt. Horrifying to the patriarchal Macon, who demands that his concept of order be followed at all times and by everyone he controls, Pilate with her disregard for the trappings of humanity—cleanliness, good food, suitable clothing—remains an enigma to him. He denies their loving childhood as brother and sister, their traumatizing witnessing of their loved father's execution, their months of fear and conspiracy as they escaped from the hostile South. Along with his name, Macon Dead wipes clean his memory; in one stroke, he loses his childhood, his family, and his little sister. In many ways, his mistreatment of Pilate and her family is even worse than his punishing hatred of his wife Ruth and his utter disregard for his daughters. When Macon Dead sends his son into Pilate's home to rob her of what he thinks is gold, only to have Milkman steal his grandfather's bones, he makes a travesty of all his family relationships.

In the midst of a life of abject poverty, Pilate manages to find her own satisfying route to spirituality. She is so untouched by desire for the material, however, that she ignores Hagar's understandable need for cosmetics, beautiful clothes, jewelry—and the bitterly manic scene of Hagar shopping, her wealth of purchases ruined in the rain, impresses the reader with one possible weakness of Pilate's otherworldly existence. Like Macon in some respects, Pilate assumes that what makes her happy is what everyone else wants. Hagar's willed madness and death prove that Pilate too is vincible; she has judged her granddaughter inaccurately, and because of her errors in assessing the girl's state of mind, a human life—a life beloved to her—is lost.

The perplexity of the reader in Morrison's *Song of Solomon* derives largely from the recognition that none of the characters is exemplary; not even Pilate is heroic. Morrison structures the text so that the painful scene of Hagar's mad shopping trip—followed by the inevitable scene of her funeral—comes near the end, carefully juxtaposed between segments of Milkman's discovery of his ancestry, the first triumph of his own adult will. The shape of narrative, then, tends to undermine the evident success of Milkman's discovery of the magical line from which both he and Hagar descend: Morrison's description of both Hagar's bitterly pathetic madness and Pilate's inconsolable grief at the loss of her "sweet sugar lumpkin . . . my baby girl" overshadows Milkman's success.

The narration itself changes tonality in the last quarter of the novel. As if to fit her method to the story being told, Morrison grows more elliptical, the tale more fragmented, the characters more surreal. Much of the factual information that Milkman seeks comes through children's songs; more from the (perhaps) addled older women—Circe, living with a cadre of dogs in the Butler mansion she systematically destroys, room by room; Susan Byrd, measuring her life in sugar cookies as she hides the reality of her Indian blood from her close companions. Single words hold the key to Milkman's history, but those words are dulled through repetition: is the name "Jay" or "Jake"? "Crow" or "Crowell"? "Sing" or "Singing" Byrd? "Solomon" or "Shalimar" or "Sugarman"? The twists in spoken language, the purveyor of the tribal tales, can change history as easily as even the best-intentioned teller can. What Milkman learns is to trust his instinctual ear rather than his literal one, and to accept a conglomerate of images in place of any systematic genealogical record.

What he learns is that his father, Macon, and his aunt, Pilate, are descended from the Solomon who flew back to Africa. In Miss Susan Byrd's account, a macabre mixture of fantasy is told as fact, and detail resonates with a kind of truth: "Some of those Africans they brought over here as slaves could fly. A lot of them flew back to Africa. The one around here who did was this same Solomon, or Shalimar. . . . it's just foolishness, you know, but according to the story he wasn't running away. He was flying. He flew. You know, like a bird. Just stood up in the fields one day, ran up some hill, spun around a couple of times, and was lifted up in the air. Went right on back to wherever it was he came from. . . . It like to killed the woman, the wife . . . she's supposed to have screamed out loud for days" (326). Susan Byrd continues to describe Ryna's maddening grief, which destroyed her just as Hagar's grief over the loss of Milkman's love destroyed her life— another clear legacy of the family line.

Morrison counters the tale of absence and madness, flight and grief so powerful they derange, with two important scenes of Milkman's ritual bathing—the bath the idealized and perfect woman Sweet gives him on his way to making his discovery, and the triumphant, exuberant swimming scene just after he hears the complete tale of Solomon's flight. In Milkman's first clear happiness, existing in his own empowerment and out of range of his father's troubled shadow, he begins to sense who he might come to be. His line is not only African; it is the noblest of Africa's people, the flying man.

Through his understanding of how meaningful his heritage is, despite the fact that his father (Jake, not Macon) has tried to deny that lineage, Milkman is able to bring peace to Pilate, temporarily distraught by the death of Hagar. His information to her, about the identity of the bones she had carried throughout her life, as well as about what her father's ghost meant by its cryptic words, enabled Pilate to save her own tormented soul. In burying her father's bones before her own death, she too was freed to fly. The only woman to attain that kind of nobility, Pilate was the final center of Milkman's full realization of humanity. After her death, he too was free to let circumstances take him, not in the sense of a preordained fate but in the sense of his own acceptance of whatever came.

Rather than being apologetic for her unresolved ending, Morrison points out (about *Song of Solomon* as well as *Beloved* and *Jazz*), "It's important not to have a totalizing view. In American literature we have been so totalized— as though there is only one version. We are not one indistinguishable block of people who always behave the same way. . . . I try to give some credibility to all sorts of voices each of which is profoundly different. Because what strikes me about African American culture is its variety" (Schappell, 117).

Morrison's *Song of Solomon* is an amazingly varied text. As the reader succumbs to the power of unraveling the mystery of Milkman's ancestry, the fascination of the varieties of his contemporarily dysfunctional family, and his own offensively limited maturity, the obvious ironies of her novel's title first resonate, and then dissipate. The wisdom of Solomon, who saved the life of a baby by threatening to divide it, seems nonexistent at first, until the reader sees that the hardly heroic Milkman has learned through dogged persistence to unearth some basic truths. Armed with the knowledge he gleaned from the children's songs that he was not too sophisticated to hear, he could then advise both Pilate and Macon about their heritage, and instruct them in suitable roles as peacemakers for the family line.

Similarly, the biblical book of "Songs," "Solomon's Song of Songs," with its highly erotic lyricism, seemed remote from the young black man's use of women. There was little discourse of affection in Milkman's life, and part of Guitar's disgust with his friend stemmed from his callous treatment of Hagar.

The meaning of Morrison's title, however, need not be only Christian or Westernized; and it clearly does reveal the "Song of Solomon" most relevant to Milkman Dead's own story. Whether his ancestor's name was Solomon or Shalimar, his legendary flight was the stuff of a song that echoed throughout his Virginia province, the mythic community of Shalimar not recorded on maps, living still in the songs and narratives of a vital culture. Morrison's task in her novel has been, in part, to rescue the "song of Solomon" from its near-oblivion in legend, and to provide a frame, a text, and an agency for its revitalized meaning.

B. Teaching the Work

1. The most useful approach is to locate the tropes of the novel in the relevant African American folkloric traditions. Trudier Harris's *Fiction and Folklore* is the standard source for information about the flying motif, the source of one's soul, and innumerable other items for all of Morrison's fiction.

2. Placing the story of Milkman and Guitar's coming to maturity in the bildungsroman tradition is another means of broadening reader focus. The narrative of young male characters leaving the shelter of their home to earn their living and maturity, through education and, often, sexual experience, shows the re-visioning of Morrison's schemata. Responding to Annis Pratt's *Archetypal Patterns in Women's Fiction, Song of Solomon* shows again that marginalized characters often are forced to respond to the pressure of maturing by growing down, not up. Milkman's stunted adulthood, before his real quest starts, is a paradigm of the life that developed without knowing challenge or promise.

Unlike the steady evolution of the protagonists in Charles Dickens's *Great Expectations* or *David Copperfield*, Milkman's development moves in bursts of discovery. His humanization near the end of the novel is a radical change, not a gradual realization. At places in *Song of Solomon*, his character resembles that of the protagonist in Thomas Hardy's *Jude the Obscure*, as sexual activity seems to deter him from self-realization.

More significant comparisons can be made between Rudolfo A. Anaya's *Bless Me, Ultima*, where the ostensible protagonist, the young man, draws on the aging *curandera* for his essential wisdom and direction; and in a negative way, with the young protagonists in the stories of Richard Wright's *Uncle Tom's Children.* By comparing Milkman's narrative with the various stories of the latter collection, the reader sees how non-adversarial Morrison's characters are drawn to be: in *Song of Solomon,* the worst enemies are within rather than without. The brotherhood of Guitar and Milkman gone awry is an apt illustration of the doubleness of identity.

Outcomes also differ from those of a traditional novel of education. Instead of a firmly positive resolution, Milkman's fate is purposely unresolved.

3. The quest pattern as an ironic undergirding supports the reader's investigation of Morrison's concept of hero. Unlike Odysseus's search for adventure and self-fulfillment, or Jason's search for the Golden Fleece, or the Arthurian knights' search for the Holy Grail, Milkman (who remains sorely in need of a name more suitable for a conventional hero throughout the book) searches for a family history. The concept of a self no longer depends on some spiritual, religious system but only on finding a trace of unique identity; Milkman's search is inherently non-patriarchal. At times he seems to be in pursuit of gold, but that is his father's (Dead) search, not his. Again, Milkman looks for the identity of Pilate's burden, her sack of bones, a trial that she understands is the purpose of her life—giving reverence to the dead, no matter who they are. But Milkman's primary search is for himself.

4. The richest source, in any study of the way Morrison achieves omnipresent irony, is that of the biblical parallels with her narrative, or, perhaps more important, the differences between her text and the biblical base. Her use of the title of the book of Songs has been mentioned; and the novel itself draws attention to the ambiguity of Pilate being named for the ruler who killed Jesus Christ. Pilate's positive character surely is a way of questioning the myth of the Christ. Pilate struggles throughout the book to define herself and her role in ways that are separate from what she would have been—and the role she would have been asked to play—in a ritualized Christian culture. Born without a navel, separated from everyone she knows because of that difference, Pilate learns to find a successful road through life even after breaking many of the Ten Commandments. She, her daughter, and her daughter's daughter—complete with their chain of Biblical names— exist in spaces separate from those of their community or their ostensible religion. And at Hagar's funeral, it is Pilate who mourns, turning herself into the priest of grief, voicing the truly important commemoratives about her granddaughter's life.

Within Macon Dead's own family, Ruth Foster shows the confusion her biblical name suggests: Ruth, here cast as a daughter who loved her male

parent to the exclusion of all else (rather than her mother-in-law), suc-
ceeded only in offending her husband and in bringing him the male child
he desired through a shamanistic trickery that forever alienated him from
her. But her revenge came through the wisdom of Paul in his First Letter to
Corinthians, for which she named her daughter (First Corinthians): the
roles of husband and wife as described there are repeatedly twisted and
defied by Macon Dead's treatment of her and her daughters.

The book of First Corinthians can, in fact, provide the alternative text
for Morrison's *Song of Solomon*. It begins by questioning concepts of conventional wisdom, and urges readers to find themselves and then look to
their individuality to lead them to truly wise behavior. Paul's words inter-
rogate the received patriarchal principles of religion, and there is a tone of
defensive apology throughout the book: in his urging people to know themselves before they apply Christian liturgy to their lives, Paul becomes a significant voice himself rather than just another preacher. More directly, as
Corinthians follows her passion for the apparently unsuitable Porter—who
is, in fact, an illiterate murderer—she finds tranquillity and love, satisfac-
tions her mother has never known.

Song of Solomon shows how well Morrison knows her Bible, and nearly
every chapter includes some reversal of a biblical plot or trope that could be
studied with good effect, time permitting.

5. The fast-paced text opens well to role playing, to acting out key scenes (as,
for example, Milkman in Shalimar, with the hostile villagers forcing him through
the various rites of passage—until he emerges, strong from his bonding with
the natural, clutching the heart of the bobcat, ironically NOT a coon). The
musical elements can also provide a way into information and discussions about
folksong, and those can be avenues for performances. Vital as Morrison's writing is, it is also dramatic and stage-worthy—and students love to see the
language come off the page.

C. Bibliography

1. Related Works

Anaya, Rudolfo A. *Bless Me, Ultima*. Berkeley, Calif.: Tonatiuh International,
        1972. Narrative of young Antonio's realization of the powers of the
        curandera, Ultima, in a life-and-death struggle for him as he attains ma-
        turity.
Dickens, Charles. *David Copperfield*. 1849–50. *Great Expectations*. 1860–61.

Reprints, New York: Penguin, 1982 (and many other paperback editions). The classic stories of young English men coming to maturity through adversity, hard work, sexual experience, and some deus-ex-machina intervention.

Hardy, Thomas. *Jude the Obscure.* 1895. Reprint, New York: Norton, 1978. A dark treatment of the classic bildungsroman, told with stentorian didacticism and harsh naturalism.

Morrison, Toni. *The Bluest Eye.* New York: Washington Square Press, 1972. The narrative of three young girls (rather than men), focused primarily on that of Pecola Breedlove, an incest victim driven mad by her tragic childhood.

Wright, Richard. *Uncle Tom's Children.* 1938. Reprint, New York: Harper and Row, 1965. Linked stories of black adolescent male characters who stunt their lives in battling the oppressive white culture.

2. Best Criticism

Blake, Susan L. "Folklore and Community in *Song of Solomon.*" *MELUS* 7 (1980): 77–82. Early source study of dynamic tropes in the text.

Clarke, Deborah L. "'What There Was Before Language': Preliteracy in Toni Morrison's *Song of Solomon.*" In *Anxious Power: Reading, Writing, and Ambivalence in Narrative by Women,* ed. Carol J. Singley and Susan Elizabeth Sweeney, 265–78. Albany: State University of New York Press, 1993. Sophisticated reading from a Lacanian and linguistic axis.

Harris, Trudier. *Fiction and Folklore: The Novels of Toni Morrison.* Knoxville: University of Tennessee Press, 1991. An essential work on the way Morrison grounds her fiction in various kinds of African American cultural and folkloristic beliefs.

Holloway, Karla F. C., and Stephanie A. Demetrakopoulos. *New Dimensions of Spirituality: A Biracial and Bicultural Reading of the Novels of Toni Morrison.* Westport, Conn.: Greenwood Press, 1987. A dialogue that opens the works to differing, but compatible, interpretations.

Hovet, Grace Ann, and Barbara Lounsberry. "Flying as Symbol and Legend in Toni Morrison's *The Bluest Eye, Sula,* and *Song of Solomon.*" *CLA Journal* 27 (December 1983): 119–40. Important early study that broadens discussion to other Morrison works.

LeClair, Thomas. "'The Language Must Not Sweat': A Conversation with Toni Morrison." *The New Republic* 184 (March 21, 1981): 25–29. The best interview with the author until the one published in 1993, below.

Schappell, Elissa, with Claudia Brodsky Lacour. "Toni Morrison, The Art of Fiction CXXXIV." *The Paris Review* 35, no. 128 (Fall 1993), 80–125. Useful questions lead the author to some of her most helpful commentary.

3. Other Sources

Awkward, Michael. *Inspiriting Influences: Tradition, Revision, and Afro-American Women's Novels.* New York: Columbia University Press, 1989.

Baker, Houston A., Jr. *Workings of the Spirit: The Poetics of Afro-American Women's Writing.* Chicago: University of Chicago Press, 1991.

Bell, Bernard. *The Afro-American Novel and Its Tradition.* Amherst: University of Massachusetts Press, 1987.

Campbell, Jane. *Mythic Black Fiction: The Transformation of History.* Knoxville: University of Tennessee Press, 1986.

Carby, Hazel V. *Reconstructing Womanhood: The Emergence of the Afro-American Woman Novelist.* New York: Oxford University Press, 1987.

Christian, Barbara. *Black Women Novelists: The Development of a Tradition, 1892–1976.* Westport, Conn.: Greenwood Press, 1980.

Coleman, James W. "Beyond the Reach of Love and Caring: Black Life in Toni Morrison's *Song of Solomon.*" *Obsidian* 2, no. 1 (Winter 1986): 151–61.

Gates, Henry Louis, Jr. *The Signifying Monkey: A Theory of African-American Literary Criticism.* New York: Oxford University Press, 1988.

Jones, Bessie W., and Audrey L. Vinson. *The World of Toni Morrison: Explorations in Literary Criticism.* Dubuque, Iowa: Kendall/Hunt, 1985.

Lee, Dorothy H. "*Song of Solomon:* To Ride the Air." *Black American Literature Forum* 16 (Summer 1982): 64–70.

Marshall, Brenda. "The Gospel According to Pilate." *American Literature* 57 (1985): 486–89.

McKay, Nellie Y., ed. *Critical Essays on Toni Morrison.* Boston: G. K. Hall, 1988.

Morrison, Toni. *Song of Solomon.* New York: Knopf, 1977.

———. "Rootedness: The Ancestor as Foundation." In *Black Women Writers (1950–1980): A Critical Evaluation,* ed. Mari Evans, 339–345. Garden City, N.Y.: Anchor/Doubleday, 1984.

———. *Playing in the Dark: Blackness and the Literary Imagination.* New York: Knopf, 1992.

A Fairy-Tale Life:

The Making of Celie in Alice Walker's *The Color Purple*

DANIEL W. ROSS

A. Analysis of Themes and Forms

Winner of the Pulitzer Prize, *The Color Purple* has been a highly acclaimed novel since its publication in 1982. The novel presents several plots in a coherent narrative: the plots of Celie's development of selfhood, her relationships with Shug Avery and other women, and her reunion with her children and her sister Nettie (who has raised the children in Africa). In addition, the stories of several other characters (Albert, Harpo, Shug, Mary Agnes, and Sofia) are told in connection to Celie's story. In some respects, *The Color Purple* adheres to the oldest traditions of the English and American novel: its epistolary narrative form harkens back to the novel's eighteenth-century genesis, and its focus on family conflicts is as traditional a theme as literature offers. In other respects, however, *The Color Purple* is distinctively contemporary: the novel features gender conflicts, racial politics, and issues of African American heritage that have become part of our more recent cultural dialogue.

Students often miss the novel's traditional elements. They may be surprised and delighted to find that it follows the pattern of other rags-to-riches stories or of fairy tales. Some readers have seen similarities between Celie's story and those of Cinderella or Chaucer's patient Griselda. Awareness of this fairy-tale structure helps students who might be ill at ease with the number of coincidences or miracles in *The Color Purple*; such events are the stock in trade of fairy tales. With its many traditional elements, *The Color Purple* could serve as an appropriate final text in a course on the history of the novel. Some of the major themes and issues of the novel are outlined in the following subheadings.

Celie's Transformation: Restoring the Body

Celie's physical and spiritual transformation, the novel's major action, invites psychoanalytic and feminist readings. The first page records the rape of Celie by her stepfather; by the third page Celie has given birth to her second child, and her own mother has died cursing her. Celie's stark language reveals these events in a manner that is bound to shock readers. Her descriptions indicate that she lacks a language to understand the traumatic actions inflicted on her: "A girl at church say you git big if you bleed every month. I don't bleed no more" (15). Even such personal knowledge comes to Celie secondhand.

Readers must confront the brutal effects of Celie's life. Married to Albert, she receives no peace: he performs sexual intercourse on her without love and demands that she keep his house and care for his unruly children. Celie's only release is to annihilate her own body in her imagination: "He beat me like he beat the children. . . . It all I can do not to cry. I make myself wood. I say to myself, Celie, you a tree" (30). Celie's development of selfhood depends upon reversing this pattern and accepting her own body as beautiful. Because of the brutality of Albert and her stepfather, she cannot see herself as beautiful or worthy of love.

Walker's portrayal of Celie's eventual acceptance of her body provides one of her connections to contemporary feminism. Though Walker has distanced herself somewhat from that movement (calling her work "womanist" rather than "feminist"), *The Color Purple* dramatizes many feminist issues. While white and black women have not experienced degradation of their bodies in exactly the same ways, the analogies are close. Two of the most noteworthy spokespersons of modern feminism, Adrienne Rich and Virginia Woolf, have focused on women's needs to accept, understand, and value their bodies. Rich's description of women's imperative to overcome negative attitudes toward their bodies certainly applies to Celie:

> But fear and hatred of our bodies had often crippled our brains.
> Some of the most brilliant women of our time are still trying to
> think from somewhere outside their female bodies—hence they are
> still merely reproducing old forms of intellection. (284)

In "Professions for Women," Woolf described her chief difficulty as a writer as telling the truth about herself as a body. Woolf recognized that culture teaches women to ignore or even feel ashamed of their bodies. Recovering the body from male domination is a primary theme of contemporary feminism and of *The Color Purple*.

Respect and appreciation for the body are necessary for self-esteem and, ultimately, for life. In Celie's case, the repossession of her body is even necessary for the development of meaningful speech. That repossession requires a helper and guide, Shug Avery. Shug plays a critical role in bringing Celie to terms with her body. Celie's repossession of her body encourages her to seek selfhood and then to assert that selfhood through language. During this process, Celie learns to love herself and others and even to address her letters to a body, her sister Nettie, rather than to the disembodied God that she has blindly inherited from white Christian mythology. This process begins when Shug forces Celie to examine her body in a mirror; here Celie first comes to terms with the body that men have so harshly appropriated. This process changes her life forever.

Celie's Sexual Awakening

One of the most difficult problems a teacher faces with *The Color Purple* is getting students who may be uncomfortable with frank portrayals of sexuality to discuss the novel's treatment of this subject. It may help if students see that Celie's sexual experiences with Shug are part of a larger pattern of growth and development that she needs to undergo because she did not have those experiences earlier. Celie, in effect, has been robbed of childhood, a deprivation that has seriously affected her response to sexuality. The mirror scene demonstrates the role of sexuality in Celie's development of selfhood.

Though Celie is not a child, her language and her lack of self-esteem indicate an arrested psychological development. Psychoanalysts such as Katherine Dalsimer report that girls often "regress" during adolescence, returning to preoedipal or pre–mirror stage fantasies of union with the mother (25–26). Girls normally break out of this cycle as they progress through adolescence, but Celie, fourteen and friendless at the beginning of *The Color Purple,* seems trapped in this infantile stage throughout her teenage years. In this regressive stage, girls tend to imagine their bodies as fragmented, mutilated, or dismembered. It is easy to see why Celie, victim as she is of male brutality, would continue thinking of her body in this way. Even her memory of childbirth is marked by images of mutilation; she recalls the "bursting open of the body" as her "stomach started moving and then that little baby came out [her] pussy chewing on it fist" (12). Celie's fragmentation is reinforced when her stepfather presents her to her future husband as less than a whole woman: "God done fixed her. You can do everything just like you want to and she ain't gonna make you feed it or clothe it" (18). This blunt language provides many implications of potential masculine domination and control of a female body.

Celie has no desire to get to know her body, or to imagine it as anything other than fragmented, until the arrival of her husband's lover, Shug Avery. Ironically, because Shug arrives in poor health, Celie first serves her in the traditional female role of nurse. In this capacity, Celie feels her first erotic stirrings and associates them with a new spirituality: "I wash her body, it feel like I'm praying" (53). Guided by Shug, Celie's stirrings foreshadow her discovery, under Shug's guidance, of a new God that allows her to love sexual pleasure guiltlessly. Shug introduces Celie to the mysteries of the body and sexual experience, making possible both Celie's discovery of speech and her eventual freedom from masculine brutality. But the introduction requires that Celie see her body and feel its components first. For this a hand-held mirror is necessary, as is Shug's encouragement that there is something worth seeing.

When Shug urges her to look at herself, Celie reacts much like a child who fears being caught by a parent: she giggles and feels "like us been doing something wrong" (80). Even Shug, for all her promiscuity, talks like a child in preparing Celie for what she will find: "Listen, she say, right down there in your pussy is a little button that gets real hot *when you do you know what with somebody*. It gets hotter and hotter and then it melt. That the good part" (79; my emphasis). The simplicity of Shug's language must be designed in part to titillate Celie, but her uncharacteristic euphemism ("when you do you know what with somebody") suggests that even the free-spirited Shug has trouble speaking straightforwardly about sex or the body. Strange as it may seem for Shug to be so childish, that behavior nonetheless emphasizes the fact that she and Celie are engaged in a juvenile drama that must be played through before Celie can reach a more mature stage of development. In her adulthood, Celie is experiencing the kind of self-discovery that she never experienced in her childhood. So, while Celie looks in the mirror, Shug guards the door like a naughty schoolgirl, letting Celie know when the coast is clear.

Celie is astonished by what she sees in the mirror: "Ugh. All that hair. Then my pussy lips be black. The inside look like a wet rose" (79). It is important for students to recognize the sequence of Celie's responses, from the initial revulsion ("Ugh") to a recognition of feminine beauty, symbolized by the rose. When Shug asks Celie what she thinks, her response abnegates her previous annihilation and rejection of her body: "It mine, I say" (80). In discovering and accepting with pride her own body, Celie initiates a desire for selfhood. Next, she begins to find an identity through a network of female relationships with Shug, Nettie (whose letters she soon discovers), Sofia, and Mary Agnes. With her newfound identity, Celie is able to break free from the masculine prohibition against speech and to join a community of women, thus freeing herself from dependence on and subjection to male brutality.

Celie's Discovery of Selfhood

The Color Purple is rich in symbolism; making students aware of the symbols, particularly those associated with Celie's perceptions of her body, provides a good way of helping them to chart Celie's progress. The symbols we use to describe ourselves, or others, invariably communicate attitudes regarding our self-esteem or lack of it. Upon examining herself in the mirror, Celie discovered three symbols of her body: the hair, the lips, the rose. Each symbolizes an important part of Celie's attitude toward her body, an attitude that must change if she is ever to become free from male brutality. The hair represents Celie's old attitude of self-revulsion, evident in her spontaneous "Ugh." The pubic hair no doubt arouses Celie's memories of her stepfather raping her; he came to her with scissors in hand, ostensibly to have her cut his hair. But inside herself Celie finds a wet rose, a symbol of her new attitude, which includes not only love but an entirely new perspective on God and Creation. Shug teaches Celie to find God in herself, in nature, and in her own feelings, including erotic ones: "God loves all them feelings," Shug says (178). In between are the lips, symbols of Celie's present ambivalence. Celie's first love-making experience with Shug is purely oral. They "kiss and kiss until [they] can't hardly kiss no more" (109). The scene culminates in an ecstasy that is both maternal and infantile for Celie:

> Then I feels something real soft and wet on my breast, feel like one of my little lost babies mouth. Way after while, I act like a lost baby too. (109)

Both maternalism and infantilism provoke negative memories for Celie: her stepfather raped her because her mother did not satisfy him, and her mother died screaming and cursing at Celie, who, pregnant with her first child, could not move fast enough to be an efficient nurse. But Celie does effectively nurse Shug's ills, a compensation for failing her mother, and Shug, in turn, plays a maternal role by teaching Celie how to love. She sucks from Celie's breast as Celie's lost children never did; we must recall that Celie's children were taken from her before she could "nurse" them, leaving her with "breasts full of milk running down [her]self" (13). Celie's orgasm suggests a rebirth or even an initial birth into a world of love, a reenactment of the primal pleasure the child enjoys at the mother's breast. No such rebirth would have been possible without Shug's guidance; certainly one of the most interesting subjects for class discussion regarding *The Color Purple* involves Walker's portrayal of the remarkable relationship between Celie and Shug.

Celie and Shug: Friendship as Theme

Celie has had few close friendships of any kind before Shug enters her life. As we have seen, Celie received little nurturing from her mother; she has also had virtually no close family relationship, particularly after Nettie's departure for Africa. Not only does Celie have no one in whom to confide, but she has no one to help her think of her body differently, not as fragmented and lacking. The example and friendship of Shug Avery, a woman who embodies sexual power, is exactly what Celie needs. In the fairy-tale context mentioned earlier, Shug represents a magic helper, the kind of assistant (like Cinderella's fairy godmother) who seems to be sent to a needy character by special Providence.

It almost seems as though Celie first created Shug in her own imagination. Long before they meet, Celie begins fantasizing about Shug. Even though Shug, as Albert's mistress and the true object of his sexual desire, should be Celie's rival, Celie makes her, in her imagination, an ego ideal. Celie thinks of Shug while Albert rapes her on her wedding night, and even though his lovemaking is as uncaring as her stepfather's, Celie begins to imagine the sexual act with some affection: "I know what he doing to me he done to Shug Avery and maybe she like it. I put my arm around him" (21). Even as an imaginary construct, Shug stirs Celie's first erotic feelings and guides her response to sexual experience. When the real Shug steps into Celie's life, these feelings become activated.

Even though Shug arrives ill and weak, she exudes a sexual power that Celie has never before imagined in woman or man. Given Celie's earlier imaginings of Shug, readers might even wonder if Celie has not projected much of Shug's sexuality on her. In light of Shug's sexuality, Celie reassesses Albert:

> I look at his face. It tired and sad and I notice his chin weak. Not much chin there at all. I have more chin, I think. And his clothes dirty, dirty. When he pull them off, dust rise. (52)

This three-sentence fixation on Albert's chin represents Celie's first inkling of an anatomical superiority and hence is an important first step in her reassessment of her own body. Celie and Shug take turns playing the supporting or maternal role, Celie going first by nursing Shug through her illness. During this nursing process, Celie connects her feelings for Shug to her lost daughter and mother: "I work on her like she a doll or like she Olivia—or like she mama" (57). The doll is an intriguing symbol in this context; the psychoanalytic school of object relations recognizes dolls as

transitional devices, helping girls break out of the pattern of childhood dependence as they begin preparing for the nurturing role they will experience as mothers. With this symbol, we see that Celie has begun to employ
some typical mechanisms of female psychic growth and development.

After Shug's recovery the roles shift, with Shug becoming Celie's nurse.
Celie's illness, however, is not physical, but psychological. Shug awakens
Celie's desire for an identity most explicitly when she sings a song she has
written just for Celie. As Celie gratefully notes, "first time somebody made
something and name it after me" (75). The act of naming something after
Celie assures the integrity of Celie herself: she must be somebody to be the
subject of a song. This act is also Celie's first clue that language need not
come under the jurisdiction of male authority.

Celie's Development: Language and the Needle

Two signs of full psychological growth are the coherent use of language
and the development of aggressivity. *The Color Purple* shows both of these
developments in Celie. Celie's aggressive nature peaks when, shortly after
her early sexual experiences with Shug, the two women find that Albert has
been hiding Nettie's letters. In one memorable scene, Celie contemplates
killing Albert with a razor, but Shug holds her back. Celie then finds herself
following the destructive path of Sofia, longing for revenge:

> All day long I act just like Sofia. I mutter to myself. I stumble bout
> the house crazy for Mr. _____ blood. In my mind, he falling dead
> every which a way. By time night come I can't even speak. Every
> time I open my mouth nothing come out but a little burp. (115)

What meager powers of speech Celie has at this time are overpowered by
her desire for revenge.

Celie learns to control her aggressive desires by two means of sublimation: assertive speech and the substitution of one cutting instrument, the
needle, for another, the razor. The needle symbolizes Celie's hard-won au-
tonomy; by learning to make pants (another appropriately symbolic object), Celie finds a means of freeing herself from Albert's domination. When
Celie does finally confront Albert for his lies and abuse of her, she does so
with assertive speech. Catching Albert off guard, she announces that she,
Nettie, and her children will "whup [his] ass" (181). Celie feels a wonderful
and mysterious power when she shouts Albert down at the dinner table:
"Look like when I open my mouth the air rush in and shape words" (187).
Celie further recognizes the power of her speech when the curse she places

on Albert sinks him into a life-threatening depression. That curse forces Albert to do what Celie has demanded—return Nettie's letters to her.

In tracing this theme, teachers can show students just how coherent Walker's novel is by demonstrating her use of other characters and their stories to comment on Celie's story. Walker uses Mary Agnes to foreshadow this power found in speech. Mary Agnes exemplifies again a woman who sacrifices for another, as Celie and Shug do for each other. In contrast, Sofia's masculine violence leads her to misery. Mary Agnes, once beaten up by her rival Sofia, helps free Sofia from prison by submitting to rape by the warden, the man who had fathered her out of wedlock. The parallels between Mary Agnes and Celie are striking: each is a victim of incest (or so it seems until Nettie reveals to Celie that "Pa is not our pa"), each dominated by a father and a husband. Each also finds freedom and power in her voice. After submitting to the warden, Mary Agnes limps home, her dress torn, a heel from her shoe missing. But in this disheveled condition, she repudiates her derogatory nickname ("Squeak") and demands that she be called by her real name. Not only does Mary Agnes no longer "squeak," she also begins to sing. Soon, she emulates Shug's success, using her voice to give her a new freedom from, and power over, men. She begins to travel, choosing when to move in and out of Harpo's life. Mary Agnes's story, like Celie's, is one of triumph, a tale of a victim gaining moral power over her oppressors. She is Celie's foil in the novel.

Celie's aggressivity is further sublimated in the development of her own form of art: sewing. Artistic creation is a major source of sublimation, of channeling anxieties and frustrations into more positive pursuits. It is no small irony that Celie adopts a traditionally feminine form of art to complete her separation from the violent masculine world; song, the art of Shug and Mary Agnes, is another form of art traditionally used by women for independence. Because sewing is such a typically feminine activity, students are likely to think of Celie's sewing principally as a demonstration of her femininity. But, by sewing, Celie actually narrows the gap between the sexes, making pants for both men and women. Sewing links Celie to woman's primordial power that predates patriarchy. As Adrienne Rich describes it, sewing or weaving emphasizes woman's "transformative power":

> the conversion of raw fibers into thread was connected with the power over life and death; the spider who spins the thread out of her own body, Ariadne providing the clue to the labyrinth, the figures of the Fates or Norns or old spinning-women who cut the thread of life or spin it further, are all associated with this process. (101)

In *The Color Purple,* women do seem to be the mythic purveyors of life and death. Rich further notes that the ultimate symbol of such transformative power is menstrual blood, "which was believed to be transformed into the infant" (101). Menstrual blood is a significant symbol in *The Color Purple,* both as part of Celie's story and as part of her daughter's coming of age in Africa; Walker has explored this symbol in further depth in her recent novel *Possessing the Secret of Joy.* Nettie also recounts such Olinka patriarchal practices as making menstruating women stay out of sight and initiating girls undergoing menarche with a ritual that Nettie describes as "so bloody and painful, I forbid Olivia to even think about it" (172).

Celie's sewing is another aspect of the novel that links her to a tradition of literary women who use their art to cast their "shame" onto their male oppressors. Hawthorne's Hester Prynne is the most prominent member of this group (see "Related Works," below). Celie's art has a more immediate effect than Hester's. Rather than revealing the source of shame to a later generation, Celie's needlework helps Albert face his own shame and even begin a process of self-regeneration. At the end of the book Albert is a new man, capable of loving and sharing. The change in him is symbolized by his sewing, side by side, with Celie. Having had his lifelong view that "men spose to wear the pants" (238) revised, Albert joins Celie in a communal act that, as Celie describes it, helps eradicate the differences that perpetuate sexual domination: "Now us sit sewing and talking and smoking our pipes" (238).

Matrifocality: The Community of Women

Ultimately, Celie learns not to be too dependent on Shug as she develops her identity and, in the process, finds a network of friends "matrifocal" in structure but open to men who can put aside their desire to dominate. Celie's participation in a matrifocal community is another measure of her progress. Early in the novel, before Celie's transformation, Harpo had asked Celie how he might better control Sofia. Shockingly, the abused Celie took the patriarchal line and advised Harpo to beat Sofia. Not only did this advice alienate Sofia from Celie, but it also proved counterproductive to Harpo's desires.

Matrifocality dissolves the old hierarchies that perpetuate dominance and oppression. The loss of such hierarchies changes one's perception of the self in society and in relation to God. Thus, it is only a short step from a belief in women's independence from man to Shug's concept of a nonracial, genderless God. In her version of God, Shug stresses joy and pleasure, not merely surviving and waiting for a reward in heaven, as Celie did earlier. Shug's nongendered God deconstructs the fountainhead of patriarchy, the Lacanian Name-of-the-Father who is the source of law and power, replacing it with a belief that one must become engaged in the Creation as Celie does, creating one's own self, art, and community. Demonstrating a parallel commitment to matrifocality, Sofia and Mary Agnes share Harpo and the responsibility of raising each other's children as a way to maintain freedom while avoiding the permanent dependence on one man that perpetuates masculine power. In Africa, Nettie first assists Corinne in raising Adam and Olivia and, after Corinne's death, replaces her as wife and mother before returning the children to their true mother, Celie. Corinne's suspicions of Nettie indicate her own inability to accept matrifocality; this suspicion may serve as a critique of Corinne's traditional Christianity and of her education at Spelman.

Community is certainly a major theme in *The Color Purple,* where happiness depends less on individual efforts than on belonging to a community of loving supporters and friends. Celie's is a healing community, one which generously bestows forgiveness on all previous offenders and provides a mythic home to which all wanderers can return. This mythic aspect of community is emphasized by the novel's conclusion, when Celie and Nettie are reunited, when Celie regains her children, and when all members of the community are brought together for the first time. The conclusion contains all the mystery and miracle of a fairy tale:

> Then us both start to moan and cry. Us totter toward one nother like us use to do when us was babies. Then us feel so weak when we touch, us knock each other down. But what us care? Us sit and lay there on the porch inside each other's arms. (250)

Celie's determined survival, her construction of selfhood, her entry into a community of women, and her establishment of independence have made such a happy ending possible, not just for her, but for all. How ironic that a man, Harpo, would comment that such a process allows us to "spend the day celebrating each other" (250).

B. Teaching the Work

Certainly, *The Color Purple* has many themes and forms that can stimulate good classroom discussion. But it is also open to a variety of critical perspectives, so a class can be challenged to consider multiple strategies for interpretation. I find it best to begin with a general discussion of themes so students have concrete ideas to work with. One way to initiate a discussion that uses multiple perspectives is by placing students in groups, giving each group a perspective and some suggestions that they might investigate. Here is one model for such a project:

Group One: In what ways is *The Color Purple* a psychological novel? (Suggestions: Consider, for example, Celie's psychological growth in the novel, her changing perspective on sexuality, the importance of her self-examination before a mirror.)

Group Two: In what ways is *The Color Purple* a feminist novel? (Suggestions: Consider, for example, the theme of Celie's discovery and repossession of her own body, the regeneration of Albert, Celie's triumph over sexual abuse, Nettie's report of Olinka rituals for young women, the theme of matrifocality.)

Group Three: In what ways is *The Color Purple* a novel about race? (Suggestions: Consider, for example, the parallels Walker draws between the colonization of the Olinkas and the colonization of African Americans, the possibility that the brutal behavior of many males in the novel is part of the legacy of slavery, the story of Sofia and the mayor's wife and daughter.)

Group Four: In what ways is *The Color Purple* a mythic novel? (Suggestions: Consider, for example, the novel's similarity to fairy tales, the theme of transformation, Celie's sewing as parallel to the Ariadne myth, Shug's role as a magic helper in Celie's life, the Odysseus-like journey and return home of Nettie, Olivia, and Adam.)

Students could approach these topics by using the text alone, but some research will enrich their understanding. For instance, members of Group Two might read the article in the bibliography by Dianne Sadoff to learn about matrifocality; members of Group Four will find Rich's discussion of the Ariadne myth and Walsh's article (also in the bibiography) enlightening. Members of different groups may find themselves working with similar passages or themes from the novel; if so, the exercise provides a good opportunity to show how a reader's perspective can affect interpretation.

Teachers who wish to take a more formalist approach can develop a similar group exercise that focuses attention on clusters of symbols. Here is one possible grouping:

Group One: the mirror, hair, vaginal lips, the rose;
Group Two: letters, song, speech;
Group Three: the Olinka community, menstrual blood, the female body;
Group Four: Celie's needle, sewing, pants.

Clusters can be arranged in other ways as well: Shug's and Mary Agnes's singing can be grouped with Celie's art of sewing. Discussions of these clusters of symbols should give students an appreciation of the novel's integrity: for instance, members of Group Three are likely to see and report parallels between the ways in which Olinka and African American men treat women.

Some students might know that the novel and the movie based on it have been harshly criticized for portraying black men as brutal and inhumane (see Stade in "Best Criticism"). This issue can be very emotional in the classroom, but it can also be stimulating. Teachers can approach this issue by asking the following question: If Walker is portraying black men as brutal, why? What historical evidence validates such a portrayal? Such questions can help students put the novel in a historical context and might lead to research projects on the novel's relation to history. Though *The Color Purple* is set in the twentieth century, it implies that modern black men are less liberated than black women and that men need to look to the examples women have set in order to shake off the lingering effects of slavery. Of course, some might argue that male slaves endured greater psychological abuse; knowing and sometimes seeing their wives raped and being powerless to stop such abuse, male slaves may have been left with a fractured sense of their own masculinity. Whether or not students approve of Walker's portrayal of men, they should realize that the ruthlessness of Albert and Celie's stepfather resembles the pattern of the worst slavemasters, who assumed they owned their slaves body *and* soul.

In its portrayal of Albert's transformation, *The Color Purple* seems to confirm that modern black men are still imprisoned by the legacy of slavery. Albert's transformation challenges readers to reconsider cultural stereotypes about masculinity. In fact, Albert has to surrender many of the forms of behavior associated with that stereotype to become a responsible, loving, and happy individual. To some readers, Albert's transformation may seem unrealistic, but realism is not Walker's genre. *The Color Purple*'s fairy-tale structure invites readers to suspend some of the hard questions that usually apply to realistic fiction and allow for miraculous events (such as the return of Celie's children) to occur.

This question of historical accuracy makes for a challenging writing topic. Other topics for writing might include the role of friendship in the novel, the power of speech, the role of the African subplot, the impact of Celie's epistolary form on readers, or the means women use for empowering themselves.

Study Questions

1. How does Celie change in the course of the novel? What actions in the novel seem to influence her change most?

2. Describe the role in the novel of each of the following symbols:

    (a) mirrors

    (b) song

    (c) speech

    (d) Celie's needle and sewing

    (e) the female body

    (f) the color purple

    (g) Africa/the Olinka community

    (h) the rose

    (i) letters

    (j) menstrual blood

3. How many plots parallel to Celie's do you find in the novel? How do these plots enhance or comment on Celie's story?

4. What roles do friendship and community play in Celie's growth?

5. In what ways is the novel like a fairy tale? What events seem improbable or miraculous like fairy-tale events? Why do you suppose Walker wanted to use parallels to fairy tales?

6. How does the novel portray black men? Does the portrayal seem fair or accurate to you?

7. How do Celie's language and the epistolary (letter) form affect your response to the novel?

8. Why is Celie's sexual relationship with Shug so important to her development as a character?

9. Does the novel seem to comment at all on the heritage of black Americans? Is the impact of slavery an implicit or explicit theme in the novel?

10. Is Nettie's story of life in Africa thematically appropriate to the novel? How or how not?

11. To what degree is *The Color Purple* a psychological novel?

12. To what degree is *The Color Purple* a feminist novel?

13. To what degree is *The Color Purple* a religious novel?

14. To what degree is *The Color Purple* a novel about racial inequality?

15. What do you regard as the most important scene in the novel? How does that scene affect your reading of the novel or your response to the novel's characters?

16. What are the novel's most important themes? Are those themes relevant to today's world?

C. Bibliographies

1. Related Works

Carter, Angela. *The Bloody Chamber.* Harmondsworth: Penguin, 1981. Carter retells fairy tales from a feminist perspective. Because *The Color Purple* has a fairy-tale structure of its own, the two books offer interesting parallels.

Hawthorne, Nathaniel. *The Scarlet Letter.* 1850. Reprint, ed. Harry Levin. Boston: Houghton Mifflin, 1960. Like Celie, Hester Prynne is a victim in a male-dominated society. Both women use sewing to transcend their sufferings, achieve independence, and assert their strength.

Morrison, Toni. *The Bluest Eye.* New York: Holt, Rinehart, 1970. Parallels between Celie and Pecola are astonishing and horrifying. Each is raped and impregnated shortly after puberty by a father figure. Morrison's novel, however, does not follow Pecola into later life. Thus, where Walker gives us a fairy tale, Morrison offers grim realism.

————. *Beloved.* New York: New American Library, 1987. The brutal treatment Sethe receives from the plantation over–seer and his nephews rivals Celie's abuse by Alfred and her stepfather. Both women are deprived by domineering men of opportunities to nurse a child of their own.

Smith, Lee. *Fair and Tender Ladies.* New York: Ballantine, 1988. There are interesting parallels between Ivy Rowe and Celie as characters. Both tell their stories by using the epistolary method; both are modern women who try to assert their identities without abandoning all of the traditional roles women play. The development of sexual identities in the two characters is another interesting similarity.

2. Best Criticism

Abbandonato, Linda. "'A View from Elsewhere': Subversive Sexuality and the Rewriting of the Heroine's Story in *The Color Purple.*" *PMLA* 106 (1991): 1106–15. This article closely examines the novel's place in the epistolary tradition, citing parallels to such works as Richardson's *Clarissa.*

Cheung, King-Kok. "Don't Tell: Imposed Silences in *The Color Purple* and *The Woman Warrior.*" *PMLA* 103 (1988): 162–74. This article elaborates the theme, cited in the above discussion, of woman's struggle to break through silence and find a way of speaking for herself. Cheung's comparisons of Walker's novel to *The Woman Warrior* serve as a reminder of how women in many cultures face barriers of language and silence.

Dalsimer, Katharine. *Female Adolescence: Psychoanalytic Reflections on Literature.* New Haven: Yale University Press, 1986. Dalsimer is a psychoanalyst, so readers with no background in the subject might find her a bit difficult. Also, there is no discussion in the book of *The Color Purple*. Still, the book offers rich insights into the psychology of women and especially of young female friendships.

Fifer, Elizabeth. "The Dialect and Letters of *The Color Purple*." In *Contemporary American Women Writers: Narrative Stratagies,* ed. Catherine Rainwater and William J. Scheick, 247–63. Lexington: University of Kentucky Press, 1985. Fifer offers one of the best available treatments of language in *The Color Purple*. She makes fine points about the novel's epistolary method and the problems that language presents for Celie.

Hymer, Sharon. "Narcissistic Friendships." *Psychoanalytic Review* 71 (1984): 423–39. This is a very readable piece of psychoanalytic scholarship, which indicates the valuable role a "mirroring" friendship can play in the life of a girl. Hymer's concepts give solid psychological grounding to the impact of Shug's friendship on Celie.

Ostriker, Alicia. "Body Language: Imagery of the Body in Women's Poetry." In *The State of the Language,* ed. Leonard Michaels and Christopher Ricks, 247–63. Berkeley: University of California Press, 1980. Focusing on women poets such as Sylvia Plath and Anne Sexton, Ostriker makes us aware of how intensely conscious women writers are of the body. Her major conclusions are certainly relevant to Walker also.

Rich, Adrienne. *Of Woman Born: Motherhood as Experience and Institution.* New York: Norton, 1976. This classic work of feminist thinking provides excellent background for several of the themes Walker portrays in *The Color Purple*.

Ross, Daniel W. "Celie in the Looking-Glass: The Desire for Selfhood in *The Color Purple*." *Modern Fiction Studies* 34 (1988): 69–84. A longer version of the present essay. It traces in depth, with more emphasis on psychoanalytic themes, the central problems of Celie's attempt to establish her own identity.

Sadoff, Dianne F. "Black Matrilineage: The Case of Alice Walker and Zora Neale Hurston." *Signs* 11 (1985): 4–26. By adopting Harold Bloom's theory of poetic influence, Sadoff traces the relationship between Walker and Hurston and explains the role of matrifocality in African American women's communities.

Stack, Carol B. "Sex Roles and Survival Strategies in an Urban Black Community." In *Women, Culture, and Society,* ed. Michelle Zimbalist Rosaldo and Louise Lamphere, 113–28. Stanford, Calif.: Stanford University Press, 1974. Stack is an anthropologist who has studied the "adaptive strategies" used by urban black women to create a community of helpers and caregivers. Mary Agnes's willingness to help raise Sofia's children while she is in jail provides an excellent example of the way black women assist each other.

Stade, George. "Womanist Fiction and Male Characters." *Partisan Review* 52 (1985): 264–70. Though very biased, Stade presents key issues in the debate about the novel's male characters.

Wall, Wendy. "Lettered Bodies and Corporeal Texts in *The Color Purple.*" *Studies in American Fiction* 16 (1988): 83–97. Readers interested in the theme of women's mutilated bodies will find this essay informative.

Walsh, Margaret. "The Enchanted World of *The Color Purple.*" *Southern Quarterly* 25 (1987): 89–101. Though the article has some significant weaknesses, its analysis of the fairy-tale elements in the structure of *The Color Purple* is an important contribution. Many undergraduates will find it accessible.

3. Other Sources

Berlant, Lauren. "Race, Gender, and Nation in *The Color Purple.*" *Critical Inquiry* 14 (1988): 831–59.

Elsley, Judy. "'Nothing Can Be Sole or Whole that Has Not Been Rent': Fragmentation in the Quilt and *The Color Purple.*" *Women's Studies* 9, no. 2 (1992): 71–81.

Gates, Henry Louis, Jr. "Color Me Zora: Alice Walker's (Re)Writing of the Speakerly Text." In *Intertextuality and Contemporary American Fiction,* ed. Patrick O'Donnell and Robert Con Davis, 144–67. Baltimore: Johns Hopkins University Press, 1989.

Hite, Molly. "Romance, Marginality, Matrilineage: Alice Walker's *The Color Purple* and Zora Neale Hurston's *Their Eyes Were Watching God.*" *Novel* 22 (1989): 257–73.

Proudfit, Charles L. "Celie's Search for Identity: A Psychoanalytic Developmental Reading of Alice Walker's *The Color Purple.*" *Contemporary Literature* 32 (1991): 12–37.

Tavormina, M. Teresa. "Dressing the Spirit: Clothworking and Language in *The Color Purple.*" *Journal of Narrative Technique* 16 (1986): 220–30.

Tucker, Lindsey. "Alice Walker's *The Color Purple:* Emergent Woman, Emergent Text." *Black American Literary Forum* 22 (1988): 81–95.

Walker, Alice. *The Color Purple.* New York: Washington Square Press, 1981.

———. *Possessing the Secret of Joy.* New York: Harcourt, Brace, 1992.

Mexican American Literature

Preface

"I live smack in the fissure between two worlds," says San Diego visual artist Guillermo Gómez-Peña, "in the infected wound: half a block from the end of Western Civilization and four miles from the start of the Mexican-American border, the northernmost point of Latin America."[1] The four chapters in this section, and the literary texts they discuss, address the fractured world suggested by Gómez-Peña.

Rudolfo Anaya's novel *Bless Me, Ultima* (1972) presents the growth of a young Hispanic boy, torn between two ways of growing up. Luis Valdez's play *Zoot Suit* (1978) captures the conflict of southwestern Chicano experience in Henry Reyna, who is simultaneously drawn to his family and his peers. Richard Rodriguez's autobiography *Hunger of Memory* (1982) portrays the author's assimilation into the American mainstream at the cost of alienation from his family, his past, and his ethnic heritage. And Sandra Cisneros's *The House on Mango Street* (1983) is also, like *Bless Me, Ultima*, a story of growing up, but involves a quest to find a house and to overcome the barriers presented by her Hispanic background and her gender.

Readers will discover rich and diverse critical perspectives in these four chapters. Antonio C. Márquez focuses his discussion of *Hunger of Memory* in terms of Wernor Sollors's notion of ethnicity as an "invention," showing how Rodriguez's autobiography achieves "a sense of self not grounded on a collective ethnic identity, but on a metaphor of self as writer and instrument of change." Juan Bruce-Novoa shows how *Bless Me, Ultima* is a novel "about learning to read," one in which readers and the main character Antonio must go "beyond passive reception into a praxis, an application in one's own life of the lessons learned." Julián Olivares's analysis of *The House on Mango Street* places the novel in the context of a male Chicano "bildungsroman," but shows how it overturns "masculine discourse" in favor of the writer's commitment to her own "writing" and "her solidarity with the people, the women, on Mango Street." And Elizabeth Ramírez introduces a critical apparatus for understanding *Zoot Suit* by providing a history of both Chicano theater and the actual historical events in Los Angeles, the Zoot Suit Riots and the Sleepy Lagoon murder trial of 1942, upon which the play is based.

Finally, readers will find a myriad of teaching strategies focusing on genre, cultural context, and intertextual connections, among other things. Márquez asks students to look at *Hunger of Memory* in terms of immigration, assimilation, the urban and rural experience, and perhaps most interestingly, in the context of "cultural memory": how are *Hunger of Memory, Bless Me, Ultima, The House on Mango Street,* and *The Moths and Other Stories* related to family history and cultural memory? Ramírez asks students to create short "*actos*" and dramatize them as a means of understanding Chicano drama, while Olivares and Bruce-Novoa wisely ask students to develop a "sensitivity" to ethnic writers by writing and sharing a narrative of a specific experience. As these four essays suggest, there are a number of ways of looking at these and other texts either in terms of genre (for example, *Hunger of Memory, Black Boy,* and *America Is in the Heart* provide interesting variations on ethnic autobiography) or theme (for example, family, as in *Their Eyes Were Watching God, The Joy Luck Club,* and *Zoot Suit*).

Notes

1. Guillermo Gómez-Peña, "Documented/Undocumented," in *Multi-Cultural Literacy: Opening the American Mind,* ed. Rick Simonson and Scott Walker (St. Paul: Graywolf Press, 1988), p. 127.

Learning to Read (and/in) Rudolfo Anaya's *Bless Me, Ultima*

JUAN BRUCE-NOVOA

A. Analysis of Themes and Forms

Rudolfo Anaya's *Bless Me, Ultima* is a bildungsroman, a growing-up text about a young boy passing through rites of passage that eventually turn him into a mature product of that experience. The specifics of how, where, when, and with whom not only determine who and what the adult character becomes, but communicate to both the character and the reader the cultural values that serve as the code of conduct—the code of personal and social identity—that the author has chosen to convey. Whether or not the author judges, and wants readers to judge, that code as admirable and even exemplary is evidenced in the presentation of the experience; that is, the experience is beneficial, leading to triumph within the narrative time or implied for the future, or, in cases in which the protagonist suffers defeat, the circumstances are shown to be wrongfully oppressive of the positive ideals. Anaya clearly intends his novel to be read as a positive message of a lesson that merits learning, or—in the case of the narrator/protagonist, the adult Antonio—relearning.

Bless Me, Ultima is thus a didactic novel. Lessons are taught through Antonio's maturing process. More than simply relating an interesting story about a boy growing up in World War II New Mexico, the novel offers readers a useful response to their own time and place. In other words, the novel calls for a reading that then goes beyond passive reception into a praxis, an application in one's own life of the lessons learned. The text's values, a code of behavior, are to be embodied by the reader, who is likely suffering from similar, even essentially the same, ills as the character who seeks an answer. Given this, the question arises: what is this lesson?

Bless Me, Ultima—a book so replete with fascinating details and diverse thematic lines that even experienced critics follow tangents that reveal more about themselves than about the novel—is about learning to read. Trite, but true. Antonio, from the first pages portrayed as a boy troubled by the familial conflict in which he lives and in search of the knowledge to understand his identity with respect to his specific context—familial and social—

learns how to read. But lest we fall into one of the traps set by the author, we must qualify the statement: while reading is often associated with print, and print in turn is linked to reason, linear logic, and the differentiation of elements into oppositional categories—this is this and not that—Antonio's reading lesson goes beyond to the great text of signs through which all life is experienced. And those who associate reading with the rational must be reminded that in the signifying code that Antonio learns, letters are magical. Instead of limiting one to strictly defined meanings, true reading, as taught to Antonio, sensitizes one to the great web of interrelated meanings that binds all living things into a mutually dependent/supportive system. Reading for Antonio goes from the semantics of oppositional difference to the semiotics of similarity, from suffering contingency to perceiving and fostering coherence, from a rationality of perception to an ecology of participation—from understanding to sympathy.

Given that the lesson is imparted to readers as well as to Antonio, readers also receive instruction on the reading process. And just as in Antonio's case, readers can easily derive superficially partial messages from the "facts" of the content. This is the danger in attempting to list the novel's central themes or key incidents. It is too easy to misread them.

For example, a significant context for Antonio's passage into maturity is the conflict between his mother's farming family, the Lunas, and his father's pastoral family, the Márez. These are two age-old occupations in New Mexico, so together they represent facets of a heterogeneous Hispanic tradition. However, for Antonio the tradition of settled land cultivation seems impossible to reconcile with the equally strong tradition of working livestock on the open range. Readers can fall into viewing the two in the terms used by the characters themselves, and at times by the narrator: that of the freedom loving Márez (the name means "The Sons of Sea") and their opposite, the firmly rooted Lunas (Moon).

The binary opposition of apparent opposites is reinforced by the implicit values assigned to each side. The Márez are MALE, while the Lunas, through the female quality associated with the moon, are FEMININE. Thus, the question of Antonio's passage into maturity becomes one of having to decide between his father or mother, with added implications about his own sexuality. Will he be forever a "Mama's boy," or will he cut her apron strings to go out into the realm of men? Goodness is associated with the former; evil with the latter. The Lunas are quiet, calm, religious men; the Márez, loud, unsettled, and hard drinking.

This opposition is unavoidable for Antonio; it is evident in the location of his home, on a hill outside town, neither in the fertile valley nor fully in the "llano" (plains). There, he performs chores—familial training rituals—associated with both parental lines: he feeds the livestock, but also ekes out a garden for his mother from the stony and arid fringe of the plain. In the opening paragraph of the novel, although seemingly fully immersed in the wonderful memory of Ultima, the narrator conveys Antonio's spatial orientation before her actual entrance into the text by opposing the "sun-baked llano" to "the green river valley" under "the blue bowl which was the white sun's home" (1).[1]

This symbolic distribution of space echoes Alfonso Ortiz's explanation of the three concentric environments of Tewa people of San Juan Pueblo. The women's inner space "consists of the village, the farmlands, and other lowlands near the village." This inner space, called the navel of the earth mother, is subsectioned into the four directions. A second circle, "of hills, mesas, and washes, is a mediating environment in every important sense." While open to women and men, "women and children did not usually go unless accompanied by men," who were in charge of the area. "Both hunting and gathering are done there, by both sexes. In a spiritual sense, it is an area defined by four sacred mesas, or flat-topped buttes, one in each direction." It is believed that entrances to the underworld exist in these hills, making them dangerous to uninitiated women and children. The outermost circle is the "clear cut domain of men . . . the destination of purely male religious pilgrimages." The Zunis of the region go further by locating four oceans "bounding the earth's circular coastline," as Weigle and White have explained in *The Lore of New Mexico*.

Antonio's fears arise from being torn by the conflicting pull between the inner and outer circles, and by the fact that his family inhabits an in-between space from which it is expected that he will choose one of two directions. However, Ultima arrives, the aging wise woman, and immediately Antonio begins to see his surroundings differently. This is reflected in a subtle change in the description of his environment. When Ultima takes Antonio's hand for the first time, his first impression is that of a "whirlwind" sweeping around him; that is, the circular orientation envelops this boy who previously has been torn between two poles in linear opposition. Then the narrator declares: "Her eyes swept the surrounding hills and through them I saw for the first time the wild beauty of our hills and the magic of the green river" (10). Her eyes, in their circular sweep, place into Antonio's space a geological presence that he, in his disorienting turmoil, had not seen, the hills—the characteristic landmark of the second Tewa circle. To reinforce the circular sensation, Anaya repeats the circular sweep, now with Antonio's eyes fused with Ultima. Yet, in a technique repeated throughout the novel, when the apprentice repeats the mentor's lesson, the perceived space expands even more. For example, Antonio sees not just hills, but the "wild beauty of the hills," to which yet another important feature of the environment is then added: "the magic of the river." Ultima teaches Antonio not to see merely what is there, but to interpret what he sees by recognizing attributes that the sign conveys—in other words, he learns to read, not just see. That act profoundly changes a boy who has been living in fear of his environment:

> My nostrils quivered as I felt the song of the mockingbirds and the drone of the grasshoppers mingle with the pulse of the earth. The four directions of the llano met in me, and the white sun shone on my soul. The granules of sand at my feet and the sun and the sky above me seemed to dissolve into one strange, complete being. (10–11)

Antonio experiences a mystical union with the cosmos—an epiphany—as he is converted into a classic *axis mundi,* a cosmic center of all directions, horizontal and vertical, in which nature, both animal and mineral, fuse in his being. This experience is what the novel would have readers eventually reach.

The lesson, however, is hard for readers or Antonio to grasp. Hence, it must be repeated over and over as Antonio passes through two-plus years of his passage into maturity. A similar expansion of his space comes in Chapter 2. In Chapter 1, readers are told that Antonio can see only two structures above the village: the church tower and the schoolhouse (6). These structures represent the two forces on his immediate horizon: he will start school and a little later begin preparing for his First Communion. Then, in Chapter 2, after witnessing the killing of a crazed war veteran, Antonio looks over to the town again, but this time he sees, besides the church and school, the "town's water tower" (21). Readers should recall that the discoveries provoked by Ultima's arrival also culminated in the presence of water, the magic of the river. Antonio is being led slowly but surely to discover, in Chapter 11, that the town is surrounded by water, a fact he associates with an ancient legend about the evil that pervades the world. It is no coincidence that it also reflects the Zuni concept of cosmic space.

This is not the place to trace each incident in Antonio's expanding ability to read his environment. A few key examples must suffice. In one of his frequent revelatory dreams, Antonio sees his own birth, to which the Lunas brought the fruits of the earth from their farm, while the Márez brought the implements of a cowboy's profession; the families almost battled over the right to claim the child's future. All through the novel Antonio worries about his destiny. Will he be a farmer priest as his mother dreams, or the son his father desires to help him fulfill his dream of moving to California? The opposition, however, is one of those misleading plays of signs that Antonio and readers must learn to read at a different level, where differences are revealed as parts of a whole. The families actually are not diametrical opposites. As mentioned above, they represent traditions common to New Mexican Hispano communities. Antonio is not torn between an Anglo and a Chicano world, but between two ways of being Chicano, ways which the Chicanos involved cannot, or will not, bring into harmony.

Significantly, however, the Márez way of life is no longer feasible—and this fact alludes to the encroachment of modern society, the one too simplistically called Anglo by some. Barbed wire killed the open range in the nineteenth century; then came trains and highways. The horse itself was supplanted by the car. Thus, while the Márez retain their dream of free movement, it has led them to the degradation of migrant labor. They pretend to be free wanderers, but their movements actually are determined by the demand for cheap workers. The irony is, of course, that the Márez have become second-class farmers, performing harvest chores on other people's land. When one of their sons is killed by a tractor, they lack even the consolation of knowing that he died working the family land. They are victims of exploitation, but also victims of stubborn nostalgia for an illusion they call tradition. The Lunas, however, have adapted to modernity—they drive pickups and use modern farm implements—yet they continue to cultivate in traditional ways, following the cycles of the moon, their namesake. Unlike the Márez, the Lunas remain themselves, true to their own tradition.

Antonio and readers can learn this lesson by observing events carefully. Yet, in case they miss it, Ultima comes to the rescue again. She holds the key to Antonio's future because she buried his afterbirth, a folk ritual common among rural peoples all over the world, in which an infant's destiny is determined by fixing its fleshy link to creation in a certain spot. Thus, when in another of Antonio's dreams he asks where he can find a permanent innocence—he is troubled with the conflicts around him that he associates with evil—Ultima tells him to look not to the quarreling families present at his birth, but to the moment in which his parents joined in love's embrace to conceive him. In other words, she instructs Antonio, as Anaya instructs readers, to search for the harmony in creative union, not the disintegration of focusing on difference.

This key image exemplifies Anaya's demand that images be read carefully to discover a depth of implications beyond the obvious. The anti-farmer father is cultivating the fertile soil of a Luna woman, metaphorically plowing and planting seed. At the same time, the mother is metaphorically the mount for her rider husband, leading him to free himself beyond his bodily limits. Like a Yin–Yang meshing of apparently opposite forces, the mother and father fuse into each other's metaphoric codes to form a hybrid product, Antonio, the new sign of mediated differences. Readers learn that the desired origin lies in harmony and love, not conflict; in synthesis, not resistance.

In one of Antonio's worst nightmares, he dreams the apocalypse of his small world torn apart by the opposition of cosmic forces in raging conflict. While his mother claims him as baptized in the moon's water, his father calls her a liar, insisting that the baptismal water came from the salty sea. At this point Ultima intervenes again, calms the storm, and proceeds to teach us how to read the same signs correctly.

> Stand, Antonio, she commanded, and I stood. You both know, she spoke to my father and my mother, that the sweet water of the moon which falls as rain is the same water that gathers into rivers and flows to fill the seas. Without the waters of the moon to replenish the oceans there would be no oceans. And the same salt waters of the oceans are drawn by the sun to the heavens, and in turn become again the waters of the moon. Without the sun there would be no waters formed to slake the dark earth's thirst.
>
> The waters are one, Antonio. I looked into her bright, clear eyes and understood her truth.
>
> You have been seeing only parts, she finished, and not looking beyond into the great cycle that binds us all.
>
> Then there was peace in my dreams and I could rest. (113)

Other characters misread their signs as well. The father thinks that he has lost a freedom that his fellow plainsmen still enjoy. Yet, as seen above, the wandering Márez are nothing more than slaves in the migrant-farmworkers stream. The father's dream of going to the idyllic vineyards of California rings ironic to readers who know that in the West Coast grape industry Chicanos are migrant pickers. The mother's dream is that Antonio will become a priest. She reads her son's intelligence and academic success as signs of his religious vocation. Yet Ultima reveals that the items the infant Antonio picked, when offered the tools of life, were pen and paper. The mother takes this to signify a priest's learning, while readers know that Antonio's true vocation is to become a writer.

Readers, even critics, have often misread the novel as a conflict between a utopian past and a realistic present. The lesson of the Márez could affirm this position. The Márez hang on to their wandering ways and fall victim to the exploitation of the new economic reality. The Lunas, however, survive by adapting to circumstance—a lesson learned from the founder of their family enclave, a married Catholic priest. Anaya's position is that of adaptation. Antonio learns not an old role—he will be neither cowboy nor farmer, nor "*curandero*" like Ultima—but a new one, that of writer. And he is a writer, a craftsman with the tools of sign inscription, not an oral storyteller as some would like him to be, because his tools are a writer's tools. Moreover, his mentor is too taciturn to be the model of a storyteller. Also, what he produces is a text we read, not a story to which we listen—although perhaps here too we should apply Ultima's lesson and admit the possibility that his craft is that of putting into writing the oral tradition.

We must not forget that the reading lesson includes praxis. In Antonio's case, the praxis of correct reading is to recreate the sign system of his experience, a system in which Ultima is the center and catalyst of activity. In this way he keeps his promise, made at the end of Chapter 1, to never let her die. While the surface signs seem to condemn her to death as the novel ends, Antonio the narrator resuscitates her through his writing. This is the irony of his statement when he says that the gunshot that kills Ultima and her owl shattered his "childhood into a thousand fragments that long ago stopped falling and are now dusty relics gathered in distant memories" (245).

Faced with the collapse of his world at the end of the narrative, Antonio the narrator apparently does not yet recognize in himself the power to restore the unity and order about which Ultima so often instructed him. This ironic distance between what the narrator believes and what the author has allowed the reader to learn creates a test of the reader's ability to read beyond surfaces to the greater cycle of signs in that space of the novel where words perpetually repeat themselves and the plot can be renewed over and over. In literary space, Ultima, though she dies, actually lives forever. Perhaps Antonio the narrator will have to become Antonio the reader.

We must not close before discussing Ultima's character. She also is the object of the general lesson of reading beyond the surface. From the start she is introduced as a *curandera,* or traditional curing woman, although some people think she is a witch. Antonio is convinced that she is the former, and readers are led to agree. Yet, in a key chapter in which Ultima cures one of the Lunas who is dying from a spell laid on him by three witches—an act that sets off the deadly conflict that drives the plot to its violent end—Ultima utilizes practices that most readers will associate with witchcraft. She fabricates dolls to represent the enemy witches, piercing the dolls with pins to make them waste away and die. These are signs of witchcraft. Later, when Ultima is put to the test—crossed pins to block a witch's passage—Antonio discovers that Ultima probably passed the test by distracting the witnesses while someone removed the pins. In other words, Ultima could well be a witch. Once again, readers must read beyond the system of binary opposites. As Ultima teaches Antonio, none of this is really a matter of clear choices, but of a system of harmonious balances. What appears to be evil is a temporary imbalance that must right itself. Whether Ultima is called a witch or a *curandera* is almost irrelevant. What she achieves is beneficial because it restores harmony.

Critics have tried to read *Bless Me, Ultima* within a historical context of the plot, the 1940s. Again, this is a superficial reading that limits the text. True, the specifics of the problems caused by the draft and the effects of combat on veterans, the exodus of young people to the cities, the encroachment of modernity with the changing realities of labor, and so on, were problems of the period. However, the novel's proper historical context is the 1960s, when it was written. The same problems were painfully present: the Vietnam War, the mobility of the counterculture generation, and the full-blown effects of the mass-media revolution. Social disorientation seemed rampant. Just as the country was suffering from a questioning of traditional definitions of the national identity, Chicanos were questioning who they were, where they were going, and the history that had produced them. The questions were usually stated in radically binary terms: Us versus Them. Conflict and violence were often the result. Yet the 1960s also saw responses of a different sort, those that proposed love, harmony, and the brotherhood of all creatures in a totally integrated ecology of resources. Proponents of this latter tendency often turned to "non-occidental" responses such as Zen Buddhism, the wisdom of the *I-Ching*, or Native American beliefs. *Bless Me, Ultima* belongs to the counterculture of brotherhood based on respect for all creation. In these terms, it is short-sighted to couch the novel in terms of some kind of Chicano resistance to the dominant American culture. Anaya produced the novel when resistance to traditional limits was so common that it was a major trend of 1960s American culture. Moreover, the kind of binary opposition the novel attacks was a feature of much Chicano rhetoric, so in a real way, if *Bless Me, Ultima* resists something, it is the burgeoning Chicano militancy of ethnic resistance.

B. Teaching the Work

1. There are various sources of background information that will help decipher Anaya's novel. Among several texts by the author, the best are "Rudolfo A. Anaya" in *Contemporary Authors Autobiography Series* 4 (1986): 15–28; and "The Writer's Landscape: Epiphany in Landscape," *Latin American Literary Review* 5, no. 10 (1977): 98–102. Two good interviews with the author can be found in Bruce-Novoa, *Chicano Authors: Inquiry by Interview* (1980); and David Johnson and David Apodaca, "Myth and the Writer: A Conversation with Rudolfo Anaya," in *New America* 3, no. 3 (Spring 1979): 76–85. For the folklore context, consult Marta Weigle and Peter White, *The Lore of New Mexico* (1988). For the specific topic of witchcraft in New Mexico, see Marc Simmons, *Witchcraft in the Southwest: Spanish and Indian Supernaturalism on the Rio Grande* (1974). For Native American myths of the region, see Alfonso Ortiz, "San Juan Pueblo," and Dennis Tedlock, "Zuni Religion and World View," both in *Handbook of North American Indians, Volume 9: Southwest* (1979). It should be noted that in 1994, Time Warner Company became Anaya's publishing house, releasing *Bless Me, Ultima* in both hardcover and paperback editions, as well as a Spanish translation, *Bendíceme, Ultima,* for the U.S. market.

2. *Bless Me, Ultima* lends itself to varied interpretations. One can approach it from a perspective of mythical archetypes, applying the concepts of Carl Jung or Joseph Campbell. The novel thus becomes the story of the apprenticeship of the heroic figure in his voyage from childhood into maturity. Ultima is his guide, instructing him, leading him through ritual training, and even calling on him to do battle with the forces of evil. During one of these trials, Antonio and the readers discover his other, his sacred warrior's name, Juan, an occurrence common in heroic voyages to manhood. Hector Calderón has done a similar archetypal and mythical reading à la Northrop Frye. In his method the text is not a novel, but a romance, with a different set of rules and expectations. While the novel is supposed to be a faithful picture of real life and customs, the romance is a heroic fable about fabulous persons and things. One must be careful when using this approach, however, to avoid condemning Anaya to the reactionary position of a nostalgic dreamer in search of a golden age no longer, and perhaps never, possible in reality. Anaya is clearly conscious of the malaise of modernity. He does not reject the realities of the nuclear age, as Calderón seems to imply, but rather offers, like other 1960s counterculture writers, an alternative based in the ancient wisdom of peoples and not limited to the rationalism that

sees anything but reason as escapist fantasy. It is no coincidence, in a book so concerned with shapes and spatial configurations, that the whirlwind is associated both with Ultima and the witches, nor that the same design can be traced in the windmill, the object upon which Antonio's father performs his recuperation-of-cosmic-harmony ritual, nor that the father then explains to Antonio that the atomic bomb is inherently neither good nor evil, just another force in nature—and, of course, the shape of the atomic-bomb explosion is yet another avatar of the ubiquitous whirlwind. If one has learned the reading lesson of the text, then the construction of such neat binary opposites, such as golden age versus nuclear age, should be immediately suspicious.

The study of binary oppositions is an obvious approach, since Anaya constructs so many in the novel. Yet, as pointed out above, this is misleading, since the oppositions are continually revealed as not mutually exclusive. Rather than pursue the oppositions for their own sake, one might profit by applying to them Jacques Derrida's sense of the mutual dependency of all binaries. Or even better, one can learn directly from the novel its message of synthesis and harmony within an ecological unity of a total system. While some critics may see this as nostalgic romanticism, others will see it as the wisdom of the ages. Enrique Lamadrid's essay is most enlightening in this respect. He recognizes that Anaya sets up the binary opposition in order to highlight the mediating position and function of Ultima and Antonio. By extension, the ideological message is then a call for a politics of mediation in the face of cultural forces that produce destructive conflict by insisting on the confrontation of oppositional absolutes. If one historicizes the text in the period of its creation, the 1960s, one can appreciate Anaya's response to the divisive forces that utilized the rhetoric of radical confrontation. His message is one of harmony, of sympathy for others, including enemies against which, when all other alternatives are impossible, one fights to the death.

3. Students can be assigned a short essay about a situation in which they have found themselves between two opposing positions, each of which had reason to expect their loyalty. In class, students can be asked to create a microcosm of a community divided into three parts. They must write the rules of two of the parts in terms of binary opposites: that is, light/dark, English/Other language, male/female, old/young, and so on. The third area is defined as the space of mediation. Then have them act out conflicts over specific areas of opposition, but communicating only through a designated mediator, who represents both sides.

Ask students to identify "before" and "after" situations in the novel, in which a description or an action is repeated, yet with some degree of alteration the second time around. Have them explain what has happened between the two scenes to produce the change. Have them consider how this technique affects the meaning of the narrative.

Have students do some historical research into the 1960s. Groups could be assigned different foci. The goal is for them to understand the atmosphere of great turmoil and radical conflict over social values. One group should focus on the counterculture's search for alternative social and spiritual models. Another group should explore the vogue of the mentor from another culture, that is, figures such as Don Juan from the Carlos Castaneda series, the Maharishi Yogi and his brand of Transcendental Meditation, the figure of the Master in the television series *Kung Fu,* or the figure of the poet/guide in the work of Alurista. Then have a discussion about Ultima in light of what they find.

Possible paper topics may develop from the following process: analyze what elements in the novel can be attributed to Anglo cultural influences; then consider if they actually provoke the conflicts in Antonio's life. Could they have occurred just as well without the Anglo presence?

Assign the reading of Tomás Rivera's . . . *y no se lo tragó la tierra.* Have students reconsider the Márez family as a symbol of freedom in the light of Rivera's sense of severely limited spaces associated with the migrant worker's social reality. Have students read Rodolfo Gonzales's *Yo soy Joaquín/I Am Joaquín;* this classic of Chicano literature—from the same period as *Bless Me, Ultima*—also constructs a series of binary opposition in harsh conflict. Have students consider the difference between the cultural responses called for in these two texts.

C. Bibliographies

1. Related Works

Baca, Jimmy Santiago. *Martín and Meditations on the South Valley.* New York: New Directions, 1986. Baca's collections of poems also trace a boy's development into manhood in the same area of New Mexico in which Anaya's works are set. It can be read as a version of the same experience through a darker lens.

Candelaria, Nash. *Inheritance of Strangers.* Binghamton, N.Y.: BilingualPress/ Editorial Bilingüe, 1985. Candelaria's novel, set in New Mexico at the end of the nineteenth century, narrates the impact of U.S. encroachment on the traditional Hispanic society. Candelaria, however, is much more a realist in style.

Nichols, John. *The Milagro Beanfield War.* New York: Holt, Rinehart and Winston, 1978. In this novel, Nichols creates a satirical view of the same cultural concerns and historical conflicts treated by Anaya. His humor undermines the seriousness found in many Chicano treatments of the subject.

Rivera, Tomás. . . . *y no se lo tragó la tierra / And the Earth Did Not Part.* Berkeley: Quinto Sol Press, 1971. Rivera tells a very different version of a Chicano boy's development, set on the migrant farmworker circuit coming out of Texas. The style is much more fragmented and oral. There is little of the magical. This novel was awarded the Quinto Sol Prize a year before *Bless Me, Ultima* won it.

Silko, Leslie Marmon. *Ceremony.* New York: Viking, 1977. A novel about Native Americans in New Mexico under similar acculturation pressures as those experienced by Antonio and his family. It offers a good comparison in the treatment of the landscape, the relationship of people to the sacred earth, and the function of oral tradition in a situation of changing values.

2. Best Criticism

Bruce-Novoa, Juan. "Portraits of Chicano Artists as Young Men: The Making of the 'Author' in Three Chicano Novels." *Festival Floricanto II,* 150–61. Albuquerque: Pajarito Press, 1977. One of the most influential interpretations of the novel. The author shows the novel to be about the apprenticeship of a writer, Antonio, who fulfills his training with Ultima by becoming a novelist, the author of his own text.

Cantú, Roberto. "Apocalypse as an Ideological Construct: The Storyteller's Art in *Bless Me, Ultima.*" In *Rudolfo A. Anaya: Focus on Criticism,* ed. César A. González-T., 13–63. Highly insightful article by one of the best informed scholars of Anaya's production. In spite of the unsubstantiated claim that the text is that of an oral storyteller, much valuable information can be garnered from the lengthy essay.

Cazemajou, Jean. "The Search for a Center: The Shamanic Journey of Mediators in Anaya's Trilogy, *Bless Me, Ultima; Heart of Aztlán;* and *Tortuga.*" In *Rudolfo A. Anaya: Focus on Criticism,* ed. César González-T., 254–73. The leading French critic on Anaya's production traces the fundamental theme of sacred-world centeredness in Anaya's major novels.

González-T., César A., ed. *Rudolfo A. Anaya: Focus on Criticism.* La Jolla: Lalo Press, 1990. The best collection of critical writing on Anaya's work by some of the leading critics in the field.

Lamadrid, Enrique R. "The Dynamics of Myth in the Creative Vision of Rudolfo Anaya." In *Pasó por aquí: Critical Essays on the New Mexican Literary Tradition, 1542–1988*, 243–54. Albuquerque: University of New Mexico Press, 1989. A well-informed interpretation of the utilization of New Mexican myth in Anaya's work.

3. Other Sources

Anaya, Rudolfo. *Bless Me, Ultima.* Berkeley: Tonatiuh-Quinto Sol International, 1972.

Bauder, Thomas. "The Triumph of White Magic in Rudolfo Anaya's *Bless Me, Ultima.*" *Mester* 14, no. 1 (Spring 1985): 41–54.

Castenada, Carlos. *The Teachings of Don Juan: A Yaqui Way of Knowledge.* 1968. Reprint, New York: Pocket Books, 1974

———. *A Separate Reality: Further Conversations with Don Juan.* 1971. Reprint, New York: Pocket Books, 1972.

Ortiz, Alfonso. "San Juan Pueblo." In *Handbook of North American Indians, Volume 9: Southwest.* Washington, D.C.: Smithsonian Institution, 1979.

Simmons, Marc. *Witchcraft in the Southwest: Spanish and Indian Supernaturalism on the Rio Grande.* Lincoln: University of Nebraska Press, 1974.

Weigle, Marta, and Peter White. *The Lore of New Mexico.* Albuquerque: University of New Mexico Press, 1988.

Notes

1. The page numbers in parentheses, which appear throughout this essay, refer to the third edition of 1974.

Chicano Theatre Reaches the Professional Stage:

Luis Valdez's *Zoot Suit*

ELIZABETH RAMÍREZ

A. Analysis of Themes and Forms

In 1978, *Zoot Suit* was an immediate success on one of the major regional stages in the United States. Luis Valdez, the founder and leading exponent of Chicano theatre, had ventured through an odyssey that led to the culmination of his work in theatre. The historical antecedents of Latinas/Latinos in the United States provided the roots for theatrical expression, but this heritage had remained dormant for several years before Valdez reawakened it on the contemporary stage. Where did this tradition come from?

Historical Background for *Zoot Suit*

Latinos/Latinas, the fastest-growing underrepresented ethnicity in the U.S., comprise the second largest group after African Americans to develop ethnic theatre. Many forms of Spanish-language entertainment, both amateur and professional, have flourished within the United States. Dating back to the sixteenth century, Spanish-language theatre predates the first English-speaking theatre on this continent. The tradition of educating the natives through religious drama, begun by the first friars in Mexico, was continued by the Spanish colonists throughout the Southwest. During the nineteenth century and perhaps earlier, Spanish-language acting companies arrived in the Southwest from Mexico and Spain, forming a lasting tradition in the U.S. Mexican American professional theatre that thrived for about fifty years in Texas, California, and other regions of the Southwest. With the coming of radio and film, especially during the Depression, Mexican American theatre died out, only to be revived again in the 1960s with the founding of El Teatro Campesino. The success of that company gave rise to a whole generation of Latino/Latina theatre groups.

The Evolution of Chicano Theatre

Contemporary Latino/Latina theatre represents diverse backgrounds. In 1985, a survey found 101 theatre groups: 29 Chicano, 24 Cuban, 28 Puerto Rican, and 20 of other Latino backgrounds. El Teatro Campesino, the best known of these groups, was founded by Luis Valdez in 1965. This Chicano theatre company first sought to show the plight of the farmworkers in California and subsequently broadened its scope to include social, political, and cultural issues revolving around the Chicano experience in the U.S.

Generally labeled agit-prop theatre, the Teatro began with productions of short scenes aimed at educating and politicizing its audience about the particular problems of the farmworkers, hoping to inspire the audience to social action. For over twenty-five years, the Teatro's history has been one of creativity, work, and change. From the early *actos* that first demonstrated the striking farmworkers' plight to its present position as a leader in alternative theatre, El Teatro Campesino continues to evolve and grow as it now seeks to reach a mass audience.

The earliest dramas of Luis Valdez are described by the playwright as *actos*. An *acto* is a short scene, arrived at through improvisation, usually comic in form, which strives to "inspire the audience to social action. Illuminate specific points about social problems. Satirize the opposition. Show or hint at a solution. Express what people are feeling" (Valdez, *Actos,* 6). Although the works were created collectively, individual observers as well as actors in the company generally attest that the final effect is due to the genius of Valdez.

The major characteristics of Valdez's early works are embodied in one of the first *actos* presented by El Teatro Campesino, *Las Dos Caras del Patroncito* ("The Two Faces of the Boss"). *Las Dos Caras* is concerned with educating the audience about the farmworkers' strike in California and the need for the union advocated by César Chávez as a solution to the injustices against the farmworker.

While the *acto* form allowed Valdez a means to show the plight of the farmworkers, he began to integrate the cultural heritage of Chicanos with the *mito* form. Valdez noted that "our rejection of white western European (*Gavacho*) proscenium theater makes the birth of new Chicano forms necessary—thus, *los actos y los mitos* [the *actos* and the myths]: one through the eyes of man; the other, through the eyes of God" (Valdez, *Actos,* 5). Valdez had begun seeking ways of relating indigenous myths to the present in response to a growing desire in Chicanos to investigate the roots of Chicano culture. A return to the *mito,* he felt, would help Chicanos rediscover their long-forgotten cultural heritage. *Bernabé, A Drama of Modern Chicano Mythology,* written in 1969, was the first drama in this vein.

The influence of the *acto* and the *mito,* along with another form that Valdez and the Teatro developed, the *corrido* or ballad in which the story was dramatized within its musical form, are the basic sources from which the Teatro's works stem. In terms of content, Valdez wrote:

> The teatros must never get away from La Raza. Without the *palomia* [the people] sitting there, laughing, crying, and sharing whatever is onstage, the teatros will dry up and die. If the Raza will not come to the theater, then the theater must go to the Raza. This, in the long run, will determine the shape, style, content, spirit and form of el teatro Chicano. (Valdez, *Actos,* 4)

But by 1980, after Valdez and El Teatro had gone to the people, he came to realize that the "powerful weapon of theatre" could also reach a broader audience. Through various notable works, Valdez and his internationally known company have continued to impress their audiences and critics.

Chicano History on the Contemporary Stage

While his movie *La Bamba* represents Valdez's best known work on film, *Zoot Suit* represents Valdez's greatest popular dramatic success to date. This Chicano drama with music was first produced in 1978 by both El Teatro Campesino and the Center Theatre Group of Los Angeles, commissioned by Gordon Davidson for the Mark Taper Forum. Considered the first Hispanic American play to reach Broadway, it opened at the Winter Garden Theatre on March 25, 1979, in a revised version. Under the direction of Luis Valdez and featuring Edward James Olmos and Daniel Valdez, this adaptation of real events that occurred in Los Angeles during World War II combines symbolism, the Living Newspaper technique, and agitprop theatre, along with elements of the *acto, mito,* and *corrido,* in a spectacular documentary play with music.

Unlike Valdez's previous plays, which foreground the immediacy of contemporary events as in the *actos, Zoot Suit* is based on historical fact. The Sleepy Lagoon murder trial of 1942 serves as the basis for which Valdez sheds light on an actual event in the history of Chicano–Anglo relations in Los Angeles. The events surrounding this trial greatly shaped the Chicano community of Los Angeles during World War II, though these incidents had been virtually ignored in the annals of American history.

Ricardo Romo, in his *History of a Barrio: East Los Angeles,* points out that several historians place the Chicano's social and political emergence in the post-1940 period in large part as a result of the "Zoot Suit Riots" and the Sleepy Lagoon trials of Los Angeles during the early war years. Estranged from American society, second-generation Chicano youth rebelled against American values and lifestyles during the late 1930s, forming gangs and cliques. Inadequate schooling and legal problems prevented many of these youth from eligibility for the armed forces, and racial prejudice restricted them from the workplace. Gang members soon became distinguishable by their style of dress, tattoo marks, and use of distinct English- and Spanish-slang dialogue. These groups began to use zoot suits, long ducktail hair-cuts, and pointed shoes, calling themselves "Chucos" or "Pachucos" while the press and the police referred to them as hoodlums or "zoot suiters" (Romo, 166).

On August 2, 1942, the body of José Díaz was found at the popular bar-rio swimming hole, the "Sleepy Lagoon." While the exact cause of death was never discovered, the police arrested twenty-two members of the Thirty-eighth Street gang, charging them with conspiracy to commit murder. The mass trial, heretofore unprecedented in U.S. judicial history, received na-tional attention, provoking renewed anti-Mexican sentiments in the Los Angeles community. Three defendants were found guilty of first-degree murder and sentenced to San Quentin Prison, nine were found guilty of second-degree murder and two counts of assault, five were convicted of lesser offenses, and five were acquitted on all counts. The East Los Angeles community organized the Sleepy Lagoon Defense Committee, appealing the convictions. The District Court of Appeals found the trial judge biased against the defendants and overturned the convictions. On October 4, 1944, all the defendants who remained in jail were freed as a result of the appeals court's reversal of the guilty verdicts (Romo, 166–67).

The celebration of the outcome was short-lived, with youths from the Eastside soon in conflict with soldiers and sailors stationed in the city. How the "Zoot Suit Riots" started remains unclear, yet a major confrontation began on June 3, 1943, when sailors attacked several Mexican gang mem-bers at a dance hall in Venice. Soon hundreds of marines and sailors emerged in response to rumors of an attack, and during the next few days Mexican Americans wearing zoot suits were stripped of their clothing and beaten. Blacks and Filipinos were also attacked. The riots stopped when the down-town section and the barrio were declared off limits by the local bases, but only after the Mexican government put pressure on officials in Washington to stop the disturbances, and the State Department, aware of the negative international attention, ordered the navy and the marines to act since the local Los Angeles officials seemed to be unresponsive.

The effects of these events were felt most profoundly by the returning Mexican American servicemen. Mexican Americans accounted for one-fifth of the total casualties from Los Angeles in World War II, although they made up only one-tenth of the city's population. Nationwide, Mexican Americans returned as one of the most decorated ethnic groups in the armed forces, and in the Los Angeles barrio some also returned as heroes. Upon their return to Los Angeles, they found profound changes in the Eastside. With the Sleepy Lagoon case and the "Zoot Suit Riots" still fresh, the legal defense of the Mexican American youths had led to a new political awareness among Eastside residents.

Mexican American veterans soon began to give the Eastside community a new political profile in the immediate postwar years; their new political activity was evident when thirty residents of East Los Angeles organized the Community Service Organization (CSO). Some of the veterans formed a chapter of the American GI Forum, a Mexican American organization founded in Texas by World War II veterans, and barrio residents of Los Angeles and surrounding communities found an ally in the League of United Latin American Citizens (LULAC) in challenging the segregation of children in the public schools. Clearly, the new political awareness continued through the postwar years, aimed at obtaining local political representation, metropolitan services and improvements, and equity in the judicial system. The "Zoot Suit Riots" and the Sleepy Lagoon trials during the early war years had served as major events in the awakening of a group of Americans who had heretofore been described as a "more or less voiceless, expressionless minority" (McWilliams, 302).

Valdez chose these highly significant historical events as a means to address Chicano struggles, through a professionally produced play written, directed, and performed by Chicanos. "There are a lot of talented Chicano actors and actresses in Los Angeles," Valdez noted, "and they've never had a chance to be in a real Chicano play or movie." This new direction for Valdez seemed a "natural step in the evolution of his Teatro and in his own commitments as a playwright and director" (Huerta, *Chicano Theater,* 175).

Various distinct forms and theatrical practices found in Valdez's *Zoot Suit* include distinct Brechtian traditions along with elements of the documentary form, influenced by the Living Newspaper style in which current events of the 1930s were dramatized through documentary theatre. Like the *acto, Zoot Suit* reveals social problems in a presentational style. Through a narrator, "El Pachuco," there is almost constant contact with the audience. Often the Pachuco will stop the action completely in order to illustrate a point. In contrast to this larger-than-life mythological figure, "The Press" serves as an allegorical figure that also stems from the *acto* form. The *corrido* form appears in the musical underscoring in which the historical events occur within the music of the period, and elements of the *mito* emerge in the image of the Pachuco as the sacrificial "god" of the Aztecs when he is stripped bare only to reemerge nobly. In addition, Valdez's study of the Aztec concept of the "nahual," found in his poem "Pensamiento Serpentino," appears in the use of El Pachuco as Henry's other self or alter ego who provides him with the strength to get in touch with his indigenous American ancestors.

There are several significant incidents in this two-act drama that reveal the southwestern Chicano experience. Although the play chiefly centers around Henry Reyna, his *familia* provides the core of a Chicano community in which Henry is rooted. Through this family, we are introduced to the conflict in Henry, who is both lauded by his siblings and his peers and devalued not only by his father but by the larger society as well.

Henry is drawn simultaneously to his family and to the demands of his peers. His family requires him to set a good example for his younger brother and sister; Henry is expected to protect Rudy and support his parents' demands on his sister's behavior. Henry serves as more of a father figure for the family than does his own father, Enrique, who both lauds Henry's manhood and ridicules him, his dress, and his friends. Henry's peers, on the other hand, look to him for leadership, setting him up as a near father figure within a group of young men and women who seem to have little family life of their own. The traditional roles of men and women are evident in the father and mother, with the father's domineering tone and assertiveness often silencing the mother while she feeds and serves and nurtures the family. Yet the mother also has a distinct voice and makes her sentiments heard within the family. Unquestionably, the father feels a great sense of pride in his elder son, although expressing his feelings is obviously difficult for him. Enrique compares Henry's going to the war to his own experience in fighting in the Mexican Revolution, viewing fighting for one's country as a great source of pride. Dolores, on the other hand, would prefer to have her son in jail rather than lose him to the war.

The demands on Henry to have a woman at his side who will provide him with loyalty, similar family background, and culture is sharply contrasted to Alice Bloomfield, the Anglo Jew who provides him with a fresh and lively exchange of intellect and equality that he has never before experienced. He is torn between Della, the traditionally meek and silent woman of the Chicano community who stands by her man, and the independent and opinionated Alice. Yet his loyalty and connections to his family and Chicana girlfriend prevent him from reaching out for someone outside his class and culture.

Distinct themes about the Chicano experience also emerge through the roles of the major characters in the drama, namely, Henry Reyna, El Pachuco, and Alice Bloomfield. El Pachuco provides Henry, the central character, with advice, but instead of offering moral choices, he determines his responses based on how he views the system that defines him. El Pachuco represents the defiance in Henry, fighting against the system that not only makes the Pachuco what he is but also determines how this figure will exist in his environment. The drama reaches its climax when the Pachuco is stripped of his emblematic clothes and left a sacrificial victim. Scared and emotionally drained, Henry draws his strength from his *nahual* or "other self" that he himself has created. Through his imagination, Henry is able to get in touch with the spirit of the Pachuco in order to survive in his bare cell. The audience can now view the Pachuco as a noble figure, instead of someone to be feared and mistrusted.

Sometimes the Pachuco's advice is more insightful politically than that of the defendants, giving Henry a perspective that the other boys do not have. At other times, the advice conflicts with Henry's gut instincts and those of the others, and Henry has to ignore the Pachuco. In some instances, Henry will be beaten regardless of whether he listens to his alter ego or not, and yet again Henry sometimes acts on his own moral judgment, regardless of the Pachuco's sentiments.

While the Pachuco is an enigmatic and dominant figure, the play clearly revolves around Henry Reyna, and Henry stands out as the pivotal character. Henry is a misunderstood, angry young man who reveals his inner defiance through his alter ego. Henry's deliberations about moral choice show his strengths and weaknesses. He is vulnerable to love and understanding, and he is firm in his desire to support his family and his community. It is important to remember that Henry is never alone. His family and the gang represent his links with the broader Chicano community in which he is an active participant, serving as an integral representative of that life as well. Henry places the needs of his family and friends above his own, and overcomes all obstacles, emerging as a defiant victor. Besides his inner consciousness as heard through the Pachuco, Henry's vulnerability and striving for the things that he cannot have are seen through his relationship with Alice.

Alice Bloomfield wants to be Henry's friend, not his "white woman" (84). Through this character, issues about interracial strife in Chicano communities surface. She reminds us of the token white woman who may be found in some Chicano families, often symbolizing attempts at assimilation with the dominant Anglo society or the conquering and possession of the forbidden and ideal of the dominant group. Yet she emerges as the symbol of love and friendship that she and Henry come to share. Because she has experienced oppression as a Jew, she can empathize with and understand Henry's struggle for freedom and the forces that keep him from gaining it. This Anglo and this Chicano are caught up emotionally. Bound by their equal desire for liberty from a very harsh reality, and with love and hate all around them, a passionate kiss seals them together.

The major themes in *Zoot Suit* include the role of myths and their meaning as related to the Chicano experience in the Southwest. The Chicano's ancestral past is shown through the Pachuco figure as well as through the visual and aural elements of the production (Valdez, *Zoot Suit,* 81). The Chicano subject in the position of resistance to the dominant American culture is found in the figure of the Pachuco, which Valdez describes as someone "finding a style of urban survival / in the rural skirts and outskirts / of the brown metropolis of Los" (80).

The Chicano search for identity in the struggle for cultural survival is found in both El Pachuco and in Henry. Henry's father says, "Be a man, hijo" (64), and we find a recurring conflict between father and son, even in one of the alternate endings where Henry and Enrique struggle before a final embrace (93–94). The Chicano also struggles with the demands from his family and his barrio, where "families are barely surviving" (88). Alice says: "You have to think of your family," and when Henry suggests that the barrio is a prison, George points out: "You guys have got to stop fighting, Henry, or the barrio will never change. Don't you realize you men represent the hope of your people?" (90). Other issues related to identity have to do with history and political action.

Issues about justice recall the Chicano struggles of the 1940s and the discrimination they suffered at the hands of the media and the courts (49, 78). The newspaper motif throughout makes use of captions to explain the dramatic action, showing the injustice of the dominant society. Issues of "discrimination against Mexicans in general" (70) remind us that this play is not only about the past, but also about the present. Jorge Huerta states:

"There is the danger that some audience members might see the events in *Zoot Suit* as history rather than as a reflection of today's realities, forgetting that police shootings and racist judgments are still commonplace in any city" (Huerta, *Chicano Theater*, 185). Urban survival and interracial strife make this drama profoundly timely because of the Rodney King events in recent L.A. history.

Through the context of music, spectacle, and language, customs and myths appear in the mix of American swing, Latino mambo, and boleros, each as a means of tying the dramatic action together. And just as the music and dancing serve as unifying factors that integrate the Chicano community with the American scene, the courtroom and the press serve to unify the dominant themes and ideas that the playwright wishes to express.

B. Teaching the Work

Heightened theatricality and spectacle stand out in this drama. Contrasting reviews of the Los Angeles production with the Broadway version can shed light on audience expectations and demands. This play was proclaimed as the first Latino play on Broadway, yet, while the audience loved the production, the New York critics did not. Compare and contrast the reviews in order to arrive at distinct audience demographics and interests (Huerta, *Chicano Theater*, 174–86, 253–56; *New York Theatre Critics' Reviews*, 312–16).

Performing scenes can be helpful in trying to comprehend character development and dramatic action, crisis and conflict, and the overall performance in terms of how the specific Chicano experience is revealed on the stage. Because the structure of the play is episodic, it is possible to use a small scene to grasp the dramatic intensity of the moment. Aristotle describes all drama as "man in human action." For example, by playing out the section in which the family appears (on 33–37) we can begin to understand the demands that the family makes on Henry. If the Pachuco begins that segment and ends it as well (on 33 and 37, respectively), we can also see how Henry's inner thoughts and attitudes play through his interaction with his loved ones.

The very brief Scene 2 in Act II can be played by contrasting Chicano and Anglo actors, exchanging roles according to race and gender, in order to grasp the underlying tension that affects racial strife and the desire to understand each other in a climate of dissension and desperation.

Studying Valdez's definition and description of an *acto* from his anthology of *actos* can provide a means of understanding the basic form of the drama. Students might study the *acto* form in contrast to the *mito* by examining two *actos*, *Las Dos Caras del Patroncito* ("The Two Faces of the Boss") and *Los Vendidos* ("The Sellouts"), both in Valdez's *Actos*, and two *mitos*, *Bernabé* and *Dark Root of a Scream* (Huerta, *Chicano Theater*, 18–23, 60–68, 97–103, 195–99). Once the forms are understood, students might be assigned to sketch a scene in the form of the *acto* and play it out in groups of two, using the model of the strife that occurs between Henry and Alice in Scene 2 of Act II. This scene can incorporate contemporary life issues arising out of ethnic or other concerns. In contrast, the use of Aztec myth and culture at the end of Scene 6 of Act II can be investigated further in Miguel León-Portilla's *Pre-Columbian Literatures of Mexico* and then played out in order to understand Chicano ancestral ritual and performance.

Valdez stands out for his use of the drama to educate and inform others about Chicano culture. How do costume and scenic elements reinforce cultural images or reveal resistance of the Chicano to the dominant American culture? Bringing in found natural objects, such as tree limbs and conches and flutes made from tree limbs or maracas, can help to bring the element of "pure" music that Valdez incorporates into the dramas to remind audiences about the Chicano's Aztec and Mayan ancestral past. These instruments can be incorporated in enacting a *mito* based on a contemporary myth similar to that found in either *Bernabé* or *Dark Root of a Scream*.

Getting a firm grasp on the Pachuco character as larger than life can serve to illustrate how certain figures in the Chicano experience have become enigmatic characters that stand out in Chicano history. Dressing and acting out the outstanding movements and speech can shed light on how and why this figure has become both a feared and revered historical figure. Using the slang of the Pachuco from the text and comparing it to the modern-day "Tex-Mex" or "Calo" found in poetry by Alurista and other Chicano artists can be helpful. Examining Guillermo Gómez-Peña's *Gringostroika*, a collection of border-crossing performance pieces, can provide students with various models of contemporary blending of Chicano, Mexican, and ancestral emblems and themes and ideas.

In teaching drama and performance, viewing videos and films and listening to music that typifies the style of the production can all be extremely useful. The video of the feature film *Zoot Suit* is available for in-class viewing. Other videos by Luis Valdez include the highly successful feature film *La Bamba* and the PBS productions of *Los Corridos* and *La Pastorela*, with

Linda Ronstadt and Freddie Fender. El Teatro Campesino also makes available a video featuring various scenes from their dramatic productions along with a history of their work to date. These videos can be helpful in understanding character portrayals and dramatic intensity of certain scenes found in *Zoot Suit*. For example, understanding the role of the mother and the family can be facilitated by viewing the mother and brother in *La Bamba*. The role of the Aztec ancestral figure that El Pachuco represents in *Zoot Suit* can also be found in all of the other videos. The first film produced by the Teatro, under the title of Centro Campesino Cultural, was *I Am Joaquín*, adapted from the poem by Rodolfo González, which addresses the Chicano movement at its earliest stages and can also be useful in trying to grasp character portrayals and dominant themes and ideas in *Zoot Suit*.

The use of music, dance, and comic elements intermingled with seriousness can all be better understood in looking at other work by Valdez, since the latter method of presentation is distinct in his style of production. Danny Valdez has had some of his original music recorded, and listening to his work can illustrate the blending of ancestral music with contemporary Chicano music. Listening to other *corridos,* besides those dramatized in the video of that name, can also be helpful in understanding how Valdez integrates performance with dance and music, drawing from a rich heritage of border ballads. Americo Paredes's study of border ballads, *With a Pistol in His Hand,* and the video based on Paredes's book, *The Ballad of Gregorio Cortez,* can also be informative.

The following questions may be helpful in studying *Zoot Suit* and, more broadly, in assessing the significance and contributions that Chicano theatre has made to American dramatic literature.

1. Characterize Henry Reyna. Do you think that Valdez regards Henry as a hero or, on the contrary, as the sort of Chicano who should remain in jail to keep society the same for the young soldiers and marines who are fighting for their country?

2. Characterize the Pachuco. Why is he feared? Hated? Stripped of his attire? Is he a pathetic figure or a tragic figure? What function does the Pachuco perform?

3. Are Henry Reyna and El Pachuco believable characters, or are they only allegorical types, representing larger-than-life figures that epitomize certain societal and cultural traits? Imagine a day when racial conflict no longer exists. Will this play be dated?

4. What does the family contribute to the play? If the mother were eliminated, what would be lost? If the father were eliminated, what would be lost?

5. Discuss the various possible endings suggested by the dramatist. Which do you support? Why? Compare and contrast your views with those of others who have also read the play. Does your point of view change after viewing the film version of the production?

6. After viewing the video of *Zoot Suit,* discuss the following: In what type of space was the production staged? Did it allow close-up viewing of costumes and makeup? of scenery and properties? Were details easily visible? What was the overall effect of the space on costumes and makeup and on scenery and properties? How did the lighting relate to that suggested in the script? How did lighting affect or help to create mood and atmosphere? Did mood and atmosphere change? If so, how? With what results? Were there special effects? What were the results? Did the setting suggest any specific interpretation of the play? If so, what interpretation? What did the scenery convey about the characters? about socioeconomic conditions? about period? about locale? Were the roles appropriately cast? Were certain actors especially effective? If so, how and with what effect? What special skills were required of certain actors? How effectively were these demands met? How closely did the production adhere to the playwright's script? Did the production make use of any unusual conventions? If so, which and with what effect? How did casting influence the production? Was the dramatic action clear? Did it build climactically? Were all of the elements of the production unified and coordinated? Overall, did the production accomplish its apparent goals? If not, where did it fall short? What were the overall results? Discuss the roles of women in this play. How are stereotypes enforced or changed with these women?

7. Describe your emotions at the end of the play.

C. Bibliographies

1. Related Works

Berson, Misha, ed. *Between Worlds: Contemporary Asian-American Plays.* New York: Theatre Communications Group, 1990. This anthology of six plays includes Philip Kan Gotanda's *The Wash,* David Henry Hwang's *As the Crow Flies,* and Wakako Yamauchi's *And the Soul Shall Dance. The Wash* has to do with biracial issues between blacks and Asian Americans, relationships between family members and parents.

Geiogamah, Hanay. *New Native American Drama: Three Plays.* Norman: University of Oklahoma Press, 1980. This collection of three plays, by the

Kiowa playwright who is also notable for his work with the American Indian Dance Theatre, includes an extensive introduction that surveys contemporary Native American drama from the 1960s through the 1970s. *Body Indian* shows the devastating effects of alcoholism on the Indian community. *Foghorn* shows Indian stereotypes ranging from Columbus to the 1973 incident at Wounded Knee, exposing the dangers that stereotypes pose for both Indians and non-Indians. *49* splendidly blends a contemporary social event with elements of a traditional past and a forward-looking shamanistic view.

Hansberry, Lorraine. *A Raisin in the Sun.* New York: New American Library, 1958. The first play by an African American woman to be presented on Broadway, this traditional American drama tells the story of the Younger family, all living together on the Southside of Chicago. The grandmother buys a house in a white neighborhood, raising issues of integration and separation of the races. Through the daughter, interest in African heritage is explored, and the son and his own family raise issues revolving around family unity and growing up.

Huerta, Jorge. *Necessary Theater: Six Plays about the Chicano Experience.* Houston: Arte Público Press, 1989. This anthology of six plays (*Soldierboy, Latina, The Shrunken Head of Pancho Villa, Guadalupe, Money,* and *La Víctima*) offers an additional supplement to the already published works by Chicano dramatists and introduces new writers. This anthology is distinguished from others in that each of the plays in this volume has been successfully produced by a professional company. None of these works has been previously available in print, and all of them deal with the Chicano experience.

Neihardt, John G. *Black Elk Speaks.* 1932. Reprint, Lincoln: University of Nebraska Press, 1979. This book has recently been adapted for the stage by Christopher Segal, produced to great acclaim at the Denver Center Theatre. An article on this production appears in *American Theatre* (December 1993) with several illustrations of the performance.

Osborn, M. Elizabeth., ed. *On New Ground: Contemporary Hispanic-American Plays.* New York: Theatre Communications Group, 1987. This anthology of six plays includes Lynne Alvarez's *The Guitarrón,* María Irene Fornes's *The Conduct of Life,* Eduardo Machado's *Broken Eggs,* José Rivera's *The House of Ramon Iglesias,* and Milcha Sanchez Scott's *Roosters.* Rivera's work deals with Puerto Rican family life in the U.S., and Sanchez Scott's work shows the turmoil of adolescent Chicano children growing up in the Southwest.

Valdez, Luis. *Bernabé.* In *Aztlan: An Anthology of Mexican American Literature,* ed. Luis Valdez and Stan Steiner. New York: Random House, 1972. And in *Contemporary Chicano Theatre,* ed. Robert J. Garza. Notre Dame, Ind.: University of Notre Dame Press, 1976. This play is one of the early longer works by Valdez. Almost entirely in Spanish, although an English version is available from the company in San Juan Bautista, this play's text shows how Valdez blends ancestral myth with contemporary Chicano reality.

————. *Dark Root of a Scream*. In *From the Barrio,* ed. Lilian Faderman and Omar Salinas. San Francisco: Canfield Press, 1973. This play treats the Chicano as the redeemer figure in a world that has robbed him of his ancestral past. Set in a wake in the living room of a casualty of the Vietnam War, Quetzalcóatl Gonzáles, Valdez combines the Chicano Aztec ancestry with the destructive materialistic modern civilization in which he is being slaughtered.

Valdez, Luis, and El Teatro Campesino. *Actos.* San Juan Bautista, Calif.: Menyah Productions, 1971. This anthology of the earliest plays by Valdez and El Teatro Campesino includes a brief introductory essay on "Notes on Chicano Theater" and an explanation of the *acto* form followed by nine *actos* from 1965 to 1971. The themes of these short dramatic pieces include Aztec mythology, Chicanos in the military, the conquest of Mexico, and injustices in the school system. *Los Vendidos* is one of the most notable and most often anthologized and produced of all of these earlier works. *Los Vendidos,* set in a "Used Mexican Lot," shows an assimilated female Mexican American from then-governor Reagan's office looking for a "Mexican type for the administration," to serve as a token "Brown face in the crowd," and several models provide interesting stereotypical choices.

2. Best Criticism

Broyles González, Yolanda. "Toward a Re-Vision of Chicano Theatre History: The Women of El Teatro Campesino." In *Making a Spectacle: Feminist Essays on Contemporary Women's Theatre,* ed. Lynda Hart, 209–38. Ann Arbor: University of Michigan Press, 1989. Significant article about Chicanas on stage examines stereotypical gender roles and the nature of performance from the beginning of El Teatro Campesino through the changing presence of women in the 1980s.

Huerta, Jorge A. *Chicano Theater: Themes and Forms*. Ypsilanti, Mich.: Bilingual Press, 1982. This text offers the most comprehensive analysis of contemporary Chicano drama and performance from the beginnings to early 1980s. Topics include: the Worker's Struggle, the Search for Identity: The Chicano in War at Home and Abroad, Back to the Barrio, Justice: On the Streets and In the Courts, and the Chicano and His Cosmos. An analysis of *Zoot Suit* is included. This text includes an extensive bibliography that is divided into articles and available plays and theatre reviews with detailed resources for El Teatro Campesino, Luis Valdez, and *Zoot Suit*. Several illustrations show staging and performance.

Ramírez, Elizabeth C. *Footlights across the Border: Spanish-Language Professional Theatre in Texas, 1875–1935*. New York: Peter Lang Publishers, 1990. A history of professional acting companies that shows a distinct Spanish-language theatre movement in Texas for over fifty years. Beginning in the nineteenth century, touring, resident, and combination companies traveling with stars arrived in the U.S. from Mexico and Spain to form a lasting theatrical tradition in the U.S. The contributions of male and female actor-managers and actors and actresses are analyzed, along with an investigation of the repertory, the productions, and types of audiences.

Yarbro-Bejarano, Yvonne. "The Female Subject in Chicano Theatre: Sexuality, 'Race,' and Class." In *Performing Feminisms: Feminist Critical Theory and Theatre,* ed. Sue-Ellen Case, 131–49. Baltimore: Johns Hopkins University Press, 1990. One of the few articles that examine dramatic literature by Chicanas along with the plays in performance. The author analyzes the myth of *La Malinche* as she explores pervasive traditional gender roles that have been reinforced in Chicano theatre overall, and then follows with distinct examples of alternative women's groups in the Chicano theatre movement. Cherrie Moraga's *Tongues of Fire* and women's roles in the work of two theatre groups, El Teatro de la Esperanza and El Teatro Campesino, are discussed.

3. Other Sources

The Ballad of Gregorio Cortez. Video Recording, Moctesuma Esparza Productions. Beverly Hills, Calif.: Nelson Entertainment, 1988. 105 minutes.

León-Portilla, Miguel. *Pre-Columbia Literatures of Mexico*. Norman: University of Oklahoma Press, 1975.

McWilliams, Carey. *North from Mexico: The Spanish-Speaking People of the United States*. Philadelphia: J. B. Lippincott, 1949.

New York Times Theatre Critics' Reviews 30, no. 7 (1979): 312–16.

Paredes, Americo. *With His Pistol in His Hand: A Border Ballad and Its Hero*. Austin: University of Texas Press, 1958.

Pottlitzer, Joanne. *Hispanic Theatre in the United States and Puerto Rico*. New York: Ford Foundation, 1988.

Romo, Ricardo. *History of a Barrio: East Los Angeles*. Austin: University of Texas Press, 1988.

Valdez, Luis. *Zoot Suit and Other Plays*. Houston: Arte Público Press, 1992.

Entering *The House on Mango Street*
(Sandra Cisneros)

JULIÁN OLIVARES

A. Analysis of Themes and Forms

Sandra Cisneros's *The House on Mango Street*[1] is a book about Esperanza Cordero, a Chicana girl who lives in the barrio, or ghetto, of a large city.[2] Through forty-four brief lyrical narratives, or vignettes, as Cisneros has called them ("Softly Insistent Voice," 14–15), ranging from one-half to three pages, the girl recounts her growth from puberty to adolescence within the sociopolitical frame of poverty, racial discrimination, and gender subjugation. The book's action is propelled by three major themes: the girl's desire to find a suitable house (essentially a move away from the barrio), to find her identity, and to become a writer. Identity is crucial, for it not only means coming to terms with her Latino ethnicity, but also arriving at a gender consciousness not circumscribed by the gender determinants of her culture. Consequently, the narrator is "twice a minority"; she is doubly marginated because of her ethnicity and her patriarchal society (Melville). As we will ascertain, the themes are inextricably interrelated; the resolution of the themes of house and identity is to be achieved by her role as writer.

The House on Mango Street is a book about growing up, what critics call a bildungsroman. This genre is cultivated commonly in the United States by emerging writers, often first- or second-generation immigrants, and especially within literatures emerging around the periphery of a dominant society.[3] It offers the advantage of a first-person narration that becomes the basis for the expression of subjectivity; the protagonist relates his or her experiences in the growth from childhood to maturity, the latter determined by the dialectic with culture and society. The often simplistic or naive narration proper to a child's perspective is conducive to an innocent but critical view of society and, in the case of *Mango Street*, to the formation of a counterdiscourse.

Before proceeding to our commentary on *The House on Mango Street*, it would be beneficial to briefly compare the work with its model and predecessor, Tomás Rivera's *. . . y no se lo tragó la tierra (And the Earth Did Not Devour Him)*, in order to appreciate their historical and critical contexts.

Both works are the products of working-class authors and project a counter ideology; both were published by small minority presses; both are slender works—depending on the edition, about one hundred pages each; both are episodic and are about a child's search for identity; both employ the symbol of the house; and both portray the protagonist as writer. Published in 1971, twelve years before *Mango Street,* Rivera's work deals with the tribulations of migrant farmworkers as experienced through the eyes of a Chicano boy; *Mango Street* deals with the trials of barrio migrants as recounted by a Chicana girl.

Tierra consists of fourteen stories, twelve of which correspond symbolically to the months of the year, all interspersed with thirteen vignettes. The book deals with the struggle of an alienated boy to recover the events of the immediate past year and to encounter his identity.[4] In the concluding story, we discover that the whole process of recollection has taken place under a house. As he emerges from under the house, we note that the encounter with his identity has resulted from a dialectic of the personal and the collective, and depends on a "dawning sense of solidarity with other members of [his] class and race" (J. Saldívar, 103). Throughout this book narrated by omniscient, first-person, and anonymous voices speaking as a collective "we," the child protagonist functions as the central consciousness. It is through his eyes and memory that the actions of the stories achieve a novelistic unity, especially in the concluding story where allusions to these events take the form of a stream of consciousness in the boy's mind. Although the boy encounters his identity, his name is never revealed. This anonymity reinforces the collective identity of the migrant workers and their solidarity in the face of discrimination and exploitation by agribusiness.

The structural unity of the forty-four vignettes of *Mango Street* is achieved by the first-person narration of the protagonist Esperanza Cordero. Thematically, they are held together, as in *Tierra,* by plot and character development, and the protagonist's search for a house and her identity. The structural similarity of both works is due to each writer's desire to create a work whose stories could stand alone and simultaneously communicate a sense of novelistic unity. Each writer comments on the desire to create such a hybrid genre. Tomás Rivera confirms that

> I had wanted to write a novel but I so liked the compacted dramatic elements of the short story that I finally decided to structure a work (novel) from which any element (chapter or short story) could be extracted and stand, out of context, on its own, with its own kernel of sensibility and meaning, albeit [with] its ambiguity. As I ar-

ranged the short stories and re-read for continuity, I would make changes in vocabulary, sentence structure, etc., to carry out a transitory sense. (*Complete Works*, 27)

Sandra Cisneros states that in addition to desiring such a structure, she was influenced by Jorge Luis Borges and wanted an amalgam of poetry and fiction:

> I recall I wanted to write stories that were a cross between poetry and fiction. I was greatly impressed by Jorge Luis Borges' *Dream Tigers* stories for their form. I liked how he could fit so much into one page and that the last line of each story was important to the whole in much the same way that the final lines in poems resonate. Except I wanted to write a collection which could be read at any random point without having any knowledge of what came before or after. Or, that could be read in a series to tell one big story. I wanted stories like poems, compact and lyrical and ending with a reverberation.[5] ("Do You Know Me?," 78)

Cisneros's *The House on Mango Street* is an intertextual response to Rivera's *. . . y no se lo tragó la tierra*. That is, it takes up the latter's structure, articulation with the tradition of the bildungsroman, and theme of alienation in order to respond to its model's ideological content and to address a different audience. Rivera's book was published at the height of the Chicano movement and was a literary protest of racial discrimination and socioeconomic and political injustice. The movement's goals, shared by the Chicanas, stirred in them, in turn, a desire for, first, cultural emancipation, then literary liberation. Chicanas perceived a parallel between their people's discrimination and exploitation by the dominant white society, and their own gender discrimination and subjugation by a traditional Hispanic patriarchic culture. Chicana literary protests against their condition found little sympathy among the small Latino presses that published the works of Chicano writers and were concerned with promoting *la causa*, the program of the Chicano movement. It was not until the 1980s that Chicanas began to be published,[6] principally by small Latino presses founded toward the end of the preceding decade, such as Arte Público Press and Bilingual Press.

In order to appreciate *Mango Street*'s response to *Tierra*, let us consider the ideology of the male discourse known as the bildungsroman. This genre includes any number of the following characteristics: (1) the hero leaves home or goes to school; (2) undergoes a trial by his peers; (3) is either accepted or learns to deal with his situation; (4) overcomes adversity; (5) performs an heroic act; (6) discovers who he is, as a man and as a person in society; and (7) at the end of the novel has integrated his consciousness, thereby achieving self-definition, and is prepared to deal with the world on his own terms.

As Erlinda Gonzales-Berry and Tey Diana Rebolledo have noted, traditional growing-up stories for females display a different process and outcome:

> The female adolescent may or may not go off to school, but, in any case, in these stories the young woman also undergoes trials and tribulations which teach her how she must behave in society, what she must learn in order to assume her expected position. In contrast to the young male hero who at the end of the *Bildungsroman* comes into a complete sense of integration and freedom, the female adolescent is carefully schooled to function in society, to lose her freedom and her sense of individuality in order to become a loving wife and mother. She thus integrates her destiny with that of a man who will protect her, defend her and create a life for her. Whereas in their rites-of-passage, adolescent males encounter tests of strength and valor . . . , younger girls [are] given 'tests in submission' while their older sisters [are] provided with models of behavior appropriate for success in the marriage market. Thus, rather than achieving maturity, young women of the traditional coming-of-age novels are led down the path to a second infancy. Consequently, the female *Bildungsroman* has tended to culminate in images of imprisoned women. When escape is an option, it is most often found through death or insanity. While elements of this fare may have been typical of the writings of early Chicano writers, the contemporary female growing-up story focuses on a more general sense of loss, around the realization that innocence is gone, around awareness of death and mortality, of the inability to retreat back into childhood and, at times, of the necessity to conform to a life not necessarily chosen by them. (109–10)

Tierra conforms in many respects to the paradigm of the male bildungsroman, confirming the general ideology of this discourse with regard to the male subject's assumption of a place in his society. However, it pronounces a counterdiscourse of the oppressed with regard to the discourse of the dominant society; yet, in doing so, *Tierra* also reveals the particular ideology of the obsessively male-centered Hispanic culture. In *Tierra,* women are submissive, silent, crazy; the sole but stereotypic exception is the "brazen floozy" Juanita, who, in the story "La noche que se apagaron las luces ("The Night the Lights Went Out") slaps her ex-boyfriend Ramón on a dance floor; this disgrace and loss of machismo cause Ramón to commit suicide by throwing himself on an electric generator.

The male protagonist of *Tierra* is nameless in conformity to the collective experience of the society portrayed and to the collective identity of the hero. In *Mango Street* the protagonist gives her name as Esperanza Cordero, not only an ethnic marker but a gender-specific identity. Furthermore, Esperanza's surname, meaning "lamb," operates symbolically in the text, but in an ironic manner. She refuses to sacrifice her gender to a patriarchic society. Manuel Martín Rodríguez perceives her surname as a sacrificial symbol by which the individual speaks and acts for the community (252). Through Esperanza, Cisneros gives voice to the passive and silent females of male-authored Chicano texts. Esperanza depicts the lonely and imprisoned, the physically and psychologically abused Latinas; and in this way she displays her collective identity with her sisters. But in the endeavor to establish her identity, to fit into her name, Esperanza also undertakes a personal quest to liberate herself from the gender constraints of her culture. It is by means of this defiant and political posture that Cisneros breaks the paradigm of the traditional female bildungsroman.

The image of the house is central to *Tierra* and *Mango Street*. In both, the image is socialized in order, as Ellen McCracken notes, to underscore a deprivation suffered by minorities under capitalism. McCracken affirms that "it is precisely the lack of housing stability that motivates the image's centrality in works by writers like Cisneros and Rivera. For the migrant worker who has moved continuously because of job exigencies and who, like many others in the Chicano community, has been deprived of an adequate place to live because of the inequities of income distribution in U.S. society, the desire for a house is not a sign of individualistic acquisitiveness but rather represents the satisfaction of a basic human need" (64).

On the symbolic level, the house image functions differently in these works. In *Tierra*, we note at the conclusion that the protagonist has undergone the process of the recollection and unification of the fragments of the lost year while lying in the dark under a house. The house symbolizes the collective consciousness of his people, which he comes to realize and express in the quest for his personal identity. This identification of the house and the collective consciousness is confirmed when the protagonist states that in order to remember more, he must return to the darkness under the house: "From now on, all I have to do is to come here, in the dark, and think about them [my people]. . . . I'll have to come here to recall all of the other years" (219).

The house on Mango Street is an extension of Esperanza Cordero's identity. While not as dilapidated as her previous house on Loomis Street, for her, its poor state is a sign of her poverty and shame. As her character develops in the work and she becomes more aware of her gender constraints, the wish for a pretty house becomes a desire for unfettered female space. At the conclusion, the house becomes a metaphor for the space of writing.

Esperanza Cordero is clearly conscious of self-exploration through writing. In the first half of the book, the reader has the impression of overhearing the protagonist "tell" stories. As the stories proceed, her growth and character development are signaled by her language development and her heightened poetic imagery. In the dialogue Esperanza relates with her aunt in "Bad Girl," the twenty-third piece, the protagonist reveals that she writes poetry, and with the subsequent stories it becomes clear that these are the memoirs she has written of her first year's experience of living in the barrio, in the little red house on Mango Street: "You live right here, 4006 Mango, Alicia says and points to the house I am ashamed of. No, this isn't my house I say and shake my head as if shaking could undo the year I've lived here" (*House on Mango Street*, 106). It is through writing, as her aunt tells her, that Esperanza will achieve her social and gender liberation. Like *Tierra*, the structure of *Mango Street* is circular. The text ends where the writing begins (Valdés, 66), and the first written piece is the beginning of the text. *Tierra* ends where it began, in the mind of the boy who was struggling to recover the events of the past year. Yet its open-ended conclusion points to the protagonist not as a writer, but as a potential writer. His recollections are acts of composition by which he re-creates the experiences of his people and creates his identity. At the novel's conclusion, then, it remains for him to give literary expression to his experience.

The initial and title piece of the book finds Esperanza's family arriving at their house on Mango Street. Slowly moving up the economic ladder, they have been migrating from barrio to barrio, always renting an apartment. Now they have their own house, but Esperanza is dejected. Its dilapidated condition is a far cry from their dream house. Her parents attempt to overcome their disappointment by saying this house is only temporary:

> We didn't always live on Mango Street. Before that we lived on Loomis on the third floor, and before that we lived on Keeler. Before Keeler it was Pauline, and before that I can't remember. But what I remember most is moving a lot. Each time it seemed there'd be one more of us. By the time we got to Mango Street we were six— Mama, Papa, Carlos, Kiki, my sister Nenny and me.

The house on Mango Street is ours, and we don't have to pay
rent to anybody . . . But even so, it's not the house we'd thought
we'd get. . . .

They always told us that one day we would move into a house, a
real house that would be ours for always so we wouldn't have to
move each year. . . . Our house would be white with trees around it,
a great big yard and grass growing without a fence. This was the
house Papa talked about when he held a lottery ticket and this was
the house Mama dreamed up in the stories she told us before we
went to bed.

But the house on Mango Street is not the way they told it at all.
It's small and red with tight steps in front and windows so small
you'd think they were holding their breath. Bricks are crumbling in
places, and the front door is so swollen you have to push hard to get
in. There is no front yard, only four little elms the city planted by
the curb . . . and the house has only one washroom. Everybody has
to share a bedroom—Mama and Papa, Carlos and Kiki, me and
Nenny.

Once when we were living on Loomis, a nun from my school
passed by and saw me playing out front. The laundromat down-
stairs had been boarded up because it had been robbed two days
before and the owner had painted on the wood YES WE'RE OPEN
so as not to lose business.

Where do you live? she asked.

There, I said pointing up to the third floor.

You live *there*?

There. I had to look to where she pointed—the third floor, the
paint peeling, wooden bars Papa had nailed on the windows so we
wouldn't fall out. You live there? The way she said it made me feel
like nothing. There. I lived there. I nodded.

I knew then I had to have a house. A real house. One I could
point to. But this isn't it. The house on Mango Street isn't it. For the
time being, Mama says. Temporary, says Papa. But I know how
these things go. (3–5)

Mango Street is a street sign, a marker, that, because of "white flight"
(13) now defines and circumscribes the Latino population of Puerto Ricans,
Chicanos, and Mexicans within an impoverished barrio. The house on
Mango Street is essentially the narrator's first universe. She starts here because it is the beginning of her conscious narrative reflection. Her description of the house is a metonymical description and presentation of her self.
The house is much more than a place to live; it is an extension of her identity. By pointing to this dilapidated house, she points to herself, revealing

her own poverty and shame. Consequently, she wants to point to another house and to point to another self.[7]

The initial piece is representative of *Mango Street*'s form, voice, and style. The form is a prose poem; the narrating presence is a composite of a poetic enunciating voice and a narrative voice (Valdés, 57). The style is consistent with that of a young girl speaking idiomatic English, with colloquialisms and a few Spanish expressions—a deceptively simple but richly imagistic language. The personification of the house is typical of a child's way of seeing and inventing the world, but it also points to the influence of story books and initiates a series of allusions to fairy tales that will appear throughout the book. However, these tales will be subverted. In this case, the rural red house is moved to a large city ghetto; and it is red (only in children's stories are houses red) because it is made of red bricks, but these bricks are crumbling.[8] The personification creating this defamiliarized fairy-book atmosphere functions, in turn, to underscore the shared identity of dilapidated house and dejected inhabitant.

The second piece, "Hairs," briefly describes the family and reveals that although externally the house is a picture of poverty, inside there is warmth and communion. "Boys and Girls," the third narrative, posits the theme of gender difference, the need to find a girlfriend to overcome her loneliness— "Until then I am a red balloon, a balloon tied to an anchor" (9)—and begins the exposition of the narrator's world.

The desire to live in a beautiful house is concomitant to finding another identity. But the identity she seeks must be freed from the gender oppression of her culture. In "My Name," the fourth piece, Esperanza says: "In English my name means hope. In Spanish it means too many letters. It means sadness, it means waiting. . . . It is the Mexican records my father plays on Sunday mornings when he is shaving, songs like sobbing." In this lyrical sketch, Esperanza traces the reason for the discomfiture with her name to cultural hegemony, the Mexican males' suppression of their women. Esperanza was named after her Mexican great-grandmother who was wild but tamed by her husband: "She looked out the window all her life, the way so many women sit their sadness on an elbow. . . . Esperanza, I have inherited her name, but I don't want to inherit her place by the window." A woman's place is one of domestic confinement, not one of liberation and choice. Thus, Esperanza would like to baptize herself "under a new name, a name more like the real me, the one nobody sees. Esperanza as Lisandra or Maritza or Zeze the X. Yes. Something like Zeze the X will do" (10–11). She prefers a name not culturally embedded in a male-centered ideology. In the meantime she feels herself to be like an X, an indeterminate personality in search of an identity. As María Elena de Valdés notes, "The narrative situation is a familiar one: a sensitive young girl's reflections of her struggle between what she is and what she would like to be. The sense of alienation is compounded because ethnically she is a Mexican, although culturally a Mexican American; she is a young girl surrounded by examples of abused, defeated, worn-out women, but the woman she wants to be must be free" (57).

The stories Esperanza relates fall into five categories, many of which are interrelated:

1. The family, children, and the barrio: "Hairs," "Our Good Day," "Laughter," "Gil's Furniture Bought & Sold," "Meme Ortiz," "Louie, His Cousin & His Other Cousin," "Those Who Don't," "Darius and the Clouds," "And Some More," "A Rice Sandwich," "Chanclas," "Papa Who Wakes Up Tired in the Dark," "Geraldo No Last Name," "The Earl of Tennessee," "A Smart Cookie."

2. Sexual awareness: "The Family of Little Feet," "Hips," "The First Job," "Sire," "Minerva Writes Poems," "The Monkey Garden," "Red Clowns."

3. Child and gender oppression, abuse, and abandonment: "Cathy, Queen of Cats," "Marin," "There Was an Old Woman She Had So Many Children She Didn't Know What to Do," "Alicia Who Sees Mice," "The First Job," "Born Bad," "No Speak English," "Rafaela Who Drinks Coconut & Papaya Juice on Tuesdays," "Sally," "Minerva Writes Poems," "A Smart Cookie," "What Sally Said," "The Monkey Garden," "Linoleum Roses," "Red Clowns."

4. Identity: "The House on Mango Street," "My Name," "Elenita, Cards, Palm, Water," "Four Skinny Trees," "Bums in the Attic," "Beautiful and Cruel," "The Monkey Garden," "The Three Sisters," "A House of My Own," "Mango Says Goodbye Sometimes."

5. Writing—pieces intrinsically related to the discovery of identity: "Born Bad," "Edna's Ruthie," "Minerva Writes Poems," "The Three Sisters," "A House of My Own," "Mango Says Goodbye Sometimes."

The racial identity of the barrio is evident in "Those Who Don't," in reference to those who get lost and wind up in the barrio fearing for their lives: "They think we will attack them with shiny knives. They are stupid people who are lost and got here by mistake." Conversely, while feeling safe in their own barrio, the Latinos fear to venture into other groups' neighborhoods: "All brown all around, we are safe. But watch us drive into a neighborhood of another color and our knees go shakity-shake and our car windows get rolled up tight and our eyes look straight. Yeah. That is how it goes and goes" (28).

"A Rice Sandwich" deals with latch-key children and poverty, and also articulates with the initial story. Esperanza shamefully identifies with a squalid flat; the nun assumes that because she is Mexican, that is where she lives: "Which one is your house? And then she made me stand up on a box of books and point. That one? she said pointing to a row of ugly three-flats, the ones even the raggedy men are ashamed to go into. Yes, I nodded even though I knew that wasn't my house and started to cry" (45).

The physical changes that mark the transition from puberty to adolescence are signs confirming female identity, bringing with it an awareness of sexuality. However, Esperanza's exhilaration in arriving at this stage of physical development is offset not only by her encounters with the dangers that sexuality provoke, but also with her awareness of the gender proscription that is set in place once sexuality becomes manifest. Esperanza's first encounter with sexual danger is the consequence of a typical and innocent game played by young girls. In "The Family of Little Feet," Esperanza and her friends put on cast-off high heels and take delight in pretending to be adult women. The corner grocer perceives the sexual danger that the high heels signal and tells the girls to take them off: "Them are dangerous, he says. You girls too young to be wearing shoes like that."[9] As they flee from the grocer, his admonishment is realized when, first, a boy, in typical male sexual banter, calls out to them, "Ladies, lead me to heaven"; and, second, in their encounter with male sexual aggression when a drunk asks one of the girls to come closer—"Your little lemon shoes are so beautiful. But come closer. I can't see very well"—and tells her he'll give her a dollar for a kiss. The girls run away in their high heels and take them off because they "are tired of being beautiful" (41–42). In this episode with allusions to "Little Red Riding Hood," Cisneros, as she does with fairy tales, deflates a light-hearted reading of a typical child's dressing-up episode in order to focus on the girls' introduction to a sexual power structure that they only dimly perceive (R. Saldívar, 185).

The awareness of a biological coming-of-age is expressed in "Hips," a piece that also touches on the formation of the writer:

> One day you wake up and they are there. Ready and waiting like a new Buick with the keys in the ignition. Ready to take you where?
> They're good for holding a baby when you're cooking, Rachel says turning the jump rope a little quicker. She has no imagination.
> . . .
> They bloom like roses, I continue because it's obvious I'm the only one who can speak with any authority; I have science on my side. The bones just one day open. Just like that.

Esperanza and her friends are talking about hips while jumping rope with little Nenny. At this point, the girls' game turns into a creative exercise as the now-older girls take turns improvising rhymes about hips as they jump to the rhythm of the jump rope. Esperanza sings:

> Some are skinny like chicken lips.
> Some are baggy like soggy band-aids
> after you get out of the bathtub.
> I don't care what kind I get.
> Just as long as I get hips.

Then Nenny jumps inside, but can only sing the usual kids' rhymes: "Engine, engine, number nine." Suddenly, the awareness of time passing and growing up is given a spatial dimension. Esperanza, on the outside, is looking at Nenny inside the arc of the swinging rope that now separates Nenny's childhood dimension from her present awareness of just having left behind that very same childhood: "Nenny, I say, but she doesn't hear me. She is too many light years away. She is in a world we don't belong to anymore. Nenny. Going. Going" (49–52).

In adolescence, Esperanza is attracted by what she perceives to be the romantic and liberating aspects of her sexuality, only to learn that it exposes her to peril and male domination. In "Sire," she relates her burgeoning sexuality, her attraction to boys, and her desire to escape from a child's confinement and to sit outside at night like a "bad girl": "Everything is holding its breath inside me. Everything is waiting to explode like Christmas. I want to be all new and shiny. I want to sit out bad at night, a boy around my neck and the wind under my skirt. Not this way, every evening talking to the trees, leaning out the window, imagining what I can't see" (73). "Red Clowns," however, brutally undermines her romantic notions of love and sex. Her physical coming-of-age is tragically confirmed by physical violation:

> Sally, you lied. It wasn't what you said at all. What he did. Where he touched me. I didn't want it, Sally. The way they said it, the way it's supposed to be, all the story books and movies, why did you lie to me? . . . He said I love you, Spanish girl, I love you, and pressed his sour mouth to mine. . . . You're a liar. They all lied. All the books and magazines, everything that told it wrong. Only his dirty fingernails against my skin, only his sour smell again. The moon that watched. The tilt-a-whirl. The red clowns laughing their thick-tongue laugh. (99–100)

As previously noted, in many of the pieces dealing with Esperanza's physical coming-of-age, Cisneros subverts their fairy-tale contexts and undermines romantic notions of love and sexuality. In "Red Clowns," Esperanza, as Ramón Saldívar affirms, "sees that the ideologies of romantic love serve as the propaganda for the maintenance of the sexual economy that makes women like Sally and Esperanza victims merely because they are women" (186).

Valdés notes that "Esperanza Cordero observes, questions, and slowly finds herself determined through her relationship to the others who inhabit her world" (59). These include girls a bit older than her, whom she perceives as possible role models. But her descriptions of them dwell on their loneliness, confinement, and abuse. Again, in taut and lyrical language, Cisneros deromanticizes their dreams. Marin—in the story of the same name—who will be sent back to her mother in Puerto Rico because "she's too much trouble," who wants to work downtown because "you . . . can meet someone in the subway who might marry and take you to live in a big house far away," never comes out of the house "until her aunt comes home from work, and even then she can only stay out in front. She is there every night with the radio. . . . Marin, under the streetlight, dancing by herself, is singing the same song somewhere. I know. Is waiting for a car to stop, a star to fall. Someone to change her life. Anybody" (26–27). And then there is Rafaela, too beautiful for her own good:

> On Tuesdays Rafaela's husband come home late because that's the night he plays dominoes. And then Rafaela, who is still young but getting old from leaning out the window so much, gets locked indoors because her husband is afraid Rafaela will run away since she is too beautiful to look at.
>
> Rafaela leans out the window and leans on her elbow and dreams her hair is like Rapunzel's. . . .
>
> Rafaela who drinks and drinks coconut and papaya juice on Tuesdays and wishes there were sweeter drinks, not bitter like an empty room, but sweet sweet like the island, like the dance hall down the street . . . (79–80)

In "Alicia Who Sees Mice," the narrator describes the hard life of her friend. Alicia, who aspires to an education as a way out of the barrio, must arise early to make her father's lunchbox tortillas because her mother has died, so she has inherited her "mama's rolling pin and sleepiness": "Close your eyes and they'll go away her father says, or You're just imagining. And anyway, a woman's place is sleeping so she can wake up early with the tortilla star, the one that appears early just in time to rise and catch the hindlegs hide behind the sink . . . " Here we note a barrio Latina's perception of life, a space of misery and subjugation, crystallized in the image of the "tortilla star." To Alicia, Venus, the morning star, does not mean wishing upon or waiting for a star to fall down; instead, it means having to get up early, a rolling pin and tortillas. Here we do not see the tortilla as a symbol of cultural identity, but as a symbol of a subjugating ideology, of the imposition of a role that the young woman must assume. In much of the literature, especially poetry, written by Chicanos in the 1960s and 1970s, tortillas and frijoles serve as proud ethnic and cultural markers. Cisneros draws attention away from the cultural products in order to stress the producers, women, of this cultural economy. In "Alicia Who Sees Mice," Venus—and the implication of sex and marriage as escape—is deromanticized, is eclipsed by a cultural reality that points to the drudgery of gender confinement. Alicia "is young and smart and studies for the first time at the university. Two trains and a bus, because she doesn't want to spend her whole life in a factory or behind a rolling pin. . . . Is afraid of nothing except four-legged fur. And fathers" (31–32).

Most of the girls and young women in *Mango Street,* however, cannot aspire to an education; rather, they want to grow up fast and get married. But these, like Minerva, usually have to get married, and they leave a father for a domineering husband. Such is the fate of Sally in "Linoleum Roses":

> Sally got married like we knew she would, young and not ready but married just the same. She met a marshmallow salesman at a school bazaar, and she married him in another state where it's legal to get married before eighth grade. She has her husband and her house now, her pillowcases and her plates. She says she is in love, but I think she did it to escape. . . .
>
> [Her husband] won't let her talk on the telephone. And he doesn't let her look out the window. And he doesn't like her friends, so nobody gets to visit her unless he is working.
>
> She sits at home because she is afraid to go outside without his permission. She looks at all the things they own: the towels and the toaster, the alarm clock and the drapes. She likes looking at the walls, at how neatly their corners meet, the linoleum roses on the floor, the ceiling smooth as wedding cake. (101–2)

Like "tortilla star," this vignette's title is a catachresis, an image whose incongruous and illogical terms bind the opposing ideas of confinement and freedom in a sign of considerable tension. "Linoleum roses" is a sign of household imprisonment and drudgery, in which the semes of rose—beauty, femininity, garden (the outside)—and rose as a traditional metaphor for woman are ironically treated. The roses decorate the linoleum floor that Sally must scrub. This is an image of her future. The simile of the last line, the "ceiling smooth as wedding cake," reverberates in an ironical twist revealing a wedding picture of despair.

The imagery of *The House on Mango Street* has many functions. Besides expressing the ideological message of gender subjugation, and thereby forming an element of its counterdiscourse, it can function on the three levels of form, plot, and symbolic significance. These levels are articulated in "Four Skinny Trees," an important piece in the narrative development of identity.[10] In her personification of the trees, Esperanza expresses a similarity between them and her: "They are the only ones who understand me. I am the only one who understands them. Four skinny trees with skinny necks and pointy elbows like mine." The image's referentiality situates text and narrator in a constrictive urban setting. "Four who grew despite concrete" then proceeds to develop the identity of the enunciating voice mired in a place where she and the trees do not belong: "Four who do not belong here but are here."

At the level of plot, the trees serve as an emblem of survival in a hostile environment:

> Let one forget his reason for being, they'd all droop like tulips in
> a glass, each with their arms around the other. Keep, keep, keep,
> trees say when I sleep. They teach.
> When I am too sad and too skinny to keep keeping, when I am a
> tiny thing against so many bricks, then it is I look at trees. When
> there is nothing left to look at on this street. Four who grew despite
> concrete. Four who reach and do not forget to reach. Four whose
> only reason is to be and be.

The image of the trees acquires its fullest significance at the symbolic level, at which stage the text manifests its intertextuality in the incorporation of the universal significance of trees: "Their strength is secret. They send ferocious roots beneath the ground. They grow up and they grow down and grab the earth between their hairy toes and bite the sky with violent teeth and never quit their anger. This is how they keep" (74–75). The image of the four skinny trees serves to express Esperanza's character development and the will to assert her identity. Against the many odds of her harsh environment and dominating culture, she must struggle, like the trees, to grow and to survive. Like the trees, she must be tenacious in her aspiration to greatness.

The themes of house, identity, and writing are bound together; the last is the resolution of the other themes. It is through writing, through the aesthetic perception of her reality, that Esperanza discovers who she is, affirms her identity, and finds her house. That this house may not be the material reality that Esperanza desires is augured forth in "Elenita, Cards, Palm, Water." Here, Esperanza visits a "witch woman," that is, a *curandera,* a healer and medium, whom she pays five dollars to tell her fortune through her palm and tarot cards. When Esperanza asks about a house, "What about a house, I say, because that's what I came for," the *curandera* replies:

> Ah, yes, a home in the heart. I see a home in the heart.
> Is that *it?*
> That's what I see, she says, . . .
> Baby, I'll look again if you want me to. . . .
> A home in the heart, I was right.
> Only I don't get it. (63–64)

Esperanza is left puzzled by the oracle; what she seeks is not to be found as a material presence on a street, but as a spiritual reality within her heart. Not a house but a home.

Indications of Esperanza's formation as a writer and another prediction of her eventual move from Mango Street to a new "home" are given in "Born Bad" and "The Three Sisters."[11] In "Born Bad," Esperanza reads her poetry to her aunt Guadalupe, who appears to be dying from polio. The aunt replies: "That's nice. That's very good, she said in her tired voice. You must remember to keep writing, Esperanza. You must keep writing. It will help keep you free, and I said yes, but at that time I didn't know what she meant" (61). Puzzled once about where to find a house and thinking that freedom could only be encountered outside the physical and cultural space of her barrio, Esperanza is now astonished that freedom can be found in writing.

In "The Three Sisters," three old women appear at the *velorio* (wake) of a neighbor's baby.[12] To Esperanza, their presence is a mysterious one: "They came with the wind that blows in August, thin as a spider web and barely noticed. Three who did not seem to be related to anything but the moon." Like the *curandera* and the aunt, these women appear at critical junctures to advance the narrative and to assist the heroine in her quest. Unlike the two previous stories, however, the sisters' intervention is related in the combination of the characteristic prose-poem form with an extended dialogue sequence. On the level of the plot, the elderly sisters, who appear like fairy godmothers, bring revelation and the gift of self to Esperanza (Valdés,

65). Esperanza begins to assume her name and her identity:

> What's your name, the cat-eyed one asked.
> Esperanza, I said.
> Esperanza, the old blue-veined one repeated in a high thin voice.
> Esperanza . . . a good name. . . .
> Look at her hands, cat-eyed said.
> And they turned them over and over as if they were looking for
> something.
> She's special.
> Yes, she'll go very far. . . .
> Make a wish.
> A wish?
> Yes, make a wish. What do you want?
> Anything? I said.
> Well, why not?
> I closed my eyes.
> Did you wish already?
> Yes, I said.
> Well, that's all there is to it. It'll come true.
> How do you know? I asked.
> We know, we know.
> Esperanza. The one with marble hands called me aside. Espe-
> ranza. She held my face with her blue-veined hands and looked and
> looked at me. A long silence. When you leave you must remember
> always to come back, she said.
> What?
> When you leave you must remember to come back for the others.
> A circle, understand? You will always be Esperanza. You will always
> be Mango Street. You can't erase what you know. You can't forget
> who you are.
> Then I didn't know what to say. It was as if she could read my
> mind, as if she knew what I had wished for, and I felt ashamed for
> having made such a selfish wish.
> You must remember to come back. For the ones who cannot
> leave as easily as you. You will remember? She asked as if she was
> telling me. Yes, yes, I said a little confused. . . . I didn't understand
> everything they had told me. I turned around. They smiled and
> waved in their smoky way.
> Then I didn't see them. Not once, or twice, or ever again. (103–5)

The three sisters now appear on the symbolic level as the Three Fates
who determine the heroine's destiny and leave her with the prophecy of

self-knowledge (Valdés, 65). Esperanza has received her wish, but does not understand it. How can she leave and still be Mango Street? How can she come back for the others? What is the meaning of the circle? Esperanza thought that by leaving Mango Street and living in another house, one that she could point to with pride, she would leave behind forever an environment she believed to be only temporary. Three mysterious women embed in Esperanza's psyche a cultural and political determination that will find expression in her vocation as a writer. Esperanza eventually will move away from the confining space of house and barrio, but paradoxically, within them she has encountered the liberating space of writing.

Through her creativity, Esperanza comes to inhabit the house of storytelling. The material house of her own—"Not a flat. Not an apartment in back. Not a man's house. Not a daddy's. A house all my own. With my porch and my pillow, my pretty purple petunias. My books and my stories. My two shoes waiting beside the bed. Nobody to shake a stick at. Nobody's garbage to pick up after"—lies in the future. What Esperanza can have now, however, is a magical house entered through the door of her creative imagination: "Only a house quiet as snow, a space for myself to go, clean as paper before the poem" (108). Consequently, the house is a book to be written, blank pages to be filled with her voice and with the voices of women trapped by their economic and cultural restrictions. The absence of punctuation and quotation marks often signal the fusion of these voices (Martín-Rodríguez, 251).

The attainment of identity and the realization of freedom through the space of writing are expressed in "Mango Says Goodbye Sometimes":

> I like to tell stories. I am going to tell you a story about a girl who didn't want to belong.
>
> We didn't always live on Mango Street. Before that we lived on Loomis on the third floor, and before that we lived on Keeler. Before Keeler it was Pauline, but what I remember most is Mango Street, sad red house, the house I belong but do not belong to.
>
> I put it down on paper and then the ghost does not ache so much. I write it down and Mango says goodbye sometimes. She does not hold me with both arms. She sets me free.
>
> One day I will pack my bags of books and paper. One day I will say goodbye to Mango. I am too strong for her to keep me here forever. One day I will go away.
>
> Friends and neighbors will say, What happened to that Esperanza? Where did she go with all those books and paper? Why did she march so far away?

They will not know I have gone away to come back. For the ones
I left behind. For the ones who cannot out.[13] (*sic,* 109–10)

Certainly, Esperanza longs for a new house where she can have her own
female space, and one that she can point to with pride, but she arrives at the
knowledge that this house is also in the heart and that its entrance is gained
through writing. The house is a metaphor for the house of storytelling. Put
another way, she lives in the book on Mango Street (Martín-Rodríguez).
But neither in the sad red house nor in the house of writing does Esperanza
indulge in escapism. She comes to terms with the ethnic consciousness that
the house represents through the process of creative fiction (McCracken,
66). Consequently, although Esperanza liberates herself from her physical
and cultural confinement through her fiction, she never leaves Mango Street
because instead of romanticizing or fantasizing, she writes of her reality.

Erlinda Gonzales and Diana Rebolledo confirm that the house is symbolic of consciousness and collective memory, and is a nourishing structure so that "the narrator comes to understand that, despite her need for a
space of her own, Mango Street is really a part of her—an essential creative
part she will never be able to leave." Thus she searches in (as narrator) and
will return to (as author) her neighborhood "for the human and historical
materials of which [her] stories will be made" (114–15). Through the aesthetic re-creation of her reality and her self, Esperanza transcends her condition, finding another house that is the space of literature. Yet what she
writes about—"third-floor flats, and fear of rats, and drunk husbands sending rocks through windows, anything as far from the poetic [that is, fan-
tasy] as possible"—reinforces her solidarity with the people, the women,
on Mango Street.

Cisneros's *The House on Mango Street,* like Rivera's . . . *y no se lo tragó la
tierra* and other works by Chicano authors, pronounces the counterdiscourse
of a minority people; yet, at the same time, it responds to these works' cultural ideology of Hispanic male supremacy. As Yvonne Yarbro-Bejarano
lucidly points out: "Esperanza is painfully aware of the racial and economic
oppression her community suffers, but it is the fate of the women in her
barrio that has the most profound impact on her, especially as she begins to
develop sexually and learns that the same fate might be hers. Esperanza
gathers strength from the experience of these women to reject the imposition of rigid gender roles predetermined by her culture" (142). As we have
noted, Esperanza's escape from her physical and cultural confinement is
achieved through education and writing. Determined not to wind up like
the victimized women of her barrio, she does encounter a few positive role

models who encourage her education and writing.

The rejection of her culture's gender proscription, achieved through writing, also entails moving away from the barrio to her own female space, a move that could be incorrectly perceived by some as a rejection of her class;[14] but Esperanza concludes her text with the promise to return: "They will not know I have gone away to come back. For the ones I left behind. For the ones who cannot out."[15]

Cisneros's slender but powerful fiction departs from the paradigm of the traditional female bildungsroman, which submits to the literary and ideological hegemony of masculine discourse. In her coming-of-age literary testimony, Esperanza refuses to accept her expected position in society. This determination is not only manifested by her actions—"I have begun my own quiet war. Simple. Sure. I am one who leaves the table like a man, without putting back the chair or picking up the plate" (89)—but by the empowering act of writing: "She seeks self-empowerment through writing, while recognizing her commitment to a community of Chicanas. Writing has been essential in connecting her with the power of women and her promise to pass down that power to other women is fulfilled by the writing and publication of the text itself" (Yarbro-Bejarano, 143).[16]

B. Teaching the Work

One of the most important considerations in approaching *The House on Mango Street* is that it cannot be effectively taught and discussed if it is categorized under feminist literature *per se*. The discourses of "American" literary and critical feminism, that is, of Anglo women writers and critics, generally do not take into account the questions of class and color, and mistakenly pretend to speak monolithically for all American women. These Anglo women writers and critics do not seem to perceive that women of ethnic and racial minorities are involved in racial and class struggles that directly influence the expression of their own cultural conflict of gender liberation. At times these women respond to the urgencies of class struggle and at times, probably more often, they express the tension of their double marginality. With regard to Chicana literature, Yarbro-Bejarano observes:

> Perhaps the most important principle of Chicana feminist criti-
> cism is the realization that the Chicana's experience as a woman is
> inextricable from her experience as a member of an oppressed
> working-class racial minority and a culture which is not the domi-

nant culture. Her task is to show how in works by Chicanas, elements of gender, race, culture and class coalesce. The very term
"Chicana" or "mestiza" communicates the multiple connotations of
color and femaleness, as well as historical adumbrations of class and
cultural membership within the economic structure and dominant
culture of the United States. While this may seem painfully obvious,
the assertion of this project in Chicana writing is crucial in combat-
ting the tendency in both white feminist and Chicano discourse to
see these elements as mutually exclusive. By asserting herself as
Chicana or mestiza, the Chicana confronts the damaging fragmentation of her identity into component parts at war with each other.
(140)

Chicanas and other Latinas perceive themselves as "women of color," a
term that not only includes women of other racial minorities but one that
identifies them with the working class. Thus, in order to discuss and analyze such a work as *Mango Street*, it is necessary to demonstrate how and
under what circumstances the elements of gender, race, culture, and class
coalesce and also vie with one another.

In taking the above factors into consideration, however, it is essential
not to follow another tendency, that of viewing minority literatures as sociology or anthropology instead of reading them as literature. A book such as
The House on Mango Street is fundamentally a work of art. It is not "art for
art's sake," however, but an aesthetic expression of the writer's personal and
social concerns. The meaning of *The House on Mango Street*, for example,
is what these concerns or ideas-in-this-form-do. Thus, the work should
not be read and studied only with regard to its formal elements, but with an
eye to seeing how these elements shape and give expression to its themes
and ideologies.

Another factor that may impede accessibility to the text is one's unfa-
miliarity with the experiences related by minority writers. That is, the degree of one's response and sensitivity to these texts can be related to one's
class, upbringing, education, exposure to other groups and ways of life,
and so on. Consequently, the acquisition of such a sensitivity depends on
one's own initiative in overcoming the limitations of ethnocentricity and
the willingness to benefit from a liberal education and a curriculum with a
multicultural component. Certainly, reading many of the works studied in
this collection would be a big step toward the acquisition of such a sensitivity and of a liberal formation.

Perhaps one sensitivity exercise could be the assignment to write a brief
narrative based on a specific experience, in the manner of the stories in

Mango Street. These could be turned in without a name, then read by all the students. The aim would be to see if the students can assess (1) artistic merit, and (2) detect racial, ethnic, class, and gender differences as well as similarities.

A method of approaching, and by implication teaching, *The House on Mango Street* has been given in the first part of this study. In this section, I propose some topics that can amplify and complement my reading, and sharpen the students' critical skills.

1. I deliberately excluded from my commentary "The Monkey Garden," leaving it for the student to analyze with regard to the themes and formal elements discussed in my analysis. Some very important things happen to Esperanza in this story. What are they and how are they expressed? How does this experience and this story relate to the book as a whole?

2. On the basis of the theme of rebirth, compare "The Monkey Garden" with the story "Moths," from *The Moths and Other Stories,* by Helena María Viramontes.

3. Valdés points out that Esperanza's affirmation of self-invention displaces men's stories about women and that her freedom depends on escaping from the trap of patriarchal narrativity (69). How does Esperanza achieve this? What is meant by "patriarchal narrativity" and how does she create a feminist narrativity?

4. In Rivera's . . . *y no se lo tragó la tierra / And the Earth Did Not Devour Him,* religion is an important theme. Rivera saw that religion had a negative influence on his people, the migrant workers. In their oppressed state, and with its promise of their reward in the hereafter, Catholicism promoted fatalism and resignation to a life of poverty and passivity, and consequently submission to the external elements of oppression. Inasmuch as Catholicism is an important component of Hispanic culture and promotes a passive and obedient role for women, do you believe its exclusion from the book is a serious omission? How could the author have treated this theme? Also, since education is important for Esperanza and she obviously attends a parochial school, why is her school experience omitted? If Cisneros were to rewrite the book, what suggestions would you give her?

5. Compare *Mango Street,* as a bildungsroman, with either (1) *Pocho,* by José Antonio Villarreal, or (2) *Bless Me, Ultima,* by Rudolfo Anaya. With regard to (1), take into consideration the portrayal of women and the theme of assimilation; concerning (2), discuss also the use of myth, the rural/urban contrast, and the role of religion.

6. Compare *Mango Street* with Richard Rodriquez's *Hunger of Memory,*

considering the latter as an autobiographical bildungsroman. Pay attention to the themes of shame, class rejection, and assimilation.

7. If you were to consider the poetics of women of color, what conclusions would you come to after reading, for example, Maya Angelou's *I Know Why the Caged Bird Sings*, Alice Walker's *The Color Purple*, Maxine Hong Kingston's *Woman Warrior*, Amy Tan's *The Joy Luck Club*, Cisneros's *The House on Mango Street*, and Viramontes's *The Moths and Other Stories*?

C. Bibliographies

1. Related Works

Castillo, Ana. *The Mixquiahuala Letters*. Binghamton, N.Y.: Bilingual Press, 1986. An epistolary novel and sociocultural document that encompasses both Mexican and United States Hispanic forms of love and gender conflict.

Cervantes, Lorna Dee. *Emplumada*. Pittsburgh: University of Pittsburgh Press, 1981. The first book by the best Chicana poet writing today. Her expression of womanhood is expansive enough to embrace a diversity of human experience. Her poetry is characterized by a utopian vision in conflict with the reality of social problems.

―――. *From the Cables of Genocide: Poems on Love and Hunger*. Houston: Arte Público Press, 1991. Poetry that stretches the resources of language, imagery, and the dialectics of love, hunger, and aesthetics to express a penetrating feminist and human vision of the poet's universe.

Chávez, Denise. *The Last of the Menu Girls*. Houston: Arte Público Press, 1986. Interrelated stories, humorous and serious, narrated by Rocío Esquibel about her identity crisis and her sister and mother, all of whom make do without a man. The adolescent protagonist examines available models of womanhood, tries out roles, comes to terms with the clutter of her past, and emerges as a writer.

Corpi, Lucha. *Palabras de Mediodía / Noon Words*, trans. Catherine Rodríguez-Nieto. Berkeley: University of California Press and El Fuego de Aztlán, 1980. Born and raised in Mexico, Corpi came to the United States after her divorce. She writes her poetry in Spanish, although her novels—*Delia's Song* (Arte Público Press, 1988) and *Eulogy for a Brown Angel* (Arte Público Press, 1992)—are in English. Her excellent poetry is about boundaries, those that are crossed from Mexican to American and Chicano cultures, and those that are surmounted in the flight from Mexican patriarchy.

Mohr, Nicholasa. *Rituals of Survival: A Woman's Portfolio*. Houston: Arte Público Press, 1985. A collection of five short stories and a novella that offers indelible portraits of Puerto Rican women in New York City and the rituals of survival that shape their lives.

Ortiz Cofer, Judith. *Terms of Survival.* Houston: Arte Público Press, 1987. A cultural legacy and a woman's desire to be released from rituals are the terms that the poet confronts in her dialectic of survival. Cultural icons, customs, and rites of passage take root in an imagery that is lush, tropical, and piercing.

————. *Silent Dancing: A Partial Remembrance of a Puerto Rican Childhood.* Houston: Arte Público Press, 1991. Personal recollections of the author's childhood, of growing up in Puerto Rico and New Jersey, the book treats the themes of female conditioning and feminine roles, culture shock and immigration.

Ríos, Isabella. *Victuum.* Los Angeles/Ventura: Diana-Etna, 1976. A psychological and experimental novel that eschews traditional narration in favor of a mimetic narrative where the characters speak for themselves without editorial intrusion or mediation. The novel traces the life of Valentina Ballesternos in Oxnard, California, from 1925, before she was born, to about 1965, and deals with a woman's perpetuation of patriarchy.

Vigil, Evangelina. *Thirty an' Seen a Lot.* Houston: Arte Público Press, 1982. Poems, many in a bilingual format, that reflect life in the Chicano barrio from a female perspective. The book's trajectory is from the community to the universal plight of Hispanics.

Viramontes, Helena María. *The Moths and Other Stories.* Houston: Arte Público Press, 1985. With an introduction by Yvonne Yarbro-Bejarano, this collection of eight stories examines feminine roles and expectations, from childhood through old age, in a terse language and innovative narrative technique.

2. Best Criticism

Cisneros, Sandra. "The softly insistent voice of a poet." *Austin American Statesman* (March 11, 1986): 14–15.

————. "Ghosts and Voices: Writing from Obsession." "Notes to a Young(er) Writer." "Do You Know Me?: I Wrote *The House on Mango Street.*" All in *The Americas Review* 15, no. 1 (1987): 69–79. These three essays by Cisneros and the above interview with her offer many insights into her background, her formation as a writer, and how *The House on Mango Street* was realized.

Gonzales-Berry, Erlinda, and Tey Diana Rebolledo. "Growing Up Chicano: Tomás Rivera and Sandra Cisneros." In *International Studies in Honor of Tomás Rivera,* ed. Julián Olivares, 109–19. Houston: Arte Público Press, 1986. A structural and thematic comparative approach that concentrates on the originality of a feminist work in opposition to a male-centered canonical text.

Gutiérrez-Revuelta, Pedro. "Género e ideología en el libro de Sandra Cisneros: *The House on Mango Street.*" *Crítica* 1, no. 3 (1986): 48–59. This article opposes the categorization of the work as "children's literature," due principally to its ideology of the working-class minority and to the postmodernist construct of a hybrid genre.

Martín-Rodríguez, Manuel M. "The Book on Mango Street: Escritura y liberación en la obra de Sandra Cisneros." In *Mujer y Literatura Mexicana y Chicana: Culturas en Contacto,* Vol. 2, ed. Aralia López González et al., 249–54. México: Colegio de México, 1990. The application of speech-act theory to the dialectic between the individual discourse and the collective discourse with the aim of creating a fictive space called Mango Street. In Spanish.

McCracken, Ellen. "Sandra Cisneros' *The House on Mango Street:* Community-Oriented Introspection and the Demystification of Patriarchal Violence." In *Breaking Boundaries: Latina Writing and Critical Readings,* ed. Asunción Horno-Delgado et al., 62–71. Amherst: University of Massachusetts Press. A Marxist approach that conceives the work in opposition to the "discourse of power," conceived both as that emanating from the ideology of the dominant society and, particularly, that of male-centered texts.

Olivares, Julián. "Sandra Cisneros' *The House on Mango Street,* and the Poetics of Space." In *Beyond Stereotypes: The Critical Analysis of Chicana Literature,* ed. María Herrera-Sobek, 160–70. Binghamton, N.Y.: Bilingual Press, 1985. A structural and thematic approach that demonstrates how the work opposes Gaston Bachelard's *Poetics of Space* (which Cisneros read prior to commencing *Mango Street*) and the masculine politics that informs his work.

Saldívar, Ramón. "The Dialectics of Subjectivity: Gender and Difference in Isabella Ríos, Sandra Cisneros, and Cherríe Moraga." *Chicano Narrative, The Dialectics of Difference,* 171–99. Madison: University of Wisconsin Press, 1990. A poststructuralist and historically based approach influenced by the criticism of Fredric Jameson, which attempts to demonstrate how the dialectical form of narratives by Chicano men and women is a way of dealing with their cultural representation, expression of subjectivity, and resistance to symbolic structures of cultural oppression.

Valdés, María Elena de. "In Search of Identity in Cisneros' *The House on Mango Street.*" *Canadian Review of American Studies* 23, no. 1 (1992): 55–72. A historical, structural approach that incorporates the social feminism of Naomi Black and Julia Kristeva, and examines the composite of the poetic enunciating voice and the narrative voice.

3. Other Sources

Bruce-Novoa, Juan. *Retrospace: Collected Essays on Chicano Literature.* Houston: Arte Público Press, 1990.

Cisneros, Sandra. *Bad Boys.* San José, Calif.: Mango Press, 1980.

————.*The House on Mango Street.* 1984. Rev. ed., New York: Vintage Books, 1989.

————. *My Wicked, Wicked Ways.* Bloomington, Ind.: Third Woman Press, 1987.

————. *Woman Hollering Creek, and Other Stories.* New York: Random House, 1991.

Herrera-Sobek, María, ed. *Beyond Stereotypes: The Critical Analysis of Chicana Literature.* Binghamton, N.Y.: Bilingual Press, 1985.

Herrera-Sobek, María, and Helena María Viramontes, eds. *Chicana Creativity and Criticism: Charting New Frontiers in American Literature.* Houston and Irvine: Arte Público Press and Mexico/Chicano Program, University of California, 1988.

Horno Delgado, Asunción, et al. *Breaking Boundaries: Latina Writing and Critical Readings.* Amherst: University of Massachusetts Press, 1989.

Lomelí, Franciso, ed. *The Handbook on Hispanic Cultures in the United States: Literature and Art.* Houston: Arte Público and Instituto de Cooperación Iberoamericana, 1993.

Melville, Margarita, ed. *Twice a Minority: Mexican American Women.* St. Louis, Mo.: Mosby, 1980.

Olivares, Julián, ed. *International Studies in Honor of Tomás Rivera.* Houston: Arte Público Press, 1986.

Rivera, Tomás. *Tomás Rivera: The Complete Works,* ed. Julián Olivares. Houston: Arte Público Press, 1991.

Rodríguez, Juan. *"The House on Mango Street,* by Sandra Cisneros." *Austin Chronicle* (Aug. 10, 1984). Cited in Gutiérrez-Revuelta, "Género e ideología en el libro de Sandra Cisernos," 52.

Saldívar, José D. "The Ideological and Utopian in Tomás Rivera's . . . *y no se lo tragó la tierra* and Ron Arias' *The Road to Tamazunchale.*" *Crítica* 1, no. 2 (1985): 100–114.

Yarbro-Bejarano, Yvonne. "Chicana Literature from a Chicana Feminist Perspective." In Herrera-Sobek and Viramontes, *Chicana Creativity and Criticism,* 139–46.

Notes

1. Originally published in 1984 by Arte Público Press, *The House on Mango Street,* winner of the Before Columbus Foundation's American Book Award

for 1985, enjoyed three printings and a second revised edition in 1988. I cite from the 1991 Vintage edition.

2. *Barrio* means "neighborhood," but in the context of Latino socioeconomic realities, "ghetto" is a better translation. The large city would be Chicago, where the author was born in 1954.

3. Cisneros is the only daughter of a Mexican father and a Chicana mother; she has six brothers.

4. For a study of . . . *y no se lo tragó la tierra*, as well as other works by Rivera, see the introduction to my edition of *Tomás Rivera: The Complete Works* (1991). Citations from *Tierra* are from Evangelina Vigil's translation, *And the Earth Did Not Devour Him*, which is included in *The Complete Works*.

5. Another possible influence on the structure, even ideology, of *Mango Street* is hagiography. Cisneros relates that she read "the lives of saints" in her childhood ("Ghosts and Voices," 70). Because of their martyrdom, which can be read in various ways, the lives of saints, especially the women, have appealed to female writers over the centuries. The various "pictures" of the suffering girls and women in *Mango Street* can be conceived as a type of martyrology. This is an approach that merits study.

6. Ramón Saldívar affirms that *The House on Mango Street* represents "the enormously complex process of the construction of the gendered subject. Posing the question of sexual difference within the urban working-class Chicano community, Cisneros' novel also emphasizes the crucial roles of racial and material as well as ideological conditions of oppression. It thus helps establish what over the course of the 1980s will become a virtual program for writings by Chicanas, namely a clear-sighted recognition of the unavoidably mutual overdetermination of the categories of race and class with that of gender in any attempted positioning of the Chicana subject" (181–82).

7. On the dialectics of inside/outside, alienation/integration, confinement/freedom, and the poetics of space in *The House on Mango Street,* see Olivares, "Sandra Cisneros' *The House on Mango Street,* and the Poetics of Space." The present study incorporates portions of my previous article.

8. Cisneros has said: "One of the most important books in my childhood . . . was Virginia Lee Burton's *The Little House,* a picture book that tells the story of a house on a country hill whose owner promises never to sell her 'for gold or silver.' . . . Stable and secure in the country, the little house is happy witnessing the changes of seasons and generations, although curious about the distant lights of the big city. . . . Finally, the city that has been growing ever larger, catches up with the little house, until she finds she is no longer in the country but eventually surrounded by tall buildings and noisy traffic. The inhabitants move away, and the little house, no longer able to see the stars at night, grows sad; her roof sags and the doorstep

droops; the windows that serve as eyes, one on either side of the door, are broken. Fortunately, the great, granddaughter of the man who built the house rescues her . . . Traffic is halted on the busy boulevard for the little house to be wheeled away to the country and settled on a hill just like the one it originally sat on, happy and once again loved" ("Ghosts and Voices," 70).

9. Women's shoes are a universal symbol of sexuality, marriage, and fertility.

10. I follow Valdés's analysis of the imagery in "Four Skinny Trees"; see also her commentary on "The Three Sisters" (63–65).

11. The context of death in these stories suggests perhaps that creativity is not only a means of escape from the confines of Mango Street, but also an affirmation of life and a rebirth. It merits noting that in "The Monkey Garden" Esperanza lies down, closes her eyes, and wills herself to die. When she awakens and stands up, she finds that she has left behind her childhood; in other words, she has been reborn.

12. McCracken (70) notes that this story is an expansion of Cisneros's poem "Velorio" in her chapbook *Bad Boys*.

13. The first edition has "For the ones who cannot get out."

14. As does Juan Rodríguez; for a rebuttal of this contention, see my 1988 study, 168–69.

15. The same conviction is expressed in "Bums in the Attic":

One day I'll own my own house, but I won't forget who I am or where I came from. Passing bums will ask, Can I come in? I'll offer them the attic, ask them to stay, because I know how it is to be without a house.

Some days after dinner, guests and I will sit in front of a fire. Floorboards will squeak upstairs. The attic grumble.

Rats? they'll ask.

Bums, I'll say, and I'll be happy. (87)

16. Appositely, Cisneros remarks: "I am the first woman in my family to pick up a pen and record what I see around me, a woman who has the power to speak and is privileged enough to be heard. That is a responsibility" ("Notes to a Young(er) Writer," 76). In another essay, she adds: "From [the] experience of listening to young Latinas whose problems were so great, I felt helpless; I was moved to do something to change their lives, ours, mine. I did the only thing I knew how. I wrote . . . ("Do You Know Me?," 78).

Richard Rodriguez's *Hunger of Memory* and New Perspectives on Ethnic Autobiography

ANTONIO C. MÁRQUEZ

A. Analysis of Themes and Form

Hunger of Memory is comprised of a brief prologue, suggestively titled "Middle-Class Pastoral," and six chapters: (1) "Aria," (2) "The Achievement of Desire," (3) "Credo," (4) "Complexion," (5) "Profession," (6) "Mr. Secrets." The book's subtitle explicitly announces its subject matter and the six chapters are variations on a theme. The six parts form the orchestration of Rodriguez's life; or as he describes the book, "Essays impersonating an autobiography; six chapters of sad, fuguelike repetition" (7). Rodriguez's autobiography (he mocks the term "ethnic autobiography") is about his education: "I wrote this autobiography as the history of my schooling" (6)—but it is also about the discovery of a vocation and the search for an identity. Spanning from elementary public school in Sacramento, California, to Ph.D. studies in Renaissance literature at the British Museum, Rodriguez's life-story is a querulous assessment of his heritage. In recasting his life and his educational experiences, Rodriguez raises central issues in relation to Mexican and Mexican American cultural history. The most controversial aspect of Rodriguez's book turns on his assertion that his education led to his separation from family and Hispanic cultural roots and that it was a necessary and beneficial separation. He contends that the assimilation into Anglo American culture and the mainstream of the United States is necessary to attain a public identity and to achieve success within that society. Both praised and vilified, *Hunger of Memory* has become the eye of an ideological storm. An outspoken critic of bilingual education and affirmative action, Rodriguez has quarreled for more than a decade with what he calls the "ethnic left." It is an issue that prompts a sardonic voice in *Hunger of Memory:* "I have become notorious among certain leaders of America's ethnic left. I am considered a dupe, an ass, the fool—Tom Brown, the brown Uncle Tom, interpreting the writing on the wall to a bunch of cigar smoking pharaohs" (4).

There is cause for Rodriguez's self-proclaimed notoriety. What is to be made of a Mexican American writer who says, "Thomas Jefferson is my cultural forefather, not Benito Juárez," who unabashedly claims that "the drama of my life was not an ethnic drama. . . . The writers who teach me best about the drama of my own life are not American. They are British . . . I cannot imagine writing my own life without the example of [D. H.] Lawrence" ("An American Writer," 5). Here is a man who makes no bones about what he values and what has given meaning to his life as a man and writer; and nowhere in this confessional celebration can be seen an acknowledgment of the traditional roots of Mexican American or Chicano culture—of its legends, heroes, artists, writers and those who serve as example or inspire us to rise above ourselves. No wonder that Rodriguez's *Hunger of Memory* incited an angry chorus of condemnation. It earned him derisive tags of *vendido* (sellout), *agringado* (a Chicano who aspires to Anglo middle-class values), and *tío taco* (Chicano Uncle Tom).

More expressive condemnation took the guise of academic criticism, as Chicano scholars and critics assailed Rodriguez's posturing in *Hunger of Memory*. Tomás Rivera, a major figure in contemporary Chicano literature, led the attack with "Richard Rodriguez' *Hunger of Memory* as Humanistic Antithesis." Rivera praises Rodriguez's prose style, but he rebukes Rodriguez's deliberate separation from the mainstays of family and culture. Explicit in the title, Rivera's central point is that Rodriguez in denying his heritage denies the very essence of human community and one's identity as a social being. More emphatically critical, Ramón Saldívar sees Rodriguez as a menace that threatens the social fabric and cultural integrity of Chicanos: "The individualized voice of the unique artistic sensibility represented among Chicanos by Richard Rodriguez is one example of the disruption of the organic Mexican American community" (136). Extending censure to Rodriguez's appreciative readers, Héctor Calderón decries "the moral outrage that the media and the political right have accorded Richard Rodriguez's *Hunger of Memory* for shedding his Mexican working class identity for that of a middle-class 'American' male" (217). José David Saldívar joined the chorus with these trenchant remarks: "Rodriguez's autobiography is a highly marketable lyric of rhetorical angst. . . . Although Rodriguez continually tells us that he suffers from a sense of the subaltern's lack of advantage, from the evidence it is clear that he suffers more from a profound sense of snobbery and bad taste" (136–37). Widely anthologized in college readers, *Hunger of Memory*'s currency added fuel to the charge that Rodriguez had provided a sop for "the most receptive audience imaginable: the right-wing establishment and the liberal academic intelligentsia" (R. Saldívar, 158).

Why did Rodriguez's book meet with a critical firestorm from Chicano scholars and critics, and at the same time earn recognition and praise from non-Chicano scholars and critics? Invariably, admirers of *Hunger of Memory* praised Rodriguez's expressive honesty, eloquent ruminations, and the literary bent of his autobiography. On the other hand, detractors either ignored the stylistic merits of the book or acknowledged them but were chafed by Rodriguez's refusal to celebrate ethnicity and cultural resistance. The question hinges on a more important concern created by the differences and problems in reading ethnic literature. For the sake of a general clarification, it can be argued that Chicano readers read *Hunger of Memory* differently than do non-Chicano readers. And it is reasonable to expect that these differences may extend to teachers who teach and students who read *Hunger of Memory* in the classroom. Moreover, the crucial matter is that the character of ethnic literature itself is changing and will continue to change. *Hunger of Memory* is an important work because it raises a problematical issue: *What is ethnic literature?*

Genaro Padilla, a discerning critic who has done the most extensive research and the best scholarship on Chicano/a autobiography, offers a judicious assessment and acute point on the directions that are being taken by writers like Richard Rodriguez: "Whether Rodriguez and his antecedents . . . should be disavowed is an issue different readers must decide for themselves. However, precisely because their lives refuse to conform to some of the images we have created for ourselves, especially in recent years when we have radicalized that self-image, their autobiographies do force us to recognize variations of the Chicano self" (303). The "variations of the Chicano self" in autobiographic writing exact the recognition that Chicano/a literature, like other ethnic literatures, is undergoing a complex process of evolution, change, expansion, and redefinition. Cultural anthropology submits the consensus that no culture is static; change is part of the dynamic of any culture, and it is certainly true of ethnic cultures and societies. The new forms of autobiographic writing assess, modify, qualify, transmute, and can also reject what has gone before—what is often called "traditional culture"— and seek new ways to express the sense of difference. In some cases, the certitudes of ethnic identity have given way to confusion or skepticism. "Ethnicity is only a public metaphor," Rodriguez muses, "like sexuality or age, for a knowledge that bewilders us" ("An American Writer," 8). Rodriguez's work, for better or for worse, is a harbinger of new directions in ethnic autobiography.

In several respects, *Hunger of Memory* deviates from the norms of ethnic autobiography and counters cultural-literary theories on the subject. In *The Ethnic Eye: A Sourcebook For Ethnic American Autobiography,* James Craig Holte posits a basic characteristic of ethnic autobiography: "One of the con-

ventions of the conversion narrative is that the writer becomes a spokesman for the community. . . . The development of a self takes place in a
community apart from middle class America, and the writer becomes, in
the narrative, the voice of the community" (7). *Hunger of Memory* diverges
from both prescriptions. Rodriguez calls his autobiography "a middle-class
pastoral," and he declines any representative role. Other Chicano autobiographies meet Holte's requisites. *Barrio Boy,* by Ernesto Galarza, is an excellent example and serves as a striking contrast. Especially in the light that
Galarza's autobiography has been used as a cultural-literary measuring stick;
some critics have compared *Barrio Boy* and *Hunger of Memory,* using the
comparison to praise *Barrio Boy* as a true and valuable Chicano autobiography and to condemn *Hunger of Memory* as a false, pretentious, and ultimately self-serving autobiography. Clearly, Galarza assumes a representative
voice and places himself in a collective historical experience: "What brought
me and my family to the United States from Mexico also brought hundreds
of thousands of others like us. In many ways, the experience of a multitude
of boys like myself, migrating from countless villages like Jalcocotán and
starting life anew in barrios like the one in Sacramento must have been
similar" (1). In contrast, Rodriguez takes the tack of individuality and directs the reader not to presume an ethnic representation: "Mistaken, the
gullible reader will—in sympathy or in anger—take it that I intend to model
my life as the typical Hispanic-American life. But I write of one life only.
My own" (7). Rodriguez's disavowal smacks of egotism, but we must not
lose sight of what characterizes his narrative: it is the autobiography of a
writer. The "ethnic drama" of *Hunger of Memory* is secondary to the act of
writing and to the metaphors of self that have modified ethnic autobiography.

From another quarter, William Boelhower's "The Making of Ethnic Autobiography in the United States" contends that there are several constants
in ethnic autobiography: "The infinite variations of ethnic autobiography
are always on a single theme—a hyphenated self's attempt to make it in
America. At the center of ethnic autobiography, of course, is the gnawing
absent presence of an old world heritage" (133). This view presupposes a
tension in ethnic autobiography between the necessity to assimilate and a
cherished attachment to the old country. *Barrio Boy,* again, follows the conventional format; Galarza expresses the immigrant's hope of a new life and
destiny in the United States, and he also looks back with nostalgia and holds
fond memories of "the solid Mexican homeland, the good native earth"
(196). Quite differently, Rodriguez sees "the old country" as remote from
the immediate realities that shaped his life and he is embarrassed by his

parents' sentimentality for "Mexican ways." The counterpoise of *Barrio Boy* and *Hunger of Memory* sustains Sau-Ling Cynthia Wong's acute observation that students of ethnic literature have not adequately measured the differences between *ethnic autobiography* and *immigrant autobiography*. Wong's focus is on Asian American literature, but she briefly covers *Hunger of Memory* and advances it as an example of a pattern in ethnic autobiography: "As is made clear in a recent ethnic autobiography, Richard Rodriguez's *Hunger of Memory* (1982), loss of the mother tongue and acquisition of English may fundamentally alter second generations' alignments with both the ethnic culture and Anglo culture"(152). The prime value of "Immigrant Autobiography: Some Questions of Definition and Approach" is Wong's persuasive argument that the universality of an ethnic literature is not a given and that historical periods and generational differences must be included in valuations of ethnic autobiographies.

With the clarification that *Barrio Boy* is an *immigrant autobiography* and *Hunger of Memory* is an *ethnic autobiography* (however problematic), the counterpoint and the story of the Rodriguez family must be placed against the backdrop of Mexican-Chicano history (see "Teaching The Work," below). In *Days of Obligation,* Rodriguez ironically recounts his parents' passage and how their homeland remained an enduring attachment: "My parents left Mexico in the twenties: she as a girl with a family; he as a young man, alone. . . . At some celebration—we went to so many when I was a boy—a man in the crowd filled his lungs with American air to crow over all, ¡VIVA MÉXICO! Everyone cheered. My parents cheered. The band played louder. Why VIVA MEXICO? The country that had betrayed them? The country that had forced them to live elsewhere? . . . Mexico was memory—not mine" (53). Rodriguez's play with the ironies of history and his parents' contrastive roles reiterates a significant facet of *Hunger of Memory*. Rodriguez is a native son, and he marks the sociohistorical, generational, educational, and cultural changes in Mexican-Chicano history. He recounts in *Hunger of Memory* and *Days of Obligation* how his parents made an uneasy truce and accommodation with their adopted country: his father admired the progress and opportunities offered by the United States but saw little else of value; his mother is often described as sentimentally singing Mexican songs and dreaming of returning to Mexico. In contrast, Rodriguez and many Chicanos of his generation—and more so of the present generation—feel no allegiance or nostalgia for Mexico. As Rodriguez often ruminates, mind and heart now reside north of the Rio Grande. He views with skepticism the myth of Aztlán, the retrieval of a heroic pre-Columbian past, and the celebration of an Indo-Hispano heritage. *Hunger of Memory* contains this dismissive aside: "Aztec ruins hold no special interest for me. I do not search Mexican graveyards for ties to unnamable ancestors" (5). Here, Rodriguez meets head-on the cultural nationalism that surfaced during the Chicano movement of the 1960s, which he derides as nostalgia wrapped in Zapata-Pancho Villa romanticism. Understandably, such spoutings raised the hackles of the so-called ethnic left, and *Hunger of Memory* compounds the problem when Rodriguez attacks Chicano academicians:

> The students insisted they were still tied to the culture of the past.
> Nothing in their lives had changed with their matriculation. They
> would be able to "go home again." . . . Leisured, and skilled at
> abstracting from immediate experience, the scholar is able to see
> how aspects of individual experience constitute a culture. By con-
> trast, the poor have neither the inclination nor the skills to imagine
> their lives so abstractly. They remain strangers to the way of life the
> academic constructs so well on paper. Ethnic studies departments
> were founded on romantic hopes. (157–58)

In effect, Rodriguez's attitudes and the purpose of his autobiography diverge from the sociohistorical concerns that have formed the bedrock of Chicano/a literature and criticism. In "The Evolution of Chicano Litera-ture," a key work of Chicano literary history, Raymund A. Paredes encapsu-lated the most common definition, or description, of Chicano/a literature: "This leads us to the final question: what exactly is Chicano literature. . . . Chicano literature is that body of work produced by United States citizens and residents of Mexican descent for whom a sense of ethnicity is a critical part of their literary sensibilities and for whom portrayal of their ethnic experience is a major concern." This predominant view underscores the ethnicity of Chicano/a literature, which transcends literary boundaries and where the import is placed on social, cultural, and political aspects of the experience. "In an age when the literature of the United States is marked by profound pessimism and a retreat from the national culture," Paredes also argues, "Chicano writing is notable for its celebration of ethnic values and traditions" (72–74). The last point implies an ethical component to the oppositional or alternative values endemic to Chicano/a literature. Paredes's formulation of the nature and purpose of Chicano/a literature has its un-deniable merits, but it also has limitations (acknowledged by Paredes) when it comes to works that do not fit the mold. How can it apply to or include a work such as *Hunger of Memory*? What if a work questions ethnicity or quarrels with its relevance? Is it less valuable because it does not affirm ethnicity? Does this mean that *Hunger of Memory* is not a work of Chicano literature and not an ethnic autobiography? Without a doubt, *Hunger of*

Memory is a problematic work. Part of the significance of Rodriguez's embattled autobiography is that it raises engaging questions about the relation of culture to literature, and literature to culture. Foremost, we must consider that neither "culture" nor "literature" is homogeneous, unchanging, and static.

To this end, new perspectives are being shaped by scholars who have fused ethnography and literary studies, and these perspectives have marked a new direction in cultural criticism that may prove useful in approaching ethnic literature. Werner Sollors's schema in "Nine Suggestions for Historians of American Ethnic Literature" serves as a point of departure: "Ethnicity is not merely a matter of cultural (let alone biological) survival; ethnicity is constantly recreated as people (and ethnic authors among them, of course) set up new distinctions, make new boundaries, and form new groups" (95). Sollors has significantly contributed to the perspective that has taken the rubric of "the invention of ethnicity." Part of the strategy of this line of inquiry is to place ethnic literature within the purview of postmodern cultural and literary theories. In *The Invention of Ethnicity,* Sollors advances a fundamental premise: "By calling ethnicity—that is, belonging and being perceived by others as belonging to an ethnic group—an 'invention,' one signals an interpretation in a modern and postmodern context. There is a certain, previously unrecognized semantic legitimacy in insisting on this context" (xiii). Michael M. J. Fischer, an anthropologist who had done ground-breaking work in applying postmodern literary and cultural theories to the study of ethnic literature, amplified Sollors's premise to form an engaging thesis centered on autobiographic writing:

> . . . so ethnic autobiography and autobiographical fiction can perhaps serve as key forms for explorations of pluralist, post-industrial, late twentieth-century society. . . . What the newer works bring home forcefully is, *first,* the paradoxical sense that ethnicity is something reinvented and reinterpreted in each generation by each individual and that it is often something quite puzzling to the individual, something over which he or she lacks control. (195)

Fischer's conspectus covers signal works of Chicano/a literature and he concludes his overview of *Hunger of Memory* with a point that confirms the problematic nature of Rodriguez's autobiography: "The antagonism/anxiety directed towards Rodriguez's autobiographic argument, as well as the commentary on the political didacticism of earlier Chicano writing, pose the key issues for the creation of authentically inter-referential ethnic voices, as well as alerting us to the diversity within the Chicano (not to mention the larger Hispanic-American) community"(220). This and similar critical writings confirm that *Hunger of Memory* is a key text in postmodern auto-biographic writing.

Considering Paredes's disquisition, for example, that Chicano writing offers an alternative to a mainstream literature marked by "a profound pessimism and retreat from the national culture," what happens when Chicano/a literature moves into the mainstream or departs from its oppositional roles? Can a culture and its literature remain isolated, unaffected, and pure? Again, we are faced with a problematic situation that is a prime concern of Chicano cultural studies. Renato Rosaldo, an anthropologist who has also expanded his interests to literary and cultural criticism, makes an intrepid suggestion. His work on Chicano cultural poetics, specifically the aptly titled "Changing Chicano Narratives," takes off from ethnographic studies on culture difference and historical change, and Rosaldo challenges "the received notion of culture as unchanging and homogeneous" (35). Surveying Chicano chronicles and historical narratives, he notes that the traditional role of the Chicano writer was to engage in cultural resistance, at the same time providing a social analysis and critique of the dominant society. This role has slackened, Rosaldo points out, as the culture and its literature have changed: "Once a figure of masculine heroics and resistance to white supremacy, the Chicano warrior hero now has faded away in a manner linked . . . to the demise of self-closed, patriarchial, 'authentic' Chicano culture" (148). Noting that it is young Chicana writers who have most vigorously revised the canon, Rosaldo marks the significant shift in the literature as a result of these writers' challenge of "earlier versions of cultural authenticity that idealized partriarchial cultural regimes that appeared autonomous, homogeneous, and unchanging" (161). Beyond the scope of this essay, an interesting question arises when we consider that Chicana writers, lesbian and male homosexual writers (Richard Rodriguez, for example) are at the forefront of the new wave of Chicano/a literature. The matter, here, is the clarification that determinants such as historical change, generational shifts, social class, gender, and alternative lifestyles have impacted and will continue to affect Chicano/a literature in specific and ethnic literature in general. Subsequently, previously accepted[1] views of culture and literature are being questioned and in some cases replaced by new dimensions in cultural studies. Rosaldo, for instance, concludes with the expectation that new Chicano narrative forms will create "a fresh vision of self and society" and they promise "an alternative cultural space, a heterogeneous world" (165).

Whether *Hunger of Memory* achieves a fresh vision of self and society is open to question. What is quite evident is a sense of self not grounded on a collective ethnic identity, but on a metaphor of self as writer and instrument of language. Like the general drift of postmodern literature and criticism, the most recent scholarship on ethnic literature stresses language, discourse, and intertextuality. For instance, Werner Sollors adds a postmodernist qualification to his exposition on "the invention of ethnicity": "At this juncture the category of 'invention' has been stressed in order to emphasize not so much originality and innovation as the importance of language in the social construct of reality" (x). In *Hunger of Memory*, Rodriguez explicitly announces the subject matter of his autobiographic excavation and the primacy of the literary act: "This autobiography, moreover, is a book about language. . . . Language has been the great subject of my life. . . . Obsessed by the[2] way it determined my public identity. The way it permits me to describe myself, writing" (7). Manifested throughout *Hunger of Memory* is the author's self-consciousness as a conduit of words and meditator of language. Paradoxically, this attitude accounts for the originality and uniqueness of Rodriguez's book and also for its oddness and spareness.

Peculiarly, much of *Hunger of Memory* is wrapped in indirection. The reader senses omissions or deliberate evasions, and we are faced with the curiosity that intimate, personal information is absent from Rodriguez's "autobiography." Who were his friends in school? His best friend? Who was his first girlfriend, boyfriend, or first love? What was his first sexual experience? What were his favorite songs, movies, sports, and so on? These are mundane questions, but they are the stuff of adolescent life. Moreover, did he experience the confusion, joy, and the seemingly heart-wrenching fears and doubts that come with adolescence? Such questions of childhood and adolescence, common in autobiographies that cover formative years, are conspicuously absent from *Hunger of Memory*. It is an "autobiography" by self-definition and by tacit assumption, but there is little of what we have come to expect in autobiographies. Rodriguez hits the mark in one of his self-reflexive moments (he not only writes his autobiography, he also explains it to us): "Writing this manuscript. Essays impersonating an autobiography; six chapters of sad fuguelike repetition" (7). The vital clue is that Rodriguez is an essayist who masks polemics with the autobiographical act.

Rodriguez's passion is reserved for a lengthy exposition on the social and philosophical nuances of language. His polemical thrust is that language creates and defines a public self, and this process would separate him from his ethnic roots. He maintains that the apprehension of English and the culture it articulates diminished and eventually replaced the language and culture of his parents: "At last, seven years old, I came to believe what had been technically true since my birth: I was an American citizen. But the special feeling of closeness at home was diminished by then. Gone was the desperate, urgent, intense feeling of being home; rare was the experience of feeling myself individualized by family intimates. We remained a loving family, but one greatly changed" (23). The "ethnic drama" that surfaces in *Hunger of Memory* turns on the "losses" and "gains" that Rodriguez tallies in his middle-age years. *Hunger of Memory* is a work nerved by contradictions, paradoxes, and sustained irony; at the heart of its narrative strategy is the truism that something is lost every time something is gained. Ironically, Rodriguez's autobiography is a success story and a story of failure. Rodriguez measures the losses: the language of his parents—a language of intimacy; the assurances of family identity; the shared knowledge of a heritage; and the pathos of not being able to go home again. It occasions one of the most poignant moments in *Hunger of Memory:* "If I rehearse here the changes in my private life after my Americanization, it is finally to emphasize the public gain. The loss implies the gain: The house I returned to each afternoon was quiet. Intimate sounds no longer rushed to the door to greet me" (27). He also acknowledges the gains and accepts, in balance, that they outweigh the losses: the language of Shakespeare, Wordsworth, and Lawrence; a public language and public identity that provided passages to all quarters of the world; and a sense of being "American" and part of the great experiment called the United States. The gains also provided, of course, the means and measures to write and publish *Hunger of Memory*—and for Rodriguez to become "an American writer."

The saddest inflection comes in the conclusion of *Hunger of Memory,* where Rodriguez shifts from his attack on academia and affirmative-action programs to summarize his presentation of his parents: "But I do not give voice to my parents by writing about their lives" (186). Or anyone else for that matter, since the only voice is the autobiographical I: the discovery of self that caps his exploration of the past. The pathos that laces *Hunger of Memory,* from start to end, attends Rodriguez's controlling metaphor: "What preoccupies me is immediate: the separation I endure with my parents in loss. This is what matters to me: the story of the scholarship boy who returns home one summer from college to discover bewildering silence, facing his parents. This is my story. An American story" (5). Indeed, Rodriguez's autobiography is part of a national experience. But his credo must not be seen as a joyous celebration of birthright; *Hunger of Memory* makes it amply evident that it is a sensibility that garners the confusion, ambivalences, and paradoxes that accompany the problematic task of "making it in America."

What is unequivocally clear is that *Hunger of Memory* documents an author's search for a literary voice to express and give shape to the experiences of his life. Ultimately, it is a quest for a metaphor of self. Rodriguez's metaphor of self is triparted: the impulse to write autobiography, the act of writing itself, and the self-image created through language and literature. The adage that narcissism is the pitfall of autobiography finds a variant in Rodriguez's extreme self-consciousness as a writer. From start to end, Rodriguez favors the romantic image of the lonely, isolated writer exalting his individual voice: "Each morning I make my way along a narrow precipice of written words. I hear an echoing voice—my own resembling another's. Silent! The reader's voice silently trails every word I put down. I reread my words, and again it is the reader's voice I hear in my mind, sounding my prose" (186). At the end, that is what lingers in the reader's comprehension of *Hunger of Memory:* Rodriguez's prose and a metaphor of self that subsumes ethnicity to the celebration of the autobiographical act.

B. Teaching the Work

> How long
> how long
> have we been searchers?
> . . .
>
> We searched through
> our own voices
> and through
> our own minds
> We sought with our words
> . . .
>
> We are searchers
> and we will continue
> to search
> because our eyes
> still have
> the passion of prophecy.[3]

Tomás Rivera's "The Searchers" touches on the essence of the Mexican American experience. The history of Americans of Mexican descent (Chicanos) has been a search and a struggle to find their rightful place in a nation that they did not adopt but rather adopted them. The struggle to retain their language and heritage is historic and heroic, especially in view of the fact that their culture has often been denied, devalued, and suppressed. Mexican Americans share a commonality with other ethnic groups in similarly facing the opposing or intolerant ideologies of the dominant culture. To some degree, there are parallels to the historical patterns of the European immigrant experience and Chicano/a literature also shares some similarities with African American and Native American literatures. Notwithstanding these similarities, the Mexican American experience and its literature have a distinct sociohistorical context. The social, historical, and political singularity of the Chicano experience is rooted in a tragic chapter of American history. Save Native Americans, no other ethnic group has a longer history or a closer attachment to the American West and Southwest. "As for Mexican-Americans," Sau-Ling Cynthia Wong points out, "the history of annexation makes their situation unique" (143). Indeed, it is a unique history, and the historicity is caught in a common refrain among Chicanos: We did not come to the United States; the United States came to us. The phrase not only captures the consequences of Manifest Destiny and Anglo American expansion into the Hispanic Southwest, but also differentiates the Mexican American immigrant experience from European immigrant patterns. Some historians prefer the term *migration,* noting that historically the Río Grande (formerly the Río Bravo) is an artificial, political boundary created by the United States when it imposed the Treaty of Guadalupe Hidalgo of 1848 on Mexico. The term *Mexican American* or *Chicano,* in effect, originates in 1848 with the annexation of Mexican territories; it was a historic juncture marked by the uprooting and disenfranchisement of the people who had lived and remained north of the Río Bravo.

The Treaty of Guadalupe Hidalgo guaranteed the people of these territories civil liberties, legal and property rights, and the freedom to practice their culture and language; however, as was the case with many treaties made with Native Americans, the terms were never honored and this failure fomented many years of injustice, discrimination, and segregation. The tragic consequence was that Mexican Americans became "foreigners in their own land." One commentator on Chicano history has underscored the lasting significance of these events: "Since the current status and daily existence of most Chicanos can be linked to the failed promises of the Treaty of Guadalupe Hidalgo, it figures strongly in Chicano literature, both as a historical event and as a commentary on the Chicano's place in American society" (Shirley, "Chicano History," 299).

The second most momentous event in Mexican-Chicano history was the Mexican Revolution (1910–1917), a virtual diaspora that occurred as multitudes were uprooted during these turbulent years. It is part of a historic drama and this facet of the Mexican American experience could have been a chapter in, say, Oscar Handlin's celebrated work, *The Uprooted: The Epic Story of the Great Migrations that Made the American People* (1951). Instead, this story was to be told some twenty years later in books such as *The Chicanos: A History of Mexican Americans,* where Matt S. Meier and Feliciano Rivera capture the scope of this historic event: "The 1910 Revolution, a period of great violence and confusion in Mexican history, directly affected the Southwest. . . . No one knows precisely how many Mexicans were involved in this great exodus; one estimate holds that more than one million Mexicans crossed over into the United States between 1910 and 1920" (123). This historic migration would become a major theme of modern Chicano literature. For instance, José Antonio Villarreal's prototypical novel, *Pocho* (1959), is anchored on the "North from Mexico" migration theme: "the great exodus that came of the Mexican Revolution. By the hundreds they crossed the Rio Grande and then by the thousands. . . . The bewildered people came on—insensitive to the fact that even though they were not stopped, they were not really wanted. It was the ancient quest for El Dorado, and so they moved onward, west to New Mexico and Arizona and California, and as they moved, they planted their new seed" (1).

In actual history, Leopoldo and Victoria Moran Rodriguez were part of that exodus and Richard Rodriguez was one of the new seeds planted in a new land. He was born July 31, 1944, in San Francisco, California: a native son. Later the Rodriguez family moved to Sacramento and it became the setting for Rodriguez's recollections in *Hunger of Memory.* From his parents' starting point in Mexican villages to San Francisco-Sacramento is a long distance—in time, space, and generational change.

Out of the historical whirlwind of wars, revolutions, uprootings, migrations, and the constant struggle to survive in an often hostile society came pressing issues that beset Mexican American communities and which have become common themes in Chicano/a literature. From the start, Mexican Americans were caught in a conflict between their historical-cultural roots, which extend to pre-Columbian times, and their participation in "the melting pot" of the United States. And from the start they had to wrestle with the dilemmas of assimilation and acculturation. It is a historic and present quandary that extends to other ethnic groups: "The very language used to describe ethnic and immigrant experience underscores the notion of change and conversion. The image of the melting pot . . . is both complex and confusing" (Holte, 6). The persistence of these quandaries is evident in *Hunger of Memory* and other contemporary Chicano autobiographical works (for example, Arturo Islas's *The Rain God* [1984] and *Migrant Souls* [1990]). The most immediate question that arises is: Can a balance be found? What is the reach and weight of the hyphen that often separates "Mexican American"? Is Mexican American a single term, a compound term, or even antithetical? Can that space be filled with a sense of identity or can one be invented from the ethnic materials that remain or those that have been transformed out of necessity? These questions lie at the heart of *la búsqueda de identidad* (the search for identity), the overriding theme of Chicano/a literature. Taking a nominal example, Rodriguez's parents have traditional first names, Leopoldo and Victoria. When did *Ricardo* swirl into the melting pot? At what point—and why—did their son become *Richard*? It happened to Rodriguez and it happened to many Chicanos across the generations. Some took extreme measures in attempting to deny what they were and in attempting to be what they were not. Name changes (both first and last), denial of one's ethnicity, and various forms of evasion and denial are part of the legacy of racial and ethnic discrimination. These attempts to either deny or ignore cultural roots indicate a breach in the continuity of ethnicity, and they have social, cultural, and political ramifications. Literature has taken a major role in the exploration of the exigencies and pressing problems that confront the survival and continuity of Chicano culture and ethnicity.

Rodriguez's position in *Hunger of Memory* is clear-cut, and he takes to task those who "scorn the value and necessity of assimilation" (26). Staying with Rodriguez's terms, what is the *value* of assimilation? Why is it *necessary*? Rodriguez's tally of "losses" and "gains" does not satisfy, but it does not lessen the importance of the issue. Without a doubt, the process of acculturation entails losses and gains; it is a compromise between the past and the present, the traditional and the new, the familiar and the foreign. Each generation and every ethnic group has had to deal with the paradoxes of "the melting pot" and "the American dream." The losses and gains have been dear; the measure can be found in the individual and collective ethnic experience. The most appropriate subtitle for *Hunger of Memory* is "the Americanization of Richard Rodriguez." In one very significant way his autobiography is not unique; it is a brief chapter in the larger story that frames the ethnic drama of America. Thus, it is proper to place *Hunger of Memory* in a comparative context; placed not only next to other works of Chicano/a literature, but also compared and contrasted to other contemporary ethnic autobiographies: African American (for example, Maya Angelou's *I Know Why the Caged Bird Sings* [1970]); Asian American (Maxine Hong Kingston's *The Warrior Woman* [1972], for instance); Native American (N. Scott Momaday's *The Names* [1976], for example). Cultural memory binds these diverse works in a common purpose. The retrieval of the past is a salient feature of ethnic literature and the foundation of all autobiographical writing. "History lies in persistence of memory," wrote Eudora Welty, "in lost hidden places that want to be found and to be known for what they are." There is, after all, a hunger of memory in all of us.

In specific and in relation to other works in this section, a series of questions can be considered as discussion topics or as theme topics.

1. A central concern of Chicano/a literature is the assimilationist theme and the tension between conflicting traditions and values. How does *Hunger of Memory* address this situation? Is Rodriguez's view singular or is it evident in other works of ethnic literature?

2. How convincing is Rodriguez's argument for the *value* and *necessity* of assimilation? Are there important factors that he overlooks or ethnic cultural values that he ignores?

3. The subtitle of *Hunger of Memory* is "the education of Richard Rodriguez." To what degree is formal education an instrument of acculturation? What are Rodriguez's views on the educational process? Why does he criticize bilingual education and cultural pluralism?

4. Excepting Anglophonic immigrant groups, what is the special bearing of the American experience that requires a person to lose his or her native language and accept another language? Must one, as Rodriguez argues, replace that language with English in order to succeed in American society?

5. How do literary works differ in style and outlook among writers who retained their first language (for example, Anaya and Cisneros) and writers who lost their knowledge of Spanish (Rodriguez, for instance).

6. How does the Chicano urban experience (for example, San Francisco-Sacramento in *Hunger of Memory*, Chicago in *The House on Mango Street*, and Los Angeles in *The Moths and Other Stories*) differ from the rural experience (New Mexico in *Bless Me, Ultima*, for example).

7. Richard Rodriguez in *Hunger of Memory* and Helena María Viramontes's protagonists in *The Moths and Other Stories* have "arguments with their fathers"; that is, they note a cultural transition and question the patriarchial authority of traditional Mexican culture. How do Rodriguez and Viramontes differ in presenting this concern? How are they similar? How do gender roles affect the nature or particulars of the two narratives?

8. *Hunger of Memory, Bless Me, Ultima, The House on Mango Street,* and *The Moths and Other Stories* are works of cultural memory. How is the recapturing of the past or the "invention of the past" a fundamental part of ethnic consciousness? Why is family history an important part of cultural identity? How do these works differ in their approaches to cultural memory and the valuation of the past?

C. Bibliographies

1. Related Works

Acosta, Oscar Zeta. *The Autobiography of a Brown Buffalo.* San Francisco: Straight Arrow Press, 1972. A powerful, disturbing autobiographical novel with a frank focus on cultural deracination.

Anaya, Rudolfo A. *Bless Me Ultima.* Berkeley, Calif.: Quinto Sol, 1972. The most famous rite-of-passage novel in Chicano literature; a boy comes of age in a small New Mexico town and discovers the power and lasting beauty of his cultural heritage.

Cisneros, Sandra. *The House on Mango Street.* Houston: Arte Público Press, 1983. A series of well-crafted stories or vignettes that dramatize a young Chicana's coming of age in a Latino community in Chicago.

Galarza, Ernesto. *Barrio Boy.* New York: Ballantine Books, 1971. A famous and popular Chicano autobiography which describes the author's journey after the Mexican Revolution to settlement and acculturation in California.

Islas, Arturo. *The Rain God.* Palo Alto, Calif.: Alexandrian Press, 1984. An autobiographical novel set in El Paso, Texas, in the 1950s; combines mythology and historical narrative to create a Chicano brand of magic realism.

Rivera, Tomás. *. . . y no se lo tragó la tierra / . . . And The Earth Did Not Part.* Berkeley, Calif.: Quinto Sol, 1971. A classic work of contemporary Chicano literature and one of the most influential works of fiction; existential dimensions are given to migrant life in Texas, and the migrants' loss and suffering is given the dignity of tragic drama.

Villarreal, José Antonio. *Pocho.* Garden City, N.Y.: Doubleday, 1959. The prototype of the modern Chicano novel; mixing historical chronicle and autobiographical fiction, the first sustained exploration of assimilation and its impact on cultural heritage.

Viramontes, Helena María. *The Moths and Other Stories.* Houston: Arte Público Press, 1985. "The Moths," Viramontes's best known work and an excellent example of feminist Chicana fiction, complements *Hunger of Memory* by examining and resisting traditional concepts of Chicano culture.

2. Best Criticism

Hogue, W. Lawrence. "An Unresolved Modern Experience: Richard Rodriguez's *Hunger of Memory.*" *The Americas Review* 1 (Spring 1992): 52–64. Clear, informative outline and analysis of the content of *Hunger of Memory*; focuses on complex issues of cultural heritage and unresolved issues.

Márquez, Antonio C. "Richard Rodriguez's *Hunger of Memory* and the Poetics of Experience." *Arizona Quarterly* 2 (Summer 1984): 130–41. An essay in genre criticism focusing on Rodriguez's style and the relation of his autobiography to Chicano literature.

Rivera, Tomás. "Richard Rodriguez' *Hunger of Memory* as Humanistic Antithesis." *MELUS* 4 (Winter 1984): 5–12. Arguably the best criticism on *Hunger of Memory*; criticizes Rodriguez's politics and ideas, but praises his style and literary gifts.

Saldívar, Ramón. "Ideologies of the Self: Chicano Autobiography." *Diacritics* 3 (1985): 25–34. An exercise in academic criticism and literary theory that analyzes *Hunger of Memory* and compares it unfavorably with *Barrio Boy.*

Woods, Richard D. "Richard Rodriguez." *Dictionary of Literary Biography: Chicano Series,* 214–216. Detroit: Gale Research, 1989. A library reference source and biographical essay providing general information on Rodriguez's background and career.

3. Other Sources

Boelhower, William. "The Making of Ethnic Autobiography in the United States." *American Autobiography: Retrospect and Prospect,* ed. Paul John Eakin 123–41. Madison: University of Wisconsin Press, 1991.

Calderón, Héctor. "At the Crosswords of History, on the Borders of Change: Chicano Literary Studies Past, Present, and Future," 211–235. In *Left Politics and the Literary Profession,* ed. Lennard J. Davis and M. Bella Mirabella. New York: Columbia University Press, 1990.

Fischer, Michael M. J. "Ethnicity and the Post-Modern Arts of Memory." In *Writing Culture: The Poetics and Politics of Ethnography,* ed. James Clifford and George E. Marcus, 194–233. Berkeley: University of California Press, 1986.

Holte, James Craig. *The Ethnic I: A Sourcebook for Ethnic-American Autobiography.* Westport, Conn.: Greenwood Press, 1988.

Meier, Matt S., and Feliciano Rivera. *The Chicano: A History of Mexican Americans.* New York: Hill and Wang, 1972.

Padilla, Genaro. "The Recovery of Chicano Nineteenth-Century Autobiography." *American Quarterly* 3 (September 1988): 286–306.

Paredes, Raymund A. "The Evolution of Chicano Literature." In *Three Ameri-*

can Literatures, ed. Houston A. Baker, Jr., 33–79. New York: Modern Language Association, 1982.

Rivera, Tomás. "The Searchers." In *Tomás Rivera: The Complete Works,* ed. Julián Olivares. Houston: Arte Público Press, 1991.

Rodriguez, Richard. *Hunger of Memory: The Education of Richard Rodriguez.* New York: Bantam Books, 1982.

———. "An American Writer." In *The Invention of Ethnicity,* ed. Werner Sollors, 3–13. New York: Oxford University Press, 1989.

———. *Days of Obligation: An Argument with My Mexican Father.* New York: Viking Press, 1992.

Rosaldo, Renato. *Culture and Truth: The Remaking of Social Analysis.* Boston: Beacon Press, 1989.

Saldívar, José David. *The Dialectics of Our America.* Durham: Duke University Press, 1991.

Saldívar, Ramón. *Chicano Narrative: The Dialectics of Difference.* Madison: University of Wisconsin Press, 1990.

Shirley, Carl R. "Chicano History." In *Dictionary of Literary Biography: Chicano Series,* 296–303.

Sollors, Werner. "Nine Suggestions for Historians of American Ethnic Literature." *MELUS* 1 (1984): 95–96.

Wong, Sau-Ling Cynthia. "Immigrant Autobiography: Some Questions of Definition and Approach," 142–70. In *American Autobiography: Retrospect and Prospect,* ed. Paul John Eakin.

Asian American Literature

Preface

This final section of *Teaching American Ethnic Literatures* provides a fair sampling of the diversity of Asian American literature, in the literary works by Filipino, Chinese American, Japanese American, and Japanese Canadian authors treated below. We wish we had room for Korean American writers (like Richard Kim), Asian Indians (Bharati Mukherjee), Southeast Asian Americans, and Native Hawaiians as well. But the books treated here represent a good cross-section of literary genres—including the novel (Tan and Kogowa), short fiction (Yamamoto), and nonfiction/autobiography (Kingston and Bulosan)—and the "Related Works" (C.3) bibliography in each chapter lists a variety of other literature that teachers might consider using, including many other Asian American works.

This section also demonstrates a healthy range of critical perspectives, from the theoretical approach of E. San Juan, Jr., on Carlos Bulosan, to Mitsuye Yamada's "experiential" classroom approach to Joy Kogowa's *Obasan*. Shirley Lim and Wendy Ho, treating works of Chinese American literature that have attracted both critical and popular attention, spend more time reviewing the scholarship, while King-Kok Cheung, San Juan, and Yamada, dealing with writers who are only beginning to attract that attention, can spend less time on the scholarship. In either case, as Wendy Ho reminds us, "it is important for readers to do the hard work of carefully processing" this primary literature.

The essays here foreground ideas that permeate Asian American literature and are, in fact, central to the whole ethnic experience—the themes of cultural conflict and assimilation, for example, of people caught between cultures, countries, and generations. As much as any literature, Asian American texts demand an understanding of the social and historical contexts out of which they come, and these essays provide that background: from Lim and Ho's detailed discussions of the Chinese American experience to Yamada and Cheung's descriptions of the relocation tragedy, to San Juan's references to Filipino history. The essays provide, likewise, a rich range of

teaching ideas, from annotations of useful background materials and resources (Lim) through lists of challenging discussion and writing topics
(Cheung and Ho).

The natural pairings here are Tan and Kingston, and Kogowa and
Yamamoto, but even a cursory glance at the "Related Works" bibliographies will reveal numerous other combinations, in pairing these works with
other ethnic and nonethnic American literature. Readers cannot come away
from these essays without a number of ideas for expanding their classrooms
and enlivening their teaching.

Searching for the Heart of "America"
(Carlos Bulosan)

E. SAN JUAN, JR.

A. Analysis of Themes and Forms

Originally acclaimed as a classic testimony of immigrant success when it appeared in 1946, *America Is in the Heart* (hereafter cited as *AIH*) presents a massive documentation of the varieties of racism, exploitation, alienation, and inhumanity suffered by Filipinos in the West Coast and Alaska in the decade beginning with the Depression and extending to the outbreak of World War II. Scenes of abuse, insult, neglect, brutalization, and outright murder of these colonial "wards"—natives of the United States' only direct colony in Asia—are rendered with naturalistic candor along with their craft of survival and resistance.

Except for Part I (twelve chapters), the remaining three parts (Chapters 13 to 49) of this ethnobiography—a polyphonic orchestration of events from the lives of the author and his generation of compatriots—chart the passage of the youthful narrator (doubling also as protagonist and witness of events) in a land of privation, terror, and violence. It begins with his victimization by corrupt labor contractors on his arrival in Seattle (99–100), his anguished flight from lynch mobs, his first beating by two policemen in Klamath Falls (156–57), his desperate flirtation with Max Smith's cynicism (164–65)—vicissitudes punctuated in the middle of the book by his testicles being crushed by white vigilantes (208). A hundred pages after this episode replete with more degrading ordeals, "Allos"—the fictional representative of about thirty thousand Filipinos resident in California—concludes by reaffirming his faith in "America," now the name for a metaphoric space, "sprung from all our hopes and aspirations" (327). How do we reconcile this stark discrepancy between reality and thought, between fact (the social wasteland called "United States") and ideal ("America," land of equality and prosperity)? Is this simply an astute ironical strategy to syncopate naive narrator with subversive author, thus multiplying polyvalent readings and celebrating the virtues of schizoid *jouissance* (Roland Barthes's term for the unique pleasure of reading)?

One way to approach this aporia, this impasse of divergent views, is to reject the conventional thesis that *AIH* belongs to "that inclusive and characteristic Asian American genre of autobiography or personal history" (Kim, 47) designed to promote assimilation or co-optation. *AIH* invents a new genre, the antithesis to the quest for Americanization. The address to the "American earth" at the end is cast in the subjunctive mood, sutured in an unfolding process whose future is overshadowed by Pearl Harbor and the defeats in Bataan and Corregidor. The last three chapters reiterate the bitterness, frustration, loneliness, confusion, "deep emptiness," and havoc in the lives of Filipinos in America (315–25). Whatever the pressures of the Cold War and marketing imperatives, to construe Bulosan's chronicle of the Filipino struggle to give dignity to their spoiled or damaged lives in the U.S. as an advertisement for patriotism or imperial "nationalism" is quite unwarranted. It is surely meant to erase all evidence of its profoundly radical, popular-democratic inspiration.

Perhaps the easiest way to correct this mistake is to identify the trope of personification, the wish-fulfilling Imaginary of this artifact. Who is "America"? The main protagonist answers: Eileen Odell "was undeniably the *America* I had wanted to find in those frantic days of fear and flight, in those acute hours of hunger and loneliness. This America was human, good, and real" (235). If "Eileen" functions as a synecdoche for all those who demonstrated trust and compassion to a stranger like Bulosan, then the term should not be conflated with the abstract referent "U.S.A." as a whole. Overall, the caring mother figure with her multiple personifications (including the feminized narrator) is the singular desire called "America."

Viewed from another angle, the idiomatic tenor of the title refers to an inward process of self-awareness, a mode of internalization, more precisely self-gestation or parthenogenesis: he felt "love growing inside him" (194) and "a new heroism: a feeling of growing with a huge life" (196). By metonymic semiosis, the trope of containment gestures toward pregnancy and deliverance: Bulosan feels remolded into "a new man" (224). Elsewhere, the "heart" image refers to the "American earth" likened to "a huge heart unfolding warmly to receive me" (326)—and the phrase "America in the hearts of men" (314) attributed to Macario is interpreted by Bulosan to mean "this small yet vast heart of mine . . . steering toward the stars." Earlier, when he encounters Marian after the most traumatic mutilation of his genitals in San Jose, the narrator-victim marvels at this "white woman who had completely surrendered herself to me" and counsels himself: "The human heart is bigger than the world" (215). Recalling the girl raped in the freight train, who in turn evoked his sisters in Binalonan, Bulosan could not touch the prostitute Marian even when "her heart was in my heart" (213).

Of crucial importance is the equation of "heart" with "one island" (323), the Philippines, deploying Robinson Crusoe's predicament as counterpointing metaphor. Literally and figuratively, the "heart" becomes a polysemous vehicle that signifies inclusion or exclusion. It functions as a device to reconcile warring viewpoints, tendencies, subjectivities. Its figural use serves to categorize the text as belonging to the romance or utopian genre of fiction where time and space (Bakhtin's "chronotope") are configured in such a way as to realize the vision of an organic community materializing within the confines of an anomic, disintegrated U.S. metropolis.

This utopian theme of imagining a community within the fold of an atomized society counterpoints the violent, even sensationally morbid, realism that pervades the narrative. It also explains the didactic and moralizing sections where the assured authorial voice seems to compensate for the disorientation of the protagonist and the episodic plot. The climax of Bulosan's project of educating his countrymen about the unifying trajectory of their fragmented lives allows him to understand the "simplicity of their hearts" based on a "common understanding" that America "is still our unfinished dream" (312). Purged of his narcissistic malaise, he writes, "I was rediscovering myself in their lives." This counters the Crusoe motif of individualism (together with its social Darwinist variant: the beast in every man) and replaces it with the Moses/mother motif of collective concern. The narrator's private self dissolves into the body of an enlarged "family" whose members are affiliated by purpose or principle, anticipating what Bulosan calls "the revolution" where ordinary workers would "play our own role in the turbulent drama of history . . . the one and only common thread that bound us together, white and black and brown, in America" (313).

The theme of fraternity among races (enabled by the fight against a common global enemy, fascism) had been sounded initially in Bulosan's desire "to know [the hoboes in the freight trains] and to be a part of their life" (119). It is the dominant structure of feeling and reference that motivates the obsession with the Spanish Civil War (56, 223), the key historical conflict of reaction and progress in this period and a touchstone of authentic solidarity. It is sounded in the often-quoted programmatic testament ascribed to Macario in Chapter 25, where the narrator harps on the central metaphor of the old world dying while a new world is struggling to be born; here "America is in the hearts of men that died for freedom . . . a prophecy of a new society." Framed by Bulosan's cathartic discovery of his capacity to write (180) and his acquisition of a socialist vision of "the war between labor and capital" (186), the apostrophe to the multiracial masses as

"America"in the context of the twin process of dying and birth is better grasped as part of Bulosan's strategy to rearticulate the discourse of human/national-popular rights on the terrain of hegemonic liberalism itself toward a socialist direction. This, of course, incurs risks and liabilities, hence the reference to "America" as a doublebind.

So far the theme of popular-front democracy versus fascism (Japanese aggression in the Philippines evokes earlier aggression by the U.S.) at the outbreak of World War II may be used to resolve the tension between naive idealism and realist mimesis. This is the utopian resolution that mediates the idea of "America" as a classless society and the actuality of racism and exploitation. It is achieved at the expense of extinguishing the historical specificity of what is indigenous or autochtonous, the primal event of colonial subjugation and deracination.

A dialectic of compensatory fulfillment is offered here when the fact of colonial domination becomes the repressed of the text. Bulosan himself points out that as exiles "socially strangled in America," rootless, Filipinos find it easier "to integrate ourselves in a universal ideal" (241). It is personified by Felix Razon, who connects the peasant uprising in Tayug, Pangasinan, with the Loyalist cause in Spain (240). This is the thrust of the autobiographical schema of the narrative oriented around the development or education of a young man who matures into an artist; the vocation of writer should be conceived not so much as a status with prestige—a possibility foiled by circumstance—but a consciousness able to comprehend the world through ideas and broad knowledge of other cultures, transcending locale and origin (246).

This theme of growing up, of initiation into adult reality, is the most commonly emphasized feature of AIH. From the time he learns the facts of landlord exploitation and sexist corruption in Part I to the abuses of labor contractors (101), repeated racist violence (110, 129) and his discovery that it was "a crime to be a Filipino in California" (121), together with the terror, hunger, and loneliness of the "alien" in a dehumanizing milieu, the narrator-becoming-anti-hero undergoes a test of character. He succeeds in his initial objective of linking up with his brothers Amado (123) and Macario (129): this search for deracinated kins, ostensibly to reconstitute the broken family, counterpoints the usual immigrant story of labor recruitment. Eventually, the brothers' fighting at the end (304) dissolves the mystique of kinship and impels Bulosan's entry into an emergent community whose festival is suggested in Chapter 46—but this fulfillment of a vow to unite the dispersed family serves to provide the occasion for writing, for the composition of the narrative itself. In effect, the condition of possibility for art is imperial racist violence. This occurs in the exact middle of the book, the end of Chapter 23; struggling to communicate to his brother, the protagonist narrates his own life and gains release from the prison of his silence to "tell the world what they've done to me." This is repeated later in Chapter 41, where he laments his brother's suffering and tries to piece together "the mosaic of our lives" (289). This discovery of the capacity for expression comes after he revolts against his employer at the Opal Cafe two chapters earlier: "I had struck at the white world, at last; and I felt free" (163). When he meets the socialist lawyer Pascual, Bulosan assumes his role as witness/ spokesperson for the union movement (he helps edit *The New Tide* and, later, *The Philippine Commonwealth Times*) and envisions literature as the allegory of his death/rebirth and the collective protagonist as token of a social type, of the ongoing metamorphosis of social formations.

However, this theme of the native's development as wordsmith, literally letter-writer, is quickly displaced by another narrative schema when Pascual, the first Filipino identified as a socialist, dies at the end of Part II and the first half of the book culminates in the rhetoric of "We are all America" (189). The apprenticeship with Conrado Torres in the Alaskan cannery, with Julio, Luz, Pascual, Max Smith (whose exploits mirror the duplicity of the system), and particularly Jose (whose mutilation becomes the stigmata of the outlaw/rebel), is of course a composite of many lives; its chief function is to indicate what the potential is for ethnic Filipino unity. Partly sublimated in the act of writing, Bulosan's fear of the barbarian and sentimentalist in himself, his anger at social injustice, and his desire for synthesis and participation in a "dynamic social struggle" are registered in the vicissitudes of union activism in Part II. What any reader would have noticed at this point is that the realistic style of this memoir and its affinities with picaresque naturalism (recurrent scenes of petty crimes, squalid surroundings, raw violence, rough language), however, are frequently disrupted by lyricized memories of the homeland (108, 114, 123, 127, 132, especially 139, 155, 166, 172, 187). By this time, the generic conventions of the memoir and autobiography, with their drive for chronological verisimilitude and linear plotting, have already been eroded by a strongly emergent comic rhythm of repetition and uncanny resourcefulness: characters appear and disappear with inexhaustible gusto, incidents multiply and replicate, while the narrator's comments and the dialogue he records are recycled, quoted, and redistributed in a carnivalesque circulation of energies in the narrative. The crisis of hegemonic representation arrives at this juncture.

In Part III, a decisive break occurs which permanently cancels out the model of the successful immigrant or the ethnic "melting pot" archetype:

Bulosan's "conspiracy" or dream of making "a better America," a forgetting of himself, is suspended by the breakdown of the body—product of the years of hunger, brutality, and anguish. History or the past materializes in the return of the "child" as invalid, the time of drifting and wandering displaced by the stasis of physical breakdown.

We discover contained within the disfigured bosom of "America" representatives of its other, its negative. The introduction of Marian signals the establishment of dialogue and empathy: she resurrects the "good" side of America ruined by the treachery of Helen and the patriarchal debasement of women (159). The prostitute Marian, the ambiguous embodiment of commodification and self-sacrificing devotion, resurrects all the other images of maternal/feminine care from the peasant mother, Estelle (108), the nameless girl raped in the train (113), Judith (173), Chiye (184), all the way to the most important influences in his life, Alice and Eileen Odell and Dora Travers, followed by other, lesser maternal surrogates like Mary Strandon, Harriet Monroe, Jean Doyle, Anna Dozier, Laura Clarendon, and Jean Lawson. The mysterious Mary of Chapter 44, the last fleeting incarnation of American "hospitality" (the term is used as a pun on Bulosan's hospitalization, which converts him into a reading/writing subaltern), assumes iconic significance as "an angel molded into purity by the cleanliness of our thoughts," giving Bulosan "a new faith in myself" (301). In retrospect, Bulosan's illness—his confinement at the hospital where the notion of a community larger than the male-bonding of Filipino bachelors in gambling and dance halls manifests itself—is not a gratuitous interruption but a functional device. It halts the spatial discontinuity, the alleged "Necessitous mobility" (Wong, 133), of the narrative line. It ushers him into a recognition (the numerous recognition scenes in the book comprise the comic refrain that belies individualistic fatality and environmental determinism) of his new vocation: not so much the ignored author of *The Laughter of My Father*—index of Bulosan's acknowledgment of the folk sources of his art (260)—as the historian/guardian of collective memory and covenant with the "associated producers" of the islands, the peasantry as matrix of production.

For what makes *AIH* the first example of an unprecedented genre, a popular-front allegory that articulates class, race, nation (ethnicity), and gender in a complex uncategorizable configuration, is its narrative evolution. The stages of Bulosan's awakening follow a path away from a focus on "workerist" unionizing to concern with broader social issues, first through the CPFR (Committee for the Protection of Filipino Rights), which confronted the key racist law of antimiscegenation, to an anti-vanguardist "communist" role of tribuneship for the masses (in Lenin's conceptualization, as elaborated in *What Is to Be Done*). Suspecting the orthodox left of traditional blindness to racism, Bulosan considered himself a "revolutionist" (279). Against the tribalism and national chauvinism of his compatriots, Bulosan counterposed a socialist outlook at home in the ecology of all civilizations.

But what I think constitutes the originality of the text is its rendering of what Julia Kristeva calls "woman's time," virtually its subtext or "political unconscious," informing the anti-generic heterogeneity of the text. Comedy and the symbolic dynamics of the unconscious interact with realist codes in defining this new paradigm.

The fundamental mythos of comedy, the alternation of death and rebirth in "monumental" time, organizes the allegory of a transported native who "died many deaths" (135) in his itinerary of exile and imagined return. There are two deaths whose contexts prepare us for the excavation of what is buried in the "American" heart: first, the killing by Japanese contractors of the first union cannery president, Dagohoy, after the interlude with Lily and Rosaline, when Bulosan returns to the primal scene of his arrival: "I was pursued by my own life" (222); and, second, the suicide of Estevan, whose story "Morning in Narvacan" about a peasant town in Northern Luzon catalyzes this change in Bulosan: "I began to rediscover my native land, and the cultural roots there that had nourished me, and I felt a great urge to identify myself with the social awakening of my people" (139). Those deaths impregnate the psyche, inducing the self-production noted earlier, recovering the repressed in the language of dreams.

What should be given a close symptomatic reading is the structure of the dream that Bulosan records in Chapter 40. Mislabeled as "the Filipino communist" strike leader, he flees from the police and falls asleep on a bus. He dreams of his return to his hometown in Mangusmana, Philippines, where he rejoices at seeing his mother and the whole family eating (280–81); awakened by "tears of remembrance," he asks himself how the "tragedy" of his childhood had returned in a dream "because I had forgotten it" (283). This dream functions as the crucial synecdoche for what is repressed—not only by the text but by the scholarly archive. It is the whole of Part I, in particular the resourcefulness, insurgent courage, and strength of the peasantry epitomized by the mother (Chapters 4–9), that practically most critics and scholars have forgotten and that is bound to haunt them.

Here I would like to underscore the desideratum of an interpretive framework that necessarily structures all possible "horizons of expectation," a framework centered on this insight: what the bulk of this narrative wants to forget but cannot, what is in fact the absence or lacunae whose manifold traces everywhere constitutes the text, is U.S. colonial violence—the Philippine-American War of 1899–1902 and its aftermath in the neocolonial system—which subjugated the natives, reinforced the semifeudal structure called "absentee landlordism," and drove Bulosan and his brothers into permanent exile. Its other name is "fascism," whose genealogy includes Spanish *falangists* and Filipino sympathizers, American racist vigilantes and police, and Japanese aggression—with this last evoking what the text dare not name: U.S. invasion of the islands at the turn of the century. This is what the text's archaeology of repetitions seeks to capture: the time of the islands, of the mother and all of the women who have been victimized by patriarchal law and exchanged without the singular value of their desires acknowledged. What *AIH* attempts to seize is "woman's time" whose surplus or excess value measured, calculated, and dispersed into the derelict space of "America" where Filipino men—including the witnessing sensibility named "Bulosan"—found themselves "castrated" under its regime of violence premised on the rationality of white supremacy, the logic of capital and commodity-reification.

The project of *AIH,* then, is the reinscription of this inaugural moment of colonial dispossession in the hegemonic culture by a text that violates all generic expectations and foregrounds the earth, the soil, and the maternal psyche/*habitus* as the ground of meaning and identity. *AIH* as cultural practice valorizes both the oppositional and the utopian negated by the dominant ideology. What is needed is the elucidation of the process whereby the unity of opposites (for example, individual rationality versus tradition) shifts into the protagonist's trial or *agon* of unearthing duplicities (147) and multiple causalities, and discriminating what is fraudulent from what is genuine. Finally, the text interrogates all readers with the ethico-political reflection in the penultimate chapter: "Our world was this one, but a new one was being born. We belonged to the old world of confusion; but in this other world—new, bright, promising—we would be unable to meet its demands" (324). Bulosan's species of "magical" or "fantastic" realism allegorizes this radical transformation from the old to the new, that is, from colonial bondage redeemed via analysis/critique to witness/testifier of that history of decolonization: the project of becoming-Filipino. This task is accomplished by *AIH* without the luxury of consolation afforded by traditional aesthetic form.

B. Teaching the Work

Aside from standard histories of Asian American immigration (by Ronald Takaki and Sucheng Chan), students need to consult Renato Constantino's *The Philippines: A Past Revisited* for facts about U.S. colonial policies in the Philippines in the first three decades of this century; and, for background data about peasant conditions depicted in Part I of *AIH,* David Sturtevant's *Popular Uprisings in the Philippines* (see also D. B. Schirmer and Steven Shalom). For an analysis of the Filipino immigrant experience, one needs to compare the limited functionalist inquiry of H. Brett Melendy and Antonio Pido with testimonies such as the life-history of Philip Vera Cruz told by Craig Scharlin and Lilia V. Villanueva, *I Have Lived with the American People* by Bulosan's contemporary Manuel Buaken, and others included in *Letters in Exile,* ed. Jesse Quinsaat. Useful also are the perspectives offered by Carey McWilliams and *The Labour Trade* by the Catholic Institute for International Relations.

A "new historicist" approach accords well with Bulosan's own historical-materialist perspective (143). It would compare and contrast the anecdotal account of a veteran organizer like Philip Vera Cruz operating in the Cold War arena with Bulosan's popular-front orientation. While Vera Cruz is almost an exact contemporary of Bulosan and both have peasant back-grounds, it would be fruitful for students to examine the contrastive effects of Bulosan's popular-front socialist orientation with Vera Cruz's union-centered activism. Meanwhile, Buaken's testimony as well as the oral histories of "old-timers" (firsthand interviews of surviving "Manongs" can be a group project), and certain stories of Bienvenido Santos, would be instructive in marking the limits beyond which Bulosan was able to venture by combining various genres, styles, and discursive modalities in the unique textual web of *AIH.*

The architectonics of *AIH* can be grasped most easily by a standard structuralist approach using the binary opposition of city versus countryside. The countryside is associated with "boundless affinity" of kins (10), the father's creativity as cultivator (76), cooperative sharing (81–82), vitality (273, 311), fraternity (314); it evokes "the pleasure, the beauty, the fragrance" (270) of belonging, opposed to the urban sophistication of sectarian left-ists. Bulosan's recollection of village life summons images of "flight and freedom" (207). The city, on the other hand, is the locus of corruption (gambling, prostitution, criminality); the arrogant middle class (38); commodification of bodies (67, 92); police violence (Moxee City, Stockton, San Jose, Los Angeles). From the viewpoint of postcolonial theory, the city becomes the U.S. as metropolitan power and the countryside the dependent/peripheral formation; the native sensibility in the U.S. then begins to map islands (121, 134, 285)and caverns (137), and discern ambivalence (109, 147, 228) and commonalities among races and genders (115, 230) that problematize fixed boundaries, including this dualism.

In terms of reception aesthetics, the student can describe the changing critical responses to *AIH,* from the early "patronizing" reviews to McWilliams's 1973 appraisal, and then to recent commentaries (Alquizola, Wong). Meanwhile, Cuban socialist criticism has revived José Martí's concept of "*nuestra America*" ("our America") as a hemispheric project. What will this new framework contribute to a revaluation of Bulosan's work? In this context, it would be revealing to track the itinerary of Bulosan's reading from authors like Kipling (173), Richard Wright, Faulkner, and Thomas Wolfe to R. Palme Dutt, Briffault, Engels; to the authors of the heroic spirit—Rilke, Kafka, Lorca, Heine (237)—and the socialist writers—Sholokhov, Gorki, Lu Hsun, Guillen, Malraux (246)—and finally to the ethnic pioneers Younghill Kang, Yone Noguchi, and Louis Adamic, among others. What intertextuality can be established among the texts of these authors adequate enough for us to formulate the semiotic principles of *AIH*?

But after exploring the permutations of contradictory values, what I suggest is needed is the method of metacommentary such as the one proposed by Fredric Jameson. A negative hermeneutic of demystification can be applied on such claims as U.S. democratic educational policy (14), the myth of Lincoln (70), as well as various melodramatic excesses (108). Of course, one can say that the narrative sequence of illusion and disappointment is itself auto-deconstructing; after Bulosan says that "I felt good and safe" on his arrival and he was glad to go anywhere "as long as it was in America" (104, 106), the Moxee City episode of vigilante attack follows. Accompanying this move is a search for a latent utopian impulse, a disclosure of scenes or characters invested with pleasure or desire, ascribing creative agency to the dispossessed and oppressed. Clustered around this positive hermeneutic is the comic theme of death–rebirth, and of regeneration (65, 175, 261), which is poignantly evoked upon Bulosan's receiving the news of Luciano's death (see 56–57). In the metonymy of this section, several thematic strands can be pursued by researchers: the function of the hospital in the city, the Spanish Civil War, affiliated with the quiet resistance of his father and brothers fighting for "a place in the sun"; remembrance as generator of courage and "vision of a better life" and, finally, of writing as restorer of life. A fruitful comparative study can be pursued between *AIH* and archetypal comic forms: for example, Voltaire's *Candide,* Rabelais's *Gargantua and Pantagruel,* even Kafka's *Amerika.*

From a semiotic viewpoint, metacommentary can also engage the trope of prophetic return or homecoming (76, 89, 118, 124, 172) to endow the past with meaning or, more specifically, "help liberate the peasantry from ignorance and poverty" (62, 228). Is this fantasy meant to evade the challenge of the immediate situation, or apologize for malingering and temporizing?

A feminist and psychoanalytic mode of reading would confront the enigmatic role of women in this "pilgrimage" of finding a home in inhospitable and dangerous territory (99, 104). The uncanny interventions of Marian and Mary (compared to the more secular ministry of Eileen and Alice Odell) need to be examined further; are they refigurations of the mother, of the island homeland? Patriarchal authority is suspended by this maternal signifier: "the password into the secrets of the past, into childhood and pleasant memories . . . a guiding star, a talisman, a charm that lights us to manhood and decency" (123, 230, 247). How do we explain the numerous examples of treacherous or seductive women (78, 141, 132, 151, 155, 179, 185, 259), of fallen women (92, 274–75)? With Marian, Bulosan stresses care and affection; his search for intimacy and knowledge converges on Eileen, "the god of my youth," annihilating "all personal motives" (236); but he is uneasy with Alice Odell's "disturbing sensuousness" (234), and his portrayal of the erotic experience verges on parody (159). Is Bulosan an androgynous protagonist striving for "manhood" while being emasculated? Can we consider *AIH* a protofeminist text with its unique syncopation of the nomadic and sedentary lines of action?

Finally, a postmodernist perspective (within the larger field of cultural and postcolonial studies) can explore to what degree *AIH* is modernist in privileging individual creativity (202), existential commitment (199), imaginative transcendence (246), and Enlightenment progress. Has the postmodernist taste for pastiche and parody made *AIH* obsolete? Or has the generational characteristic of the new Filipino immigrants (mostly middle-class professionals obsessed with consumerism) become the main obstacle for a renewal of those social energies that lie dormant in the interstices of Bulosan's text? Here one can compare *AIH* with cinematic texts like *Dollar a Day, 10 Cents a Dance, In No One's Shadow,* or *Dreaming Filipinos* to map the mutations in the Filipino articulation of "America."

C. Bibliographies

1. Related Works

Buaken, Manuel. *I Have Lived with the American People.* Caldwell, Idaho: The Caxton Printer, 1946. Text contemporaneous with *AIH,* but organized as a collage of documents.

Bulosan, Carlos. *America Is in the Heart.* New York: Harcourt Brace, 1946. Reprint, Seattle: University of Washington Press, 1973.

———. *The Sound of Falling Light,* ed. Dolores Feria. Quezon City: University of the Philippines Press, 1960. Most substantial collection of Bulosan's letters; essential primary source.

———. *The Cry and the Dedication,* ed., with introduction, E. San Juan, Jr. Philadelphia: Temple University Press, 1995. First published as *The Power of the People* by Tabloid Books (Guelph, Canada) in 1972, this corrected edition is now the definitive version.

———. "Selected Writings of Carlos Bulosan." Special issue, *Amerasia Journal* 6, no. 1 (1979). Initial collection of Bulosan's writings, with an interview of Aurelio Bulosan (Carlos's only surviving brother in the U.S.) and bibliography of Bulosan's writings.

———. *Selected Works and Letters,* ed. E. San Juan, Jr. and Ninotchka Rosca. Honolulu: Friends of the Filipino People, 1982. Representative stories, and collected letters from Dorothy Babb never before published.

———. *On Becoming Filipino: Selected Writings of Carlos Bulosan,* ed., with introduction, by E. San Juan, Jr. Philadelphia: Temple University Press, 1995. This anthology supersedes previous collections.

Santos, Bienvenido. *Scent of Apples.* Seattle: University of Washington Press, 1979. Themes of many stories deal with the superfluity, alienation, and exile of petit bourgeois Filipinos in the U.S.

Scharlin, Craig, and Lilia V. Villanueva. *Philip Vera Cruz.* Los Angeles: UCLA Labor Center and Asian American Studies Center, 1992. Bulosan's contemporary; mediated life-history necessary to understand the political and ethical problems that plagued the United Farm Workers of America.

2. Best Criticism

Alquizola, Marilyn. "Subversion or Affirmation: The Text and Subtext of *America Is in the Heart.*" In *Asian Americans: Comparative and Global Perspectives,* ed. Shirley Hune et al. Pullman: Washington State University Press, 1991. This article illuminates the problem of disparity between the author's rhetorical claims and the evidence of the events. It develops the argument of an earlier essay: "The Fictive Narrator of *America Is in the Heart.*"

In *Frontiers of Asian American Studies,* ed. Gail Nomura et al. Pullman: Washington State University Press, 1989.

Campomanes, Oscar. "Two Letters from America: Carlos Bulosan and the Act of Writing." *MELUS* 15, no. 3 (Fall 1988): 15–46. This essay examines the intertextuality of Bulosan's fiction and his letters, using ideas from Walter Ong and Mikhail Bakhtin.

Evangelista, Susan. *Carlos Bulosan and His Poetry.* Quezon City: Ateneo de Manila University Press, 1985. Substantial but not complete, excludes many poems found in earlier anthologies; the biographical introduction relies on questionable informants and unreliable sources.

Kim, Elaine. *Asian American Literature.* Philadelphia: Temple University Press, 1982. A typical "assimilationist" approach; sympathetic but unreflective of the ideological-political resonance of texts.

San Juan, E. *Carlos Bulosan and the Imagination of the Class Struggle.* Quezon City: University of the Philippines Press, 1972. The first full-length critical study of Bulosan's oeuvre.

————. *Bulosan: An Introduction with Selections.* Manila: National Book Store, 1983. A compendium of the most important texts, plus a substantial introduction.

————. *Racial Formations/Critical Transformations.* Atlantic Highlands, N.J.: Humanities Press, 1992. This book contextualizes Filipino writing within U.S. racial politics and updates the author's previous research.

————. *Reading the West/Writing the East.* New York: Peter Lang, 1992. Includes a summing-up of Bulosan's achievement.

————. *The Philippine Temptation: Dialectics of Philippines-United States Literary Relations.* Philadelphia: Temple University Press, 1996. This work gives a synoptic and critical review of literary relations between the two societies.

3. Other Sources

Bakhtin, Mikhail. *The Dialogic Imagination.* Austin: University of Texas Press, 1981.

Catholic Institute for International Relations. *The Labour Trade.* London: CIIR, 1987.

Chan, Sucheng. *Asian Americans: An Interpretive History.* Boston: Twayne, 1991.

Constantino, Renato. *The Philippines: The Continuing Past.* Quezon City: Foundation for Nationalist Studies, 1978.

Jameson, Fredric. "Metacommentary." In *The Ideologies of Theory.* Minneapolis: University of Minnesota Press, 1988.

Kristeva, Julia. "Women's Time." In *The Kristeva Reader,* ed. Toril Moi. New York: Columbia University Press, 1986.

McWilliams, Carey. *Brothers under the Skin.* Boston: Little, Brown and Co., 1964.

Melendy, H. Brett. *Asians in America.* New York: Hippocrene Books, 1977.

Palumbo-Liu, David, ed. *Meta-Ethnic: Critical Essays on the Constructions of Ethnic Literary Canons.* Minneapolis: University of Minnesota Press, 1995.

Pido, Antonio J. *The Pilipinos in America.* New York: Center for Migration Studies, 1986.

Quinsaat, Jesse, ed. *Letters in Exile.* Los Angeles: UCLA Asian American Studies Center, 1976.

San Juan, E. *Hegemony and Strategies of Transgression.* Albany, NY: State University of New York Press, 1995.

Schirmer, D. B., and Steven Shalom, eds. *The Philippines Reader.* Boston: South End Press, 1987.

Sturtevant, David. *Popular Uprisings in the Philippines, 1840–1940.* Ithaca: Cornell University Press, 1976.

Takaki, Ronald. *Strangers from a Different Shore.* Boston: Little, Brown and Co., 1989.

Wong, Sau-ling Cynthia. *Reading Asian American Literature.* Princeton, N.J.: Princeton University Press, 1993.

"Growing with Stories":

Chinese American Identities, Textual Identities (Maxine Hong Kingston)

SHIRLEY GEOK-LIN LIM

A. Analysis of Themes and Form

1. Themes

The Woman Warrior provides an account of an "eccentric" Californian childhood, a difficult mother-daughter relationship, and the silences that constrain the American-born daughter within a Chinese patriarchal community and within United States sexist and racist society. The narrator disrupts these silences in the memoirs' first sentence: "'You must not tell anyone,' my mother said, 'what I am about to tell you. In China your father had a sister who killed herself. She jumped into the family well. We say your father has all brothers because it is as if she had never been born'" (3). The memoirs, structured on stories about Chinese women and narrated vividly by the daughter, disobey the mother's opening injunction. Maxine, the narrator, writes the story of No Name Woman, ironically "heard" first as the mother's "talk story"—oral and illegitimate history—to claim a space for women in a patriarchal society that has written them out of existence. As many critics have noted, *The Woman Warrior* places fiction in tension with history, and self-fashioning through orality in tension with written art.

The memoirs break into five chapters, each fluidly circling around a major transgressive female figure: No Name Woman, the aunt in China who kills herself and her infant girl after the villagers punish her family for her adultery; Fa Mulan, the legendary woman warrior who cross-dresses and takes her father's place as a conscript in the Imperial Army; Brave Orchid, the narrator's mother, who becomes a midwife after her husband leaves for the United States; Moon Orchid, the narrator's aunt, whom Brave Orchid persuades to come to the United States to reclaim her bigamous husband; and Ts'ai Yen, a historical poet, captured by barbarians and exiled for twelve years before returning to her home. These relatives and heroines offer the narrator/protagonist "ancestral help" in her representative passage toward cultural self-understanding: "Chinese-Americans, when you try to understand what things in you are Chinese, how do you separate what is peculiar to childhood, to poverty, insanities, one family, your mother who marked your growing with stories, from what is Chinese? What is Chinese and what is the movies?" (5–6).

The Woman Warrior can be approached as a book about growing up, a kind of female bildungsroman or novel of development. However, unlike other American classics such as J. D. Salinger's *The Catcher in the Rye,* it is not chiefly about a sensitive young individual's identity in conflict with a corrupt social and adult world. In the opening chapter, Kingston's protagonist protests against many values of her parents' emigrant Cantonese society, particularly the notions that degrade girls as inferior and that punish women's sexuality through rape and ostracism. Yet, paradoxically, she also finds in the same culture counter-values that present women not merely as victims but as agents: "When we Chinese girls listened to the adults talk-story, we learned that we failed if we grew up to be but wives or slaves" (20).

To illustrate the heroic imperative for women in Chinese culture, the second chapter, "White Tigers," retells the well-known folktale of the woman warrior, Fa Mulan, from a first-person point of view. In Kingston's retelling, the figure of the woman warrior embraces contradictions. She succeeds as a cross-dressed male soldier, but she marries and bears a son. Transgressing narrowly prescribed gender roles, she is motivated, ironically, by nothing less than ideals of filiality and female submissiveness. The fantasy of the martial woman concludes with her kneeling "at my parents-in-law's feet . . . a legend [of] perfect filiality" (45).

In contrast, the narrator/protagonist confesses, "My American life has been such a disappointment" (45). In her American life, "What fighting and killing I have seen have not been glorious but slum grubby" (51). Maxine believes that to her parents she is "useless, one more girl who couldn't be sold" (52). In response to Chinese devaluation of the female ("They only say, 'When fishing for treasures in the flood, be careful not to pull in girls,' because that is what one says about daughters"), she insists on her "American successes," and leaves her family "to get out of hating range" (52).

The narrator, however, sees similarities between the swordswoman who revenges her family's injustices and her work as a writer to report on the crimes of racism wreaked on Chinese Americans in the United States. Thus, although the daughter criticizes her ethnic community for its patriarchal demeaning of women, she does not reject it. Instead, she hopes to prove herself worthy of its approval through her struggle to fight against racism on its behalf.

The next two chapters, "Shaman" and "At the Western Gate," focus specifically on the mother, Brave Orchid, and the mother's sister, Moon Or-

chid. The narrator both idealizes and resists the shamanistic maternal figure, for Brave Orchid's indomitability inspires and terrifies the daughter.
Hardly a stereotypical passive victim in a patriarchal China, Brave Orchid
is presented in a superhuman perspective. She is aggressive, wily, intelligent, brave, and resourceful: a ghost killer, a doctor, a big eater, a storyteller.
The daughter fears her mother's complicity with Chinese cultural attitudes
toward females. Her mother had bought a slave girl; the young Maxine believes her mother's "enthusiasm for me is duller than for the slave girl" (82).
She hopes that her mother "did not prepare a box of clean ashes beside the
birth bed in case of a girl" (86). Her fears of the Chinese practice of female
infanticide appear in recurrent nightmares, which the narrator/protago-
nist interprets as symptomatic of her struggles to negotiate the cultural differences between Chinese and U.S. society: "To make my waking life
American-normal, I turn on the lights. . . . I push the deformed into my
dreams, which are in Chinese, the language of impossible stories" (87).

The daughter has to escape matriarchal domination, the weight of the
mother('s) culture, in order to find her identity in the United States. Coun-
tering Brave Orchid's working-class anxieties and parochial fixation on ethnic nostalgia, the American daughter urges the mother to give up her
immigrant survivor mentality—"Do you really have to work like that? Scab-
bing in the tomato fields?" (103)—and advises her to accept the loss of her
land in China: "We belong to the planet now, Mama" (107). She suffers
guilt and resentment at her mother's demands that she remain in the parental home: "[My mother] pries open my head and my fists and crams
into them responsibility for time, responsibility for intervening oceans"
(108). Still, it is only when her mother gives her permission to leave that the
narrator/protagonist feels the weight "lifted from me. . . . The world is somehow lighter [as s]he sends me on my way" (108–9).

While "Shaman" traces the daughter's reconciliation and escape from
matriarchal domination, "At the Western Gate" narrates the breakdown of
a female psyche less resilient and survivalist than Brave Orchid's. Brave
Orchid brings Moon Orchid from Hong Kong to California to meet her
husband, who has remarried in the United States. Moon Orchid is unable
to fulfill her sister's plans for her to reclaim her errant husband; she is timid,
delicate, a "high-class city" person unaccustomed to work, unlike Brave
Orchid who is bold, strong, with an emigrant villager's toughness (127).
The tragicomic scene where Brave Orchid forces Moon Orchid to confront
the bigamous surgeon contrasts two kinds of women, the weak and strong
sisters, and two kinds of cultural systems, traditional Chinese kinship systems in which the first wife enjoys a privileged status and U.S. social norms

that criminalize polygamy. The scene underlines the gender asymmetry and prejudice in both societies: traditional Chinese society, which practices polygamy, and U.S. society, which privileges younger, prettier women and assimilated Chinese. The husband's rejection of Moon Orchid brutally repeats U.S. social bias against Chinese immigrants: "Look at her. She'd never fit into an American household. I have important guests who come inside my house to eat" (153).

Recentering to Moon Orchid's point of view, the narrative calls into question the raced identity of immigrant Chinese. Herself from China, Moon Orchid is able to see the differences between Chinese and Chinese Americans. Walking through Chinatown, she observes, "So this is the United States . . . . It certainly looks different from China. I'm glad to see the Americans talk like us" (136). Moon Orchid views her American-born nephews and nieces as aliens whose actions have to be decoded: "'What time is it?' she asked, testing what kinds of minds they had, raised away from civilization . . . . Moon Orchid defended them, sweet wild animals that they were" (134). Unable to assimilate, Moon Orchid suffers from paranoid delusions. Unlike the inveterate storyteller, Brave Orchid, "Mad people have only one story that they talk over and over" (159). When Moon Orchid is finally institutionalized "in a California state mental asylum," she finds happiness among a company of mad women who "speak the same language, the very same" (160).

The narrator as devalued female, a member of a Sze Yup (Cantonese) group removed from its original society, finds an uncanny resemblance between herself and various mad women. No Name Woman and Moon Orchid are just two of a number of crazy women who are memorialized. They are like the character of the "village crazy lady" (94), whose unconventional decorative costume and self-absorbed dances lie outside the villagers' understanding. Feminist critiques of patriarchal abuses of women—the severely restrictive roles imposed on women, social evils such as rape, footbinding, ostracism, and murderous violence—are implicit in these stories. Because the village crazy lady threatens this social control, the villagers kill her, "beating her head and face, smashing the little mirrors into silver splinters" (96). The story suggests that women who possess their own resources of pleasure and reflection, symbolized in the crazy lady's mirrored headdress, are seen as dangerous and must be eradicated.

The theme of female madness in response to cultural violence is further developed in the last chapter, "A Song for a Barbarian Reed Pipe." Madness, ghosts, and silence, three major themes, are drawn together in the narrativization of an autobiographical self marked by the fears and misunderstandings of a family isolated from mainstream America. In "Shaman" the narrator uses the trope of ghosts to link Chinese and American cultures. While China is transmitted to the children as a land of spirits through the mother's stories, America "has been full of machines and ghosts" (96). "Ghosts" are Americans who do not belong to the emigrant culture: "the White Ghosts and their cars," "Black Ghosts," "the Mail Ghost, Meter Reader Ghost, Garbage Ghost" (97–98).

Because America is turned ghostly by her family's nonassimilative segregation, the young Kingston "speak[s] English for the first time" (165) in kindergarten. The language/cultural difference leads to shame and silence. The narrator suggests that this silence is not a Chinese cultural trait, although "the silence had something to do with being a Chinese girl" (166). At Chinese school, the same girls "were not mute. They screamed and yelled during recess. . . . they had fist-fights" (167). The narrator/protagonist is silenced by an American culture that shames her; but she also resists a Chinese culture that appropriates the individual voice for collective identity: "You can't entrust your voice to the Chinese, either; they want to capture your voice for their own use" (169).

The young girl confuses her struggle for a voice—ironically described as "an American-feminine speaking personality" (172)—with her anger against a silent classmate. Projecting her own confusion and fear onto "the quiet one" (173), the sixth grader Maxine beats her up to force her to talk, an unsuccessful endeavor. Similarly, she is frustrated by her mother's silence on Chinese culture. In stable, homogeneous societies, culture's signs and meanings are transmitted through living it; however, a marginalized culture like that of the emigrant Cantonese loses its hegemonic signification when contested by another dominant cultural system. To the American-born daughter, the arbitrary provisional nature of social action usually reified as "Chinese tradition" becomes painfully clear. Growing up in the United States, the narrator does not query the significance of dominant American rituals such as Christmas and Thanksgiving. Her struggle is to make sense of the ethnic culture: "How can Chinese keep any traditions at all? They don't even make you pay attention. . . . The adults get mad, evasive, and shut you up if you ask" (185).

Trapped in the cultural silencing of Chinese in American society and in the gendered silencing of women in Chinese society, immigrant Chinese women retreat into insanity, a fate the young Kingston fears for herself. "I thought talking and not talking made the difference between sanity and insanity. Insane people were the ones who couldn't explain themselves" (186). As an adolescent, she rejects her parents' attempts to marry her within the immigrant community, and rehearses "a list of over two hundred things that I had to tell my mother so that she would know the true things about me" (197). To the mother, the daughter's talk is "Senseless gabbings," "craziness" (200) that she does not want to hear. In a crucial scene, the daughter vents her resentment at the mother's perceived complicity with Chinese patriarchal attitudes, and voices her choice for a less sexist, assimilated American identity: "I won't let you turn me into a wife or a slave. I'm getting out of here. . . . And I'm not going to Chinese school anymore. I'm going to run for office at American school, and I'm going to join clubs" (201–2). At the same time, the narrator ironizes this choice. In place of Chinese mysteries and complexities, American assimilation offers "simplicity," a homogeneity figured in the images of concrete, freeways, plastics, and TV dinners (204).

The closing story presents a contrasting dynamic; instead of assimilation, the figure of Ts'ai Yen, the woman poet in exile among barbarians, offers a more complicated vision of translation. Just as Ts'ai Yen's song could be understood as both Chinese words and "barbarian phrases," so too a Chinese American text like *The Woman Warrior* can be understood as speaking from two cultures, translating both to each other. In rewriting the Chinese mother's oral tales, the American-born daughter does not erase the mother('s) culture, but extends it as one continuous narrative: "The beginning is hers, the ending mine" (206).

2. Form

The Woman Warrior and *China Men,* Kingston's second book, are categorized as works of nonfiction, and Kingston makes it clear that both books are based on her parents' lives; that is, they are forms of biography. While *The Woman Warrior* is based on her mother and the talk stories her mother tells her, *China Men* is composed of stories on her father's life in China and in the United States, and on the lives of various male relatives and sojourners, including grandfathers, uncles, and brother. Kingston frequently emphasizes the organic unity of the two books. "At one time, *The Woman Warrior* and *China Men* were supposed to be one book. I had conceived of one huge book" (Rabinowitz, 179). In this interview, Kingston explains that the women's stories "have a convolution and the men's stories have more of a linear passage through time": "those men were making history" because the Chinese American male experience was within history, but the women were caught up in "old myths." Both books, however, "are much more American than Chinese"; the characters are "American people."

The work's sheer literary luminosity, even as it transgresses and adds its weight of transformation to traditions and canons, makes it a classic. To teach *The Woman Warrior*, the teacher must introduce tools of literary criticism—imagery and symbolism, narrative structure, characterization, theme analysis—and emphasize the relations of fictive imagination to personal and collective history.

In brief, the memoirs are structured on two major figures of woman: the warrior, resisting both Chinese and U.S. oppressive cultures; and the storyteller, who fashions writing out of the mother's talk stories. The two figures undermine and reinforce each other, forming a repeated self-reflexive narrative pattern. For instance, on the one hand, the retelling of the Fa Mulan legend marks a rupture between traditional patriarchal Chinese society and the American-born daughter; on the other hand, in deploying the talk story, the memoirs invite a transmission of cultural memory and the values— traditional and patriarchal—of that memorialized ethnic community.

Keenly aware of the power of myth in narrative, Kingston synthesizes, conflates, and vivifies mythic material in *The Woman Warrior*. As she has remarked, "I keep the old Chinese myths alive . . . by telling them in a new American way." An important and hitherto unnoticed element is the figure of "the West" (important in the American mythic imagination); it is used as a narrative leitmotif and a signifier for characterization and action. (Coincidentally, the journey to the West is also a key allusion in Kingston's novel, *Tripmaster Monkey: His Fake Book.*) The memoirs draw upon the mythic resonance of East and West to provide the coda in which the legendary figure of Ts'ai Yen becomes the metaphor for the narrator/writer herself (Cheng Lok Chua, in Lim, 146).

Chinese American male texts, such as Louis Chu's novel *Eat a Bowl of Tea,* work from different subject positions and materials than Kingston's memoirs. Chinese American historiography has been until recently narrowly male dominated (Robert G. Lee, in Lim, 52), and *The Woman Warrior* fills the gaps which traditional documentation does not reveal. It revises dominant male constructions to imagine the Chinese American experience in a specifically "woman"-gendered way. Indeed, it has been read in a strategically essentializing move as a woman's way of writing autobiography, what Joan Lidoff calls "the forgiving genre" (Lim, 116). Based on the permeable boundaries of the mother-daughter relation (theorized by Nancy Chodorow), a model of women's autobiography emerges that does not place the self centrally as a hero, but starts with stories of other family members, other women, especially the mother. *The Woman Warrior* is framed by the mother's voice. Modifying the mother's storytelling power that both inhibits and enables the daughter's voice, Kingston tells an innovative story that is at once her own and her culture's.

Central to an analysis of the memoirs is the provocative combination of the subjunctive mood and conditional tense, explicitly foregrounded in the text, and the categories provided in the front cover's statement, "The best book of nonfiction published in 1976" and the classification on the upper left corner of the back cover, "autobiography." The narrative strategy deliberately unsettles the genre of the "autobiography" from its conventional definition of "factual" life-story by blurring "autobiography" with fiction and fantasy. This move implies that to insert Chinese American women's subjectivities, historically absent in Asian American history, into discourse, the memoirs have to appropriate resources not traditionally associated with autobiographical modes: myths, legends, fantasies, and invented narratives.

The deliberate crossing of conventionally rigid boundaries between historical "evidence" and fictional persuasiveness, the pervasive fluidity within the text between narratives usually constructed as opposing discursive practices—one empirical, impersonal, and hence more valuable, and the other speculative, personal, and less valuable as knowledge—subtly interrogates notions of authentic raced and gendered identity. The memoirs' mixing of conventions of biographical and fictional narrative (Timothy Dow Adams, in Lim, 151) leads to a destabilization of identity discourses. Kingston's narrative strategies parallel the narrator/protagonist's troubled perceptions of the mother's talk stories: "You lie with stories. You won't tell me a story and then say, 'This is a true story,' or 'This is just a story.'" It is necessary therefore to resist reading *The Woman Warrior* as autobiography, unless we take autobiography to signify a literary form for destabilizing as well as constituting identity. As an "eccentric" genre, autobiography's claims to "truth" rest on benign denial of distinctions between categories of storytelling and lying, between history and talk story.

As in a piece of postmodern architecture where the parts call attention to themselves, *The Woman Warrior*'s successful structure is more than the sum of its parts. Fragmentation is deployed in the service of integration. The collage-effect is clearly not haphazard. The tension between its individual sections and the total text reflects both a female mentality, struggling to find voice and space in a world that would deny both to women (Marilyn Yalom, in Lim, 108), and postmodern artistic concerns. In fact, critics such as Michael Fischer argue that *The Woman Warrior* must be read as a postmodern text. It deploys mythopoetic strategies, constituting subjectivity as inseparable from language resources. Its writing challenges the boundaries between fiction and nonfiction, even as it raises concerns that operate within an ethical domain. Its linguistic and narrative features conform to what M. M. Bakhtin has described as "heteroglossia," the multiplicity of social speech types characteristic of the novel genre. Thus, overlapping and layering the opening narrative voice are multiple other voices. The memoirs, as five linked chapters composed of multiple talk stories, anecdotes, histories, legends, and so forth, form not a static and fixed text but a shifting unstable textuality that continuously reweaves, reorganizes, subverts, and undermines points of view and positions, including positions that the narrator/authorial character Maxine had earlier maintained.

The memoirs construct relationships between the fixities of a descent identity and what is consented to in the calculated appropriation of the past, or deliberate misreading: the need to choose where you come from and so make up the world that has made you. The narrator-subject lays claim to America in the name of her community. The five chapters achieve an oblique representation of the autobiographical subject through the profiles of others. By redoing the past and revealing the mixed meanings inherent in our inheritances, Kingston cunningly usurps forms (the mother's talk stories, on the one hand; classic United States literary works, on the other) that are meant for socialization and reshapes them into forms that resist normative identities.

B. Teaching *The Woman Warrior*

1. Background Materials

The Woman Warrior possesses enormous popularity and broad appeal. While it is clearly an ethnic text that comes from and addresses a Chinese American history and community, it is not ethnic-bound. Its power as a literary artifact forms its dominant appeal to mainstream teachers, and autobiography and genre studies help elucidate these aspects of the memoirs. Also, it is both an American cultural document and a strong feminist articulation, albeit complicated and nuanced by race and class. Because *The Woman Warrior* is a multivocal text, capable of being addressed to immediate and wider audiences, the background studies recommended are multidisciplinary, diverse, even divergent and loose.

Kingston uses traditional Chinese materials in her memoirs, including a number of traditional Chinese sources such as "The Ballad of Mulan," "Eighteen Stanzas for a Barbarian Reed Pipe," ghost stories, martial-arts novels, and folklore on "immortals." Essays by Sau-ling Wong, on Kingston's handling of traditional Chinese sources, and by Kathryn VanSpanckeren, on the Asian literary background, are both found in the *Approaches to Teaching Kingston's The Woman Warrior* (236–36, 44–51). Although Kingston has modified these sources, the cultural context underlines the importance of reading Kingston's chief artistic enterprise: to establish the legitimacy of a unique Chinese American (as opposed to Chinese) experience and sensibility.

To appreciate *The Woman Warrior*, it is necessary to understand something of cultural analysis. Clifford Geertz's *The Interpretation of Cultures* and Edward Said's *Orientalism* present theoretical departure points that can help situate the memoirs' cross-cultural materials outside of Eurocentric perspectives. Werner Sollors's *Beyond Ethnicity; Consent and Descent in American Culture* (1986) and William Boelhower's *Through a Glass Darkly: Ethnic Semiosis in American Literature* (1987) offer theoretical frames that help consideration of the memoirs as a piece with American literature.

In the same spirit of cross-cultural inquiry, certain studies provide useful information on Chinese and Chinese American culture and history. One resource is Margery Wolf and Roxane Witke's *Women in Chinese Society*. Wolf's essay, "Women and Suicide in China," gives the No Name Woman episode an anthropological grounding, providing a fuller appreciation of the Chinese and female cultural contexts. Kay Ann Johnson's *Women, the Family and Peasant Revolution in China* is knowledgeable in its analysis of women's roles and images in a Chinese patriarchal system. The seemingly ambiguous position of women as both strong and weak, dangerous and victimized, in the memoirs is illuminated by Johnson's discussion of how the pattern of sexually irresponsible and dangerous women juxtaposed against cultural ideals of nurturing, submissive mothers-wives is most pronounced in extended patrilineal, patriarchal societies.

To many readers, the memoirs' social background is of an unfamiliar people and history. Michael Omi and Howard Winant's *Racial Formation in the United States from the 1960s to the 1980s* is helpful in understanding the memoirs' negotiation of the constitution of Chinese American identity. Teachers will find Paul C. P. Siu's *The Chinese Laundryman: A Study of Social Isolation* useful background for understanding the lives of Chinese sojourners portrayed in Kingston's first two books. The Exclusion Laws against Chinese that were in place between 1882 and 1945, as well as other U.S.

immigration laws, prevented Chinese wives from joining their husbands in the United States. The enforced "bachelorhood" encouraged deviant and misogynistic attitudes toward women in a culture that was already strictly patriarchal.

Many histories of Chinese immigration to the United States, Chinese labor in California, and Chinese women in America provide information necessary for an understanding of the memoirs; for example, the Nees' *Longtime Californ'* and Jack Chen's *The Chinese of America*. Ronald Takaki's *Strangers from a Different Shore* and Sucheng Chan's *Asian Americans: An Interpretive History* contain histories of Chinese immigrant labor, racist legislation against Chinese on the West Coast, and the development of Chinese American communities. Chan's chapter "The Exclusion of Chinese Women" (in *Entry Denied: Exclusion and the Chinese Community in America, 1882–1943*) explains the nexus of gender, class, and race oppressions that kept Chinese women out of the United States, while Judy Yung's visual history, *Chinese Women of America: A Pictorial History*, recaptures the experiences of Chinese women caught in the intersections of race and gender in the United States. Of particular relevance is Lai et al., *Island: Poetry and History of Chinese Immigrants on Angel Island 1910–1940*, a collection of translations of Chinese detainees' poems that record the stresses of dislocation and detention in the Angel Island barracks.

When *The Woman Warrior* is placed in a canon of women's writing or of autobiographies, a range of contemporary scholarship on autobiography offers rewarding theorization on genre distinctions, from James Olney's *Autobiography*, which does not deal specifically with Kingston's book, to Sidonie Smith's subtle decoding of its stylistics in *A Poetics of Women's Autobiography*. Women theorists such as Carol Gilligan (*In a Different Voice*) and Elaine Showalter (*New Feminist Criticism*) also provide analytical tools that help to interpret the memoirs' "feminist" content.

No single biographical essay exists on Kingston. Most of Kingston's interviews skirt personal questions to focus on her writing, but biographical data relating her background to her writing process do emerge in some interviews. The interview with Arturo Islas (1980) in *Women Writers of the West Coast* gives insights into the relation between *The Woman Warrior* and Kingston's own life. These insights are further elaborated and updated in the interview with Paula Rabinowitz (1987). A taped interview with Kay Bonetti provides more background information (American Audio Prose Library, 1986); and a video interview with Bill Moyers on Public Television's *World of Ideas* is particularly useful (1989).

A comprehensive guide to teaching *The Woman Warrior* is Shirley Geok-lin Lim's 1991 edited volume, *Approaches to Teaching Kingston's The Woman Warrior*. The *Approaches* volume contains seventeen essays on teaching strategies and a section on materials that notes the rich diversity of resources for the instructor. King-Kok Cheung and Stan Yogi's *Asian American Literature: An Annotated Bibliography* has a useful bibliography on Kingston's work. While the bibliography covers other ethnic Asian writers, the relevant section on primary sources of Chinese American literature (27–58) surveys the tradition in which *The Woman Warrior* is to be read. The discussion on Kingston's work (199–213) forms a small part of Elaine H. Kim's *Asian American Literature: An Introduction to the Writings and their Social Context*, but the entire study provides a coherent background for understanding the memoirs in the gendered context of Chinese American literary tradition. Frank Chin's essay, "Come All Ye Asian American Writers of the Real and the Fake," in *The Big Aiiieeeee!* is particularly critical of Kingston's success. *Redefining American Literary History* (ed. Brown and Ward) has essays by Amy Ling and Shirley Geok-lin Lim that place Kingston's work in the comparative frame of American minority and multicultural literature.

Four recent volumes on Asian American literature—Amy Ling's *Between Worlds: Women Writers of Chinese Ancestry*; *Reading the Literatures of Asian America*, edited by Shirley Geok-lin Lim and Amy Ling; King-Kok Cheung's *Articulate Silences: Hisaye Yamamoto, Maxine Hong Kingston, Joy Kogawa*; and Sau-ling Cynthia Wong's *Reading Asian American Literature*—offer critical readings on the memoirs and on texts that enlarge interpretation of the memoirs. Ling's *Between Worlds* reads *The Woman Warrior* in the tradition of Anglophone writing by women of the Chinese diaspora. Lim and Ling's edited volume contains essays on *The Woman Warrior* (King-Kok Cheung, 163–90) and *China Men* (Donald C. Goellnicht, 191–214), as well as readings that exhibit the heterogeneity of Asian American ethnic identity and literary production. Cheung's study of how silence "can speak many tongues, varying from culture to culture" (1) seeks to modify Eurocentric premises and to explain "reticence" as a central rhetorical strategy and value in Asian American women's writing. Contextualizing *The Woman Warrior* in an evolving body of Asian American texts, Wong reads it within cultural themes: the binary of Necessity and Extravagance in immigrant writing, the racial shadow, the eating motif, and art and play. Wong carries conventional thematic analysis to more complex levels, as her interpretation weaves European psychological references, a host of Asian American texts, and feminist and ethnic theories.

The Woman Warrior has been the subject of many smaller critical studies, as a single-text reading or as part of a broader analysis of Kingston's writings and of ethnic women's literature. Among the more illuminating single-text studies are Sidonie Smith's chapter on *The Woman Warrior* in *A Poetics of Women's Autobiography*. Another instance of postmodern interpretation, the chapter reads *The Woman Warrior* as "an autobiography about women's autobiographical storytelling" (150), in which "the hermeneutics of self-representation can never be divorced from cultural representations of woman that delimit the nature of her access to the world and the articulation of her desire" (151). Other studies focus on *The Woman Warrior* and *China Men* as a paired opus. Leslie Rabine's essay in *Signs* (1987) analyzes Kingston's double ambivalence to her parents' Chinese culture and to U.S. culture and the "proliferation of gender arrangements" in *The Woman Warrior* and *China Men* to show how gender systems change across cultures as well as how symbolic and social gender change between cultures (474).

In recent years the collection of films dealing with Asian American culture has grown. These films, including historical documentaries and fictional portrayals of Asian American life, provide visual images for the situations and characters portrayed in Kingston's book. A recent documentary, "Maxine Hong Kingston: Talking Story," features interviews with Kingston, juxtaposed with significant moments in Chinese American history, commentary by the eminent *New York Times* book reviewer John Leonard, scenes in which her mother, father, and husband, Earl Kingston are introduced, and shots of Kingston in Stockton, her childhood hometown, and in Hawaii, where she had spent seventeen years during which she wrote her first two books.

2. Classroom and Teaching Strategies

The Woman Warrior has been taught in a variety of courses; for example, as a rhetorical model, in freshman and sophomore writing courses; as an instance of American ethnic literature; and as a feminist work. A contemporary text, many of whose materials are drawn from emigrant Chinese folklore, it is also situated in a tradition of California regional literature and of American cultural pluralism. It exemplifies qualities noted in standard autobiographies, such as those of Benjamin Franklin and Henry Adams. Taught alongside works by Native American, African American, and Chicano writers, ranging from *The Autobiography of Malcolm X* to Maya Angelou's *I Know Why the Caged Bird Sings,* it exhibits positions on race and gender identity politics that enrich debates on U.S. culture. The book elicits a profoundly complex response to its cross-cultural, ethnographic, postmodern narratives.

A major problem that instructors face is students' resistance to the memoirs' cultural "strangeness" and density of language. Some films help to familiarize the memoirs' background. "A Small Happiness" treats women's subordinate position in China, and so provides the cultural frame through which Kingston's depiction of emigrant villagers' attitudes toward girls can be understood. In delineating the social inferiorization of females in traditional Chinese society, the documentary also helps to explain the narrator/daughter's anger and resistance to her mother and community that makes *The Woman Warrior* more than simply a celebration of ethnic identity. The film's view of rural life and women's work in China makes concrete the material circumstances under which the suicide of No Name Woman becomes possible. "Maxine Hong Kingston: Talking Story" introduces the American context for the memoirs, and contains an overview of the Asian American scene, including the influences that Kingston's work has had on Chinese Americans. In tandem, the two films help to demystify and situate the memoirs' Chinese and American cultural referents.

Teachers should use complementary resources to help widen students' historical and social imaginations. Selected poems from *Island* help to clarify the hopes and fears of immigrant Chinese, and can be read together with the chapter on Moon Orchid, "At the Western Gate." Similarly, to historicize passages from *The Woman Warrior*, students should be assigned relevant chapters in Takaki's (79–131, 230–69) and Chan's Asian American histories (45–62, 103–20) and *Entry Denied* (57–94). For example, the memoirs treat the mother's entry into the United States in 1940, and Kingston's early childhood (96–99; 183–85). What were the conditions for Chinese immigrants and their children during the pre–civil rights period in U.S. history? How does this history relate to the family's attitude toward American "ghosts" and toward American institutions?

Students should analyze major themes, such as the process of identity (self and ethnic) formation, the place of silence in raced and gendered subordinate relations, and the tensions between mothers and daughters, as they are articulated through the figures of women characters. Teachers may wish to elucidate from students what stereotypes of Chinese and Chinese Americans are common in American popular culture. Some common stereotypes are that Chinese Americans do not speak or write English well; they are quiet, hardworking, and law-abiding; they come from large and supportive extended families: that is, they form a "model minority." In what ways do the memoirs support these stereotypes? In what ways do the narratives of women's suicides, madness, anger, silences, and confusions contradict the stereotype of the "model minority"? How are the struggles of the narrator/ protagonist against her domineering mother and patriarchal community similar to the students' experiences with their families?

Students may work on personal-narrative assignments to trace similarities between their own growing-up experiences and the memoirs. These autobiographical/analytical assignments may be enlarged to include discussions of their ethnic communities. Personal and ethnic identity topics allow students to appreciate both Kingston's Chinese American subjects and the relevance of these subjects to their own identity. Students should read materials on identity formation—for example, Omi and Winant's sociological study. Is the narrator's identity a dynamic process, or is it a fixed product or an essence? Similarly, students may discuss generational conflicts between parents and children. How do ethnic cultures affect these conflicts, as seen in the particular tensions between immigrant mothers and American-born daughters (99–109, 197–205)?

The Woman Warrior can be discussed as a series of narratives built upon central characters: No Name Woman, Fa Mulan, Brave Orchid, Moon Orchid, and Ts'ai Yen. Students should discuss the various significations that accrue to these characters. Are they wholly positive, like role models, or wholly negative? Or do they encompass complex and even contradictory values? Do students find these characters totally "alien"? What qualities do these characters possess that allow students to find them understandable and even to identify with them? Who are some of the "minor" characters in the memoirs? What roles do characters such as the wise old man and woman in "White Tigers," the bigamous husband in "At the Western Gate," and the silent girl play in the memoirs? How is the narrator/protagonist constructed? What aspects of her childhood are emphasized and for what purposes?

The analysis of character must be accompanied by an analysis of genres and of the memoirs' language strategies. Students should research what is meant by literary terms such as "autobiography," "biography," "memoirs," "history," "fiction," "fantasy," "evidence," "myths," and "legends." One class assignment could be to distinguish between different genres, to discuss if and why such distinctions are important and/or possible. What genre can be assigned to *The Woman Warrior*? What significance lies in the choice of one genre vis-à-vis another?

To discuss these questions in depth, students need to examine the memoirs' narrative strategies. A close reading of the way in which the memoirs' language moves from declarative sentences to the subjunctive (for example, 8, 10, 11), from simple past tense to the conditional past (20, for example), will help students grasp the shifts in narrative voices and hence the "instabilities" in the text between autobiographical narrative and fantasy, between the personal voice of the narrator and the other voice of the storyteller. Such exercises in close reading will help students to understand and appreciate the complexity of language in *The Woman Warrior.*

3. Writing and Discussion Assignments

The following questions may help instructors in encouraging students to analyze the memoirs.

1. Discuss the relationship between the author, the narrator, and the autobiographical subject. Although they can be seen as residing in one identity, "Maxine Hong Kingston," should they be read as one and the same? If not, what are the different functions you would assign to them, based on an analysis of the memoirs?

2. *The Woman Warrior* has been called an "autobiography" and a work of "nonfiction." What do you understand by these terms? Do you agree with this classification of the memoirs? Explain your answer with specific textual explications and illustrations.

3. Select one major female relative and examine the narrator's relationship to this relative. How does the narrator describe this relative? How is the relationship conceptualized? What does the narrator mean by "ancestral help"?

4. What are some legendary Chinese women whose stories *The Woman Warrior* reproduces? Does the narrator simply repeat these stories, or does she "revise" them for her purposes? From a close reading of these passages, what can you infer of the reasons for retelling these well-known legends?

5. According to the memoirs, what are the attitudes of immigrant Chinese, including those of the narrator's family members, toward American society and institutions? Refer to specific passages in your response. What historical knowledge do we need in order to explain these attitudes?

6. According to *The Woman Warrior,* what is the position of women in traditional Chinese culture? Discuss this with reference to at least three "talk stories." Are these women chiefly victims in a patriarchal society, or do they also resist their subordination? Explain your answer fully.

7. Summarize the daughter's construction of her mother. With reference to specific passages, analyze how the mother-daughter bonds/bounds are negotiated.

8. Although *The Woman Warrior* places some of its actions in China, it is very much an American book. Compare its representations of growing up

in the United States—for example, generational conflicts, school pressures, cross-cultural misunderstanding—with representations from another American work, such as Maya Angelou's *I Know Why the Caged Bird Sings*.

9. *The Woman Warrior* should be read together with a number of other Asian American books—for example, Amy Tan's *The Joy Luck Club*. In what ways does it influence Tan's novel? How does it revise and extend the portrayal of Chinese American daughterhood that is found in an earlier autobiography, Jade Snow Wong's *Fifth Chinese Daughter*? Or, when read against a Chinese American novel like Louis Chu's *Eat a Bowl of Tea*, contrast a male representation of a Chinatown community with Kingston's family-based memoirs.

10. Discuss the theme of silence as it is developed in the memoirs. How is the silence inscribed in the name of No Name Woman different from the silence of the emigrant Chinese villagers in U.S. society and from the silence of the Chinese American girls in the American school? Analyze the protagonist's torturing of the silent little girl to force her to talk in "Song for a Barbarian Reed Pipe." How is the theme of silence related to the figure of Ts'ai Yen, the woman poet in exile?

C. Bibliographies

1. Related Works

Angelou, Maya. *I Know Why the Caged Bird Sings*. New York: Bantam, 1971.
Chu, Louis. *Eat a Bowl of Tea*. 1961. Reprint, Secaucus, N.J.: Lyle Stuart, 1979.
Kingston, Maxine Hong. *China Men*. New York: Knopf, 1980.
———. *Tripmaster Monkey: His Fake Book*. New York: Knopf, 1989.
Lai, Him Mark, Genny Lim, and Judy Yung, eds. *Island: Poetry and History of Chinese Immigrants on Angel Island 1910–1940*. San Francisco: HOC DOI, 1980.
Liu, Wu-chi, and Irving Yucheng Lo, eds. *Sunflower Splendor: Three Thousand Years of Chinese Poetry*. Bloomington: Indiana University Press, 1975. See, especially, "The Ballad of Mulan," trans. William H. Nienhauser (77–80); and "The Lamentation," trans. Yi-T'ung Wang (36–39).
Malcolm X. *The Autobiography of Malcolm X*. c. 1965. New York: Ballantine Books, 1992.
Salinger, J. D. *The Catcher in the Rye*. Boston: Little, Brown, 1951.
Tan, Amy. *The Joy Luck Club*. New York: Ivy Books/Ballantine, 1989.
Wong, Jade Snow. *Fifth Chinese Daughter*. New York: Harper and Row, 1945.

2. Best Criticism

Brown Ruoff, A. LaVonne, and Jerry W. Ward, eds. *Redefining American Literary History*. New York: Modern Language Association Press, 1990.

Cheung, King-kok. *Articulate Silences: Hisaye Yamamoto, Maxine Hong Kingston, Joy Kogawa*. Ithaca and London: Cornell University Press, 1993.

Fischer, Michael M. J. "Ethnicity and the Postmodern Arts of Memory." In *Writing Culture: The Poetics and Politics of Ethnography*, ed. James Clifford and George E. Marcus. Berkeley: University of California Press, 1986.

Kim, Elaine H. *Asian American Literature: An Introduction to the Writings and Their Social Context*. Philadelphia: Temple University Press, 1982.

Lim, Shirley Geok-lin, ed. *Approaches to Teaching Kingston's The Woman Warrior*. New York: Modern Language Association Press, 1991.

Lim, Shirley Geok-lin, and Amy Ling, eds. *Reading the Literatures of Asian America*. Philadelphia: Temple University Press, 1992.

Ling, Amy. *Between Worlds: Women Writers of Chinese Ancestry*, 119–23, 137–53. New York: Pergamon Press, 1990.

Rabine, Leslie. "No Lost Paradise: Social Gender and Symbolic Gender in the Writings of Maxine Hong Kingston." *Signs* 2, no. 3 (1987): 471–92.

Rabinowitz, Paula. "Eccentric Memories: A Conversation with Maxine Hong Kingston." *Michigan Quarterly Review* 26 (Winter 1987): 177–87.

Smith, Sidonie. *A Poetics of Women's Autobiography*. Bloomington: Indiana University Press, 1987.

Wong, Sau-ling. *Reading Asian American Literature: From Necessity to Experience*. Princeton, N.J.: Princeton University Press, 1993.

3. Other Sources

Bakhtin, M. M. *The Dialogic Imagination: Four Essays*. Austin: University of Texas, 1981.

Boelhower, William. *Through a Glass Darkly: Ethnic Semiosis in American Literature*. New York: Oxford University Press, 1987.

Chan, Sucheng. *Asian Americans: An Interpretive History*. Boston: Twayne Publishers, 1991.

Chan, Sucheng, ed. *Entry Denied: Exclusion and the Chinese Community in America, 1882–1943*. Philadelphia: Temple University Press, 1991.

Cheung, King-Kok, and Stan Yogi. *Asian American Literature: An Annotated Bibliography*. New York: Modern Language Association Press, 1988.

Chin, Frank. "Come All Ye Asian American Writers of the Real and the Fake," 1–93. *The Big Aiiieeeee!* New York: Meridian, 1991.

Chodorow, Nancy. *The Reproduction of Mothering*. Berkeley: University of California Press, 1978.

Geertz, Clifford. *The Interpretation of Culture.* New York: Basic Books, 1973.

Gilligan, Carol. *In a Different Voice.* Cambridge: Harvard University Press, 1982.

Islas, Arturo. "Maxine Hong Kingston." In *Women Writers of the West Coast: Speaking of Their Lives and Careers,* ed. Marilyn Yalom, 11–19. Santa Barbara, Calif.: Capra Press, 1983.

Johnson, Kay Ann. *Women, the Family and Peasant Revolution in China.* Chicago: University of Chicago Press, 1988.

Nee, Victor, and Brett Nee. *Longtime Californ': A Documentary Study of an American Chinatown.* New York: Pantheon, 1972.

Olney, James, ed. *Autobiography: Essays Theoretical and Critical.* Princeton, N.J.: Princeton University Press, 1980.

Omi, Michael, and Howard Winant. *Racial Formation in the United States from the 1960s to the 1980s.* New York: Routledge and Kegan Paul, 1986.

Said, Edward. *Orientalism.* New York: Vintage, 1979.

Showalter, Elaine, ed. *The New Feminist Criticism.* New York: Pantheon, 1985.

Siu, Paul C. *The Chinese Laundryman: A Study of Social Isolation,* ed. John Kuo Wei Tchen. New York: New York University Press, 1988.

Sollors, Werner. *Beyond Ethnicity: Consent and Descent in American Culture.* New York: Oxford University Press, 1986.

Takaki, Ronald. *Strangers from a Different Shore.* New York: Viking Penguin, 1989.

Wolf, Margery. "Women and Suicide in China." In *Women in Chinese Society,* ed. Margery Wolf and Roxane Witke, 111–42. Stanford, Calif.: Stanford University Press, 1975.

Yung, Judy. *Chinese Women of America: A Pictorial History.* Seattle: University of Washington Press, 1986.

4. Video and Films

Bonetti, Kay. "An Interview with Maxine Hong Kingston." Audiotape. American Audio Prose Library, 1986.

Maxine Hong Kingston: Talking Story. Joan Saffa, director and editor. Joan Saffa and Stephen Talbot, producers. NAATA, 1990. 60 min.

Moyers, Bill. Interview with Maxine Hong Kingston. *World of Ideas.* Public Broadcasting System, 1989.

Small Happiness. Carma Hinton and Richard Gordon, directors. Long Bow Group, producers. Distributed by New Day Films, 1984. 58 min.

Experiential Approaches to Teaching
Joy Kogawa's *Obasan*

MITSUYE YAMADA

A. Analysis of Themes and Forms

When I was assigned to teach Ethnic American Literature in the 1970s to a class of predominantly white students at a community college, I learned very quickly that the historical and aesthetic approaches to literature that had served me well in teaching the "standard" American literature course were not working. I was not able to communicate to my students that these works by ethnic Americans are part of their own American culture. My students persisted in speaking about "those people" as if the experiences they were reading about were in no way related to them. What was missing in my teaching these works as literature, I realized, was the experiential approach that I used for my composition students. In the writing classes, I encouraged students to examine not only the form as it is related to content, but the way the writers seemed to fall back on their own resources, their personal histories, in telling their stories. In these writing classes they read short literary works, often excerpts from novels, as models for their own compositions. The experiential approach is particularly important in studying works by ethnic writers, for it forces students to experience the work by tapping into their own personal encounters. A novel that lends itself well to such a treatment is *Obasan* by Japanese Canadian writer Joy Kogawa.

Of course, for a full appreciation of any work, all three approaches, the aesthetic, the historical, and the experiential, must be considered by serious students of literature.[1] *Obasan* is a poignant psychological novel with astounding poetic artistry as well as historical significance and has received some well-deserved critical attention as a work of art in the past few years, most notably by three critics/scholars: King-Kok Cheung, Cheng Lok Chua, and Shirley Geok-Lin Lim. Cheung decries the "Eurocentric perspective" of mainstream critics in analyzing Asian American literary works. She argues that critics persist in writing about "silences" present in *Obasan* as if they reflected a negative Asian cultural trait. Cheung maintains that these "silences" in *Obasan* and other Asian American writings are a positive rather

than a negative force in Asian culture. She examines the numerous metaphors of silences in *Obasan* with clarity and insight. Chua's work is helpful
in that it concisely recounts the history of anti-Asian sentiment in the U.S.
and Canadian pasts, besides explaining some of the mythic and symbolic
qualities in the novel. Lim asserts that Asian American women's texts cannot be approached linearly, but that the critic must take note of "multiple
presences, ambivalent stories and circular fluid narratives" inherent in the
telling. These and other in-depth studies are extremely important for serious students of literature. However, the approach that I am suggesting will
be useful in an English composition course in which the novel is included
among the reading assignments.

Obasan is a fictionalized account of the devastating experiences endured
by Canadians of Japanese ancestry during World War II. Partly autobiographical, the story is told from the point of view of a thirty-six-year-old
Canadian Japanese schoolteacher, Naomi Nakane, thirty-one years after the
major events of the novel. Blending the historical with the psychological,
Kogawa makes a strong statement about the miracle of breaking silence.
The narrator/author fulfills a double assignment: the narrator, Naomi,
comes to terms with her past when she breaks her own silence; and the
author, Kogawa, begins a healing process for Japanese Canadians by bringing to light what the Canadian government has never publicly acknowledged until recently. The narrative strategy that Kogawa uses is a
counterpoint of dipping into a cache of family letters, diaries, and documents that triggers intermittent flashbacks into Naomi's childhood. Gradually, Naomi, who was only five years old at the beginning of the war, begins
to understand thirty years later what really happened during those war years.
As she searches, reluctantly at first, through her memory bank, she begins
to understand who she is within her family and her community. Kogawa
also makes use of actual letters and historical documents she found in the
Canadian archives for part of her story. She unmasks the psychic wounds
left on the narrator and perhaps herself, whose lives had been deeply af-
flicted by the individual, institutional, and historical racism in Canada.
Breaking the silence for Japanese Canadians (whose nationality as well as
property and freedom had been taken from them during and after the Second World War), the author redefines herself through her narrator.

Using all three approaches in reading this novel, the teacher can help
students to experience the psychological awakening of the narrator/author
during the few days of real time that the major portion of the novel covers.
They will participate in her personal journey to self-discovery and at the
same time recover some memories from their own pasts. When they be-

come conscious of their own buried past, they may come to understand that the recovery of this past can give meaning to their present identity. The involuntary memory that is aroused through a specific concrete image, such as a particular scent or taste associated with a past event, was honed into an art form by Marcel Proust in his celebrated work, *Remembrance of Things Past*. An excerpt from the "Overture" in the first volume of this work (*Swann's Way*) can be introduced and discussed at this time.

In the beginning, some discussion of context is necessary for historical/ethnic novels. This is especially true with *Obasan* because most students may admit to knowing very little about Canadian history or politics. The third necessary component, the aesthetic approach, will happen quite naturally during the discussion of this richly evocative novel.

The context of this novel, the uprooting of the Japanese Canadians from their homes during World War II, can be examined and compared to similar events in the United States, the removal and incarceration of the West Coast Japanese Americans during the same period.[2] Also, Canada's history of antipathy toward Asians from the late nineteenth century to the twentieth, it can be pointed out, was similar to attitudes that existed in the United States during that period. In both countries that antipathy directly translated into numerous racist laws against the Chinese and Japanese as well as outright social discrimination (Adachi, 41). During that period, with very little effort the propagandists were able to whip up fear among the Canadians of the encroachment of what they called the "Yellow Peril" by using a distorted Darwinian biological theory. In 1905, one Canadian newspaper columnist writes:

> . . . the Chinese, or the Japanese, through an evolutionary process which has been in progress for centuries is now, as we find him, a marvelous human machine, competent to perform the maximum of labour on the minimum of sustenance. He does not require to maintain a home as white men do; does not spend one 50th part of what the meanest white labourer considers absolutely necessary for clothing; lives in a hovel where a white man would sicken and die and with it all performs . . . unskilled laborious tasks quite as efficiently as a white man and given the training, is equally proficient at duties requiring the exercise of some skill. (Adachi, 65)

This columnist "marvels" at the efficiency of the "Oriental immigrants," but at the same time warns that these "human machines" will pose "a threat to the future of the white race" (Adachi, 65). Most Canadians, along with their neighbors, considered the attack on Pearl Harbor by the Japanese a treacherous attack on the whole Western world by an Asian race. This event was a perfect excuse for Canadian citizens to demand that the Japanese be removed from their communities for security reasons. Because the media had habitually characterized "Orientals" as not having "normal" human needs, the Canadian authorities in charge of the removal of the Japanese were able to do so without providing the most basic amenities for the Japanese families.

At the same time that this "evolutionary theory" was being espoused, Canada, herself a commonwealth of Great Britain, supported the policy of colonial aggression against "inferior" peoples. From here it was a very easy step toward the official policy adopted by the Canadian government for the treatment of the Japanese Canadians. In the United States, the government forcibly removed 120,000 Japanese Americans living on the West Coast and placed them into nine concentration camps during the spring of 1942. Canada preceded the U.S. in declaring the Pacific Coast as a military zone and removed twenty-three thousand Canadians of Japanese ancestry to what they called "interior settlements" in British Columbia. Similar to the action taken by the U.S. Federal Bureau of Investigation, which placed male leaders in the Japanese American communities under arrest and interned their families in separate camps, the Canadian government split up families by sending able-bodied men to labor camps and their families to ghost towns and abandoned mining communities. However, the Canadian government's actions were more cruel and drastic. It confiscated and sold the evacuees' properties to defray the cost of their removal. When the families arrived at the sites assigned to them, they found old makeshift shacks that were unfit for human habitation.

Somehow the Japanese families coped, and in time transformed the ruins into habitable living quarters. They built something that resembled a community among themselves. However, three years later, toward the end of the war in 1945, Mackenzie King, the Royal Commissioner of Canada, announced his "reconstruction" policy: the Japanese must agree to repatriate to Japan or disperse themselves to somewhere "east of the Rockies" to self-supporting jobs (Adachi, 258). The government did not permit them to return to their former neighborhoods until 1949, long after the need for caution—because of supposed "military necessity"—was past.

In the first chapter, we find the narrator, Naomi Nakane, and her Uncle Isamu spending an affectionate but strangely disquieting evening together at the coulee near the uncle's home in Granton. The Nakane family had finally settled in Granton after the war, their exile from exile "east of the Rockies" in southern Alberta. The year is 1972, thirty-one years after the beginning of World War II. The uncle—formerly a master shipbuilder and fisherman deprived of his livelihood when the family was moved to this interior area during that war—often walked up the hill through a prairie of tall grasses and pretended the prairie was the sea. Naomi does not quite understand why the uncle insists that she accompany him to this spot every year in August. For her the prairie evokes other thoughts: "I search the earth and sky with a thin but persistent thirst" (3). This chapter alerts us to the novel's ambiance: that "persistent thirst" that is sustained throughout the novel.

In Chapter 2 the reader is in the "real present." We discover that Chapter 1 is Naomi's nostalgic memory of her last moments with her Uncle Isamu during her visit with him and Aunt Aya a month before his death. When she is called out of her classroom and is told of her uncle's death, Naomi hurries to Granton to be with her Aunt Aya, the Obasan of the title. This aunt was the one adult who had provided continuity in the lives of Naomi and her older brother, Stephen, during their turbulent growing up years. Sorting through family papers in the house where she spent her late childhood, Naomi discovers within herself long-suppressed memories of the dead, especially "those that refuse to bury themselves."

The agency that coaxes Naomi's consciousness out of its dormant state is not only the house and Uncle's death, but a heavy package as hard as "a loaf of Uncle's stone bread." The package contains newspaper clippings, journals, letters, and notes on scraps of paper collected by her crusading Aunt Emily. While Naomi awaits the arrival of the other surviving members of the family, she browses through these papers and recalls the visits of Aunt Emily, who has been campaigning for Japanese Canadians' rights since the end of the war. The energetic Emily would talk about her meetings with various groups of political activists, but Naomi would listen quietly and say she would rather "leave the dead to bury the dead." Naomi remembers her aunt had retorted, "I'm not dead. You're not dead. Who's dead?" (42). Only through reading these documents does Naomi begin to understand Aunt Emily's anger and impatience at her niece's seeming lack of interest in the history of the Japanese Canadians. Naomi recalls her numerous conversations with Aunt Emily and finally hears her message: "You are your history. If you cut any of it off, you're an amputee. Don't deny the past."

Because many young students with very little sense of history often think that only the present is important in their lives, they may agree with Naomi that the past is of little relevance to the present. A discussion of the value of recovering the past in general terms would be very appropriate during the early part of this novel.

Without being aware of it, Naomi begins a slow healing process of recovering from a sense of incompleteness. The "persistent thirst" that has been tormenting her throughout her life was the need to know why adults around her kept a total silence about the disappearance of her mother when she was five years old. Many students will be drawn into this process of rediscovery. They may agree at first with Naomi saying to Aunt Emily early in the novel, "Life is so short, the past is so long. Shouldn't we turn the page and move on?" (42). They may not quite understand at this point Aunt Emily's retort, "The past is the future," but will acknowledge that "speech that frees comes forth from that amniotic deep." They should be reminded of the second epigraph, where we are told before we know what is to come that "beneath the dreams is a sensate sea." Not only Naomi and her older brother, Stephen, the author suggests, but the Canadian government, the Christian church, and the dominant culture all suffer from historical amnesia.

Gradually, old photographs and documents bring back "a collage of images" in the "caverns" of Naomi's mind. She cannot become whole again until the intuited knowledge that is accrued in childhood and the "real" information that she discovers in Aunt Emily's documents, letters, and journal come together and become part of her.

Students can be encouraged at this point to recover their own family histories from old photographs that have been in the family for a long time, and old letters that have been stashed away somewhere in some family member's attic. The memories evoked from these articles need not necessarily be their own, but they can be encouraged to talk to older members of the family who will be more than willing to talk about their experiences. The process of how lost memory can well up quite spontaneously from the subconscious mind (as familiar concrete images from the past are brought out) can be demonstrated in this way.

In the novel, the adult Naomi recalls that her remembered childhood is peppered with inexplicable occurrences she is left to sort out for herself. Students will remember from their own memories how the world looked to them when they were children and begin to understand how children store knowledge that only becomes clear to them years later. Developmental psychologists tell us that between the ages of two to seven, a child's cognitive growth increases at a tremendous rate. The child begins to conceptualize the world around her by piecing together what she sees and hears. Often this concept formation is incomplete when much of what is happening makes no sense at all at the time and the adults around them offer no satisfactory answers.

Shirley Geok-lin Lim has suggested that the "novel presents itself on one level as a mystery story, a historical and psychological riddle" and that the narrator's personal quest "for the lost mother is also the political quest/ion that the novel explores. What happened to the Japanese Canadians between 1941 and even after the Pacific War ended?" (Lim, 308). Until the "mystery" is (re)solved, the novel shows us that the adult child will continue to suffer the pain of feeling "abandoned" by her mother and that a whole generation of Japanese Canadians will continue to feel the tenuous nature of their position as citizens of Canada.

There are many layers of symbolic images that can be explored in this novel, but the metaphor that works best with the experiential approach is that of the lost mother as a metaphor for the lost self. Having been rejected by her mother country (Canada), the land where she was born and to which she thought she belonged, the narrator is in search of an anchor. Contemporary examples abound, such as the voice of a Palestinian woman: "It's the obsession of the exiled in retrieving the lost homeland, the lost piece of heart, stability, continuity and constancy."[3]

Naomi's need for stability is so great that she grasps at signs of it in her early childhood, but the memories of the innocence of that childhood may be questioned. Memories of the innocence of early childhood are invariably clichéd. Students will tell us that what they remember of their early childhood has been "romanticized" just as Naomi's seemed to be. There was warmth and security in the Nakane household when her mother was around to read Japanese fairy tales to her. Her mother and grandmother were always alert to her needs: "When I am hungry, and before I can ask, there is food. If I am weary, every place is a bed. No food that is distasteful must be eaten and there is neither praise nor blame for the body's natural functions" (56). She remembers that "simply by existing a child is a delight."

However, even at the age of five, Naomi had sensed that some things are both fascinating and dangerous at the same time. She remembers the molestation by "Old Man Gower," but that "his hands are frightening and pleasurable" (65). Around the same time, her mother (a Canadian-born Japanese woman who grew up in Japan) leaves for Japan to visit the great-grandmother. Aya Obasan, who is childless, becomes Naomi's surrogate mother throughout Naomi's and Stephen's childhood and tells the children that their mother must go because great-grandmother is asking for her. Naomi wonders why great-grandmother's needs are greater than her own. The child is never told that the outbreak of the war has left her mother stranded in

Japan and she cannot return. The two events, the molestation and the mother's disappearance, become linked in the child's mind. The physical and psychological separation from her mother torments Naomi with guilt and confusion.

The students can be asked to think about some of the contradictory images of their own past. Are there fragile memories in their past that they have cherished and nurtured through the years that can be easily contradicted by some simple facts that they remember but failed to process?

Except for the disappearance of the mother, young Naomi's life appears to be "normal." The direct consequences of the war on Naomi's once closely knit extended family were devastating, but the adults around her (her father, her Aya Obasan, Uncle Isamu, and her paternal grandparents) all manage to put on a good face for the sake of the children. Nevertheless, through "whispers and frowns and too much gentleness" (73), the child cannot help sensing that there is a "heavy mist of fear" that pervades the air.

Some students may recall instances in their childhood when they felt something was being withheld from them. They could be asked, Is the pall of unhappiness or uneasiness that pervades the family mood often more terrifying than the truth itself to small children? Through the documents, Naomi discovers that her paternal grandparents both died in camp away from the family, the father contracted tuberculosis and was hospitalized, and Uncle was sent to a labor camp. Even as the closely knit extended family gradually disintegrated during those years, Naomi's surrogate parents did everything in their power to let the children think all was well and normal. The child Naomi did not understand the gravity of the family situation.

The adult Naomi learns from reading Aunt Emily's journal that there was chaos, anger, and fear among the adults throughout those years. She sees what she had not seen as a child: the adults had every reason to be demoralized. The journal contains painfully poignant letters to Naomi's mother (Emily's older sister in Japan), in which Emily bares her heart and soul. Although the letters could not be sent, Emily hopes that someday when the war is over, her Nesan (older sister) will know what happened to the family during her absence. Naomi thinks as she reads, "I feel like a burglar as I read, breaking into a private house only to discover it's my childhood house filled with corners and rooms I've never seen. Aunt Emily's Christmas 1941 is not the Christmas I remember" (79).

Internal stress within the family during the holiday season, when everyone in the world is supposed to be joyfully celebrating, is such a common occurrence that for some students this part of the novel will be very real to them.

Naomi's surrogate parents, Uncle Isamu and Aunt Aya, tried to provide Naomi and her brother, Stephen, as comfortable a life as was possible under the circumstances. They appeared quite calm on the surface, but Emily's letters tell another story. Those months after the bombing of Pearl Harbor, the government seized Uncle Isamu's prized fishing boat and suspended his fishing license. The Canadian authorities rounded up the men and sent them to labor camps. "We're like a bunch of rabbits being chased by hounds," writes Emily (90). But for the sake of the children they manage to put on an air of resignation.

By entering into the mind of the child Naomi while the adult Naomi is reading these letters and documents, we, the readers, understand the sense of total helplessness and powerlessness that was felt by the Japanese Canadians as they responded to the orders of the Canadian government. Her Aunt Emily understood this process in purely human terms. "Bureaucrats find it so simple on paper and it's translated willy-nilly into action—and the pure hell that results is kept 'hush hush' from the public, who are already kicking about the 'luxury given to Japs'" (92).

Chapter 25 is a pivotal chapter that occurs about two-thirds into the novel, when the family and neighbors gather for their last communion service before they disperse to parts unknown. Students with some background in Christian ritual will understand that there is something quite significant happening here. The students by this time will be aware that they have been reading this novel at multiple levels. What they know of ambiguity and irony should come into play in this chapter quite readily. On the historical level, we know from the documents that the Canadian government has launched its program to disperse the evacuees to "east of the Rockies." After three years of living in the ghost town, there is another separation. Inexplicably, the families are sent to different camps. "It's happening again," the child thinks as she watches her father's eyes, "the same stare, the eyes searching elsewhere" (172). Naomi does not understand why they are moving again, and the adults, again, fail to answer her questions. Stephen, who is three years older, is no help at all. To her question, "Why can't we go home?" he simply says crossly, "Because. That's why." At another point in answer to the same question, her father says rather vaguely, "itsuka," someday.[4]

While they are packing boxes to leave the ghost town, the minister and several friends gather at their cabin to share the Holy Communion. The words of the service from the *Book of Common Prayer* are steeped in double meanings: "Almighty God, unto whom all hearts be open, all desires known and from whom no secrets are hid . . . *Zenno no Kami yo subete no hito no kokoro wa Shu ni araware . . .* " (175). As if one cannot believe the words, they needed to be repeated in both languages, English and Japanese. " . . . in the same night that He was betrayed He took Bread . . . " The child Naomi retells this event almost verbatim because the ritual of the communion service had felt as unfathomable to her as all the events in her life that lead up to that moment. Stephen, who restlessly fidgets during prayers, accidentally breaks a phonograph record in one of the crates on which they are sitting. The incident is a welcome distraction to the children during the boring service and neither of them realize the significance of breaking their absent mother's favorite song, "Silver Threads among the Gold." Naomi notices that the broken record looks like a large cookie with a bite taken from it. At that moment the priest is breaking the large wafer, the body of Christ, into smaller pieces that he will offer to his communicants. In remembering this event, the adult Naomi connects the broken record, the broken wafer, and the broken family and understands with clarity, perhaps for the first time, the impossible contradictions in the lives of the Japanese Canadians at that time.

Even for students who are not Christians, the supreme irony of the family celebrating the last communion at this juncture in the Nakane family's lives should be quite apparent. There is the allusion to the Last Supper, but the meaning of that event is now completely distorted.[5] At the first Last Supper, the betrayed Christ gathers his disciples and proclaims oneness with his community. Ironically, his submission to be crucified was an act of resistance against the state. Christ offers communion to His disciples to empower them to resist their oppression, their colonization, and their captivity. In the context of the novel, however, Kogawa shows how these Christian symbols have been turned around. Nakayama sensei at this ghost town communion service attempts to bring comfort to the now totally dispirited Japanese Canadians who are being shunted off to nowhere, the families separated again and "permanently destroyed." By giving his congregation the personal strength to face their dire circumstance, he is encouraging them to take the path of least resistance and become more obedient. Nakayama sensei adheres strictly to the scripted words of the communion as if he dare not deviate from the service as it is written. At this point in the novel, the author, who was raised in a Christian family herself, delivers the most forceful indictment of the Christian church's complicity in the persecution of the Japanese Canadians during this time.

The discussion of symbols, religious and otherwise, is very appropriate at this point in the novel because Kogawa carries the communion symbols even further. Do symbols often take on different meanings, under different circumstances? in different people's lives? or even in one person's life? Are these symbols used to empower or to further oppress?

In thinking about this dispersal twenty-seven years later and remembering the last communion service, Naomi realizes that "we were the unwilling communicants receiving and consuming a less than holy nourishment, our eyes, cups filling with the bitter wine of a loveless communion" (182). She says she is tired and wants to get away "from the past and all these papers, from the present, from the memories, from the deaths, from Aunt Emily and her heap of words." In spite of her disclaimers, the documents from the past that she had been reading with mild interest at the beginning of this journey become "materials of communication" for her, like the communion wafer.

As Naomi reads an old newspaper article entitled "Facts about evacuees in Alberta" (194), she suddenly explodes. "I cannot bear the memory. There are some nightmares from which there is no waking, only deeper and deeper sleep." Naomi, who has been searching through a life that had been shut away for too long, finally gives herself permission to express anger. She compares Aunt Emily to a "surgeon cutting at my scalp." She is tired of all the denials that have been very much a part of her life. She yearns for the truth just as she had yearned for her mother throughout her life. She realizes that Aunt Emily's political activities in urging Canadian governments to do right by the Canadians of Japanese ancestry cannot succeed until the Japanese Canadians themselves stop becoming the "unwilling communicants." She comes to realize the necessity for unifying the past and present psychologically.

The students, even the skeptics who were thinking "let bygones be bygones" in the beginning, should understand by this time what it means to "look for the truth" in one's life.

There is another important truth that Naomi comes to articulate more clearly toward the end of the novel: the truth of the "ordinary" white Canadian's racist attitude toward the Japanese Canadians, and their complicity in the "official" Canadian government's decisions. In Chapter 34, Mr. Barker, the Nakanes' next-door neighbor for many years, comes to pay his respects with his new wife after the uncle's death. Mr. Barker is characterized as a basically decent Canadian. He treats them with condescension (at one point Naomi bristles when he refers to them as "our Japanese") and is completely oblivious to his own racism. On the other hand, Naomi can see that Mrs. Barker sees herself as a superior being who "represents the Barker Kingdom, a tiny but confident country" (224). Naomi observes Mrs. Barker's expressions and her body language and finds herself "donning her restless eyes like a pair of trick glasses" and assessing her surroundings through Mrs. Barker's critical eyes: "She must think the house is an obstacle course. . . . The patterns and colours all clash. . . . She must be wondering how any mind can rest in such surroundings" (223). Similar encounters with white Canadians were described before, but what is different this time is Naomi's response. We remember the disastrous date Naomi recalls having had with the father of one of her students, "a widower," at the beginning of the novel, but at the time she attributed their lack of rapport to her own social ineptitude. The taunts of the white children in Vancouver after the attack on Pearl Harbor and again in Slocan are reported simply as incidents not quite understood by the child Naomi. It appears that this single visit calls up memories of all the past offensive remarks she has had to endure as a Japanese Canadian: "'How long have you been in this country? Do you like our country? You speak such good English. Do you run a café? My daughter has a darling Japanese friend. Have you ever been back to Japan?' Back?" (225).

Because the Barkers' visit occurs toward the end of the novel (after the students have had the opportunity to examine their own pasts in conjunction with Naomi's experiences), Naomi's conclusions at the end of this chapter become significant. "Where do *any of us* come from in this cold country?" (italics mine). "We come from our untold tales that wait for their telling" (226).

The interesting thing about this chapter is that students' reactions usually fall into two categories: they identify with either Naomi or Mrs. Barker depending on their personal backgrounds and experiences. Some students who have felt silently "put down" by someone because of being different in some way (class, race, religion, physical appearance, and so on) will identify with Naomi's extreme uneasiness during this visit. They understand that Naomi's lack of self-esteem is the result of always being made to feel as though she did not "belong." On the other hand, students who feel somewhat ashamed about having done exactly what Mrs. Barker appears to be doing in this chapter (or what Naomi thinks she is doing) identify with Mrs. Barker. They feel defensive about Naomi judging Mr. and Mrs. Barker unfairly. With a mixed class of white and minority students, this discussion could become quite lively.

The truth that is kept from Naomi and the reader until the end of the novel is the most important one for Naomi: the story behind her mother's disappearance. Like all the other "truths," this story is uncovered among the papers Naomi is studying, but unlike the others, it is couched in a language she cannot read. Some time after the end of the war, the maternal grandmother sends a long letter describing the plight of the mother during the war. She writes that Naomi's mother had gone to Nagasaki during the war and had become one of the victims of the atom bomb that destroyed that city. The grandmother describes the mother's suffering, her death, and her request that Naomi and Stephen be spared the truth of what happened to her. The surviving adults had honored the mother's wishes and withheld the news from the children, but finally decide to translate the contents of the letter to the now adult children at the uncle's wake. They (and the reader) learn for the first time about their mother's agonizing and lingering death in the days and years following the bombing of Nagasaki. After reading the letter, Nakayama sensei is speaking of "forgiveness," but Naomi is not ready to forgive, not just yet; her head is too full of images of the lost mother's horrors that she has just heard. "Gentle Mother, we were lost together in our silences. Our wordlessness was our mutual destruction" (243).

However, both the reader and Naomi are "prepared" for the revelation after having shared Naomi's living memories. Now we know what is meant by "The speech that frees comes forth from the amniotic deep." We begin to understand the references to "hidden manna" and "white sound." We understand the epigraph and the first five chapters that poetically establish the themes of the novel. We understand that the question that was asked at the very beginning of the novel, "After all these many earth years, where is she now?" (27) has wider implications. Naomi at this point envisions a Canadian maple growing where her mother is commemorated among the dead in Nagasaki. Moments later, she comes full circle: she is able to forgive.

The following day, with the new knowledge of her mother's death, Naomi returns to the coulee where we met her and her uncle in the opening chapter of the novel. She now knows why her uncle and she went there every year on August 9: to commemorate the dropping of the atom bomb on Nagasaki.

Perhaps the "new name" that has been written may be the names of the main characters as we know them. The Canadian government's treatment of its citizens of Japanese heritage has affected Naomi, Stephen, Aunt Emily, and Obasan in dramatically different ways. In the end, Naomi's reconciliation comes through her recognition of where she does not want to be. There is Stephen, who has entered the dominant world so completely that he is uncomfortable with anything "too Japanese." He briefly returns after Uncle's death to attend the services, but it appears to Naomi that "he already looks as if he would like to run out" (231). After the reading of the letter about the mother's death, Naomi must grieve alone because her brother, the only other surviving member of their nuclear family, has become an "amputee," a well-assimilated Canadian who completely denies his heritage. There is Aunt Emily, whose in-your-face crusading style makes Naomi uncomfortable. Naomi thinks that a "lot of academic talk just immobilizes the oppressed and maintains [the] oppressed and maintains oppressors in their positions of power" (34). There is her Aya Obasan, the Issei woman who, Naomi discovers later, holds the key to the "puzzle" about her mother, but remains silent out of her misguided kindness. The older generation "does not dance to the multi-cultural piper's tune or respond to the racist's slur" (226), and Aya Obasan represents the generation of Japanese that prefers silence, discretion, and peace.

But this type of silence was the cause of much turmoil in Naomi's life. Naomi comes to realize that the denial of her past was as costly for the whole community, her own and the country's, as it was for her as an individual. Analogically, the student of this work should be able to see what the lack of awareness of our history (for example, in both Canada and the U.S.) has done to the psyche of the "dominant" culture. There is a process at work here that Asian American critic Walter J. Ong calls "interactive organization":

> A minority literature often mixes what is unfamiliar to the majority culture with what is familiar. It thus provides not only an organization of experience different from that of the majority culture (and of other minorities) but also an interactive organization. A minority literature often negotiates for its own identity with the majority culture and constantly redefines itself, ultimately bringing the majority culture to define itself more adequately, too. Cultures, whether majority or minority, are remarkably like persons, born both to isolation and to community. (Ong, 3)

Only recently have we in the United States and Canada barely begun to accept the experiences of the minority peoples among us as legitimate parts of our history. However, most of us trained in various disciplines in both countries are still woefully lacking in our understanding of how we have become the multicultural/multiracial societies that we are today. It is important for our students to understand that *Obasan* is not confined to Japanese Canadians. It is part of the cultural history of all Americans. The experiential approach need not, of course, be confined to this novel. The process can be replicated and has possibilities of opening up new ways for the student to read any great work of art.

"Any great literature is culturally/nationally rooted. Whether it be Tolstoy or Camus, they are intensely human stories with which we could or must identify. Otherwise, anything 'foreign' will forever not be human, and to that extent we 'dehumanize' ourselves and we become ethnocentric, which is probably one of the basic problems of white dominant 'America.'"[6]

B. Suggested Questions for Students

The following questions are presented in the order the issues were raised in this essay. Each question should be followed by a suggestion to "explain," "describe," or "elaborate" with "specific details."

1. What were the similarities/differences between the treatment of the Japanese Americans and the Japanese Canadians by their respective governments?

2. Have you ever had occasion to revisit a place (house, school, park, or some other) familiar to you in your childhood? What memories were evoked by your returning to these "old haunts"?

3. What can we learn by "recovering" our past?

4. What old memories have been "resurrected" by the sudden discovery of an old photograph, a letter or an object connected with your past?

5. Read the "Overture" in *Swann's Way* by Marcel Proust and compare and contrast the way Kogawa seems to use the involuntary process of recovered memories in her novel.

6. To what extent do you think you have "romanticized" your childhood? Are there events you remember that might alter that image in some way?

7. Do you remember family holidays during your childhood when you sensed an underlying tension that disturbed you?

8. Do you remember a family ritual (not necessarily religious) that the adults appear to think had great import but that you didn't understand at all as a child?

9. Do symbols take on different meanings under different circumstances? in different people's lives? or even in one person's life?

10. How are symbols used? to empower or to oppress?

11. In the incident where the Barkers visit the Nakanes (Chapter 24), do you identify more with Naomi or Mrs. Barker? Why?

12. Explain why Mr. Barker's remark about "our Japanese" summons unpleasant memories in Naomi. Why is she insulted?

13. Do you and your siblings remember certain events in your childhood in completely different ways?

14. What do you think Joy Kogawa meant by the question she appears to be asking herself and the reader: "Where do any of us come from in this cold country?"

C. Bibliographies

1. Related Works

Kogawa, Joy. *Itsuka*. Toronto: Bantam Doubleday Dell Publishing Group, 1992. A sequel to *Obasan*. *Itsuka* follows the character Naomi Nakane to adulthood. It is the story about the Japanese Canadian fight to receive government compensation for the lost property that was never returned.

Houston, Jeanne Wakatsuki, and James D. Houston. *Farewell to Manzanar*. Boston: Houghton Mifflin Co., 1973. In work co-authored with her writer-husband, James D. Houston, Jeanne Wakatsuki Houston recalls her life in Manzanar, a Japanese American internment camp in the desert country of California during World War II and its aftermath.

Proust, Marcel. *Swann's Way*. From *Remembrance of Things Past*, trans. C. K. Scott Moncrieff. New York: Random House, 1956. A fifteen-volume novel that Proust spent a lifetime writing. The student might read the "Overture" in *Swann's Way* to understand the Proustian vision. Like the overture of an opera, the opening chapter of this work delineates the broad themes and methods of the author. Proust suggests that the only access to the truth about our personal past is through involuntary memories that are recalled through accidental encounters with sensory images in the present. Students should be encouraged to read the most famous passage of all in this work: the images recalled when Marcel dips a piece of madeleine in a cup of tea.

Sone, Monica. *Nisei Daughter*. Seattle: University of Washington Press, 1979. The author describes her childhood in Seattle, coping with being both Japanese and American, her experiences in a concentration camp in Idaho during World War II, and her adjustment to life after her release from camp.

Uchida, Yoshiko. *Desert Exile: The Uprooting of a Japanese American Family.* Seattle: University of Washington Press, 1982. An autobiographical account of the removal and detention in Topaz, Utah, of a Japanese family, told from the point of view of a child.

Yamamoto, Hisaye. "The Legend of Miss Sasagawara." In *Seventeen Syllables and Other Stories.* Latham, N.Y.: Kitchen Table: Women of Color Press, 1988. A haunting story of an "eccentric" middle-aged nisei woman who is perceived as an "outsider" by her fellow inmates at Poston, Arizona, in one of the internment camps during World War II, and who eventually suffers a mental breakdown. The story is written from the point of view of a somewhat immature young woman to whom the title character is a source of curiosity and idle gossip with her friends. As in a dramatic narrative, the narrator reveals more than she realizes.

2. Best Criticism

Cheung, King-Kok. "Attentive Silence: Obasan." In *Articulate Silences: Hisaye Yamamoto, Maxine Hong Kingston, Joy Kogawa.* Ithaca, N.Y.: Cornell University Press, 1993.

Chua, Cheng Lok. "Witnessing the Japanese Canadian Experience in World War II: Processual Structure, Symbolism, and Irony in Joy Kogawa's *Obasan.*" In *Reading the Literatures of Asian America,* ed. Shirley Geok-lin Lim and Amy Ling, 97–108. Philadelphia: Temple University Press, 1992.

Fujita, Gayle K. "'To Attend the Sound of Stone': The Sensibility of Silence in *Obasan.*" *MELUS: Multiethnic Literature of the United States* 12, no. 3 (1985): 33–42.

Lim, Shirley Geok-lin. "Japanese American Women's Life Stories: Maternality in Monica Sone's *Nisei Daughter* and Joy Kogawa's *Obasan.*" *Feminist Studies* 16, no. 2 (1990): 289–312.

Ueki, Teruyo. "*Obasan:* Revelations in a Paradoxical Scheme." *MELUS* 18 (Winter 1993): 5–20.

3. Other Sources

Adachi, Ken. *The Enemy that Never Was: A History of the Japanese Canadians.* Toronto: McClelland and Stewart, 1976.

Arasoughly, Alia. *Torn Living* (film). Cambridge: August Light Productions, 1993.

Broadfoot, Barry. *Years of Sorrow, Years of Shame: The Story of the Japanese Canadians in World War II.* Toronto: Doubleday Canada Limited, 1977. Commission on the Wartime Relocation and Internment of Civilians.

Personal Justice Denied. Washington, D.C.: U.S. Government Printing Office, 1982.

Fisher, Anne Reeploeg. *Exile of a Race.* Seattle: F and T Publishers, 1965.

Kitagawa, Muriel. *This Is My Own: Letters to Wes and Other Writings on Japanese Canadians, 1941–1948,* ed. Roy Miki. Vancouver: Talonbooks, 1985.

Kogawa, Joy. *Obasan.* Boston: David R. Godine, Publisher, 1982.

Leighton, Alexander H. *The Governing of Men: General Principles and Recommendations Based on Experience at a Japanese Relocation Camp.* Princeton, N.J.: Princeton University Press, 1945.

Nakano, Takeo Ujo, with Leatrice Nakano. *Within the Barbed Wire Fence: A Japanese Man's Account of His Internment in Canada.* Toronto: University of Toronto Press, 1980.

Ong, Walter J. "Introduction: On Saying We and Us to Literature." In *Three American Literatures,* ed. Houston A. Baker, Jr. New York: Modern Language Association Press, 1982.

Sunahara, Ann Gomer. *The Politics of Racism: The Uprooting of Japanese Canadians during the Second World War.* Toronto: James Lorimer and Company, Publishers, 1981.

Takashima, Shizuye. *A Child in Prison Camp.* Montreal, Quebec: Tundra Books, 1971.

Weglyn, Michi. *Years of Infamy, The Untold Story of America's Concentration Camps.* New York: Morrow and Company, 1976.

Notes

1. I thank my former officemate, Dr. Margaret Boegeman, for her careful reading of this essay and for her helpful suggestions about teaching strategies.

2. There are many books about the forcible removal of the Japanese Americans from the West Coast, but the most comprehensive reference on the subject is Michi Weglyn's *Years of Infamy, The Untold Story of America's Concentration Camps.*

3. Alia Arasoughly's moving film, *Torn Living,* about the displaced Palestinians today puts a personal face on situations that we hear about in the news every day. It is a terrifying reminder that yearning for "home" has become too common a human condition among thousands of victims of political powerplay in the world today.

4. Kogawa's new novel, *Itsuka,* deals with the gradual empowerment of the Japanese Canadians, which finally enables them to seek reparations from their government.

5. Some of the thoughts about the levels of meaning of the communion

service were formulated during a conversation with my brother, a priest in the Episcopal church, the Reverend S. Michael Yasutake.

6. A quote from a sermon delivered by the Reverend Yasutake on the political nature of racism in the United States.

Reading between the Syllables:

Hisaye Yamamoto's *Seventeen Syllables and Other Stories*

KING-KOK CHEUNG

A. Analysis of Themes and Forms

In portraying the interaction among diverse Americans and in expressing feminist and polyethnic sympathies, Hisaye Yamamoto is ahead of her
time. She is best known for her depiction of early Japanese immigrants and
their children: the cross-cultural constraints of manhood faced by issei men,
the frustration and rebellion of issei women, the ambivalence of nisei daughters toward their Japanese American legacy. A virtuoso storyteller, Yamamoto
excels in fusing humor and pathos, deploying irony and understatement,
and constructing muted plots through the use of naive narrators.

Much of Yamamoto's work harks back to the places and the events of her
own life. She discloses that "Seventeen Syllables" is her mother's story,
though all the details are invented. "The Legend of Miss Sasagawara" is set
in Poston, Arizona, where Yamamoto was interned during World War II.
"After Johnny Died" records the tragic death of a brother killed in combat
at the age of nineteen in Italy. "A Fire in Fontana" traces her experience as a
staff writer for the *Los Angeles Tribune,* a black weekly. "Epithalamium" is
set in a Catholic Worker community farm on Staten Island, where she lived
from 1953 to 1955 as a volunteer worker.

Just as Yamamoto's life encompasses historic events, multiple locales,
and cross-cultural encounters, her writing commands a wide range of subject matter. Yet several themes recur in her work: the tension between religious precepts and human desires, the interaction among various ethnic
groups in the American West, the uneasy adjustment of the issei in the New
World (especially the constrictions experienced by Japanese American
women), and the cultural and generational barrier between Japanese immigrants and their children.

Intent on depicting human complexity, Yamamoto seldom casts her characters as heroes or villains; her characters are often caught in circumstances
that render unqualified condemnation or approval difficult. Though she
persistently confronts religious and moral issues, she refrains from passing

judgment. But her very reticence frequently prompts us to reexamine conventional beliefs. The sentiment expressed by Yuki, the narrator in "Epithalamium," is illustrative. Yuki, who has been taking Catholic instruction, does not wish to get baptized: "to reject Buddhism entirely and to accept the Catholic theory that, as heathens, the most that good Buddhists could hope for was . . . Limbo . . . would be equivalent to rejecting her mother and father, and Yuki could not bring herself to cause this irreparable cleavage" (68).

Having lived among people of all colors, Yamamoto captures both the tension and the rapport among people from diverse ethnic backgrounds. Like Ann Petry, she can portray instances of racism in realistic and galling detail. Like Flannery O'Connor, she can do so without explicit accusations but with stabbing irony. The white protagonist of "Underground Lady," for example, betrays her own bigotry while complaining about her Japanese American neighbors. In "Wilshire Bus," a story set in postwar Los Angeles, a drunk on a bus heaps racist slurs on a Chinese couple and demands that they return to where they came from; soon the couple get off—at the veterans' hospital—most likely to visit a son who is an American soldier injured in the war. "Life among the Oil Fields" shows the insolence of a neighboring white couple who run over a Japanese American child in their car, but refuse to apologize or make compensation, as though the child were literally invisible. By framing the incident with allusions to F. Scott Fitzgerald and his wife Zelda, and by linking this couple to the heartless couple in the story, Yamamoto suggests that the callous insouciance divulged in her story is often naturalized, if not glamorized, in American belles lettres.

In contrast to these inimical encounters are instances of cross-cultural bonding. "The Eskimo Connection" describes a friendship that develops through correspondence between a middle-aged Japanese American housewife and a young Eskimo prisoner. "Epithalamium" registers the thrills and heartaches of a Japanese American woman in love with an Italian alcoholic. In "A Fire in Fontana," the nisei narrator finds her inner self turning "black" in empathy after reporting on a fire that has "accidentally" killed a black family residing in a white neighborhood.

Humor and pathos are often interwoven in Yamamoto's interracial episodes. "The brown house"—the eponymous gambling establishment—does not discriminate between races. During a police raid, "the windows and doors of the brown house began to spew out all kinds of people—white, yellow, brown, and black" (42). A black man seeks refuge and is granted shelter in the car of a Japanese woman, Mrs. Hattori, who with her five children is waiting for her husband to emerge from the gambling den. Before long, Mr. Hattori joins them and drives away without knowing that his car carries an extra passenger. When the black man reveals his presence, the driver receives a shock:

> Mrs. Hattori hastily explained, and the man, pausing on his way
> out, searched for words to emphasize his gratitude. He had always
> been, he said, a friend of the Japanese people; he knew no race so
> cleanly, so well-mannered, so downright nice. (42)

This comic episode is laden with irony. Once the fugitive is gone, Mr. Hattori reproaches his wife for offering sanctuary to a black person; Mrs. Hattori retorts that her husband has no misgivings about mixing with other races inside the brown house. Mr. Hattori, whom the black man thanks profusely, has performed an act of charity against his will. Assumed to be "well-mannered" and "downright nice," he refers to the thankful man derogatorily as "*kurombo*" ("Blackie") as soon as the man is out of earshot, and he beats his wife that evening (42).

Another theme that Yamamoto explores repeatedly is the precarious relationship between issei parents and nisei children. Language barriers and disparate cultural values intensify their generational differences. Rosie in "Seventeen Syllables" cannot appreciate her mother's haiku, though she pays lip service to its beauty: "Yes, yes, I understand. How utterly lovely" (8). But the truth is that "English lay ready on [Rosie's] tongue but Japanese had to be searched for. . . . It was so much easier to say yes, yes, even when one meant no, no" (8). The mother and daughter in "Yoneko's Earthquake" likewise talk at cross-purposes. Out of guilt, Mrs. Hosoume, who has undergone an abortion and then lost a son, envisions a causal link between the two premature deaths: "Never kill a person, Yoneko, because if you do, God will take from you someone you love" (56). The mother's cryptic moral is entirely lost on Yoneko, who merely replies, "I don't believe in that, I don't believe in God" (56).

Despite difficulties and failures, these mothers at least attempt to impart their hard-earned wisdom to their daughters, but the fathers—either preoccupied by livelihood, or bent on spiritual enlightenment, or shackled by vice—communicate even less effectively with their children. Mr. Hayashi in "Seventeen Syllables" and Mr. Hosoume in "Yoneko's Earthquake" are earthbound men oblivious to the artistic or romantic inclinations of their wives and daughters. The Buddhist father in "The Legend of Miss Sasagawara" is too absorbed in his spiritual pursuit to notice that his sensuous daughter is disintegrating right under his saintly nose. Both Mr.

Hattori and Charley (the title character of "Las Vegas Charley") are inveterate gamblers unfit to set examples for their children. Ineffectual as these issei fathers are, Yamamoto never reduces them to unsavory stereotypes. Noriyuki's mixed reaction to his deceased father, at the end of "Las Vegas Charley," exemplifies Yamamoto's oblique characterization:

> Noriyuki . . . had lived through a succession of emotions about his father—hate for rejecting him as a child; disgust and exasperation over that weak moral fiber, embarrassment when people asked what his father did for a living; and finally, something akin to compassion, when he came to understand that his father was not an evil man, but only an inadequate one with the most shining intentions . . . limited, restricted, by the meager gifts Fate or God had doled out to them. (85)

The passage alludes to the aspirations and difficulties of the early Japanese immigrants, and the temptations and frustrations that await them in America. Yamamoto's understanding of the hardships that beset the newcomers to American soil allows her to paint incorrigible souls such as Charley and Mr. Hattori with occasional tender strokes. Once a successful farmer, Charley turns to gambling after the death of his beloved wife. Twice he tries to kick the habit, but renews his addiction when the monotony of camp life and his isolation in Las Vegas become too much for him. By delineating the circumstances that turn this well-meaning man into a compulsive gambler, Yamamoto gives us insights into a life that is otherwise all too easily condemned. Mr. Hattori, who gambles in the hope of making a quick fortune after losing money on his strawberry crop, has less claim on our sympathy. Yet even this gambler disarms us with his sincere though short-lived resolutions to reform.

If Yamamoto portrays the failings of Mr. Hattori with tolerance, she extends the strongest sympathy to his long-suffering wife, who does not have the heart to leave her reckless husband permanently. At the end of the story, her family is mired in debt and she is pregnant again. Looking at Mrs. Hattori, Mrs. Wu (the Chinese proprietress of the gambling house) "decided she had never before encountered a woman with such bleak eyes" (45).

Mrs. Hayashi in "Seventeen Syllables" is another female immigrant caught in an unhappy marriage. She struggles to express herself through writing haiku, but her husband sulks whenever she engages in long discussions of poetry with people who share her interests. The conflict comes to a head when she wins a haiku contest sponsored by a Japanese American newspa-

per. On the day the editor comes to deliver the award—a Hiroshige print—
the family is busy packing tomatoes. Mr. Hayashi becomes increasingly
impatient while his wife discusses poetry with the editor in the house, and
finally stalks inside and emerges with the prize picture. The wrenching scene
that follows is seen through the eyes of Rosie:

> he threw the picture on the ground and picked up the axe. Smash-
> ing the picture, glass and all (she heard the explosion faintly), he
> reached over for the kerosene that was used to encourage the bath
> fire and poured it over the wreckage. . . . [Rosie] burst into the
> parlor and found her mother at the back window, watching the
> dying fire. They watched together until there remained only a feeble
> smoke under the blazing sun. Her mother was very calm. (18)

This description, which sears into our consciousness the husband's fury
and the wife's desolation, attests to Yamamoto's genius in creating scenes
that are powerful literally and symbolically. The external calmness of the
mother suggests the depth of her anguish. Although we are not immediately told of her inner reaction to her husband's outrage, the incinerated
picture speaks for her: she is consumed by seething rage and smoldering
despair. The burning of the award signals the end of her poetic career.

Another striking use of a near epiphany to convey repressed emotions
occurs in "Yoneko's Earthquake," when Mr. Hosoume drives his wife to the
hospital to abort an illegitimate child. On the way, the father hits a beautiful collie, but drives on as though nothing has happened. The unblinking
killing of the animal enables us not only to perceive the father's anger and
his indifference to the life about to be destroyed, but also to imagine the
mother's contrasting psychological state. She must cringe inwardly as she
witnesses the act that foreshadows the fate of her unborn child.

Two other narrative techniques contribute to the exquisite telling of "Seventeen Syllables," "Yoneko's Earthquake," and "The Legend of Miss
Sasagawara": the use of a limited point of view and the juxtaposition of a
manifest and a latent plot. "Seventeen Syllables" is told from young Rosie's
point of view. While we are informed of Mrs. Hayashi's poetic interest from
the beginning, the first part of the story revolves around Rosie's adolescent
concerns, especially her secret rendezvous with Jesus, the son of the Mexican couple who work for her family. Only at the end of the story do we
learn the submerged tragedy of her mother, made pregnant and then abandoned by a lover in Japan before her marriage. As Mrs. Hayashi and Rosie
watch the award burn, the lives of mother and daughter intertwine. Rosie,
still in the flush of her first romance, is confronted with her mother's dev-

astating love affair and troubled marriage. Yamamoto fuses their conflicting emotions in the dramatic last paragraph when, with a desperate plea, the mother pits her disenchantment against the daughter's hopes.

Rosie's story and Mrs. Hayashi's story are inexorably enmeshed at the end. But in "Yoneko's Earthquake," one of the plots remains hidden throughout. Also told from a daughter's point of view, the seemingly lighthearted tale ostensibly describes ten-year-old Yoneko's crush on Marpo, the Filipino farmhand who works for her family. Yoneko confides to us matters of utmost concern to her while reporting in passing the daily occurrences in her family, such as getting a ring from her mother one day and being driven by her father to a hospital on another. But her random digressions allow us to infer a liaison between Yoneko's mother and Marpo and the mother's subsequent abortion. Yoneko's passing crush on Marpo and fleeting sorrow after his departure at once parallel and contrast with her mother's passionate affair and unremitting sorrow at being deserted.

Unreliable narration assumes strategic as well as thematic significance in "The Legend of Miss Sasagawara," a story that insinuates the harmful effects of rumors and questions societal definitions of insanity. The title character, Mari Sasagawara, is a nisei woman driven "insane" by the combined pressures exerted upon her as an "other"—in her own family, in her ethnic community, and in American society at large. The word *legend* nicely calls into question the veracity of the information provided in the story, in which we are often misled into looking at a character or an event in a certain way, only to have our perceptions radically altered later. Both Miss Sasagawara and her father, a devout Buddhist priest, are introduced to us through various secondhand reports, made up of gossip and rumors, the gist of them being that Miss Sasagawara is highly eccentric, if not completely deranged. At the end of the story, however, the narrator discovers a poem written by Miss Sasagawara in which she intimates the torment of being confined with a saint:

> But say that . . . someone who had not achieved this sublime condition and who did not wish to, were somehow called to companion such a man. Was it not likely that the saint . . . would be deaf and blind to the human passions rising, subsiding, and again rising, perhaps in anguished silence, within the selfsame room? The poet . . . would describe this man's devotion as a sort of madness. (33)

This veiled record of a passionate daughter's anguished remonstration with an ascetic father not only gives us insight into Miss Sasagawara's tragedy, but also revises our earlier judgment of who is sane and who is not. The daughter, who feels circumscribed emotionally and aesthetically in the presence of her father, is also literally incarcerated. Because of the internment, father and daughter are condemned to live "within the selfsame room." Her mental illness seems an unconscious act of resistance against the chilling influence of her father and against the senseless decree of the U.S. government. By contrast, the other internees conduct their lives in camp as though they were at liberty. Miss Sasagawara's father, who "had felt free for the first time in his long life" during this confinement (32), offers the most bizarre example.

The line between sanity and insanity keeps shifting in this story, which weaves together a particular tale about human passion and saintly impassiveness, a feminist critique of conventional gender expectations (defining who is normal and who is not), and a political allegory of racial prejudice. Yet none of these motifs is explicit. In terms of the coding strategies feminist critics have associated with women writers, this tale is thrice muted: there is neither direct confrontation with the father, nor explicit criticism of the Japanese American community, nor open protest against the government.

Reminiscent of the verbal economy of haiku, in which the poet "must pack all her meaning into seventeen syllables only" (8), Yamamoto's stories exemplify precision and restraint. We must be attentive to all the words on the page to unbury covert plots, fathom the characters' repressed emotions, and detect the author's silent indictment and implicit sympathy. Many of her stories give added pleasure with each new reading, but some may actually require a second perusal to be fully appreciated. Only then may we echo Rosie without her glibness: "Yes, yes, I understand. How utterly lovely."

B. Teaching Ethnic Literature[1]

1. Preparatory Materials

Japanese American history and culture inform Yamamoto's fiction. Most Japanese immigrants came to the United States between 1885 (the year the Japanese government officially permitted the emigration of Japanese nationals) and 1924 (the year the Asian Exclusion Act was passed). The first waves of immigrants consisted mainly of single young men who saw America as a land of opportunity. Only after establishing themselves in the new country did they contemplate marriage and family. Many marriages were arranged by means of photographs exchanged across the Pacific. Hence a large number of Japanese "picture brides" came to America after the turn of the century to meet bridegrooms they had never seen in person. Most of these women were much younger than their husbands. *Giri* (obligation or duty) rather than romance formed the basis of issei marriages. Such information will help students better understand the relationships between Mr. and Mrs. Hayashi, and between Mr. and Mrs. Hosoume.

Equally important is knowing how World War II affected Japanese Americans. Michi Weglyn's *Years of Infamy* is especially helpful in providing such background. Within four months of the bombing of Pearl Harbor over 110,000 Japanese Americans had been forced to abandon homes, farms, and businesses all through the West Coast and were detained in various internment camps. "The Legend of Miss Sasagawara" is full of allusions to the circumstances leading to the internment and to the condition of the camps. One of the most unbearable features of camp life was the total lack of privacy. The narrator mentions passing in front of the Sasagawara "apartment," which was "really only a cubicle because the once-empty barracks had soon been partitioned off into six units for families of two" (22). We know the exact measurements from Weglyn: "A degree of uniformity existed in the physical makeup of all the [relocation] centers. A bare room measuring 20 feet by 24 feet was . . . referred to as a 'family apartment'; each accommodated a family of five to eight members; barrack end-rooms measuring 16 feet by 20 feet were set aside for smaller families. A barrack was made up of four to six such family units" (84). Furthermore, "evacuees ate communally, showered communally" (80). In this light, Miss Sasagawara's decision to dine and shower alone seems not abnormal but eminently sensible. Also implicit in the story is the stockade around these tight quarters. The evacuees are surrounded by barbed-wire fences and watched by armed military police. Like Miss Sasagawara, they are under unrelenting and unnerving surveillance.

Thus the politics of the time not only contribute directly to Miss Sasagawara's distress, but also figure allegorically. Within the individual story, the congestion at camp intensifies the gaze on Miss Sasagawara and accelerates the spreading of gossip. On the allegorical level, the scandal-loving and finger-pointing community has a counterpart in the white majority that allowed themselves to be swayed by prejudice and hearsay into endorsing the imprisonment of an entire people. Just as the rumors about Miss Sasagawara accord well with the stereotypes of dancer or spinster, much of the incriminating "evidence" leading to the persecution of Japanese Americans conformed to the ruling culture's historical prejudice against people of Japanese descent. Tendentious information snowballed in a manner analogous to the tattle concerning Miss Sasagawara. The communal assumption of her pathology echoes the government's speculation that many people of Japanese descent residing on the West Coast were devious spies. The isolation and eventual institutionalization of Miss Sasagawara correspond to the exclusion and ultimate detention of the race.

Placing Yamamoto's fiction in historical and cultural contexts also enables us to see her art of indirection as overdetermined. Her predilection for naive narrators and muted plots, though undoubtedly influenced by modernist experimentation with limited point of view, is also inseparable from her position as a nisei woman writer. Feminist critics have argued that indirection in women writers is a means to avert the masculine gaze. As a woman writing at a time when feminist sensibilities were scarcely publishable, Yamamoto understandably couched her sympathy in a disarming style that keeps alarming subtexts below the surface. But she also had to reckon with the restrictions particular to her race and culture. Belonging to a racial minority inevitably heightened her "anxiety of authorship," especially in face of the anti-Japanese sentiment that broke into the open after the bombing of Pearl Harbor. Though the incarceration of people of Japanese ancestry ended with the war, the lingering hostility of the dominant culture necessitated textual constraints beyond the duration of the physical confinement.

Finally, as a nisei brought up to observe Japanese etiquette, Yamamoto is influenced by concepts such as *enryo* and *gaman,* terms associated with proper behavior. The rules related to *enryo* (self-restraint, reserve, and deference) and *gaman* (suppression of emotion and quiet perseverance) are imparted early in a Japanese family, discouraging children from verbal confrontation and open protest. These modes of interaction can be found in many of Yamamoto's stories, in which neither men, women, nor children voice their protest.

But Yamamoto also transforms cultural rituals into art. She not only capitalizes on the infrequent verbal communication between issei spouses and between issei parents and nisei children, but also makes strategic use of a conversational technique that sociologist Stanford Lyman has associated with the nisei: "Conversations among Nisei almost always partake of the elements of an information game between persons maintaining decorum by seemingly mystifying one another" (53). Issei parents (especially fathers) tend to be authoritative and protective toward the young, so that free verbal exchange between parents and children is frequently suppressed. By playing the naive nisei point of view against the pregnant silence of the issei in "Seventeen Syllables" and "Yoneko's Earthquake," Yamamoto constructs hidden plots and deflects attention from unsettling messages; only through the ingenuous telling of the nisei daughters do we catch nuances of the adult silence. "The Legend of Miss Sasagawara" similarly engages us in an "information game" in which we must decode the ostensibly random observations of various onlookers.

2. Group Activities

To provide the cultural context for Yamamoto's fiction and to help students appreciate Yamamoto's elliptical narrative strategies, teachers may wish to show *Hot Summer Winds,* an one-hour film produced by KCET (Los Angeles) for the PBS's American Playhouse series. The film, loosely based on "Seventeen Syllables" and "Yoneko's Earthquake," will give students a sense of the prewar rural setting and of the interaction of a Japanese American family. But many unspoken details in Yamamoto's stories are spelled out in the movie. Students can learn much about Yamamoto's art of silence by contrasting her narrative indirection and open-endedness with the cinematic explicitness and closure (see Payne).

Students may also be asked to describe their reactions to the characters' behavior in the stories (or the film) and how they would react in similar situations. The ensuing discussion can alert them to different cultural expectations. I have found in teaching these two texts that readers tend to react to the characters according to their own cultural persuasions. Japanese-born students are invariably more sympathetic than their American-born counterparts to the husbands, and more critical of the wives.

3. Discussion Questions

1. Discuss Yamamoto's use of the naive narrator. (Or: Compare the use of naive narrator in the fiction of Yamamoto and Wakako Yamauchi/Sandra Cisneros/Helena María Viramontes.)

2. Discuss the theme of communication in Yamamoto's fiction.

3. In what ways does Yamamoto's stylistic restraint mirror the verbal and emotional restraint of her characters?

4. Discuss the encounters among people of different races in Yamamoto's fiction.

5. Discuss Yamamoto's treatment of religion. (Compare, for instance, her depiction of Buddhism and of Christianity.)

6. Compare the theme of "insanity" in "The Legend of Miss Sasagawara" and Charlotte Perkins Gilman's "The Yellow Wallpaper."

7. Compare the theme of female repression in Yamamoto's "Seventeen Syllables" and Tillie Olsen's "Tell Me a Riddle."

8. Compare Yamamoto's "Yoneko's Earthquake" and Wakako Yamauchi's "Songs My Mother Taught Me."

9. Compare "Seventeen Syllables" and "Yoneko's Earthquake" with the film *Hot Summer Winds*.

C. Bibliographies

1. Related Works

Cisneros, Sandra. *The House on Mango Street*. Houston: Arte Público Press, 1988. This novella uses naive narrators and describes the confusing initiation into womanhood; compare "Seventeen Syllables."

Gilman, Charlotte Perkins. *The Yellow Wallpaper*. 1901. Reprint, New York: Feminist Press, 1973. The themes of female creativity and madness have parallels in "The Legend of Miss Sasagawara."

Olsen, Tillie. *Tell Me a Riddle*. Philadelphia: J. B. Lippincott, 1961. Like "Seventeen Syllables," this title story portrays the conflict between domestic responsibility and literary aspiration.

Viramontes, Helena María. *The Moths and Other Stories*. Houston: Arte Público Press, 1985. The shifting points of view in "Cariboo Cafe" can be compared with those in "The Legend of Miss Sasagawara."

Yamauchi, Wakako. "And the Soul Shall Dance." 1966. In *Aiiieeeee! An Anthology of Asian-American Writers*, ed. Frank Chin, Jeffery Paul Chan, Lawson Fusao Inada, and Shawn Wong, 232–39. Washington, D.C.: Howard University Press, 1983.

———. "Songs My Mother Taught Me." *Amerasia Journal* 3, no. 2 (1976): 63–73.

———. "Handkerchief." *Amerasia Journal* 4, no. 1 (1977): 143–50. All three of Yamauchi's stories use naive narrators to hint at parental discord, as does "Yoneko's Earthquake."

2. Best Criticism

Cheung, King-Kok. "Thrice Muted Tale: Interplay of Art and Politics in Hisaye Yamamoto's 'The Legend of Miss Sasagawara.'" *MELUS* 17, no. 3 (1991–92): 109–25. This article contains a comparison of Yamamoto's story and Charlotte Perkins Gilman's "The Yellow Wallpaper."

Cheung, King-Kok, ed. "*Seventeen Syllables*," by Hisaye Yamamoto. New

Brunswick, N.J.: Rutgers University Press, 1994. This casebook includes an introduction, a chronology, the texts of "Seventeen Syllables" and "Yoneko's Earthquake," two essays ("Writing" and ". . . I Still Carry It Around'") by Yamamoto, an interview with Yamamoto, a comprehensive bibliography, as well as critical essays by Charles L. Crow, Donald C. Goellnicht, Elaine H. Kim, Dorothy Ritsuko McDonald, Zenobia Baxter Mistri, Katharine Newman, Robert M. Payne, Robert T. Rolf, and Stan Yogi.

Crow, Charles L. "Home and Transcendence in Los Angeles Fiction." In *Los Angeles in Fiction: A Collection of Original Essays,* ed. David Fine, 189–205. Albuquerque: University of New Mexico Press, 1984. This essay contains a discussion of "Yoneko's Earthquake."

Kim, Elaine H. *Asian American Literature: An Introduction to the Writings and Their Social Context.* Philadelphia: Temple University Press, 1982. This book contains a chapter on Japanese American literature and a section on Yamamoto.

Yogi, Stan. "Rebels and Heroines: Subversive Narratives in the Stories of Wakako Yamauchi and Hisaye Yamamoto." In *Reading the Literatures of Asian America,* ed. Shirley Geok-lin Lim and Amy Ling, 131–50. Philadelphia: Temple University Press, 1992. This essay compares Yamamoto's "Seventeen Syllables" and "Yoneko's Earthquake" with Yamauchi's "And the Soul Shall Dance" and "Songs My Mother Taught Me."

3. Other Sources

Cheung, King-Kok. *Articulate Silences: Hisaye Yamamoto, Maxine Hong Kingston, Joy Kogawa.* Ithaca: Cornell University Press, 1993.

———. "The Dream in Flames: Hisaye Yamamoto, Multiculturalism, and the Los Angeles Uprising." *Bucknell Review* 39, no. 1 (1995): 118–130.

Crow, Charles L. "A *MELUS* Interview: Hisaye Yamamoto." *MELUS* 14, no. 1 (1987): 73–84.

Koppelman, Susan, ed. *Between Mothers and Daughters.* New York: Feminist Press, 1985.

Lyman, Stanford M. "Generation and Character: The Case of the Japanese Americans." In *Roots: An Asian American Reader,* ed. Amy Tachiki et al., 48–71. Los Angeles: UCLA Asian American Studies Center, 1971.

Nakamura, Cayleen. *"Seventeen Syllables": A Curriculum Guide for High School Classroom Use in Conjunction with "Hot Summer Winds."* Los Angeles: Community Television of Southern California, 1991.

Payne, Robert M. "Adapting (to) the Margins: *Hot Summer Winds* and the Stories of Hisaye Yamamoto." *East-West Film Journal* 7, no. 2 (1993); reprinted in *"Seventeen Syllables,"* by Hisaye Yamamoto, ed. King-Kok

Cheung, 203–218.

Weglyn, Michi. *Years of Infamy: The Untold Story of America's Concentration Camps.* New York: William Morrow, 1976.

Wong, Sau-ling Cynthia. *Reading Asian American Literature: From Necessity to Extravagance.* Princeton, N.J.: Princeton University Press, 1993.

Yamamoto, Hisaye. "After Johnny Died." *Los Angeles Tribune,* Nov. 26, 1945. Reprinted as "Life and Death of a Nisei GI: After Johnny Died," in *Pacific Citizen* (Dec. 1, 1945): 5.

———. "A Fire in Fontana." *Rafu Shimpo* (Dec. 21, 1985): 8–9, 16–17, 19. Reprinted in *Rereading America: Cultural Contexts for Critical Thinking and Writing,* 2d ed., ed. Gary Columbo, Robert Cullen, and Bonnie Lisle, 366–73. Boston: Bedford Books, 1992.

———. *Seventeen Syllables and Other Stories.* Latham, N.Y.: Kitchen Table Press, 1988.

Notes

1. Because of space limitations, this section focuses solely on "Seventeen Syllables," "Yoneko's Earthquake," and "The Legend of Miss Sasagawara."

Swan-Feather Mothers and Coca-Cola Daughters:

Teaching Amy Tan's *The Joy Luck Club*

WENDY HO

A. Analysis of Themes and Forms

Amy Tan's *The Joy Luck Club* is not a book in praise of "Oriental exotics" or passive victims. Nonetheless a number of critics and readers think that Amy Tan writes stories about a tantalizing, mysterious, and romanticized Old China or an exoticized Other. Some reviewers comment more about Tan than about the book, referring to her as "the flavor of the month, the hot young thing, the exotic new voice" (Streitfeld, F8); others invoke stereotypes in their review of the book: "Snappy as a fortune cookie and much more nutritious, *The Joy Luck Club* is a jolly treatment of familiar conflicts" (Koenig, 82). Another critic asserts that the Joy Luck mothers' memories of China are not anchored in "actual memory," but overtaken by "revery" for the China of their childhood past. He disappoints in encouraging readers to "dream" through the Old China sequences in Tan's book (Schell, 28). In *The Big Aiiieeeee!,* a groundbreaking anthology of Asian American literature, the writer-editors are highly critical of what they perceive as Tan's exoticization of China and the Chinese for a white mainstream audience. For them, her book simply resurrects racist images of an inscrutably corrupt East; of heartless, sexist (if not invisible) Chinese men; and of fragile, lotus-blossom women who appear to be too good for the decadent, ignorant society and culture from which they come (Chan et al.). Such one-dimensional Western representations are indeed destructive to the Asian American community. They are derived from the Orientalist school that Edward Said has so eloquently critiqued in his two books *Orientalism* and *Culture and Imperialism.*

But contrary to what the above critics may say or think, Amy Tan is not out to resurrect shallow stereotypes or Chinese exotica in *The Joy Luck Club.* As teachers, we need to seek out new and empowering interpretive strategies for reading Tan's texts rather than appropriating to ourselves—consciously or unconsciously—ways of reading our emerging writers that are based on racist, sexist perspectives. In this regard, I think it is important for readers to do the hard work of carefully processing the new literary, talk-story texts as intimately anchored not only in the psychodynamic tensions between Chinese immigrant mothers and their Americanized daughters within different familial situations, but also in the concrete socioeconomic, cultural, and historical realities of a hybrid diaspora culture in the United States.

The Joy Luck mothers' imaginations are not so overtaken by "revery" that they cannot comprehend the intersecting struggles of their lives in China or America, or the sexism and racism that they and their families must deal with in their lives. Tan resurrects women's untold personal stories of daily survival and resistance as a form of countermemory: Their multiple stories counter, rather than support, the monolithic imperialist, patriarchal gaze and narratives that have denied them agency, complexity, and visibility in not only their own ethnic communities but also in the dominant Western culture in the U.S. Through her semiautobiographical fiction, Amy Tan advocates the value of reclaiming and understanding these Chinese women's neglected stories in China and America and of preserving and reimagining their Chinese heritage even as they tell of their bewildering new dilemmas as Chinese women in the United States. (For the semiautobiographical nature of her book, consult personal interviews by Seaman; Somogyi and Stanton; Tan, 1990.) Her book is dedicated to her mother, Daisy Tan: "To my mother and the memory of her mother. You asked me once what I would remember. This and much more." From these mother roots, daughter-writers such as Tan draw strength to survive, adapt, and create new stories and myths, new definitions of self-in-community, new strategies for cultural/historical survival that will honor their mothers and communities as well as their Chinese pasts. (See Friedman on the importance of group identity in the discussion of self in the writings of women, minorities, and many non-Western peoples.) Such links of the self in new and old communities will sustain them in the dangerous minefields of Anglo American life and culture.

Tan's *The Joy Luck Club* is structured around four central mirroring pairs of mothers and daughters: Suyuan Woo and Jing-mei "June" Woo; An-mei Hsu and Rose Hsu Jordan; Lindo Jong and Waverly Jong; and Ying-ying St. Clair and Lena St. Clair.[1] In *The Joy Luck Club,* the stories of these four pairs are interwoven in four major segments, with the mothers and daughters telling their stories of how it is they came to be where they are in life. Each of the four major segments of the book opens up with a vignette, which is followed by four chapters. The first and last segments involve the Joy Luck mothers' individual stories ("Feathers from a Thousand Li" and "Queen Mother of the Western Skies"). These two mother segments figuratively embrace the two middle segments ("The Twenty-Six Malignant Gates" and "American Translation") in which their daughters speak as second-generation Chinese women in America. In an interesting twist, Jing-mei, the daughter who has reluctantly assumed the place of her deceased mother Suyuan at the mah jong table at the beginning of the book, tells her mother's story in the final chapter, "A Pair of Tickets." She fulfills her mother's dream of returning to China to see her twin daughters—Jing-mei's lost sisters. She finally begins the process of re-identifying with a mother whom she had long neglected—whom she had often dismissed as an exotic Other. The daughter's recognition and reclamation of the intimate bonds with her mother is in counterpoint to the cultural and institutional images and definitions of women as mirrored in patriarchal/imperialist discourse. There is an impending change of guard at the end of the book which suggests the potential for continuity and transformation of mother-and-daughter bonding among a new generation of Chinese American women.

Tan's multiple pairings of mother-daughter stories mirror the strong links between the individual mothers and daughters as well as among all the women of the Joy Luck Club. Rather than focusing on a single primary mother-daughter relationship, Tan gives the reader a sense of the diversity of mother-daughter bonds within Chinese American families. As Tan says, "And when you talk to 100 different people to get their stories on a situation, that's what the truth is. So it's really a multiple story" (Seaman, 256). The links between these mothers and daughters in America are further complicated by the bonds between the Joy Luck mothers and their mothers (and foremothers) in China. Tan enriches the reader's understanding of a single woman's history and of these Chinese American mother-daughter pairs by extending the resonances to the past and to the spidery links to mother-daughter bonds embedded in Chinese culture and society. For example, we witness Lindo Jong's sad separation from her beloved mother and the development of her feisty and clever private self in an arranged marriage—a self that is reflected in a complicated relationship with her own strong-willed daughter. In An-mei Hsu's story, we explore the roots of her frustrations and anger as a woman in the telling of her mother's oppressive life and death as a concubine in feudal China. We begin to understand the links between her personal liberation and the revolutionary changes in China— of a woman and a nation finding a new voice. Tan links Hsu's personal-political struggles with a sociohistorical awareness and participation in her people's struggle for justice and equality. Through the book's intersecting storylines, the reader is exposed to the rich variations and interconnections in the relationships and communications between Chinese mothers and daughters in China and/or in America as they attempt to talk out the silences and distances and to process what is really being described and felt by each other as women.

In *The Joy Luck Club*, the mothers and daughters continually struggle not only to reclaim and speak their stories, but also to "talk back" as complex subjects. But in order to speak up in the larger community and to transform women's lives in a sexist, racist society, Tan's mothers and daughters have to learn to be friends and allies to each other. For women, one important place to begin this primary, necessary work is in the problematic relationships and communications between mothers and daughters. (For an introduction to mother-daughter writing, see, for example, Hirsch.) In *The Joy Luck Club*, mothers and daughters find a compelling need to set the record straight on the specific actualities of their lives in China and America; but they find it difficult to articulate their honest intentions, emotions, and experiences to each other. Jing-mei Woo's mother gives her an heirloom jade pendant—her life's importance—by which she will know her mother's meaning. But as Jing-mei notes, it seemed that she and other jade-pendant wearers were "all sworn to the same secret covenant, so secret we don't even know what we belong to" (198). Much miscommunication takes place between the mothers and daughters. It is a tricky and risky task for them to dredge up and decipher each other's personal stories—these palimpsests that are shrouded in layers of silence, secrecy, pain, ambiguity, collusion, and prohibition within the varied discourses, institutions, and power relations in a society.

However, this is precisely the work that Tan takes up. Each woman has her story of hopes and ambitions, of failure, of survival and resistance. The mothers, for example, must confront the personal archive of tragedy, alienation, suffering, and loss in their own lives; they must negotiate the shame and guilt of leaving country, family, home, and mother. Each woman must wrestle with what to tell the other amid the false images and narratives that obscure or silence their personal stories as Chinese American women. They must overcome the sense that their daughters often look upon them as outcasts, as Other, in America. Jing-mei thinks of her mother's mah jong gatherings as "a shameful Chinese custom, like the secret gathering of the Ku Klux Klan or the tom-tom dances of TV Indians preparing for war" (28). In this less than hospitable context, Suyuan Woo struggles continually to translate her tragic war stories to a resisting daughter. Tan does not neglect to portray the serious dilemmas and ironies that these mothers confront in creating and maintaining a protective environment, a material, cultural and psycho-political bastion, for themselves or their families in America.

Nevertheless, the Joy Luck mothers work painfully to decipher and speak the buried, bittersweet pain of their lives in order to reclaim their own stories and to protect their bewildered daughters from similar pain and oppression as women in America. Through their personal recall, they begin to recognize the insidious links between their pasts and present struggles in America and between their pasts and their daughters' present lives. It is important to read these women's stories as the complicated physical, psychological, cultural, and sociohistorical positionings for personal and communal survival and resistance in the Chinese diaspora communities of the United States. In this light, these stories record not detached reveries or myths about China but, rather, daily heroic actions of many of the Joy Luck mothers, who struggle to raise children under stressful political and sociohistorical conditions.

Like their mothers, daughters must overcome their personal anger, resentment, guilt, and fear toward their mothers. Tan demonstrates how the daughters tend to stereotype their mothers—to freeze them in time as old-fashioned ladies; they do not often give their mothers the space to particularize themselves or to cross over into their lives. They are second-generation, English-speaking Chinese American women, who are located or positioned in an Anglo American homeland that has a long history of oppressing Asian Americans. In living in America, the daughters assimilate certain stereotypical and racist views of the Chinese that alienate them from their own mothers and heritage. They find it distasteful to be identified with their mothers or their stories; with speaking the Chinese language, or with keeping the old ways and customs. Joy Luck daughters often fail to recognize the difficult but vital work and nurture of their working-class, immigrant Chinese mothers. Yuppie Waverly Jong, for example, makes up jokes to tell her friends about her mother's arrival in America and about her parents meeting and marriage. She trivializes their stories of struggle and joy. Waverly does not know the true story about the difficulties of her feisty immigrant mother; the poignant story of how her parents courted by surmounting ethnic and linguistic difficulties; or the story of how her name was chosen to express her mother's love and hopes for her.

Within this problematic framework, the Joy Luck women struggle to maintain vital communication with each other and to piece together the fragmented memories and talk-story of their actual lives. In *The Joy Luck Club,* it is a struggle, with varying successes and failures, for the mother-daughter pairs to know and love each other for their own strengths, weaknesses, and contexts. As we see in the individual stories, it is easy for mothers and daughters to get lost in the intense psychodynamic love–hate struggles within themselves and with each other. Both can be nurturing and suffocating, protective and negligent, trusting and distrustful, arrogant and humble, powerful and weak, affiliative and competitive toward each other. Each Joy Luck mother-daughter pair attempts to articulate positions that are rooted in their intertwined needs for individuation, mutual respect, and attachment to each other and their communities.

In addition, these psychodynamic tensions are embedded in particular socioeconomic and historical circumstances in China and in America that further complicate their relationship and communications with each other; that is, internal tensions between mothers and daughters are exacerbated and even generated by external factors. In *The Joy Luck Club,* mothers and daughters often have a difficult time smoothly negotiating the great sociohistorical expanses of their specific *weltanschaung.* For example, mothers and daughters are separated by historical time, cataclysmic natural disasters and wars, generations, classes, sociocultural systems and values, and languages. The traumatic translation of devalued and ambitious Chinese-speaking immigrant mothers from their motherland to an unfriendly and alien country and the assimilation of their second-generation, English-speaking Chinese daughters into mainstream America cause serious fractures in their relationship and communication with each other.

For the Joy Luck women to communicate with each other and to speak up as women against the invisibility—the distorted images and stereotypes of women in China and America—is to begin to imagine the histories that have been left out. (For instance, see Kim, especially 3–22, on stereotypes of Asian American people in literature, media, and society.) As some of their own mothers struggled to teach them, Joy Luck mothers want to teach their daughters how to acknowledge and deal with pain; how to know true friends; how to trust that their mothers know them inside and out; how to be free of confusion; how to survive under tricky and marginal circumstances with grace and joy luck. Some of the mothers especially desire to pass on to their daughters a sense of *shou,* a respect and honor for their mothers; *nengkan,* an ability to accomplish anything they put their mind to; and *chuming,* an inner knowing of each other as women. Most desire to reclaim their daughters by fighting for their hearts and minds and by responsibly educating them to survive and to subvert the oppressive systems in which they live. Joy Luck mothers teach their daughters that personal and cultural identity need to be maintained not only through the preservation of Chinese heritage but also through a continually active, fluid, multidimensional agency that can negotiate the fluctuations of oppressive social, cultural, and historical processes.

On the one hand, Asian American women have suffered under imperialist and patriarchal power structures. To deny these oppressive factors in any culture—whether in China or America—is, as Frank Chin likes to say, to live in the "fake world," not the "real world." The Asian American mothers and daughters in *The Joy Luck Club* are struggling subjects and agents encountering a not very perfect world in China and in America. Sometimes they lose their battles in the oppressive systems in which they live and position themselves; they comply, negotiate, and/or betray themselves and others in their search for sheer survival or status within systems of power. Tan shows us the complicity and compromise that can mire her female characters as they struggle to come to consciousness and voice about their lives and circumstances. For example, women are complicit in destroying An-mei's mother through the patriarchal power arrangements of family and society. Wu Tsing's childless Second Wife arranges to entrap An-mei's mother as a concubine for her husband. As a rich woman, Second Wife uses the borrowed class, wealth, and power of her husband to oppress and manipulate other women. This oppression of the other wives is her attempt to guarantee her own tenuous position and status in Wu Tsing's competitive female household. Tan is not out to valorize or privilege all women's language and actions. She paints a painfully problematic picture of women's complicity not only in another woman's oppression, but in their own continuing oppression in and maintenance of male-dominated culture.

On the other hand, Asian women are not always or simply powerless, passive, exploited dupes and sexual objects, domestic drudges, illiterates, and/or traditional women in patriarchal or imperialist systems (see Mohanty). In teaching this book, one must not neglect to take into account that Tan shows us how ordinary women, located in the specific context of their own times and personal circumstances, have challenged and subverted the socioeconomic and political systems under which they have lived and are living in many different ways. At the same time that their lives bespeak oppression and tragedy, the Joy Luck mothers do not neglect to pass on empowering interventions to their daughters. These resistances counter the patriarchal and imperialist systems that they are exposed to in China and America, which have forced them to speak, see, think, and act often in disempowering terms.

Such communication provides vital entry into the past, present, and future. The mothers' life-stories are the valuable maps not only of the powerlessness, servility, frustration, defeat, and compromise, but also of the powerful strategies of intervention and subversion that help women survive with a certain amount of grace, anger, strength, connectedness, and love. Mothers and daughters come to realize their fierce love and respect for each other as friends and survivors. They come to realize that there are rich challenges and meanings embodied even in the silences, fragments, tensions, and differences.

Doing the work of talk-story as a way to resist oppressive, monolithic patriarchal and imperialist institutions and metanarratives can lead to the inscription of new and fluid woman-centered spaces for women. In *The Joy Luck Club,* we learn just how vital it is for mothers and daughters to continually talk-story—not to wait, for instance, to speak only until spoken to or given authority to do so or till one can speak perfect American English. It can be personally and politically empowering and heroic for women to tell their stories and attend to each other—not to be decentered objects whose stories are continually co-opted or translated for them or to them by those in power. In this way, women can be empowered to challenge society. During the Chinese Revolution, Chinese women learned to stand up and speak against not only their landlords but also their husbands and fathers. The slogan for this emancipation of people was *fanshen,* which meant "to stand up and overturn the oppressing classes." Women learned to speak the bitterness in their daily lives. Within their consciousness-raising women's groups in the countryside and cities, women learned, first of all, to speak up about the poverty, the hunger, the physical and psychological abuse and fear, the socioeconomic and political inequities. (See description of *suku,* or the "indictments of bitterness," in Ono, 170–75.) Women had access to each other's true feelings and contexts in an affiliative, nurturing environment. In this way, they learned they were not alone, separate from other women or other oppressed groups. Many Chinese women were empowered to speak and act together in transforming their lives and society. Likewise, Tan's mothers want to teach their daughters how to read situations clearly and how to stand up and fight for themselves. They want their daughters to be bolder, more self-assured women; to be independent from their husbands; to have status and voice on their own merit. As the critic bell hooks has powerfully stated, talking back is a way of speaking up for oneself as a woman, boldly and defiantly. It is "not solely an expression of creative power; it is an act of resistance, a political gesture that challenges politics of domination that would render us nameless and voiceless. As such it is a courageous act—as such, it represents a threat. To those who wield oppressive power, that which is threatening must necessarily be wiped out, annihilated, silenced" (8).

Like Maxine Hong Kingston, Amy Tan is a daughter-writer, who has come to realize that locating, defining, and reporting women's stories and the crimes against women and community are part of the constructive, articulated anger and revenge against the narratives and institutions that oppress them. To recover multiple histories and to talk back as women united is to do real battle against oppression in their personal and communal lives. In reading Tan, one becomes acutely aware that this is serious, painful, complicated excavatory work; it is also subversive, creative, freeing, and responsible work for mothers and daughters who wish to connect as women-allies.

B. Teaching *The Joy Luck Club*

An understanding of the Joy Luck mothers' (and their foremothers') Chinese past can help make the problematic interactions with their second-generation Americanized daughters—how they perceive and treat them and why—more accessible to readers. Teachers can assign introductory background readings on women in Chinese and Chinese American history.[2] The mother-and-daughter relationships cannot be fully understood as simply personal, internal problems to be worked out between Chinese mothers and their daughters. The bonds are problematized or complicated, in part, by their embeddedness in the particular psychological, socioeconomic, cultural, and historical realities of a traditional Confucian society that socialized and oppressed women in China.

As Julia Kristeva notes, Confucianists saw women as small human beings (*hsiao ren*) to be categorized with babies and slaves (Ling, 3). Women were not suited by nature for the intellectual life of a scholar or a statesman. Women's lives were to revolve around the Three Obediences and Four Virtues:

> The Three Obediences enjoined a woman to obey her father before marriage, her husband after marriage, and her eldest son after her husband's death. The Four Virtues decreed that she be chaste; her conversation courteous and not gossipy; her deportment graceful but not extravagant; her leisure spent in perfecting needlework and tapestry for beautifying the home. (Ling, 3)

These delimiting societal prescriptions for women's gender roles and for a "true" Chinese womanhood can permit the physical and psychological abuse of women. The Joy Luck mothers experience their mothers' as well as their own difficult compromises and failures in a restrictive patriarchal culture and society. For example, An-mei Hsu learns the lessons that attempt to strain and destroy her relationship with her mother. Both An-mei and her mother live in traditional familial and societal structures, which often deny their personal needs, sufferings, and struggles and ask them to conform to a male-dominated culture against their own individual and common interests as women. An-mei grows up with stories, which attempt to break the spirit of strong-willed girls, the disobedient types—like her hidden self. These patriarchal stories are powerful forms of socialization into her proper and public roles in traditional Chinese society as a daughter, wife, mother, woman. The film version of Tan's *The Joy Luck Club* (Wayne Wang) dramatically depicts the tragic experiences of the mothers in China and its parallels and consequences in the lives of their daughters in the United States. A viewing of the film—a real tearjerker—could provide another way to access the psychodynamic tensions between the mother-daughter pairs in the book. For a view of women's lives in prerevolutionary China, students can read the Chinese novel *The Family* by Pa Chin. The film *Small Happiness* (Carma Hinton and Richard Gordon) can provide a sense of women's lives in a specific Chinese context. In exploring the impact of a Chinese Confucian system on women's socialization into gender roles and identity, students can better understand the relationships of the Joy Luck mothers to their own mothers in China. In addition, this information can help students to understand the complex interactions between the Joy Luck mothers and their own daughters in America.

The historical events and natural disasters in China also play a role in shaping the Joy Luck mothers. They and their mothers before them, in one way or another, experience a range of horrific wars and chaos, evacuations, deaths, economic turmoil, revolutionary changes, poverty, floods, and famines that seriously impinge on their personal relationships and communications with their daughters. In the 1800s to middle 1900s, there were horrendous wars for colonial dominance over China waged by imperialist powers such as England, the United States, and Japan. There was bloody civil war between the Chinese Communist Party (Mao Zedong) and the Guomindang (Chiang Kai-shek) rumbling through China (see Ono). Chinese women suffered the terrible consequences of these chaotic events, especially the toll they took on the socioeconomic and political situations in their daily lives. For instance, Suyuan Woo's life, fears, and ambitions are clearly influenced by the chaos and brutalities of war, separation from family, death of a husband, and loss of her baby daughters. Suyuan's abandonment of her twin daughters during her escape from the invading Japanese is vividly portrayed in the film version of *The Joy Luck Club*. Young Lindo Jong remembers the painful, lonely separation from her beloved mother: she is sent to her boy-husband's household after disastrous floods, famine, and poverty make it difficult for the family to keep a "useless" daughter. Ying-ying St. Clair's concerns for her daughter's safety and her own fears at being sexually harassed on an Oakland street by a stranger could be rooted in her own bitter experiences as a lone married woman migrating from the poor countryside to Shanghai, a city notorious for its foreign decadence and the murder, rape, kidnapping, and prostitution of Chinese women in the early to middle 1900s. However, it was also a significant revolutionary period of change, not only in terms of women's rights but also for the Chinese nation. Students need to keep in mind that the Joy Luck mothers are the products of these revolutionary times. They are women of old and new China.

Besides an understanding of the Joy Luck mothers' Chinese roots, it is important to consider their traumatic translation to the United States. The mothers are excited by the potential opportunities in America for themselves and their families. But they are also socialized into silence by American racism and haunted by the history of immigration policies that have excluded Asians from entry into America. Before the arrival of the Joy Luck mothers in 1949, America already had a long and ugly record of discriminatory attitudes and policies aimed not only against successive groups of Asians, but also specifically against the Chinese (see S. Chan, Daniels, and Wong). Besides numerous Chinese immigration exclusionary laws enacted between 1882 and 1904, there were also a number of immigration policies that specifically deterred the immigration of Chinese women to America (such as the 1875 Page Law and the 1924 Immigration Act). These restrictive forms of social and legal legislation affected the numbers of Asian women entering the country and the subsequent formation of Asian families in America. Racist/sexist stereotypes portrayed Chinese women as lewd and immoral women, who were unfit to enter the country. Sensational newsmedia coverage on the evils of Chinese prostitution created the long-standing stereotype of Chinese women as prostitutes. As audiovisual resources, films such as *Slaying the Dragon* (Deborah Gee) and *New Year* (Valerie Soe) can provide a visual introduction to the many stereotypes of Asian American women/people. With this long history of racism and sexism in the United States, Tan shows us why it is not difficult to understand the Chinese immigrant mothers' fear of the police, deportation, and backlash from white Americans based on their race and gender.

Despite all her years in America, An-mei Hsu lives with fears of deporta-tion. An-mei's fears are well grounded, especially if one remembers America's severe anti-communist paranoia of the 1950s. Likewise, Ying-ying St. Clair is forced to invent a fictive self that is oriented to her present and future life in America, but which does not account for her frightening past life. In this foreign and suffocating space, she feels numb, off balance, and lost, living in small houses, doing servant's work, wearing American clothes, learning Western ways and English, accepting American ways without care or com-ment, and raising a distant daughter. Upon her arrival in America, Ying-ying is processed at Angel Island Immigration Station, where agents try to figure out her classification: war bride, displaced person, student, or wife. She is renamed Betty St. Clair; she loses her Chinese name and identity as Gu Ying-ying and gains a new birthdate. In the Chinese lunar calendar, she is no longer a tiger but a dragon. It takes her a long time to recover and pass on her tiger spirit to her daughter Lena.

In contrast to the mothers, the daughters, born and raised in contempo-rary America, have assimilated more easily into the dominant society. But Tan portrays the great cost of assimilation in the miscommunications be-tween the Joy Luck mothers and daughters. Under such circumstances, how can mothers tell their stories to their insider/outsider daughters? How can the Joy Luck mothers articulate their stories fully if they feel they must hide or deny their past? their language in America? How can Americanized Chi-nese daughters begin to understand the fractured narratives that surface, made up, as they are, of so many lies and truths, so many protective layers set up against the outsiders' *chuming,* an inner knowing, of them? What are the advantages and disadvantages of assimilation for these mothers and daughters? How can these women learn to be friends and allies to each other? How are language and strategies for survival and resistance passed from mothers to daughters? She demonstrates how many intertwined di-lemmas can impede or frustrate clear access by daughters to their mothers and to the full stories of their mother's and family's life and history in China and America. Nevertheless, Tan's text emphasizes that this difficult work of recovery is vital to women's well-being and solidarity with each other.

Another way of accessing Tan's book is to analyze her use of traditional Chinese legends (for example, the Moon Lady story) and images to articu-late the concerns of Chinese American women. For instance, the Joy Luck mothers want their daughters to turn into beautiful swans—perfect, happy, successful, and independent women. In traditional Chinese stories, swans symbolize married, heterosexual love. Tan subverts and re-interprets the traditional image of swans by applying it to the silenced and intimate pairings between women. In this case, a mother and her daughter. The traditional symbols and narratives are being appropriated, reconstructed, or ruptured by writers like Tan (and Maxine Hong Kingston) who do not wish to focus on the master narratives of patriarchy, but to focus instead on the powerful stories of love and struggle between mothers and daughters, between women in China and in America. The stories in *The Joy Luck Club* give voice to the desires and experiences of female characters who have not had the advantage to write or tell their stories as men have had. It is their neglected stories that they tell and attempt to transmit to their daughters in the oral traditions of talk-story. These hybrid talk-story narratives challenge those who would deny or lessen the power, beauty, value, and pain in these women's lives. This is what Maxine Hong Kingston spent a lot of time learning in her memoir *The Woman Warrior:* "The reporting is the vengeance—not the beheading, not the gutting, but the words" (63). The personal stories of the Joy Luck mothers do battle through gossip, circular talking, cryptic messages/caveats, dream images, bilingual language, and talk-story traditions—not in the linear, logical, or publicly authorized discourse in patriarchal or imperialist narratives. This is talk that challenges the denial of Asian American women's voices and identities—denials not only by a male-dominated Chinese society and a Eurocentric American society but also by their very own daughters who have become so Americanized that they can barely talk-story with their mothers. In many ways, Tan's book can be fruitfully compared with *The Woman Warrior.* As heroic paper daughters in quest of their mothers' stories, Tan and Kingston empower not only their mothers but also themselves and their racial/ethnic communities through a psychic and oral/literary birthing that keeps alive the intimate, ever-changing record of tragedies, resistances, and joy luck for all people.

In the following section, I have included a number of additional discussion and paper topic questions that would be useful in teaching Tan's *The Joy Luck Club.*

1. What are the experiences most remembered by the mothers? Where is "home" for them? How do the experiences of the mothers resonate in the lives of their daughters? Can one see parallels in the daughters' lives? What expectations do individual mothers have for their daughters? and vice versa? What are the obstacles—social, economic, psychological, cultural, historical—that impact on the communications between the mothers and daughters? How does assimilation into dominant Anglo American culture affect their relationship? Is it important for daughters and mothers to communicate with each other? Why? How do mothers and daughters specifically find

ways to survive and resist their multiple oppressions as Chinese American women?

2. Discuss how Tan portrays the acquisition of gender identity and roles in the early childhood of the Joy Luck mothers in stories such as "The Moon Lady," "The Scar," or "The Red Candle." How does Tan convey through the language and images the particular conflicts and tensions within the different women? Do they simply adjust to the repression of their own private desires and dreams? How do they negotiate or resist patriarchal/imperialist oppression? Do they succeed and/or fail in their attempts?

3. Discuss the style or structure of Tan's text—for example, her use of a first-person point of view in the text. Or why and how does Tan use and/or transform the Chinese talk-story tradition or the images and legends in her own Chinese American stories? In regard to these topics, students could expand the discussion by comparing and contrasting two other Chinese American mother-daughter literary texts—Jade Snow Wong's *Fifth Chinese Daughter* (1945) and Maxine Hong Kingston's *The Woman Warrior* (1977).

4. (a) For a broader analysis of Asian American mother-daughter interactions, compare/contrast *The Joy Luck Club* with Tan's second novel *The Kitchen God's Wife,* which focuses on the difficult relationship and revelations between the immigrant mother Jiang Weili and her Chinese American daughter Pearl. *The Joy Luck Club* can also be used with Faye Myenne Ng's first novel *Bone,* which reveals the trauma and grief of a San Francisco Chinatown family attempting to deal with the suicide of one of their three daughters. Tan's book also works well with Joy Kogawa's *Obasan* or Hisaye Yamamoto's *Seventeen Syllables and Other Stories.* Both writers deal with the multiple tensions between immigrant mothers and their second-generation daughters in the Japanese American community before, during, and after World War II. There are also a good selection of essays, short stories, and poems by other Asian American writers on this topic in Asian American anthologies listed in section C, "Related Works," below.

(b) Other mother-daughter writing that can be used with Tan's book include Kim Chernin's *In My Mother's House: A Daughter's Story,* Edwidge Danticat's *Breath, Eyes, Memory,* Audre Lorde's *Zami: A New Spelling of My Name,* and Paule Marshall's *Brown Girl, Brownstones.* For example, Paule Marshall's novel, set in Brooklyn during the period of the Depression and World War II, depicts the struggles of a Barbadian immigrant family as it confronts poverty and racism in the United States. In the story, Selina Boyce, a young daughter searching for identity, must confront and resolve the contradictory feelings she has toward her hardworking, ambitious mother. Possible questions to help promote discussion around these novels include the following: What personal, cultural, and sociohistorical struggles do women encounter in their families and mixed cultures in the United States? In what ways do they attempt to construct multiple selves, subjectivities, or positionings that have value against the meaninglessness, oppression, and violence (psychic and physical) that they encounter in their lives? Do they succeed and/or fail in their attempts? How do women empower or destroy other women? How do these diverse writers find innovative ways to rupture racist/sexist language and institutions through their creative use of language and/or narrative strategies? Are there similarities and/or differences in their writing strategies/tactics, stories, experiences? What type of identification and valorization of a women's culture is portrayed in the texts?

5. To provide for more inclusive and personal participation in the discussion of the book, students can compare their own relationships with their mothers and families and how they are situated and constructed in specific and diverse racial/ethnic, social, cultural, and historical contexts. This can be done in small group discussions, journal entries, and/or an oral history project.

6. (a) Students might wish to see the film version of *The Joy Luck Club* and discuss how the film might significantly differ from the book. What stories were left out? which ones kept? and why? Were there any modifications in the stories portrayed in the film? Why? How are men depicted in the book and film? Are the issues of racism and sexism in the United States discussed or left invisible in the film? Why and/or why not?

(b) Compare/contrast the portrayals of the mother-daughter relationship in *The Joy Luck Club* with another film directed by Wayne Wang, entitled *Dim Sum*, which also portrays the daily interactions between an immigrant Chinese mother and her daughter. What are the similarities and/or differences in the representations of Chinese Americans and their experiences in these two films? What were the production contexts (such as funding, decision-making process, studio, writing, and directing) for these two films by Wayne Wang? How do these institutional contexts impact on the final aesthetic product that is produced? Who are the audiences for these two films?

C. Bibliographies

1. Related Works

Chernin, Kim. *In My Mother's House: A Daughter's Story.* New York: Harper and Row, 1983.

Danticat, Edwidge. *Breath, Eyes, Memory.* New York: Soho Press, 1994.

Kingston, Maxine Hong. *The Woman Warrior: Memoirs of a Girlhood among Ghosts.* New York: Vintage, 1977.

Kogawa, Joy. *Obasan.* Boston: David Godine, 1981.

Lorde, Audre. *Zami: A New Spelling of My Name.* Freedom, Calif.: Crossing Press, 1982.

Marshall, Paule. *Brown Girl, Brownstones.* 1959. Reprint, New York: Feminist Press, 1981.

Moraga, Cherríe, and Gloria Anzaldúa, eds. *This Bridge Called My Back: Writings by Radical Women of Color.* New York: Kitchen Table/Women of Color Press, 1981. There are a number of excellent texts on how the issues of race, class, gender, and sexuality impact on the lives of immigrant mothers and second-generation daughters-writers: Cherríe Moraga's "La Güera," Merle Woo's "Letter to Ma," and Gloria Anzaldúa's "La Prieta."

Ng, Fae Myenne. *Bone.* New York: Hyperion, 1993.

Tan, Amy. *The Kitchen God's Wife.* New York: G. P. Putnam's Sons, 1991.

Watanabe, Sylvia, and Carol Bruchac, eds. *Home to Stay: Asian American Women's Fiction.* New York: Greenfield Review Press, 1990. A diverse selection of writing that may be helpful in situating Tan's work with other contemporary Asian American women writers.

Wong, Jade Snow. *Fifth Chinese Daughter.* 1945. Reprint, Seattle: University of Washington Press, 1989.

Yamamoto, Hisaye. *Seventeen Syllables and Other Stories.* Latham, N.Y.: Kitchen Table/Women of Color Press, 1988.

2. Best Criticism

Cheung, King-Kok. *Articulate Silences: Hisaye Yamamoto, Maxine Hong Kingston, Joy Kogawa.* Ithaca, N.Y.: Cornell University Press, 1993. Though she does not discuss Tan's work, Cheung provides a useful study of the thematic and rhetorical uses of silences in the articulation of the unspeakable and in defiance of the hegemonic culture that denies the voices/experiences of Asian American women.

Ho, Wendy. "Mother-and-Daughter Writing and the Politics of Location in Maxine Hong Kingston's *The Woman Warrior* and Amy Tan's *The Joy Luck Club.*" Ph.D. diss., University of Wisconsin, Madison, 1993. Reprint, Ann Arbor: UMI, 1993. I examine (1) the complex negotiations that Chinese

American immigrant mothers and their second-generation daughters perform daily in dealing with diverse, and often conflicting, socioeconomic, cultural, historical, and political frameworks and (2) how Kingston and Tan invent alternative literary-political strategies and positionings to tell their mothers' stories and their own.

Kim, Elaine. *Asian American Literature: An Introduction to the Writings and Their Social Context.* Philadelphia: Temple University Press, 1982. This early classic in the study of Asian American literature provides a sociohistorical introduction to the literary works by Americans of Chinese, Japanese, Korean, and Filipino descent from the nineteenth century to the early 1980s.

Ling, Amy. "Focus on America: Seeking a Self and a Place." *Between Worlds: Women Writers of Chinese Ancestry.* The Athene Series. New York: Pergamon Press, 1990. Ling examines the mother-daughter theme and its links to the notions of the motherland and to the "between-worlds" tensions in the work of Chinese American women writers such as Kingston and Tan.

Lowe, Lisa. "Homogeneity, Hybridity, Multiplicity: Marking Asian American Differences." *Diaspora* 1, no. 1 (Spring 1991): 24–44. By using *The Joy Luck Club* as one of her examples, Lowe explores the concept of hybridity and heterogeneity in Asian American experiences and the importance of considering the complex intersections of race, class, and gender in the mother-daughter trope.

Schueller, Malini Johar. "Theorizing Ethnicity and Subjectivity: Maxine Hong Kingston's *Tripmaster Monkey* and Amy Tan's *The Joy Luck Club.*" *Genders* 15 (Winter 1992): 72–85. Using a poststructuralist framework, Schueller examines the socially constructed discursive nature of ethnic and gender identity in Kingston and Tan. She argues that these writers provide alternative ways of resisting authoritarian and essentialist definitions of ethnicity and gender identity that have been used to marginalize oppressed peoples.

Wong, Sau-ling Cynthia. *Reading Asian American Literature: From Necessity to Extravagance.* Princeton, N.J.: Princeton University Press, 1993. In a stimulating critical study, Wong argues for an intertextual framework for reading Asian American texts, which she demonstrates through the study of four motifs. In the food and eating motif, there are brief references to *The Joy Luck Club.*

3. Other Sources

Chan, Jeffrey Paul, Frank Chin, Lawson Fusao Inada, and Shawn Wong, eds. *The Big Aiiieeeee!: An Anthology of Chinese American and Japanese Literature.* New York: Meridian, 1991.

Chan, Sucheng. *Asian Americans: An Interpretive History.* Twayne's Immigrant
    Heritage of America Series. Boston: Twayne Publishers, 1991.

Daniels, Roger. *Asian America: Chinese and Japanese in the United States since
    1850.* Seattle: University of Washington Press, 1988.

Friedman, Susan Stanford. "Women's Autobiographical Selves: Theory and Prac-
    tice." In *The Private Self: Theory and Practice of Women's Autobiographical
    Writings,* ed. Shari Benstock, 34–62. Chapel Hill and London: University
    of North Carolina Press, 1988.

Hirsch, Marianne. "Mothers and Daughters." *Signs: Journal of Women in Cul-
    ture and Society* 7, no. 1 (Fall 1981): 200–222.

hooks, bell. *Talking Back.* Boston: South End Press, 1989.

Koenig, Rhonda. "Heirloom China." *New York Magazine,* March 20, 1989, 82–83.

Mohanty, Chandra Talpade. "Cartographies of Struggle: Third World Women
    and the Politics of Feminism." In *Third World Women and the Politics of
    Feminism,* ed. Chandra Mohanty, Ann Russo, and Lourdes Torres.
    Bloomington and Indianapolis: Indiana University Press, 1991.

Ono, Kazuko. *Chinese Women in a Century of Revolution:* 1850–1950, ed. Joshua
    Fogel. Stanford, Calif.: Stanford University Press, 1989.

Schell, Orville. "'Your Mother Is in Your Bones.'" Review of *The Joy Luck Club*
    by Amy Tan. *New York Times Book Review,* March 19, 1989, 3+.

Seaman, Donna. "The Booklist Interview: Amy Tan." *Booklist* (Oct. 1, 1990):
    256–57.

Somogyi, Barbara, and David Stanton. "Amy Tan: An Interview." *Poets and
    Writers* 19, no. 5 (September/October 1991): 24–32.

Streitfeld, David. "The 'Luck' of Amy Tan." Review of *The Joy Luck Club* by Amy
    Tan. *Washington Post,* Oct. 8, 1989, sec. F1+.

Tan, Amy. *The Joy Luck Club.* New York: G. P. Putnam's Sons, 1989.

———. "Amy Tan on Amy Tan and *The Joy Luck Club.*" *California State Library
    Foundation Bulletin* 31 (April 1990): 1–10.

Wolf, Margery, and Roxane Witke, eds. *Women in Chinese Society.* Stanford,
    Calif.: Stanford University Press, 1975.

Wong, Diane Yen-Mai, and Asian Women United of California, eds. *Making
    Waves: An Anthology of Writings by and about Asian American Women.*
    Boston: Beacon Press, 1989.

Yung, Judy. *Chinese Women of America: A Pictorial History.* Seattle: University
    of Washington, 1986.

Notes

1. Note that mirror imagery is pervasive in Tan's book. For instance,
Lindo Jong looks into the mirror and discovers a private self. Waverly also
looks into the hairdresser's mirror. Jing-mei looks into the mirror to dis-

cover her secret "prodigy" self. There are many references to mothers as mirrors and to the placement of mirrors in rooms. Tan attempts to break down the binary polarizations that patriarchy demands and the separation between one woman and another. Before the freeing bonds between mother and daughters can be re-membered, the miming/doubling in the false mirror of patriarchy and imperialism must be ruptured.

2. On the important roles played by Chinese women in peasant strikes, silk-factory communities, labor movements, and uprisings in pre-and post-revolutionary China, consult Ono and Wolf and Witke. For Chinese American women's history, consult S. Chan, Wong, and Yung.

Contributors

Juan Bruce-Novoa is a poet and critic and the author of a number of works, including *Chicano Poetry: A Response to Chaos* (University of Texas Press, 1982), *Retrospace: Collected Essays on Chicano Literature, Theory, and History* (Arte Público Press, 1990), and *Only the Good Times,* a novel forthcoming from Arte Público. He is presently chairman of the Department of Spanish at the University of California, Irvine.

King-Kok Cheung is associate professor of English at the University of California, Los Angeles, and the author of *Articulate Silences: Hisaye Yamamoto, Maxine Hong Kingston, Joy Kogowa* (Cornell University Press, 1993). She also edited *"Seventeen Syllables": A Collection of Critical Essays* (Rutgers University Press, 1994) and compiled *Asian American Literature: An Annotated Bibliography* (Modern Language Association Press, 1988).

G. Thomas Couser is professor of English and co-chair of American Studies at Hofstra University. He is the author of *American Autobiography: The Prophetic Mode* (University of Massachusetts Press, 1979) and *Altered Egos: Authority in American Autobiography* (Oxford University Press, 1989). He is currently completing a study of contemporary life-writing about illness and disability.

Yoshinobu Hakutani, professor of English at Kent State University, is the author or editor of many books, including *Young Dreiser: A Critical Study* (Fairleigh Dickinson University Press, 1980), *Critical Essays on Richard Wright* (G. K. Hall, 1982), *Selected Magazine Articles of Theodore Dreiser: Life and Art in the American 1890s, Selected English Writings of Yone Noguchi: An East-West Literary Assimilation* (1990–92), and *The City in African American Literature,* with Robert Butler (1995), (all three from Fairleigh Dickinson University Press).

Wendy Ho is an assistant professor of Asian American Studies and Women's Studies at the University of California, Davis, where she teaches courses in Asian American literature, Asian American women, literature by women of color, feminist theory, and cultural studies.

Helen Jaskoski, professor of English at California State University, Fullerton, is completing a volume on Leslie Marmon Silko for the Twayne series in short fiction. She has published on American Indian, African American, Asian American, and Jewish American literature, as well as on poetry therapy and composition instruction. Her book *Poetry/Mind/Body* is available from University Press of America.

Shirley Geok-lin Lim edited *Approaches to Teaching Kingston's "The Woman Warrior"* (Modern Language Association Press, 1991), and is the author of two recent critical studies, *Nationalism and Literature* (New Day Publishers, 1993) and *Writing South East/Asia in English* (London: Skoob, 1994). She has published four volumes of poetry, and a second collection of her short stories (*Life's Mysteries*) is forthcoming. She is currently professor of English and Women's Studies at the University of California, Santa Barbara.

John R. Maitino is associate professor of English at California State Polytechnic University, Pomona, where he teaches English and coordinates the English education program. He has written widely on teaching, on film and fiction, and on multicultural literature.

Antonio C. Márquez is associate professor of English and Comparative Literature at the University of New Mexico. He co-edited *Cuentos Chicanos: A Short Story Anthology* (University of New Mexico Press, 1980), and his critical essays have appeared in *The Arizona Quarterly, The Bilingual Review, Dictionary of Literary Biography, Essays in Literature,* and *MELUS.*

Susan Meisenhelder is professor of English at California State University, San Bernardino, and is the author of *Wordsworth's Informed Reader: Structures of Experience in His Poetry* (Vanderbilt University Press, 1989) and *Hitting a Straight Lick with a Crooked Stick: Zora Neale Hurston's Literary Craft* (forthcoming), as well as articles on American and African women writers.

Jeanne-Marie A. Miller is professor of English and director of the Graduate Studies Program in English at Howard University, where she teaches American and African American literature and drama. For ten years she edited the *Black Theatre Bulletin* for the American Theatre Association and also served as an associate editor of *The Theatre Journal.* She has published, in a variety of books and journals, numerous articles on the works of African American authors.

Julián Olivares is professor of Spanish at the University of Houston and has published widely on Latino literature. A former senior editor of Arte Público Press and *The Americas Review,* he is the author of *Tras el espejo la musa escribe: lírica femenina de los Siglos de Oro* (Siglo XXI, 1993) and critical editions of the works of Tomás Rivera.

David R. Peck is professor of English at California State University, Long Beach, and teaches courses in American literature. He is the author of *Issues in Teaching Multicultural Literature* (a teacher's guide to accompany the sixth edition of Kennedy and Gioia, *Literature: An Introduction,* HarperCollins, 1995) and *American Ethnic Literatures: An Annotated Bibliography* (Salem Press, 1992).

John Purdy is the editor of *Studies in American Indian Literatures* and contributed the essay on Louise Erdrich to the *Dictionary of Native American Literature,* edited by Andrew Wiget (Garland, 1994). In 1993 he was a Fulbright lecturer in American literature at the University of Canterbury, New Zealand.

Elizabeth C. Ramírez, is professor of Theatre Arts at the University of Oregon and is the author of *Footlights across the Border: A History of Spanish-Language Professional Theatre in Texas, 1873–1935* (Peter Lang, 1990) as well as numerous articles and reviews on American theatre. Dr. Ramírez works professionally as a dramaturg.

Daniel W. Ross is assistant professor of English at Columbus College in Columbus, Georgia. He has published a number of articles on American literature, including "Celie in the Looking-Glass: The Desire for Selfhood in *The Color Purple*" (*Modern Fiction Studies,* 1988), and is currently finishing a book on William Styron.

E. San Juan, Jr., currently teaches at Bowling Green. His *Racial Formations/ Critical Transformations* (Humanities Press, 1993) won awards from the Asian American Studies Association and the Gustavus Myers Center. State University of New York Press will publish this year his *Hegemony and Strategies of Transgression,* while Temple University Press is putting out his edition of two volumes of Carlos Bulosan's writings. He co-edits *The Arkansas Review* and *Nature, Society, and Thought.*

William W. Thackeray is professor of Humanities and Native American Studies at Montana State University—Northern, where he founded the degree programs in Native American Studies. He has written extensively on American Indian literatures.

Linda Wagner-Martin is Hanes Professor of English and Comparative Literature at the University of North Carolina, Chapel Hill. She has written a number of works on American literature, most recently *The Modern American Novel* (Twayne, 1989), *Telling Women's Lives: The New Biography* (Rutgers University Press, 1994), and *The Oxford Companion to Women's Writing in the U.S.* (Oxford, 1995). Her biography of Gertrude Stein is forthcoming.

Norma C. Wilson, professor of English at the University of South Dakota, has written many articles on Native American literature, including essays on Joy Harjo, Linda Hogan, Wendy Rose, and Roberta Hill Whiteman in *Dictionary of Native American Literature*, ed. Andrew Wiget (Garland, 1994). She has also published a book of poetry, *Wild Iris*, and co-authored with Jerry Wilson a film script, *South Dakota: A Meeting of Cultures* (1985).

Mitsuye Yamada is an internationally known poet and critic (*Camp Notes and Other Poems* [Shameless Hussy Press, 1976]; *Desert Run: Poems and Stories* [Kitchen Table/Women of Color Press, 1988]) as well as the co-editor of *Sowing Ti Leaves: Writings by Multicultural Women* (MCWW Multicultural Women Writers of Orange County, 1990).